The
Television
Will Be
Revolutionized

Amanda D. Lotz

NEW YORK UNIVERSITY PRESS

New York and London

NEW YORK UNIVERSITY PRESS
New York and London
www.nyupress.org

Library of Congress Cataloging-in-Publication Data
Lotz, Amanda D., 1974–
The television will be revolutionized / Amanda D. Lotz.
p. cm.
Includes bibliographical references and index.
ISBN-13: 978-0-8147-5219-7 (cloth : alk. paper)
ISBN-10: 0-8147-5219-5 (cloth : alk. paper)
ISBN-13: 978-0-8147-5220-3 (pbk. : alk. paper)
ISBN-10: 0-8147-5220-9 (pbk. : alk. paper)
1. Television broadcasting. 2. Television broadcasting—United
States. 3. Television—Technological innovations. 4. Television
broadcasting—Technological innovations. I. Title.
PN1992.5.L68 2007
384.550973—dc22   2007023407

New York University Press books are printed on acid-free paper,
and their binding materials are chosen for strength and durability.

Manufactured in the United States of America

c 10 9 8 7 6 5 4 3 2 1
p 10 9 8 7 6 5 4 3 2 1

For Robert and Linda Lotz,
with gratitude and affection

Contents

Acknowledgments

Perhaps one reason that the examination of the operation of cultural industries is a less common pursuit among media studies scholars is that this type of research holds particular challenges. Executive offices and the day-to-day operation of cultural industries are not easy for critically minded academics to access, but over the last five years I've attended a wide range of industry events and forums that offered meaningful glimpses into these worlds and informed my research in crucial ways. This research is built upon four weeks of participant observation of media buying, planning, and research departments, as well as immersion in a number of industry conferences, including the Academy of Television Arts and Sciences Faculty Seminar, November 2002; the National Association of Television Program Executives Conference and Faculty Seminar (NATPE), 2004–2007; the Future of Television Seminar sponsored by Television Week, September 2004; the International Radio and Television Society Foundation Faculty/Industry Seminar, November 2004; the International Consumer Electronics Show, January 2006; the National Cable and Telecommunications Association National Show, April 2006; and the Future of Television Forum, November 2006. Visiting these industry meetings and reading the trade press extensively provided more information about the industry than I could meaningfully report. The precise sources of all of the anecdotes, cases, and analyses in the following chapters are not always explicitly acknowledged—but my understanding of industry operations and struggles derive primarily from these sources. Immersing myself in the space of these industry events helped me understand the paradigm of thought that dominated the industry at various points in the adjustment chronicled here; everything from formal conference presentations to casual conversations overheard in hallways and ballrooms contributed to my sense of industry concerns and perspectives.

Many organizations, individuals, and funding sources facilitated my research in crucial ways. I am incredibly grateful to the National Association of Television Program Executives Educational Foundation, expertly managed by Greg Pitts, for the various ways a Faculty Development Grant, a Faculty Fellowship, and the organization's educator's rate and programming provided firsthand access to many of the executives making decisions about the industrial changes chronicled here. The Faculty Development Grant, and generous hosting by Mediacom, also offered invaluable perspective on the upfront buying process.

The Advertising Education Foundation's Visiting Professor Program allowed me to spend two weeks observing the operation of media buyer Universal McCann, and a schedule carefully arranged by Charlotte Hatfield exposed me to the many dimensions of buying, planning, and research that were exceptionally helpful in composing the advertising chapter. Thanks also to Sharon Hudson for her work on this great program and to all those in the industry who support it.

I was honored by the International Radio and Television Society Foundation in November 2004 as the Coltrin Professor of the Year as a result of a case study exercise I wrote to explore issues with my students which are examined in this book. In addition to bestowing such a fine honor, IRTS constructed a number of excellent panels featuring industry executives who provided valuable information and perspectives. I am also grateful to the faculty from many institutions who joined me in New York and participated in the case study. Thanks to IRTS, Joyce Tudryn, Stephen H. Coltrin, and all those who support IRTS for these opportunities.

Funding and support from the Denison University Research Foundation and the NATPE Educational Foundation, along with a University of Michigan Rackham Faculty Grant and Fellowship, all helped with various aspects of travel and industry conference fees. A course release in the winter of 2006 and a summer stipend allowed me to attend a marathon of industry conferences and also enabled me to focus on the writing of this book, which I hope will provide a timely contribution.

Many working in the industry offered insight in formal and informal interviews and responded to email queries. The degree of descriptive detail I offer here would have been impossible without their generous explanations. Thanks to Laura Albers, Pamela Gibbons, Todd Gordon, Heather Kadin, Deb Kerins, Michele Krumper, Jon Mandel, Mitch Oscar, Rob Owen, Francis Page, Brent Renaud, Shawn Ryan, Andy Stabile, Stacy Sullivan, and Susan Whiting for their time and the information they provided.

After I completed my research, a number of kind and generous colleagues offered suggestions that were tremendously helpful in crafting and then in revising the book. Thanks to Jason Mittell for early feedback, detailed notes, and catching some important final points. Suggestions from Jonathan Gray, Kathy Newman, Sarah Banet-Weiser, and Michael Curtin also proved exceptionally useful. Russ Neuman joined me in spirited debates over lunch that helped me identify central arguments, and Susan Douglas reviewed preliminary manuscripts and offered valuable advice in helping this book find a publisher. Thanks as well to Janet Staiger for her introduction to New York University Press. I'm also very grateful to have found a small community of scholars and friends also examining the practice of critical media industry studies—conversations with Tim Havens, Serra Tinic, and Vicki Mayer were and continue to be important to my thinking about the methods and goals of this type of work.

Thanks also to Erin Copple, Nic Covey, Vanessa Miller, and Alex Green who contributed to this work in various ways and inspired me with their enthusiasm and ability. Finding students passionate about and interested in the industry and research is a tremendous reward and enables connections between teaching and research that enrich both pursuits as well as the day-to-day work of academic life. The community of colleagues I joined in the Communication Studies Department at the University of Michigan has also enhanced my work tremendously. Their generosity and intellectual engagement have added new richness to my work, and their friendships have helped make Ann Arbor home.

Horace Newcomb and Christopher Anderson have been crucial influences in my thinking about the connections among culture, art (my word), and commerce, although I take full responsibility for any shortcomings in my treatment of these topics. I tremendously value their continued collegiality and engaged critique. Perhaps unintentionally, they've also offered admirable models of intellectual generosity and humility, as well as of ways to balance the pursuits of work and life that have been helpful in my career.

Thanks as well to Emily Park and other members of New York University Press for their help in making this book the particular contribution to the field that I sought it to be. Their commitment to the project and identification of its specific needs will, I hope, enable the book to reach beyond specialists.

I'm grateful as well to a range of friends, old and new, who have been supportive and offered a world outside of television. I'm frankly humbled xii | *Acknowledgments*

by their curiosity about my work and willingness to read my intellectual musings. My fondest regards to Heather Buchanan, Megan French, Sonya McKay, Courtney Paison, Sharon Ross, Faith Sparr, Scott Campbell, and the 8 Balls and their fabulous wives. Thanks also to Katherine Ferguson and Jay Rogers for their kind hospitality on many different trips to New York.

This project, and the speed with which I completed it, required the support of my generous partner, Wesley Huffstutter. Mere thanks seem inadequate in acknowledging his patience with the things that were delayed in my pursuit of deadlines, his willingness to keep me fed and sane, his not begrudging my travels, and his provision of many lifts, often at unreasonable hours, to the airport. We've already had a long trip together, and I look forward to the next stretch and the new challenges and rewards it is sure to offer.

I dedicate this book to my parents, Robert and Linda Lotz as a small acknowledgment that I owe so much of who I am and what I've accomplished to them. So few people seem to be graced to find an avocation that rewards them as thoroughly as I find mine to do. Their life lessons—whether sticking with things you're not great at, cultivating an inner life, or a myriad others—helped me make the most of the opportunities I've been fortunate to encounter. Their faith in me and support when I ventured off of the known path made a world of difference and have helped me find a happy and fulfilling life.

Introduction

　　As I was dashing through an airport in November of 2001, the cover of *Technology Review* displayed on a newsstand rack caught my eye. Its cover announced "The Future of Television," and the inside pages provided a smart look at coming changes.[1] Even by the end of 2001, which was still long before viewers or television executives truly imagined the reality of downloading television shows to pocket-sized devices or streaming video online, it was apparent that the box that had sat in our homes for half a century was on the verge of significant change. The future that author Mark Fischetti foresaw in the article depicts my current television world fairly accurately, although I am admittedly an early adopter of television gear and gadgetry and there are still some aspects of this world beyond my reach. And right there in his third paragraph is the sentiment that television and consumer electronics executives uttered incessantly in 2006 as the mantra of the television future: "whatever show you want, whenever you want, on whatever screen you want."

　　But even though Fischetti presciently anticipated the substantial adjustments in how we view television, where we view it, how we pay for it, and how the industry would remain viable and vital, many other headlines in the intervening years have predicted a far different situation. A 2006 IBM Business Consulting Services Report announced "The End of Television As We Know It," and an otherwise sharp *Slate.com* article proclaimed "The Death of Television"; a *Business Week* article explained "Why TV Will Never Be the Same," and the *Wall Street Journal* opined on "How Old Media Can Survive in a New World."[2] By 2007, a *Wired* article better captured the contradictions emerging with the title "The TV Is Dead. Long Live the TV."[3] Predicting the coming death of television seemed to become a new beat for many of the nation's technology and culture writers in the mid-2000s.

The journalists weren't alone in their uncertainty about the future of television or even what television was, as new ways to use television and new forms of content confounded even those who used the device everyday. In 2004, a student relayed a conversation with a colleague in which this colleague told her that he did not own a TV. The student knew my colleague's child enjoyed an expansive video collection, and it seemed unlikely that he could have tossed out the set and videos without good reason. So she asked, incredulously, why had he thrown away the set? He looked at her with confusion and responded that he still had the set, but he made plain that his family doesn't watch TV; they watch videos. She wondered aloud in my office, "But they do watch the videos on a television?" Her story reminded me of an anecdote that Rich Frank, a long-time broadcast television executive, told a Las Vegas ballroom full of television executives a few weeks earlier. Frank shared that he had recently visited with his young grandson and asked the boy which network was his favorite. Frank expected to hear a broadcast network or perhaps Nickelodeon in response, but what the boy replied, without a moment's hesitation, was "TiVo." Now clearly, if young children watch videos without watching television and believe TiVo is a channel, then either the future of television has arrived or we are well on our way.

We may continue to watch television, but the new technologies available to us require new rituals of use. Not so long ago, television use typically involved walking into a room, turning on the set, and either turning to specific content or channel surfing. Today, viewers with digital video recorders (DVRs) such as TiVo may elect to circumvent scheduling constraints and commercials. Owners of portable viewing devices download the latest episodes of their favorite shows and watch them outside the conventional setting of the living room. Still others rent television shows on DVD, or download them through legal and illegal sources online. And this doesn't even begin to touch upon the viewer-created television that appears on video aggregators such as YouTube or social networking sites. As a result of these changing technologies and modes of viewing, the nature of television use has become increasingly complicated, deliberate, and individualized. Television as we knew it—understood as a mass medium capable of reaching a broad, heterogeneous audience and speaking to the culture as a whole—is no longer the norm in the United States. But changes in what we can do with television, what we expect from it, and how we use it have not been hastening the demise of the medium. Instead, they are revolutionizing it.

This book offers a detailed and exhaustive behind-the-screen exploration of the substantial changes occurring in television technology, program creation, distribution, and advertising, why these practices have changed, and how these changes are profoundly affecting everyone from television viewers to those who study and work in the industry. It examines a wide range of industrial practices common in U.S. television and assesses their recent evolution in order to explain how and why the images and stories we watch on television find their way to us at the beginning of the twenty-first century. These changes are so revolutionary that they have initiated a new era of television, the effects of which we are only beginning to detect.

What Is Television Today?

Television is not just a simple technology or appliance—like a toaster—that has sat in our homes for more than fifty years. Rather, it functions both as a technology and a tool for cultural storytelling. We know it as a sort of "window on the world" or a "cultural hearth" that has gathered our families, told us stories, and offered glimpses of a world outside our daily experience. It brought the nation together to view Lucy's antics, gave us mouthpieces to discuss our uncertainties about social change though Archie and Meathead, and provided a common gathering place through which a geographically vast nation could share in watching national triumphs and tragedies. A certain understanding of what television was and could be developed during our early years with the medium and resulted from the specific industrial practices that organized television production processes for much of its history. Alterations in the production process—the practices involved in the creation and circulation of television—including how producers make television programs, how networks finance them, and how audiences access them, have created new ways of using television and now challenge our basic understanding of the medium. Changes in television have forced the production process to evolve during the past twenty years so that the assorted ways we now use television are mirrored in and enabled by greater variation in the ways television is made, financed, and distributed.

We might rarely consider the business of television, but production practices inordinately affect the stories, images, and ideas that project into our homes. Consequently, the industrial transformation of U.S. television has begun to modify what the industry creates. Industrial processes are normally nearly unalterable and support deeply entrenched structures of power that determine what stories can be told and which viewers matter most. But from 1985 through 2005, the U.S. television industry reinvented itself and its industrial practices to compete in the digital era by breaking from customary norms of program acquisition, financing, and advertiser support that in many cases had been in place since the mid-1950s. This period of transition created great instability in the relationships among producers and consumers, networks and advertisers, and technology companies and content creators, which in turn initiated uncommon opportunities to deviate from the "conventional wisdom" or industry lore that ruled television operations. Industry workers faced a changing competitive environment triggered by the development of new and converging technologies that expanded ways to watch and receive television; they also found audiences willing to explore the innovative opportunities these new technologies provided.

Rather than enhancing existing business models, industrial practices, and viewing norms, recent technological innovations have engendered new ones—but it is not just new technologies that have revolutionized the television industry. Adjustments in how studios finance, make, and distribute shows, as well as in how and where viewers watch them occurred simultaneously. None of these developments suggested that television would play a diminished role in the lives of the nation that spends the most time engaging its programming, but the evolving institutional, economic, and technological adjustments of the industry have come to have significant implications for the role of television in society. In the mid-2000s, the industry was on the verge of rapid and radical change as the television transformation moved from a few early adopters to a more general and mass audience. Likewise, as new uses became dominant and shared by more viewers, television's role in culture underwent changes. Understanding these related changes is of crucial interest to all who watch television and think about how it communicates ideas, to those who study media, and to those who are trying to keep abreast of their rapidly evolving businesses and remain up-to-date with new commercial processes.

Despite changing industrial practices, television remains a ubiquitous media form and a technology widely owned and used in the United States and many similarly industrialized nations. Yet the vast expansion in the number of networks and channels streaming through our televisions and the varied ways we can now access content has diminished the degree to which any society encounters television viewing as a shared event. Although once the norm, society-wide viewing of particular programs is now an uncommon experience. New technologies have both liberated the place-based and domestic nature of television use and freed viewers to control when and where they view programs. Related shifts in distribution possibilities that allow us to watch television on computer screens and mobile phones have multiplied previously standard models for financing shows and profiting from them, thereby creating a vast expansion in economically viable content. Viewers face more content choices, more options in how and when to view programs, and more alternatives for paying for their programming. Increasingly, they have even come to enjoy the opportunity to create it themselves.

Thus, although television remains a mass medium that can in principle always be capable of serving as the cultural hearth around which a society shares media events—as we did in cases such as the Kennedy assassination or Challenger explosion—it increasingly exists as an electronic newsstand through which a diverse and segmented society pursues deliberately targeted interests. The U.S. television audience now can rarely be categorized as a mass audience; instead, it is more accurately understood as a collection of niche audiences. Although television has been reconfigured in recent decades as a medium that most commonly addresses fragmented and specialized audience groups, no technology emerged to replace its previous norm as a messenger to a mass and heterogeneous audience. The development and availability of the Internet substantially affected the circulation of ideas and enabled distribution to even international audiences, yet the Internet allows us to attend to even more diverse content and provides little commonality in experience. Television's transition to a narrowcast medium—one targeted to distinct and isolated subsections of the audience—along with adjustments within the broader media culture in which it exists, significantly altered its industrial logic and has required a fundamental reassessment of how it operates as a cultural institution.

For the last fifty years we have thought about television in certain ways because of how television has been, but the truth is that television has not operated in the way we have assumed for some time now. Few of the norms of television that held from the 1950s into the 1980s remain in place, and such norms were already themselves the results of specific industrial, technological, and cultural contexts. In particular, the presumption that television predominately functions as a mass medium continues to hold great sway, but the mass audiences once characteristic of television were, as media scholar Michael Curtin notes, an aberration resulting from Fordist principles of "mass production, mass marketing and mass consumption."[4] Consequently, previous norms did not suggest the "proper" functioning of the television industry more than did subsequent norms; rather, they resulted from a specific industrial, technological, and cultural context no more innate than those that would develop later.

Understanding the transitions occurring in U.S. television at this time is a curious matter relative to conventional approaches to exploring technology and culture. Historically, technological innovation primarily has been a story of replacement in which a new technology emerged and subsumed the role of the previous technology. This indeed was the case of the transition from radio to television—as television neatly adopted many of the social and cultural functions of radio and added pictures to correspond with the sounds of the previous medium. The supplanted medium did not fade away, but repositioned itself and redefined its primary attributes to serve a complementary more than competitive function. But it is not a new competitor that now threatens television; it is the medium itself.

The changes in television that have taken place over the past two decades—whether the gross abundance of channel and program options we now select among or our increasing ability to control when and where we watch—are extraordinary and on the scale of the transition from one medium to another, as in the case of the shift from radio to television. And it is not just television that has changed. The field of media in which television is integrated also has evolved profoundly—most directly as a result of digital innovation and the audience's experiences with computing. Various industrial, technological, and cultural forces have begun to radically redefine television, and yet paradoxically, it persists as an entity most still understand and identify as "TV."

This book explores this redefinition of television specifically in the United States, although these changes are also redefining the experience with television in similar ways in many countries around the world. From its beginning, broadcasting has been "ideally suited" technologically to transgress national borders and constructs such as nation-states; however, the early imposition of strict national control and substantially divergent national experiences prevailed over attributes innate to the technology.[5] Many different countries experienced similar transitions in their industrial composition, production processes, and use of this thing called television at the same time as the United States, but precise situations diverge enough to make it difficult to speak in transnational generalities and lead to my focus on only the U.S. experience of this transition. The specific form of the redefinition—as it emerges from a rupture in dominant industrial practices—is particular to each nation, yet similarly industrialized countries shared in experiencing the transition to digital transmission, the expansion of choice in channel and content options, the increasing conglomeration of the industry among a few global behemoths, and the drive for increased control over when, where, and how audiences viewed "television programs." The development of an increasingly global cultural economy also has integrated the fate and fortune of the television industry beyond national confines.

Situating Television Circa 2005

During its first forty years, U.S. television remained fairly static in its industrial practices. It maintained modes of production, a standard picture quality, and conventions of genre and schedule, all of which led to a common and regular experience for audiences and lulled those who think about television into certain assumptions. Moments of adjustment occurred, particularly at the end of the 1950s when the "magazine" style of advertising began to take over and networks gained control of their schedules from advertising agencies and sponsors, but once established, the medium remained relatively unchanged until the mid 1980s. First, the "network era" (from approximately 1952 through the mid-1980s) governed industry operations and allowed for a certain experience with television that characterizes much of the medium's history. The norms of the network era have persisted in the minds of many as distinctive of television, despite the significant changes that have developed over the past twenty years. I therefore identify the period of the mid-1980s through the mid-2000s as that of the "multi-channel transition." During these years various developments changed our experience with television, but did so very gradually—in a manner that allowed the industry to continue to operate in much the same way as it did in the network era. The final period, the "post-network era," begins in the mid-2000s and is certainly not complete as this book goes to press. What separates the post-network era from the multi-channel transition is that the changes in competitive norms and operation of the industry have become too pronounced for old practices to be preserved; different industrial practices are becoming dominant and replacing those of the network era.

These demarcations in time, which are intentionally general, recognize that all production processes do not shift simultaneously and that people adopt new technologies and ways of using them at varied paces. By the end of 2005, adjustments in how people could access programming enabled a small group of early adopters to experience television in a manner characteristic of the post-network era.[6] Change of this scale is necessarily gradual. Even as I made final edits to this manuscript in early 2007, it still remained impossible to assert that a majority of the audience had entered the post-network era or that all production processes had "completed" the transition, but the eventual dominance of post-network conditions does appear to be inevitable.

The characteristics of the three phases of television, summarized in Table 1, are reviewed below.

TABLE 1
Characteristics of Production Components in Each Period

Production Component	Network Era	Multi-Channel Transition	Post-Network Era
Technology	Television	VCR Remote control Analog cable	DVR, VOD Portable devices (iPod, PSP) Mobile phones Slingbox Digital Cable
Creation	Deficit financing	Fin-syn rules, surge of independents, end of fin-syn conglomeration and co-production	Multiple financing norms, variation in cost structure and aftermarket value; opportunities for amateur production
Distribution	Bottleneck, definite windows, exclusivity	Cable increases possible outlets	Erosion of time between windows, and exclusivity; content anytime, anywhere
Advertising	:30 ads, upfront market	Subscription, experimentation with alternatives to :30 ads	Co-existence of multiple models—:30, placement, integration, branded entertainment, sponsorship; multiple user supported-transactional and subscription
Audience Measurement	Audimeters, diaries, sampling	People Meters, sampling	Portable People Meters, census measure

The Network Era

The series of fits and starts through which U.S. television developed complicates the determination of a clear beginning of the network era. Early television unquestionably evolved from the network organization of radio. This provides a compelling argument for dating the network era to the first television broadcasts of the late 1940s, if not to the days of radio. Alternatively, the industrial conditions of early television enabled substantial local production and innovation, which made these early years uncharacteristic of what developed in the early through the mid-1950s and became the network-era norm. Dating the network era as beginning in 1952 takes into account the passage of the channel allocation freeze (during which the FCC organized its practice of frequency distribution), color television standard adoption, and other institutional aspects that regularized the network experience for much of the country.[7]

Television certainly began as a network-organized medium, but many of the industrial practices and modes of organization that eventually defined the network era were not established immediately. By the early 1960s, network-era conventions were more fully in operation: the television set (and for some, an antenna) provided the extent of necessary technology; competition was primarily limited to programming supplied to local affiliates by three national networks that dictated production terms with studios; the networks offered the only outlets for high-budget original programming; thirty-second advertisements—the majority of which were sold in packages before the beginning of the season—supplied the dominant form of economic support and were premised upon rudimentary information about audience size; and audiences, which exercised no control over when they could view particular programs, chose among few, undifferentiated programming options.

The network era of U.S. television was the provenance of three substantial networks—NBC, CBS, and ABC—which were operated by relatively non-conglomerated corporations based in the business center of New York. These networks were organized hierarchically with many layers of managers, and each was administered by a figurehead with whom the identity and vision of the network could be identified.[8] Established first in radio, the networks spoke to the country en masse and played a significant role in articulating post-war American identity.[9] Networking was economically necessary because of the cost of production and the need to amortize costs across national audiences. Achieving economies of scale, networking recouped the tremendous costs of creating television programming by producing one show, distributing it to audiences nationwide, and selling advertising that would reach that massive national audience. Gathering mass audiences through a system of national network affiliates enabled networks to afford "network quality" programming with which independent and educational stations could not compete.

The financial relationships between networks and the production companies that supplied most television programming have changed throughout the history of television, but the dominant practices of the network era were established by the mid-1960s. Film studios and independent television producers had only three potential buyers of their content and were thus compelled to abide by practices established by the networks. In many cases the networks forced producers to shoulder significant risk while offering limited reward through a system in which the producers financed the complete cost of production and received license fees (payments from the networks) often 20 percent less than costs. Studios also sold the programs to international buyers or in syndication to affiliates after the program had aired on a network, but the networks typically demanded a percentage of these revenues, as detailed in Chapter 3.

The conventions of advertising and program creation were multifaceted in television's early years. As was the case in radio, much early television featured a single sponsor for each program—as in the *Texaco Star Theater*—rather than the purchase of commercials by multiple corporations, a practice that later became standard. The networks eliminated the single sponsorship format, thereby wresting substantial control of their schedule away from advertising agencies and sponsors, only in the late 1950s and early 1960s. The earlier norm eroded precipitously in part as a result of the quiz show scandals that revealed advertisers' willingness to mislead audiences, but as explored in Chapter 5, this erosion also had much to do with adjustments in how the networks sought to operate, as well as with differences in the demands of television relative to radio. After the elimination of the single sponsorship format, networks earned revenue from various advertisers who paid for thirty-second commercials embedded at regular intervals within programs in the manner that is still common today. Advertisers made their purchases based on network guarantees of reaching a certain audience, although many of the methods used to determine the size and composition of the audience were very limited.

Viewers had comparatively few ways to use their televisions during the network era. Most selected among fewer than a handful of options and optimally chose among three nationally distributed networks, inconsistently dispersed independent stations, and the isolated and under-funded educational television stations that became a slow-growing and still under-funded public broadcasting system. As the name implies, in the network era, U.S. "television" meant the networks ABC, CBS, and NBC.

In addition to lacking choice, network-era viewers possessed little control over the medium. Channel surfing via remote control, an activity taken for granted by contemporary viewers, did not become an option for most until the beginning of the multi-channel transition—although, as established, there was little to surf among. Viewers possessed no recourse against network schedules, and time-shifting remained beyond the realm of possibility. If the PTA bake sale was scheduled for Thursday night, that week's visit with *The Waltons* could not be rescheduled or delayed.

In the network era, television was predominantly a non-portable, domestic medium, with most homes owning just one set. Even by 1970, only 32.2 percent of homes had more than one television.[10] Communication scholar James Webster distinguishes the characteristics of television in this era as that of an "old medium" in which television programming was uniform, uncorrelated with channels, and universally available.[11] Such basic characteristics of technological use and accessibility contributed to the programming strategies of the era in important ways. Network programmers knew that the whole family commonly viewed television together, and they consequently selected programs and designed a schedule likely to be acceptable to, although perhaps not most favored by, the widest range of viewers—a strategy CBS vice president of programming Paul Klein described as that of "least objectionable programming."[12] This was the era of *broad*casting in which networks selected programs that would reach a heterogeneous mass culture, but still directed their address to the white middle-class. This mandate was integral to the business design of the networks and led to a competitive strategy in which they did not attempt to significantly differentiate their programming or clearly brand themselves with distinctive identities, as is common today. The fairly uniform availability of the three broadcast networks in each market forced viewers nationwide to choose among the same limited options, and the variation between daytime and prime-time schedules indicated the extent of targeted viewing in this era of mass audiences.

The network era featured very specific terms of engagement for the audience regardless of the broader distinctions in how the industry created that programming or how the business of television operated. Viewers grew accustomed to arbitrary norms of practice—many of which were established in radio—such as a limited range of genres, certain types of programming scheduled at particular times of day, the television "season," and reruns. These unexceptional network-era conventions appeared "natural" and "just how television is" to such a degree that altering these norms seemed unimaginable. However, adjustments in the television industry during the multi-channel transition revealed the arbitrary quality of these practices and enabled critics, industry workers, and entrepreneurs to envision radically different possibilities for television.

As the arrival of technologies that provided television viewers with unprecedented choice and control initiated an end to the network era, the multi-channel transition profoundly altered the television experience. To be sure, many network-era practices remained dominant throughout the multi-channel transition, but during the twenty-year period that began in the mid-1980s and extended through the early years of the twenty-first century these practices were challenged to such a degree that their preeminent status eroded.

The Multi-Channel Transition

Beginning in the 1980s, the television industry experienced two decades of gradual change. New technologies including the remote control, video-cassette recorder, and analog cable systems expanded viewers' choice and control; producers adjusted to government regulations that forced the networks to relinquish some of their control over the terms of program creation;[13] nascent cable channels and new broadcast networks added to viewers' content choices and eroded the dominance of ABC, CBS, and NBC; subscription channels launched and introduced an advertising-free form of television programming; and methods for measuring audiences grew increasingly sophisticated with the deployment of Nielsen's People Meter. As in the network era, this constellation of industrial norms led to a particular viewer experience of television and enabled a certain range of programming. Many of these industrial practices are explored in greater depth in Chapters 2 through 6, which focus on explaining new norms emerging in production processes including technology, program creation, distribution, advertising, and audience measurement and how these norms adjusted the type of programming the industry creates. In introducing this distinction between the multi-channel transition and post-network era here, it is most helpful to first establish the difference in viewers' experience of television. The subsequent chapters then detail the modifications in industrial practices that introduced these changes for viewers.

The common television experience was altered primarily as a result of expanded choice and control introduced during the multi-channel transition. As competition arising from the creation of new broadcast networks, such as FOX (1986), The WB (1995) and UPN (1995), expanded viewing options, a rapidly growing array of cable channels also drew viewers away from broadcast networks—so much so that the combined broadcast share, the percentage of those watching television who watched broadcast networks, declined from 90 to 64 during the 1980s.[14] Moreover, despite the arrival of new broadcast competitors during the 1990s, viewers continued to switch their prime-time viewing to cable, although not at such a precipitous rate as before. Still, broadcast networks (ABC, CBS, FOX, NBC, The WB, and UPN) collected an average of only 58 percent of those watching television at the conclusion of the 1999–2000 season, and only 46 percent by the end of the 2004–2005 season.[15] Alternative distribution systems such as cable and satellite enabled a new abundance of viewing options, and 56 percent of television households subscribed to them by 1990—a figure that grew to 85 percent of households by 2004.[16] And with homes receiving an average of 100 channels in 2003, up from 55 just two years earlier and 33 in 1990, the range of programming choices for viewers also grew considerably.[17]

The development of new technology that increased consumer control also facilitated viewers' break from the network-era television experience. Audiences first found this control in the form of the remote control devices (RCDs) that became standard in the 1980s. The dissemination of VCR technology further enabled them to select when to view content and to build personal libraries. For many, the availability of cable, remote control devices, and VCRs provided significant change all at once. The diffusion of these technologies was complexly interrelated. Viewers did not need to purchase a new remote-equipped set to gain use of an RCD. Many who acquired cable boxes and VCRs first accessed RCDs with these devices, while the new range of channels offered by cable and the control capabilities of VCRs expanded viewers' need for remotes.[18]

Substantial changes within the walls of the home also altered how audiences used television during the multi-channel transition. The limited options of the network era led programs to be widely viewed throughout the culture, but the explosion of content providers throughout the multi-channel transition enabled viewers to increasingly isolate themselves in enclaves of specific interests. As Webster explains, "new media" provide programming that is diverse and is correlated with channels, and they make content differentially available.[19] For example, although many cable channels can be acquired nationwide, the varying carriage agreements and packaging of the channels by locally organized cable systems create different availability based on geography and subscription tier.

Webster argues that this programming multiplicity results in audience fragmentation and polarization.[20] While much of the concern within the industry about audience fragmentation focuses on the consequences of smaller audiences for the commercial financing system that supports U.S. television, cultural critics are now considering how the polarization of media audiences contributes to cultural fissures such as those that emerged around social issues in the 2000 and 2004 elections. Here, polarization refers to the ability of different groups of viewers to consume substantially different programming and ideas, rather than simply to the dispersal of audiences. New technologies contribute to this polarization in various ways; for example, control technologies, which enable audiences to view the same programs at different times, decrease the likelihood of viewers sharing content during a given period, while the new surplus of channels spreads the audience across an expansive range of programming.[21] Moreover, viewers' ability to use recording technologies to develop self-determined programming schedules also diminished the already languishing notion of television as an initiator of water-cooler conversation—a notion once enforced through the mandate of simultaneous viewing.

The emergence of so many new networks and channels changed the competitive dynamics of the industry and the type of programming likely to be produced. Instead of needing to design programming likely to be least objectionable to the entire family, broadcast networks—and particularly cable channels—increasingly developed programming that might be most satisfying to specific audience members. At first, this niche targeting remained fairly general with channels such as CNN seeking out those interested in news, ESPN attending to the sports audience, and MTV aiming at youth culture. As the number of cable channels grew, however, this targeting became more and more narrow. For example, by the early 2000s, three different cable channels specifically pursued women (Lifetime, Oxygen, and WE), yet developed clearly differentiated programming that might be "most satisfying" to women with divergent interests. These more narrowly targeted cable channels increased the range of stories that could be supported by an advertising-based medium. By the mid- to late 1990s, some cable channels built enough revenue to support the production of "broadcast quality" original series such as *La Femme Nikita* and *Any Day Now,* and their particular economic arrangements allowed them to schedule series with themes and content unlikely to be found on broadcast networks.[22] Their niche audience strategy and the supplementary income they gained from the fees paid by cable providers led cable channels to develop shows such as Lifetime's female-centered dramas *Any Day Now* and *Strong Medicine* or FX's edgy dramas *The Shield* and *Nip/Tuck* which have much more specific target audiences than those of broadcast series. The ability of cable channels to succeed with smaller audiences made broadcasters' mission difficult as viewers chose the most satisfying program over that which was least objectionable. Yet the cable channels were also simultaneously constrained by their much smaller audiences and related lower advertising prices.

Indications of a Post-Network Era

The choice and control that viewers gained during the multi-channel transition only continue to expand during the post-network era. Others (myself included) have previously used "post-network" to indicate the era in which cable channels created additional options for viewers—similar to the way I use the phrase "multi-channel transition" here. The term "post-network" is best reserved, however, as an indicator of more comprehensive changes in the medium's use. Here, "post-network" acknowledges the break from a dominant network-era experience in which viewers lacked much control over when and where to view and chose among a limited selection of externally determined linear viewing options—in other words, programs available at a certain time on a certain channel. Such constraints are not part of the post-network television experience in which viewers now increasingly select what, when, and where to view from abundant options. The post-network distinction is not meant to suggest the end or irrelevance of networks—just the erosion of their control over how and when viewers watch particular programs. In the early years of the post-network era, networks and channels have remained important sites of program aggregation, operating with distinctive identities that help viewers find content of interest.

Chapters 2 through 6 provide detailed considerations of the new industrial conditions that suggest that a post-network era is coming to be established. These conditions include emerging technologies that enable far greater control over when and where viewers watch programming; multiple options for financing television production that develop and expand the range of commercially viable programming; greater opportunities for amateur production that have arisen with and been augmented by a revolution in distribution that exponentially increases the ease of sharing video; various advertising strategies including product placement and integration that have come to co-exist with the decreasingly dominant thirty-second ad; and advances in digital technologies that further expand knowledge about audience viewing behaviors and create opportunities to supplement sampling methods with census data about use. Once again, adjustments in the production process change the use of television as viewers gain additional control capabilities and access to content variation. Additionally, other new technologies have expanded portable and mobile television use and have removed television from its domestic confines.

Unlike the fairly uniform experience of watching television in the network era, by the end of the multi-channel transition, there was no singular behavior or mode of viewing, and this variability has only increased in the post-network era. For example, research of early DVR adopters found that they sometimes engaged television through the previously dominant model of watching television live. However, at other times and with other types of programming they also exhibited an emergent behavior of using the device not only to seek out and record certain content but also to pause, skip, or otherwise self-determine how to view it. Control technologies have effectively added to viewers' choice in experiencing television, as they have enabled far more differentiated and individualized uses of the medium.

Two key non-television related factors also figure significantly in creating the changes in audience behaviors that characterize the post-network era: computing and generational shifts. The diffusion of personal computers relates to changing uses of television in significant ways. During the multi-channel transition, when viewers increasingly experienced television as one of many "screen" technologies in the home, the initial contrast between the experience of using computers and watching television led users to differentiate between screen media according to whether they required us to push or pull content, lean back or lean forward, and pursue leisure or work. Subsequently, however, digital technologies have come to dismantle these early differentiations and tendencies of use and have allowed for the previously unimagined integration of television and computers in the post-network era. This integration has occurred concomitantly with the growth in home computer ownership, which rose from 11 percent in 1985 to 30 percent in 1995 and reached equilibrium by 2003—growing only 2 percent by 2005 from 65 to 67 percent.[23] The technological experience of personal computing is important beyond the growing convergence of media in the latter part of the multi-channel transition era because of the new technological aptitudes and expectations embodied in computer users. The presumption that technologies "do" something useful and that we "do" something with them has played a significant role in adjusting network-era behavior with regard to television. New media theorist Dan Harries refers to the blending of old media *viewing* and new media *using* as "viewsing."[24] Thinking about such activities as being merged, rather than as being distinct, takes important steps beyond the binaries between computer and television technologies commonly assumed in the past and addresses the multiple modes of viewing and using that audiences began to exhibit by the end of the multi-channel transition.

Related generational differences have also played a key role in changing uses of television.[25] Many of the distinctions such as broadcast versus cable—let alone between television and computer—that have structured understandings of television are meaningless to those born after 1980. Most members of this generation (dubbed "Millennials" or "digital natives") never knew a world without cable, were introduced to the Internet before graduating from high school, and carried mobile phones with them from the time they were first allowed out in the world on their own.[26] The older edge of this generation provoked a new economic model in the recording industry through rampant illegal downloading, while their younger peers made their first music purchases from online single-song retailers such as Apple's iTunes.

Acculturated with a range of communication technologies from birth, this generation moves fluidly and fluently among technologies. Anne Sweeney, co-chair of Disney media networks and president of the Disney-ABC television group, recounted research in 2006 indicating that 40 percent of Millennials went home each evening and used five to eight technologies (many simultaneously), while 40 percent of their Boomer parents returned home and only watched television.[27] Similarly, a 2006 report by IBM Business Consulting Services emphasized the "bi-modality" of television consumers in coming years. It predicted a "generational chasm" between "massive passives" who were mainly Boomers who retained network-era television behaviors, "gadgetiers" who were members of the middling Generation X who were not acculturated with new technologies from birth, but were more willing to experiment with them, and "kool kids," the Millennials.[28] Younger generations, who have approached television and technology in general with very different expectations than their predecessors, have also introduced new norms of use. For example, television scholar Jason Mittell reflects on the significance of the arrival of a DVR in his home at the same time as his first child, and notes that when she came to ask "what is on television?" the question referred to what shows might be stored on the hard drive, as she had no sense of the limited access to scheduled programming assumed by most others.[29] The widespread availability of control technologies provides a different experience for younger generations who may never associate networks with television viewing in the same manner as their antecedents. As the generation that came of age using television to watch videos and DVDs and to play video games becomes employed in the industry, it will enable even greater re-imagining of television content and use.

At a summit on "The Future of Television" sponsored by the trade publication *Television Week* in September 2004, all but one of the panelists used evidence drawn from observations of their children's approach to television as justification for their arguments about the new directions of the medium. In addition to their children not operating with a model of television organized by networks and linear schedules, the executives noted, with awe, the mediated multi-tasking that defined their children's television use. Research that continues to show growth in all media use supports these anecdotes. For example, as of 2007, time spent viewing television had not diminished despite continued expansion in time spent using the Internet; instead, multiple media have come to be simultaneously used. Generations who are growing up with computers and mobile phones are accustomed to using multiple technologies to achieve a desired end—whether to access information, find entertainment, or communicate with friends. Such comfort in moving across technologies, or what those in the industry refer to as "media agnosticism," has been crucial to the adoption of devices for watching television and ways of doing so that further facilitate the shift to the post-network era.

In sum, while features of a post-network era have come to be more apparent, such an era will be fully in place only once choice is no longer limited to program schedules and the majority of viewers use the opportunities new technologies and industrial practices make available. Post-network television is primarily non-linear rather than linear, and it could not be established until dominant network-era practices became so outmoded that the industry developed new practices in their place. The gradual adjustment in how viewers use television, and corresponding gradual shifts in production practices, have taken more than two decades to transpire, which is why I distinguish this intermediate period as the multi-channel transition. During this time, viewers experienced a marked increase in choice and achieved limited control over the viewing experience. But the post-network era allows them to choose among programs produced in any decade, by amateurs and professionals, and to watch this programming on demand and for viewing on main "living room" sets, computer screens, or portable devices.

And So, the Television Will Be Revolutionized

> The world as we knew it is over.
> —Les Moonves, President of CBS Television, 2003

> The 50-year-old economic model of this business is kind of history now.
> —Gail Berman, President of Entertainment, FOX, 2003[30]

These bold pronouncements by two of the U.S. television industry's most powerful executives only begin to suggest the scale of the transitions that took place as the multi-channel transition yielded to new industrial norms characteristic of a post-network era. Television executives commonly traffic in hyperbolic statements, but the assertions by Moonves and Berman did not overstate the case. Here they reflected on the substantial challenges to conventional production processes as a result of scheduling and financing the comparatively cheap, but widely viewed unscripted ("reality") television series. Yet, the issues brought to the fore by the success of unscripted formats offered only an indication of the broader forces that threatened to revise decades'-old business models and industrial practices.

A confluence of multiple industrial, technological, and cultural shifts conspired to alter institutional norms in a manner that fundamentally redefined the medium and the business of television. The U.S. television industry was a multifaceted and mature industry by the early years of the twenty-first century, when Moonves and Berman made these claims. As post-network adjustments became unavoidable, many executives expressed a sense that the sky was falling—and indeed, the scale of changes affecting all segments of the industry gave reasonable cause for this outlook. A single or simple cause did not initiate this comprehensive industrial reconfiguration, so there was no one to blame and no way to stop it.

An important harbinger of the arrival or near arrival of the post-network era occurred in mid-2004 when the rhetoric of industry leaders shifted from advocating efforts to prevent change to accepting the inevitability of industrial adjustment. This acceptance marked a transition from corporate strategies that sought to erect walls around content and retard the availability of more personalized applications of television technology to efforts to enable content from traditional providers to travel beyond the linear network platform.[31] In his detailed history of the invention of media technologies, Brian Winston illustrates how existing industries have repeatedly suppressed the radical potential of new technologies in an effort to prevent them from disrupting established economic interests. Unsurprisingly, the patterns Winston identifies also appear in the television industry, in which "supervening social necessities" led inventors to create technologies that provided markedly new capabilities, while those with business interests threatened by the new inventions sought to curtail and constrain user access.[32] Nonetheless, many of the conventional practices and even the industry's basic business model proved unworkable in this new context, which resulted in crises throughout all components of the production process. Considerable uncertainty arose about the new norms for programming and how power and control would be reallocated within the industry.

New technological capabilities and consumers' response to them forced the moguls of the network era to imagine their businesses anew and face fresh competitors who had the vision to foresee the new era. As suggested by the duration of the multi-channel transition, this industrial reconfiguration often produced unanticipated outcomes and developed haphazardly. Much of the sense of crisis within the industry resulted from the inability of powerful companies to anticipate the breadth of change and to develop new business models in response. Those who dominated the network era sensed their businesses to be simultaneously under attack on multiple fronts, which often led to efforts to stifle change or deny the substance of the threats to conventional ways of doing business.[33] Entrenched network-era business entities consequently did not lead the transition to the post-network era; rather, mavericks such as TiVo, Apple, and YouTube connected with viewers and forced industrial evolution.

Contrary to the contemporary headlines, television was not on the verge of death or even dying. Although indications of all kinds of change abounded, there was no suggestion that the central box through which we viewed would be called anything other than television. Adjustments throughout the television industry would not turn us into "screen potatoes" or lead us to engage in "monitor studies." We have, and will continue to process coming changes through our existing understandings of *television*. We will continue to call the increasingly large black boxes that serve as the focal point of our entertainment spaces *television*—regardless of how many boxes we need to connect to them in order to have the experience we desire or whether they are giant boxes or flat screens mounted on walls in the manner once reserved for art and decoration. The U.S. television industry may be being redefined, the experience of television viewing may be being redefined, but our intuitive sense of this thing we call television remains intact—at least for now.

The following pages update understandings about television's industrial practices from which others might build analyses of the substantial adjustments occurring within media systems and their societies of reception. The book also contributes to the necessary rethinking of "old" media in new contexts. The deterioration of the foundational business model upon which the commercial television industry long has operated suggests that a substantive change is occurring. Examining the industry at this time sheds light on how power is transferred during periods of institutional uncertainty and reveals the way that new possibilities can develop from emerging industrial norms. There is a similarity between the industrial moment considered here and that examined in Todd Gitlin's 1983 book, *Inside Prime Time*.[34] Both books chronicle the consequences of industrial practices of the television industry at the close of an era. Gitlin, however, captured this moment unintentionally. This work, in contrast, is reflexively aware of the transitory status of the practices it explores.

Examining the "television" that so confounded executives such as Moonves and Berman requires that I also consider many of the other boxes we connect to our televisions to expand our ability to use television, such as cable/satellite boxes and digital video recorders. At last count, a neat pile of no fewer than six rectangular black boxes was stacked below my television. Each serves a different function: some enhance my ability to access and control television programs, while others allow the set to function independently of the content made to stream through it. Here, I focus upon devices that deliver and enhance content produced and understood as "television"—so that the VCR derives its importance from its function of recording content transmitted as television programming. Likewise, I emphasize the DVD as a means to distribute television series, despite its other and equally important functions that connect it to the film industry.

As new distribution methods allowed viewers to share "television" content among their televisions, computers, and mobile phones, content boundaries among screen technologies disintegrated. I do not intend to denigrate, displace, or suggest a hierarchy of importance in the contemporary uses of television by focusing on the content and industrial practices culturally and historically defined as that of "television" rather than also including a detailed examination of applications previously perceived to be more particular to the computer.[35] At the same time that I circumscribe this understanding of television, I acknowledge there are complicated tensions and inconsistencies: Rich Frank's grandson may prefer to watch TiVo, but he probably considers himself to be watching "television" in a manner different from my colleague, who claims to watch videos, not "television."

Perhaps paradoxically I take a particular type of television—"prime-time programming"—and the national broadcast networks as the book's focus. Despite significant industry changes, as I completed the book, prime-time programming remained the most viewed and dominant form of "television." The post-network era threatens to eliminate time-based hierarchies, but the distinctive status of prime time is determined as much by its budgets and production practices as by the time of day in which it airs. Changing industrial norms bore consequences for all programming. Adjustments in production components also affected affiliate and independent stations in significant and particular ways, but the breadth of these matters prevents me from addressing them here. Although the affiliates represent a large part of the television industry, the consequences of post-network shifts affected these stations in substantially different ways depending, among other things, on whether the station was owned and operated by a network, located in a large or small market, and the network with which the station was affiliated.

The next chapter briefly steps away from the book's main focus on how shifts in industrial practices and business norms affect programming to meditate on some of the more abstract and bigger issues—some might say theories—called into question by these institutional adjustments. Concerns about how television operates as a cultural institution, the adaptation of tools used to understand it, and the development of new ones aid us in thinking about intersections of television and culture that may not be the primary concern of those who work in the industry. Such questions and concerns are nonetheless of crucial importance to the rest of us who live in this world of fragmented audiences and wonder about the effects of the erosion of the assumptions we have long shared about television.

Each aspect of production examined in Chapters 2 through 6 changed on a different timetable in the course of the multi-channel transition. By 2005, technological capabilities and distribution methods characteristic of post-network organization had emerged, while other production components were not as substantially developed. Thus, each of these chapters focuses on a particular production component—technology, creation, distribution, advertising, and audience measurement—and explores the process of transition, what practices have changed, and their consequences with regard to how television functions as a cultural institution.

With a focus on technology, Chapter 2 explores how new devices have made television more multifaceted and enabled more varied uses than were common during the network era. By 2005, new television technologies enabled three distinct capabilities—convenience, mobility, and theatricality—that led to different expectations and uses of television and created a diversified experience of the medium in contrast to the uniform one common in the network era. Technologies including DVRs, portable televisions, and high-definition television—among many others—produce complicated consequences for the societies that adopt them as viewers gain greater control over their entertainment experience, yet become tethered by an increasing range of devices that demand their attention and financial support.

Chapter 3 explores the practices involved in the making of television, particularly the institutional adjustments studios and networks made during and after the implementation of the financial interest and syndication rules, as well as the effects of these adjustments on the content the industry produces. Studios have responded to changing economic models by battling with creative guilds and unions to maintain new revenue streams, shifting production out of union-dominated Los Angeles, and creating vertically integrated production and distribution entities. Changing competitive practices among networks have borne significant adjustments in the types of shows the industry produces and expanded the range of profitable storytelling. The chapter thus examines how redefined production norms have created opportunities for different types of programming and required new promotion techniques.

Some of the most phenomenal adjustments in the television industry result from viewers' expanded ability to control the flow of television and to move it out of the home. Whereas a distribution "bottleneck" characterized the network era and much of the multi-channel transition, the bottleneck broke open in late 2005 with nearly limitless possibilities for viewers to access programming. Chapter 4 explores how viewers gained access to television in an increasing array of outlets that featured differentiated business models. New distribution methods made once unprofitable programming forms viable and decreased the risk of unconventional programming, opening creative opportunities in the industry and contributing to the fundamental changes in the production processes discussed throughout the book.

Chapter 5 examines how commercial television's financiers—the advertisers—also helped advance its redefinition by embracing both new and much older advertising strategies in the early 2000s. Various alternatives to the thirty-second advertisement emerged, such as product placement, integration, branded entertainment, and sponsorship, but these strategies did not threaten to supplant the thirty-second advertisement as a dominant form. Rather, the diversified strategies were symptomatic of the conditions of a multifaceted post-network era that relies upon multiple, co-existing advertising strategies. At the same time, though, these different advertising techniques have come to enable a new variety of programming and to yield significant implications for television as a cultural institution. The chapter closes with examinations of *The Shield, The Days,* and Super Bowl XXXVIII to illustrate the narrative differentiation made possible by advertiser support of a fragmented media environment and the breadth of content such an environment can sustain.

Following the examination of advertising, Chapter 6 explores the often-unconsidered role of audience measurement that proved particularly contentious in the late years of the multi-channel transition. Industry leader Nielsen Media Research endeavored to introduce technological upgrades that reallocated advertising dollars, while new distribution methods and advertising strategies required impartial measurement for validation. The existing paradigm of audience measurement proved increasingly insufficient for the variation characteristic of post-network television. This chapter considers the crucial role of audience measurement and developments during the tumultuous early 2000s, as well as the consequences adjustments in this sector might bring to the production of television in the future.

While Chapters 2 through 6 include many examples that apply somewhat abstract industrial practices to specific shows and circumstances, Chapter 7 takes a detailed look at how technology, creation, distribution, advertising, and audience measurement intersect in five very different programs. Each of the five cases explored here owe their existence or success to production practices uncharacteristic of the network era and tell a particular and distinctive story about production processes at the end of the multi-channel transition. These shows, *Sex and the City, Survivor, The Shield, Arrested Development*, and *Off to War*, illustrate how changes in multiple practices interconnected to expand the range of stories that could be profitably told on U.S. television, as well as pointing to some of the implications of this expanded storytelling field for the industry and culture.

The perspective here involves looking ahead, not to predict, but to prepare for a new era of television experience and criticism. The precise form that the technologies and uses of television will take are not definite, but substantial industrial ruptures are already apparent, and the need for practical information and conceptual models to rethink the medium are evident. The following pages may consequently serve as both a eulogy to the television we have experienced to this point and prepare our understanding of the medium yet to come.

1

Understanding Television at the Beginning of the Post-Network Era

Early in every semester I survey my classes in search of a show we all share in common in order to draw examples from it throughout the term. This was a pretty easy feat in my first few years of teaching. Usually I found a show on my first (*Friends*) or second (*ER*) try. In recent semesters I have all but given up on such unanimity. Instead I gather a sense of what different factions of students might be watching, as it has been a while since I taught a class in which we had all seen the same show at least once (yes, even *American Idol*). This development illustrates an important consequence of the choice in viewing provided by the post-network era. The hundreds of channels offering programming by the end of the multi-channel transition has significantly fragmented the audience. By mid 2006, viewers could readily access hundreds of television shows from any era on DVD or online, and an amateur video clip could reach as large an audience as a network show. Although only early adopters may have been viewing television in these new ways by this time, these developments suggest additional coming fragmentation.

In early August 2006, "The Evolution of Dance," a humorous six-minute amateur performance of the progression of popular dance styles from the 1950s through the present, had been on YouTube.com for four months and had been played at least thirty million times.[1] Site users reposted the video multiple times, and in at least three different languages, taking advantage of one of YouTube's technological strengths—the ease with which videos can be linked to other sites—but making it difficult to sum up how many times it had been viewed across these multiple postings and on other sites. As a point of comparison, the most watched television show of the preceding season—*American Idol*'s Tuesday night performance episodes—averaged 31.2 million viewers each week. FOX's blockbuster hit included judges paid roughly $30 million a year, and the network earned $700,000 for a thirty-second advertisement, in addition to the at least $25 million per season paid by each of the three series sponsors.[2] In contrast, "The Evolution of Dance" featured the negligible production values of a video camera set up in the audience of a comedy club and was originally posted by the video's creator and dancer, Judson Laipply. Laipply did not profit directly from the millions of viewers, although stories about the video's popularity appeared on the *Today Show, Good Morning America,* and *Inside Edition* and drew attention to his work as a public speaker and "inspirational comedian." YouTube benefited from the high traffic to the site that may have clicked through some of the banner advertisements, and the video figured prominently in increasing cultural awareness of the site. When I queried my classes later that fall about their familiarity with the video, some had seen it—although fewer than I had expected and by no means as many as had seen various television shows. When I asked co-workers (faculty and staff over the age of thirty), most responded by asking what YouTube was—until a few months later when Google's $1.65 billion purchase of the site drew much attention.

The changes in how we view, experience, and use television made evident by these anecdotes have massive implications for how we think about television and its role in culture. The increased fractionalization of the audience among shows, channels, and distribution devices has diminished the ability of an individual television network or television show to reinforce a certain set of beliefs to a broad audience in the manner we long believed to occur. Although television can still function as a mass medium, in most cases it does so by aggregating a collection of niche audiences. The narrowcasting that became common to television during the multi-channel transition has thus required adjustments in theories about the mass nature of the medium, while the exponential expansion in viewers' choice and control since the network era has necessitated an even more substantive reassessment of television. Taking up these issues, this chapter provides an overview of some of the central ideas that have governed the study of television and culture as well as some preliminary tools for making sense of television in the post-network era.

Defining Television

The industrial changes that developed during the multi-channel transition made the very object that we are exploring uncertain as new forms and ways of using television required us to reconsider "what is television?"

The anecdote about my colleague's claim of viewing "videos" and not television at the beginning of the introduction illustrates the growing ambiguity about the boundaries of the medium, just as one might wonder whether or not "The Evolution of Dance" should be considered television. Although the term "television" has been broadly used to refer to a singular technology—a box with a screen—the range of experiences has long made the object of study quite uncertain. We have commonly assumed shared knowledge of "television," although few have deliberated extensively on this point.[3]

Television is more than just a technology—more than a composite of wires, metal, and glass. It possesses an essence that is bound up in its context, in how the box is most commonly used, in where it is located, in what streams though it, and in how most use it, despite the possibility for broad variation in all the factors. What is the distinction, then, between a television and a monitor, particularly in the context of contemporary technological convergence and the manufacturing of digital "televisions" that have no tuning capability—i.e., the ability to receive signals over the air? Recent work by Lisa Gitelman argues for a definition of media as "socially realized structures of communication, where structures include both technological forms and their associated protocols."[4] Protocols include "normative rules and default conditions" such as the greeting "Hello," monthly billing cycles, and a system of wires and cable for the U.S. phone service. Understanding that the protocols of television contribute to distinguishing the medium helps us rectify some of the inadequacy of defining the medium only in terms of the piece of equipment and addresses how the technology becomes a television when it receives signals via broadcast, cable, or satellite transmission. A television is not just a machine, but also the set of behaviors and practices associated with its use. Consequently, it may not be a "television" when it functions merely as a conduit through which video games, computer signals, or a DVD may pass, but its reception of networks and channels does make it a television—even though both uses now require the connection of certain boxes to the set for it to fulfill these functions. New questions are also emerging. What if this "network" content we perceive as characteristic of television is displayed elsewhere, such as on a laptop or mobile phone screen? Does one still watch "television" in these contexts?

I approach television with the presumption that our cultural understanding of this medium does indeed conceive of it as more than a monitor, piece of hardware, or gateway to programming, and that television is less defined by how the content gets to us and what we view it on than by the set of experiences and practices we've long associated with the activity of viewing. All of these technical attributes unquestionably contribute to how a culture uses and understands television, yet inherited meanings, expectations, and habits also circumscribe it in particular ways. New technologies and industrial practices have introduced radical changes in technological aspects of television, its use, and its consequent cultural significance, but various aspects of socio-cultural experience still define television in our minds in specific and meaningful ways—particularly for those generations who knew television in the network era.

The transition of radio in the 1940s provides an illustrative parallel. As television first entered homes, radio had to fundamentally redefine itself—both its programming and in how and where listeners used it. Before television, radio was primarily a domestic-bound technology that played particular programs on a known schedule; after television usurped the captive home audience, radio became a portable medium and shifted to emphasize ongoing music or talk formats. Nonetheless, after television, the technology remained commonly understood as "radio" despite the substantial difference in the medium and adjustments to its role as a cultural institution. Likewise, in recent years, as the television experience has encompassed new capabilities and spread to additional screens, established cultural understandings have shifted accordingly so that we still continued to comprehend different experiences as watching "television." Television may not be dying, but changes in its content and how and where we view have complicated how we think about and understand its role in the culture.

In introducing a collection of essays that considers various aspects of the wide-ranging transitions that occurred by the beginning of the twenty-first century, Lynn Spigel reflects on the title of the anthology— *Television After TV: Essays on a Medium in Transition*. She notes that, "Indeed, if TV refers to the technologies, industrial formations, government policies, and practices of looking that were associated with the medium in its classical public service and three-network age, it appears we are now entering a new phase of television—the phase that comes after 'TV.' "[5] Although the title of the collection is eye-catching and provocative, it suggests a far more absolute rupture than that which occurred; it is also arbitrary in affording the norms of the network era such eminence as determinant of the medium. Still, attention to transition and uncertainty about the present status and likely future of television evident in the anthology and its title were not uncommon by late in the multi-channel transition. Another title of an important article queries, "What is the 'Television' of Television Studies?"—a question that similarly asserts concern about ambiguity regarding the fundamental attributes of television.[6] Those who write about television have never adequately addressed which of the "technologies, industrial formations, government policies, and practices of looking," to borrow from Spigel, might particularly establish the ontological boundaries of the medium—the things that make television "television." We err in allowing those norms established first to "determine" the medium; they are as arbitrary as any subsequent formation.[7]

Thinking about Network-Era Television

Scholars in fields as diverse as literature, film studies, political science, sociology, psychology, and communication developed different ways of thinking about television and its role in culture. Those in the area of "media studies" have attended most closely to the ways in which programs, audiences, industries, and socio-cultural contexts intertwine in the creation and circulation of television, and their ideas are most relevant here. Scholars of media studies—and critical television studies in particular—have developed detailed theories and empirical studies that examine the multifaceted nature of cultural production common to television. But in the network era, there was no need for esoteric discussions of "what is television" as it was assumed to be a simple technology whose variation spanned little more than screen size and color or black and white.[8] Most television theory continues to presume network-era norms in explaining the cultural and institutional functions of television, and draws from distinctive national experiences with the medium. This book and the conditions of the post-network era call many of these assumptions into question.

Foundational understandings of television view it as a—if not the—central communicative and cultural force within society. Its centrality derived from its *availability* and *ubiquity*; as early as 1960 more than 87 percent of U.S. households had televisions, and the technology increasingly was available in spaces outside of the home such as taverns and hospitals.[9] The accessibility of television was in many ways enabled by the low cost of acquiring its programming. Either as a result of advertising support in the United States or public funding in most other countries, viewing television programs did not require the same type of per-use fee associated with most other entertainment and informational media such as films, newspapers, and magazines. To be sure, commercial media "cost" societies in ways obscured by simple presumptions that proclaimed that network-era television was "free"; nonetheless, it was reasonable to assert that television's low barriers to access greatly contributed to its cultural importance in the network era.

During that time, the medium gained its status as a primary cultural institution precisely because network-era programming could and did reach such vast audiences. Television derived its significance from its capacity to broadly share information and ideas and facilitate an "electronic public sphere" of sorts.[10] Its stories and ideas reached a mass audience that some have argued enabled television programs to negotiate contradictory and contested social ideas, while others have proposed that this reach allowed television to enforce a dominant way of thinking.[11] Significantly, both perspectives ascribed importance to television because of its pervasiveness.[12] Viewers' lack of control over the medium and the limited choice at this time aided its ability to function as both forum and ideological enforcer. Network-era norms imposed the synchronicity of linear viewing, and television earned its status as an instigator of "water-cooler conversation" by providing shared content for discussion. Co-workers and neighbors chose from the same limited range of programs each night, and thus were likely to have viewed the same program.

Assessments of television that consider how it contributes to the sharing and negotiation of ideas understand it to operate as a "cultural institution"—that is, as a social conduit that participates in communicating values and ideas within a culture by telling stories and conveying information that reflects, challenges, and responds to shared debates and concerns. Educational systems, clubs and societal orders, and religious organizations are also cultural institutions, although we may more readily identify and accept the influence of these sites on how we know and understand the world around us.[13] At the same time television functions as a cultural institution, however, it is also a "cultural industry." That is, in a context such as the United States, the television industry operates as a commercial enterprise that primarily seeks to maximize profits, while nonetheless producing programs that are important creative and cultural forms that communicate social values and beliefs. Industry workers may primarily make decisions based on what types of programming they perceive to be most profitable, yet these decisions still have important cultural implications for what stories are told, by whom, and how society comes to understand the worlds that television presents. Remembering the commercial mandate of television—again, particularly in the United States—is imperative: in the cultural industry of television, business and culture operate concurrently and are inextricable in every aspect.

Studies that explain the economic and industrial norms of television in the network era are particularly relevant to the focus here upon television as a cultural industry. Until recently, few attempted to bridge the chasm between humanities-inflected theories about the operation of media in culture and political economy research that emphasizes economics and industrial operations.[14] This history of avoidance, and at times hostility, between approaches is increasingly being corrected by theories and methods that deliberately merge aspects of culture and economics or explore quotidian industrial processes to better understand the agents, organizations, and processes involved in cultural production—as I attempt here.[15]

As is the case of dominant cultural theories about television, most political economy work assumes television to be a mass medium and attributes much of its importance to this characteristic. The notion of mass media and the scale of such businesses are important to political economy approaches examining the assemblage and distribution of labor and capital, while the mass audience was crucial to cultural approaches because of the necessity for programs to be widely shared within the culture. In both cases, the breadth of the audience reached by network-era programming allowed television to circulate ideas in a way that asserted and reinforced existing power structures and dominant ways of thinking within a society.

In many cases, the changed industrial context has not negated the value of theoretical tools provided by these perspectives, but some require reconsideration and adjustment. For example, Horace Newcomb and Paul Hirsch's argument that television programs provide a cultural forum to negotiate ideas within society makes sense insofar as television continued to facilitate this cultural role after the network era on certain occasions; however, broad and heterogeneous audiences now rarely share individual programs in the manner they assumed. Television might continue to provide a cultural forum for those who tune in to a particular show, but it has become increasingly unlikely that television functions as a space for the negotiation of contested beliefs among diverse groups simply because audiences are now more narrow and specialized.[16]

Other theories, such as Raymond Williams' network-era theory of "flow," require more significant revision.[17] Williams used the idea of flow to comment on the nature of the steady stream of programming through the set and the manner in which narrative, advertisements, and promotions all intermixed. The continuous infiltration of control devices into television use has greatly disrupted flow as a fundamental characteristic of the medium—at least in terms of television flow being determined by someone other than the individual viewer.

Television's transition from its network-era norm as a mass medium toward its post-network-era function as an aggregator of a broad range of niche and on-demand viewing audiences has required significant adjustments to industrial assumptions about the medium. For example, in his 1989 book, *The Capitalization of Cultural Production,* Bernard Miege located television among media industries that operate under a "flow" model (this use of the term differs substantially from that of Williams) and rely on "home and family listening," "an undifferentiated, indirect mass market," the "instant" obsolescence of content, and the use of a programming grid that creates daily interaction and cultivates viewer loyalty, all of which eroded during the multi-channel transition. By the mid-2000s, the market characteristics of U.S. television have come instead to resemble those of his "publishing" model, which features a "segmented mass market" and the "dialectic of the 'hit and catalogue,' " along with the purchase of individualized objects—in this case, particular episodes of television shows.[18]

Noting that " 'television' now functions as a bookstore, a news stand, or a library," Newcomb has recently departed from the "cultural forum" concept of organization he and Hirsch offered in 1983 and produced a construction of the medium similar to Miege's publishing model.[19] Television adopted multiple possible revenue streams in ways that mirror the bookstore (DVD sell-through, iTunes downloading), magazine subscription (premium cable networks such as HBO), and the library (free on demand), as well as other related venues, such as the subscription library model of NetFlix, which was initially envisioned as a film rental service, but was used by many to watch television on DVD as well. Each of these possible transactions of capital for content created new and distinct relationships between the economic model, programming, and how these forms of television might function as a cultural institution. And, as Newcomb notes, these alternative transaction or publishing models thrive on specialty, distinction, and niche taste—all of which unmistakably distinguish the practices of the multi-channel transition and post-network era from network-era norms that privileged the opposite characteristics.

Post-network-era practices have led the television audience not only to fracture among different channels and devices, but also to splinter temporally. The control over the television experience that various technologies offer has ruptured the norm of simultaneity in television experience and enabled audiences to capture television on their own terms. Moreover, as *New York Observer* columnist Tom Scocca notes, the ephemerality once characteristic of the medium has also come to be less prominent; for example, the video experiences offered by YouTube allow for archiving images so they may be called up at will.[20] New devices have provided tools to capture television and consequently have produced a norm of asynchronous viewing that has altered the interaction of the culture with the medium in crucial ways. Television devices remained ubiquitous and accessible in the post-network era, but the ubiquity of specific content has been eliminated as broad audiences have come to share little programming in common and less frequently view it simultaneously.

The adjustments to the U.S. television industry chronicled here provided as extraordinary a shift for those who work in it as those trying to understand it. Much of the slow pace of change throughout the multi-channel transition resulted from the lack of clear business models that could reflect the dynamics of a new era. Those who long profited from the norms of television's operation under a flow model were unwilling to relinquish their dominant status or pursue actions likely to hasten greater change. The diversification in economic models, changing industrial relationships, and challenges to regulatory practices posed by new technologies all required revisiting many of the foundational industrial assumptions of television and how it operated.

Theorizing Niche Media: Identifying Phenomenal Television

Regardless of whether we have truly reached the post-network era, the U.S. television industry and its norms of operation have changed significantly. The most noteworthy adjustment evident by 2005 was the erosion of television's regular operation as a mass medium. Although it has continued to play this role in isolated moments, television is no longer organized in this way and has not been since the mid-1990s. By then, it was already apparent that we needed to reassess television and see it as a medium that primarily reaches niche audiences. Continued transition in television's core economic models would only further adjust the type of programming that could be profitably produced and television's operation as a cultural institution.

No mass medium arose to supplant television in the wake of its industrial change, and it might be that mass media as they existed in the twentieth century were remnants of a particular set of industrial and economic relations from another era.[21] Niche-focused media long have played an important role in society by communicating cultural beliefs, albeit to narrower groups than mass media. Women's magazines provide an illustrative example, as ample critical scholarship has explored how this media form that targets a specific audience consistently reproduced certain discourses of beauty, identity, and female behavior.[22] Niche media are identified as important voices to specific communities, but have received less critical attention than mechanisms of mass messaging.

Theorizing the cultural significance of niche media might begin by exploring those industries that have operated in this organization for some time, and the magazine industry—with its era of mass distribution earlier in the century—may provide the most relevant point of comparison. Joseph Turow considers the process through which this industry transitioned from mass market publications with titles such as *Life, Look,* and the *Saturday Evening Post* to more narrowly targeted magazines and argues that demand from advertisers to reach ever more specific audiences fueled the fragmentation.[23] While acknowledging the economic value and efficiency targeting provides to advertisers, he raises a cautionary flag about such fragmentation and rightly notes the dangers for ideals of democracy and community that result from what develop into "gated informational communities."[24] The redefinition of television in the course of the multi-channel transition as a medium that supports fragmented audiences and polarized content consequently has exacerbated the cultural trends and outcomes that Turow identified in the magazine industry.

Television's new abundant offerings make it difficult to determine a proper frame through which to examine programming and assess its significance. We are accustomed to moral panics and activism that develop from concern about the vast reach of mediated messages. Thinking about television in the age of narrowcasting requires that we take into account the substantial variation now encompassed by its programming. "Successful" television programs might now gather audiences that range from tens of thousands to tens of millions, while channels might be accessible in anywhere from three million to one hundred million homes. Some programs stream into the home without any viewer payment, others require a subscription for a channel of programming (HBO), and viewers now can buy specific programs on DVD or as single-show downloads. With such ample variation in the availability and ubiquity of television programming, we need more specific models for understanding television's operation in the culture, ones that will enable us to differentially assess its significance.

Toward this end, I propose "phenomenal television" as a particular category of programming that retains the social importance attributed to television's earlier operation as a cultural forum despite the changes of the post-network era. In the network era, television content derived its relevance simply from being on the air, which necessarily meant that it was widely viewed because of the vast and substantive audiences programs had to draw to survive. Often popular shows were particularly important sites of analysis because broad viewership on a mass medium denoted a certain scope of influence. In a narrowcast environment, content must do more than appear "on television" to distinguish itself as having cultural relevance, since now much that appears on television might be seen by just a few viewers. For example, the particular economic model of advertiser-supported cable networks allows them to produce shows viewed by 1 percent of the available audience and for these shows to still be considered hits. Network-era theories might still apply to some programming produced in this narrowcast environment, and phenomenal television denotes such programming. Although the task of determining relevance and distinction is more difficult in the post-network era, phenomenal television does have identifiable attributes, as specified below.

Themes, topics, and discourses that appear in multiple and varied outlets indicate a form of phenomenal television. The criterion here is not purely quantitative—as in a topic that appears in seven shows is "more" phenomenal than one appearing in six; rather, multiplicity might indicate a society-wide negotiation of an issue or a crisis in existing understandings in the same manner it did in the network era. Trans-show or trans-network themes derive importance in a narrowcast environment because such scope indicates content that has achieved or is likely to achieve uncommon audience breadth despite fragmentation and polarization. Ideas appearing in multiple shows—particularly different types of shows—might indicate concerns relevant to the broader society rather than distinct subcultures.²⁵ For example, in the year after the September 11, 2001, attacks on New York and Washington, multiple narratives exploring fictional renditions of the aftermath appeared across at least twelve shows on seven networks.²⁶ Cultural critics could not look to just one of these shows as indicative of cultural sentiment on the subject, or even just that of television; instead, the niche media environment required a more holistic evaluation of the multiplicity of stories that likely reached varied audiences. This attribute responds to the way that individual programs and episodes rarely have the cultural significance previously common because of the fragmentation of audiences, although when thematically similar content is viewed and considered in aggregate, television has the potential to operate much as it did in the network era.

Attention to institutional factors such as *what network or type of network airs a show relative to the network's common audience* derives increased importance after the network era and plays a role in determining phenomenal television. Despite all being forms of television, broadcast, basic cable, and subscription cable have different regulatory and economic processes that contribute to their norms of operation and the possible programs they can create. These outlets also vary amply in audience size—and this, too, is a factor we must address in considering the reach and importance of a program or theme. Many programs—particularly those on premium and basic cable—reached narrow audiences throughout the multi-channel transition, but too often particular audience conditions were not addressed in framing analyses of or concerns about programs. Additionally, factors such as whether viewers watch content as part of linear schedules or on demand further have come to distinguish contemporary television programming as more viewers incorporate new control devices into their regular viewing habits. In the network era, we could assume a broad and heterogeneous audience who viewed linear schedules of network-planned programs. Now we cannot presume that the audience represents the culture-at-large; instead, it embodies only a distinct segment or component thereof. Assessing the type of network providing programming offers significant insight into the audience of a particular program.

Programs that achieve *"water-cooler status"* earn a certain degree of importance due to their ability to break through the cluttered media space, but this alone does not indicate phenomenal television. We must also explore how and why a program achieves this prominence. A water-cooler show that is supported by a particularly large promotion budget might be less meaningful than a show that captures the zeitgeist of the moment or gains its attention from the way that it resonates with a cultural sentiment or a struggle percolating below the surface of mainstream discourse. Phenomenal television can "go under the radar" and circulate out of sight or beyond the awareness of most of society, but examinations of such television must attend to how and why such shows are important. In the network era, water-cooler shows were often those that were somehow boundary defying, but few boundaries remain and merely airing on television has become less indicative of social significance than was once the case.

Incongruity suggests another feature of phenomenal television, which has a tendency to break into unexpected gated communities. For example, incongruity might exist in cases where the ideology of a story conflicts with the dominant perspective anticipated to be shared by the audience of that network. The ability for like to speak only to like is one of the greatest consequences of narrowcast media because it decreases the probability of incongruity and disables the type of negotiation theorized to be central to the ability of network era television to operate as a cultural forum. In many ways, the significance of a show such as *All in the Family* resulted from the heterogeneous audience that had their views alternatively challenged and reinforced by the differing perspectives articulated by Archie and Meathead. Similarly, a show such as *The Cosby Show* was particularly important because its depictions of upper-middle-class black life reached both black and white homes in a segregated society accustomed to representations of African Americans as being poverty-stricken or criminals. It remains significant to have a dramatic series focused on the lives and sexuality of a group of gay men (*Queer as Folk*) or lesbian women (*The L Word*), but these shows aired on a subscription channel that built an identity as the destination for gay and gay-friendly people, which made the content of these shows far more congruous than if it had aired elsewhere. Incongruous moments, such as the sophisticated negotiation and deconstruction of hegemonic masculinity provided by *Playmakers* and aired on ESPN or the critical exploration of the abuses of the Taliban against women on The WB family drama *7th Heaven*—which notably aired before September 11, 2001—expose audiences to ideas they may not normally self-select. The incongruity of these shows relative to what the audiences of these channels and their programs might expect can defy the tendency of narrowcasting to perpetuate gated media communities.

Programming affirmed by *hierarchies of artistic value and social importance*—those programs imbued with what Pierre Bourdieu terms "cultural capital"—indicate another distinction of phenomenal television. I do not wish to suggest that what I term "phenomenal television" is categorically "better" than other television—in the manner that "quality" television has been inconsistently used. Rather, what I am proposing is that television programming of specific aspiration and accomplishment —whether this be an ambitious period drama, a rigorous piece of investigative journalism, or a pointed political satire—might also distinguish itself as phenomenal because of its particular effort to enrich or expand cultural dialogue or thinking and to maximize the creative potential of the medium.

This delineation of characteristics of phenomenal television is not intended to suggest that programs that do not meet any of these criteria are unimportant. Rather, it marks a preliminary effort to develop a multifaceted theory in response to the growing multiplicity of television and its operation as a niche medium. The conditions of the post-network era require reconsidering everything we once knew about television and more clearly differentiating among its many forms. Size of audience is a significant consideration, but there are also features that distinguish programs in terms of content and in ways that are important to assess. The idea of phenomenal television provides a way to adjust our assumptions of television while keeping its increasingly niche operation in mind.

In many cases, the presumptions of network-era theory remain relevant in thinking about the cultural role of niche media and require only slight modification. For example, in 1978 John Fiske and John Hartley described the "bardic" role of television, noting how programs could "articulate the main lines of the established cultural consensus about the nature of reality."[27] Such a premise remains relevant in a narrowcast environment, but with the difference that television articulates the main lines of cultural consensus for the particular network and its typical audience member rather than for society in general. A so-called "boundary defying" program such as *The Shield,* which explores the psyche and actions of a corrupt detective, may seem too far outside of the accepted reality of the television audience on the whole, but the ambiguity of right and wrong it represents does appeal to a specific group of viewers who accept the complexity of human action and the arbitrariness of the justice system.

A category such as phenomenal television is just an initial tool for understanding the role of niche media in society; much more thinking in this area is certainly needed. Theories of niche media can in most cases reasonably assume certain characteristics of the audience—as niche media succeed because of their ability to tap into certain affinities that bring audience members together. But even though television programming of the multi-channel transition and post-network era increasingly targeted niche audiences, the breadth of content transmitted through the medium remained accessible to many beyond those targeted audiences. Those who watch niche content, but for whom it was not intended, might be viewed as "cultural interlopers"—as when teens' parents watch MTV or liberals view Fox News; although not all niche programming is equally susceptible to such practices. Industrial and economic factors such as how media are paid for vary the likelihood of interlopers across different types of television and in comparison with other niche media such as magazines. For example, subscriptions that provide access to a package of cable channels readily allow cultural interloping; subscriptions to specific programs, as in the case of pay-per-view, do not. Television watching is also often a shared activity in households, which increases the probability of co-habitants exposing others to television content not geared toward them.

Such possibilities for cultural interloping may further change as post-network distinctions solidify. Television purchased on a transactional basis, such as the pay-per-episode model available on iTunes, may be less likely to reach interlopers because of the added fees required to access this content. By contrast, subscriptions to channels might better facilitate interloping—as in the case of a viewer who subscribes to Showtime for the movies, but samples *Queer as Folk* because it has no added cost. Important similarities and differences might be identified with other media such as magazines that have a fee per use and tend to be consumed in solitude, but can often be picked up in places like waiting rooms and read for free. These discrepancies and variations suggest the degree to which a one-theory-fits-all-media—and even a one-theory-fits-one-medium—framework is inadequate for theorizing niche media and post-network-era television. Similarities among media might exist, but specific contexts remain crucial in assessing the particularities of varied media.

The Persistence of Television as a Cultural Institution

The ubiquity that earned television much of its perceived significance has also been changing as a result of post-network reconfigurations. As the possibilities for portable and mobile television explored in the next chapter indicate, television is everywhere it has ever been and in many more places. Paradoxically though, individual "pieces" of television (shows, episodes) are shared by fewer and fewer viewers. Together, these developments further the need to consider specific contexts and factors that are far narrower than "television" per se allows. For example, in March 2006, two University of Chicago professors released a study widely reported in newspapers across the country that found that children who watched television were not substantially harmed by the behavior.[28] Such reports—with varied findings—appear yearly (even monthly) from researchers in many different fields. With rare exception these studies talk about the effect of "television," as though there were no differences in the experience of it, no differences in what is watched or how. Certainly, effects studies are not the only form of research to suffer from such unspecified generalizations concerning television, but the point is that variations in the medium that emerged throughout the multi-channel transition indicated how untenable these generalizations had become, if they were ever meaningful.

Instead of utilizing uniform assumptions and explanations of television, we might diversify our thinking by establishing "modes of television" that group similar functions of the medium. Indeed, for all the differences in viewing, every instance is not so distinctive as to be fundamentally unlike any other. Establishing some frequent modes of television use aids in distinguishing characteristics in a great many of television's iterations. At least four distinctive modes of television function existed by 2005: Television as an electronic public sphere; Television as a subcultural forum; Television as a window on other worlds; and Television as a self-determined gated community.

Television as an *electronic public sphere* identifies the operation of television in the network era as it was explained by Horace Newcomb and Paul Hirsch's cultural forum model, Todd Gitlin's delineation of television's ideological processes, or John Fiske and John Hartley's notion of the medium's bardic role.[29] Drawing primarily on Newcomb and Hirsch, we might say that television operates as an electronic public sphere when it reaches a vast and heterogeneous audience and offers a shared experience or content that derives its importance from the scope of its reach, its ability to provide a space for the negotiation of ideological positions, and as a process-based system of representation and discourse. Now, however, television decreasingly operates in this way. When it does, it usually does so on unplanned occasions, except for a few remaining events such as the Super Bowl. At the same time, though, it is helpful to see the electronic public sphere as existing on a continuum. Thus, for example, in comparison with the network-era reach of television—when top shows were watched by 40 to 50 percent of television households—popular contemporary shows such as *American Idol* have a narrower scope—only 15.7 out of a universe of 109 million homes watch it.[30] But even with only an average of 14 percent of U.S. television households watching the show, it is among the most widely viewed regular programs in a given year.

Television operates as *subcultural forum* when it reproduces a similar experience as the electronic public sphere, but among more narrow groups that share particular cultural affinities or tastes. MTV is likely to be the best example, in that the network provides the lingua franca for adolescents and operates as "must-see TV" in order for teens to achieve cultural competence. The key difference between the electronic public sphere and a subcultural forum (note the embedded "cultural forum" in the terminology) is that the latter is characteristic of television that reaches smaller and more like-minded audiences. Many Spanish-language networks may speak to similar experiences in immigrant audiences, just as Fox News provides a version of daily news and events that serves viewers who choose to watch a news outlet with its particular sensibility. Importantly, when television operates as a subcultural forum, it is often integrated with the use of other media that similarly reflect subcultural tastes and sensibilities. Viewers incorporate a television network or set of programs into a broader set of media, reproducing particular silos of specific worldviews.

Post-network television also can function as a *window into other worlds*. In some ways this is a corollary to its function as a subcultural forum, as the ubiquity and availability of television make it a convenient means for exposing oneself to programming targeted to a different audience—or to interlope. Television makes it easy to be a casual anthropologist and travel in worlds very different from one's own, although by no means are all those worlds equally available. Viewers engage in television as a window into other worlds when, as cultural interlopers, they view niche media not targeted to them. Parents trying to understand teen culture can gain glimpses into it on MTV—although understanding how teens receive the content or how any intended audience makes meaning of programming is another matter entirely. In leaving my own silo of information and taste culture, I have explored the excessive and regressive masculinity offered by Spike or the stories of masculinity in crisis aired on FX shows *Rescue Me* and *Nip/Tuck*. Ever-expanding cable systems make available ever more worlds—including networks and content originating from outside of the United States, although, again, all worlds and perspectives are far from equally available. Perhaps one of the most telling aspects of post-millennium U.S. culture emerges from the uncommon use of television as a window into other worlds relative to television as a subcultural forum.

Finally, a fourth mode of television as a *self-determined gated community* has emerged particularly as a result of increasing flexibility in distribution and opportunities for viewers to access programming on demand. Here, television's cultural role is even more specific than when it functions as a subcultural forum. This mode encompasses particular uses and personalized organizations of television—as well as individuals' pursuit of specific content, including that which may be amateur-created. The operation of this more nascent mode can be observed in the videos submitted to aggregators such as YouTube or in those attached to social-networking sites such as MySpace. Here self-created television becomes a forum of expression and a way for viewers to communicate—most likely with established peers—which they do by sharing their television. As television and web viewing become more integrated and convenient, viewers will also share recommendations, links, and viewing line-ups that contribute to the personalization of television. Self-determined viewing behaviors include deliberately shifting among the variety of modes of use noted here and creating specialized viewing communities.

Certainly other modes may already exist that I have not included. The expanding fan cultures facilitated by the web perhaps suggest another distinct mode of television that might be labeled "television as cult conduit." The point I wish to highlight is the variety and differences in just the few functions given here. Each mode features varied characteristics and leads to very different cultural outcomes—television "means" differently in each of these modes—and does so in ways that previous explorations of television have not considered. I do not intend these four modes to account for all of television viewing; rather, I hope that identifying them will encourage others to consider television in terms of specific contexts and uses, rather than thinking about television-related phenomena as characteristic of television-at-large.

Delimiting the different ways television functions leads us to foreground the multifaceted nature of television and the growing diversity of uses viewers may adopt. You use the television that you flip on in the background while making dinner differently from the way you use the set to record a show you reserve for a time when all other distractions can be avoided—and that content consequently has different meaning and importance. Likewise, the television you view on a portable device on a daily train commute or the videos you search out online also indicate still other relationships between content and use. Each of these examples illustrates fundamental distinctions among use, content, and audience. In each case, the viewer may be watching television, but to understand the behavior and its cultural function, we need to develop more specific frameworks to explain differentiation among types of television content —such as phenomenal television—and why viewers watch in particular ways.

Key Ideas for Thinking about Television's Revolution

Finally, I turn to the key ideas and definitions particularly important for the reconsideration of television offered in the remaining pages. Most viewers remain unaware of the business of television, such as the intricate processes involved in deciding what shows to produce, selling them to networks, and finding advertisers, but understanding the business of television and how it is changing is crucial to comprehending why the industry produces certain shows and how to intervene in this system. Those who have sought changes in the cultural output of television—shifts in depictions of ethnic groups and women, for example—have been most successful when they have illustrated that their goal was a matter of "good business" for the industry, as has been the case for many social initiatives.[31] The production of expressive forms like television shows is a challenging business, and no matter the extent of market research, many of the tools other sectors of business use to understand what their consumers want and to predict success are ineffective in the creation of cultural forms.

I closely examine many components of production that figure centrally in the creation of U.S. television programming and focus exclusively on the commercial sector despite the existence of a small public broadcasting system. As I noted in the introduction, rather than thinking of production as just the making of a show, I define production as *all of the activities involved in the creation and circulation of television program-*

ming. I organize this broad conception of production into five "production components"— technology, creation, distribution, advertising, and audience research—and explore each in subsequent chapters. I do not intend any prioritization in the production components catalogued here. Sometimes technologies and distribution practices enhanced preceding developments intentionally (as in creating access to shows for video iPods), while other adjustments occurred independently (Slingbox).

Although I distinguish these five components as different activities, they must be understood as interrelated processes connected by multi-directional influences. Thus, for example, changes in advertising can introduce adjustments in how producers create programs, while changes in the creation of programs can likewise affect how advertisers are integrated in programming, as well as how much advertiser support networks or studios need. Moreover, the relations among the five components are constantly in flux. During the multi-channel transition in which adjustments in distribution capabilities affected economic models, the altered economic models then enabled certain creative norms—all of which affected the type and range of programming likely to be produced. Such an approach to production differs considerably from ideas about industry operation that assume power and influence operate in a one-way, top down, hierarchical manner and that allow factors such as ownership structures a more deterministic role in the creation of expressive forms and day-to-day industry operations.

Just as production encompasses multiple components, production also exists as one "cultural process" in what some have termed the "circuit of culture" and others a "circuit of media study."[32] These circuit-based models or frameworks for studying media such as television provide a sophisticated conceptualization of the relationship between the creation of culture and the imperatives of commercial industries. Processes and factors other than production, such as reception, socio-historical context, and particular cultural artifacts, are interconnected, with each affecting and being affected by the others. The production of television involves the negotiation of many different interests and requires a complicated model to adequately address the intersections of varied commercial and regulatory interests that also mediate in the creation of cultural forms.

Because of my focus on production, other parts of the circuit of culture receive minimal attention despite their relevance to the changes that mark the emergence of the post-network era. Often, these other cultural processes serve as structuring forces that significantly affect the conditions of production. For example, regulatory actions dating to the 1920s continue to determine the fundamental characteristics of the competitive terrain upon which the television industry operates. However, I attend little to the details of many of these broad, structuring regulatory actions, except in the instances that they particularly affect specific production practices, because of their consistency throughout the history of broadcasting and the existence of other works that attend to regulation and policy in great detail.

Here, though, I must emphasize the significance of the deregulatory policy that the government began implementing at the beginning of the multi-channel transition, even though it is not a topic examined extensively in the book. This policy produced considerable regulatory consequences despite the reduced regulatory influence that "de" regulation might suggest. Most notably, deregulation allowed massive consolidation and conglomeration of all aspects of television and much of the media industry. Ownership of the roughly 1,400 television stations nationwide was substantially consolidated by the networks and a few station groups while conglomerates also gathered broadcast networks, cable channels, production facilities, and even distribution routes such as cable and satellite providers into common ownership. New media entities were often integrated into these vast media conglomerates—as in the case of the AOL/Time Warner merger—although in many cases the architects of the new media age (Yahoo!, Microsoft, Google, Apple) and the consumer electronics industry remained separate from conglomerates dominating television (News Corp., Viacom, Time Warner, and Disney) and many other "old" media.

Regulators had the perfect opportunity to intervene in broadcast norms during the digital transition mandated by the Telecommunications Act of 1996. The forced transition to digital transmission could have allowed Congress and the Federal Communications Commission to revisit the vaguely defined mandate that stations operate in the "public interest, convenience, and necessity" in exchange for the opportunity to use public airwaves to secure billions of dollars in profits, but regulators largely ignored this opportunity. Although regulatory rhetoric might have proclaimed that deregulation would lead to competition, most of the actions of the FCC since the end of the network era have been strongly influenced by the powerful industries the agency was created to regulate.[33] For the most part, the changes in industry operation chronicled here did not result from the competition deregulation was supposed to inspire; instead, they came largely from the actions of companies outside of FCC purview (consumer electronics and computing).

The degree to which the medium and the industry redefined themselves with remarkably little re-regulatory input introduced notable challenges by the late multi-channel transition. The interventions made by the regulatory sector—seen most distinctly in the fin-syn rules (explained in Chapter 3), shifting cable policies, and deregulation of ownership—had massive implications for the industry's operation and in structuring the norms of production. At the same time, the relative swiftness with which production components responded to changes in various production practices decreased the relevance of the lumbering regulatory sector in establishing the regulatory conditions appropriate to emerging post-network norms. Regulators could radically adjust the playing field for the industry at any time—as the intermittent threat of mandating à la carte cable service suggested throughout the mid-2000s—but they seemed unlikely to deviate from the "market-driven" logic underscoring their decisions for the previous two decades—that is, except in the case of content regulation. The developments of the multi-channel transition merited sweeping regulatory action that revisited broadcasting's regulatory foundations; however, by the beginning of 2007, regulators had established no clear principles that reflected the substantial industrial adjustments occurring.

Each of the following five chapters focuses on a different aspect of production in order to explain the broad changes that have taken place over the past twenty years, the new norms being established in the post-network era, and why these changes in how television is made affect both the types of programs that are produced and the role of these stories in the culture. The next chapter looks at the changing technologies viewers used to watch television and how new devices enabled viewers unprecedented control over how, where, and what they viewed—and increasingly, to even make their content.

2

Television Outside the Box
The Technological Revolution of Television

Never before have the balance sheets, strategies, constituent relationships and very existence of media conglomerates been shaped
so radically by technology and changing consumer habits. Never
before has so much revenue been put on the line, and never before
has there existed the potential for so much content, distribution,
packaging and pricing to be placed beyond the reach of the media
giants.

　　　　　　　　　—*The Hollywood Reporter.com*, September 13, 2005[1]

TV has evolved in the past, but the current digital revolution shock
is unprecedented. And, just as in earlier periods of fecundity, TV
production, distribution, and consumption are all being redefined
and refreshed by outsiders, from Apple's Steve Jobs to the new amateur producers peopling YouTube or Blip.tv.

　　　　　　　　　　　　　　　—*Wired*, April 6, 2007[2]

The commentary of the first epigraph, taken from an uncharacteristically
forward-looking think piece by one of the industry's key trade publications, captures the uncertainty and anticipation of the industry in 2005.
Industry workers knew technological change was approaching. Many
had seen the diverse platforms and applications debuting at electronics
shows, but none could be certain of how audiences would use the new
technologies, how quickly they might adopt them, which devices would
prove essential, or what might be the next "killer application."

Technologies involved in the digital transition enabled profound adjustments in how viewers used television and necessitated modifications
in many other production processes. Many devices considerably enhanced viewers' ability to control television in many different ways. The
increased control over how, when, and where to view provided by DVRs,

DVDs, electronic programming guides, and portable devices such as the Microsoft Personal Media Player and Sony's PlayStation Portable (PSP) expanded *convenient* uses of television. These devices enhanced the capabilities afforded by analog technologies such as VCRs and allowed viewers far more viewing flexibility.

Simultaneously, convergence among televisions, mobile phones, and the Internet yielded a nearly limitless expansion of television's physical presence by enabling reception of live television almost anywhere. Viewers no longer needed to leave their office desks, cars, or leisure venues to watch breaking news or coverage of a live sporting event as new devices and distribution methods made television *mobile*. Viewers could take television anywhere they could receive a broadcast signal, access a wireless Internet environment, or even receive a mobile phone signal—which meant virtually anywhere in the United States. This capability substantially eroded the degree to which television tethered its audience to a specific physical space, which had been a defining attribute of the medium in the network era.[3]

Additionally, technological advancements in audio and visual quality —many of which resulted from the digital transmission of television signals—expanded the *theatricality* of television until the distinction intended by the word, as in of real life or perhaps film quality, became insignificant. The emergence of high-definition sets as replacements for the long inferior NTSC television standard particularly contributed a technological revolution in the quality of the television experience. Digital transmission alone allowed some enhancement of television's audio and visual fidelity, but the high-definition images in particular appeared as crisp as reality and offered the detail available on film.

Each of these attributes of post-network technologies—convenience, mobility, and theatricality—redefined the medium from its network-era norm. Their significance results from the considerably revised and varied uses of television that consequently have emerged and that contrast with the unstoppable flow of linear programming, the domestic confinement, and the staid aesthetic quality of the network era. Rather than these technological assassins causing the death of television, as many writing about television in the mid-2000s claimed, the unprecedented shift of programming onto tiny mobile phone screens, office computers, and portable devices ultimately reasserted the medium's significance. The new technological capabilities also required adjustments in television distribution and business models in order to make content available on the new screens.

These technologies produced complicated consequences for the societies that adopted them. Viewers gained greater control over their entertainment experience, yet became attached to an increasing range of devices that demanded their attention and financial support. Many viewers willingly embraced devices that allowed them greater authority in determining when, where, and what they would view, although as fees and services proliferated, they also struggled with the burden of many costs previously borne by advertisers. In many cases, the "conventional wisdom" forecasting that the new technologies would have negative consequences for established industry players proved faulty, as empowered viewers initially used devices to watch *more* television and provided the industry with unexpected new revenue streams at the same time they eroded old ones. The emergence of these technologies consequently resulted in contentious negotiations within and between factions as viewers assessed what capabilities were worth the cost, the consumer electronics industry endeavored to imbed its products in the daily use of as many as possible, old media (such as broadcast networks) evolved their business models, and old and new media services (cable providers and Internet aggregators like Yahoo! and YouTube) developed mechanisms to make new technologies useful and programming accessible.

Network-Era and Multi-Channel Transition Technologies

The lack of technological variation during the network era enforced a fairly uniform television experience for viewers. Television sets that received very few signals over the air functionally defined the technological experience in the network era, while the use of antennas and CATV added complexity and limitations for some viewers. These devices, however, tended to only enable viewers in rural or mountainous areas the same access to the medium as enjoyed by their more urban located brethren. Either way, viewers had no technological control over television and little choice among content. Certainly, the transition to color was significant, and many of the technologies that began to revolutionize television use during the multi-channel transition were introduced to early adopters while all other characteristics of the network era remained firmly intact. For most, however, a single television in the home without remote control or VCR characterized the network-era technological experience with television. This uniformity of use aided the industry's production processes because it enabled the industry to assume certain viewing conditions and rely on viewers to watch network-determined schedules.

Technological developments of the multi-channel transition introduced profound changes for users, first by enhancing choice and control with analog technologies such as cable network distribution, VCRs, and remote control devices. Experiments with remote controls began in the early days of radio and continued through its refinement and into the television era.[4] The industry sold as many as 134,000 remote equipped televisions as early as 1965, though definitive penetration rates for the device are uncertain because the primary data collected counted set sales and consequently did not account for homes with more than one set or homes replacing one remote-equipped set with another. Despite these early starts, Bruce Klopfenstein argues that 1984 to 1988 marked the period of most rapid overall remote control diffusion due to the simultaneous distribution of cable and VCR remote controls in concert with those of television sets.[5]

The VCR is one of the first technologies to trouble understandings of "television." The distribution of the VCR as an affordable technology, which achieved mass diffusion at the same time as the remote control, significantly expanded viewers' relationship with and control over television entertainment. Nearly 50 percent of U.S. homes owned VCRs by 1987;[6] this figure increased to 65.4 percent by 1990, 88.1 percent at the end of the century, and peaked at 98.4 percent in 2003, after which VCR rates declined and DVD rates grew.[7] The recording devices allowed viewers to negate programmers' strategies through time-shifting and introduced new competitors such as the home video purchase and rental market. In addition to enhancing viewers' television capabilities by allowing them to record and review television shows, the VCR also enabled the television set to function entirely independently of the networks' linear program schedules. "Watching television" became acceptable to those who previously denigrated the device once it could be used to screen the works of master filmmakers, as in the case of my colleague who watches videos but not "television."

Another key characteristic of the early multi-channel transition resulted from the arrival of cable, which introduced profound changes in both technology and distribution. As a technology, cable substantially altered the viewers' experience with its introduction of a vast array of channels. In 1988, 50 percent of U.S. households subscribed to cable, which was the subscription base analysts believed necessary for cable operators to provide a large enough audience to achieve profitability.[8] This sub-scription level marked an increase from just 19.9 percent in 1980, grew to 56.4 percent by 1990, and reached 68 percent in 2000. By 2000, nearly ten million additional households received programming via Direct Broadcast Satellite (DBS—services such as DirecTV or Dish Network).[9]

Broadcasters maintained many of their network-era programming practices throughout the multi-channel transition even though the audience they reached decreased in scope. The growth of program outlets significantly shifted the size and composition of the audience watching the Big Three networks, but it required decades for this change to reach an economic crisis point. In some ways, a paradox of remaining the "most mass" programming outlet reaffirmed the status of broadcasters and allowed them to remain disproportionately dominant throughout much of the multi-channel transition despite their slipping share of the audience. Cable channels drew audiences, but the multiplicity of cable channels was only significant in aggregate; any one channel drew a small fraction of the audience still reached by a broadcaster. The broadcast net-works achieved some cost-cutting by scheduling more programs from cheaper genres such as newsmagazines and early "reality" shows such as *Cops,* but the broadcast networks were able to maintain many of their core practices throughout the multi-channel transition. Broadcasters' continued dominance and cable channels' limited encroachment enabled a conciliatory coexistence that ruptured once cable channels began pro-ducing "broadcast quality" series and other shifts in production processes forced broadcasters to substantially adjust their practices by the late 1990s.

Analog technologies enabled limited control and choice during the multi-channel transition, but the arrival of digital television technologies at the end of the century vastly reconfigured technological capabilities and introduced characteristics of a post-network era. The shift from an analog technology such as the VCR to the DVR and DVD may seem in-significant in terms of the similar capabilities each provide, but the arrival of digital technologies fundamentally changed television.

Digital Media and the Post-Network Era

Welcome to the age of fast-food TV: nuggets of news and entertainment that can be consumed on cellphones, video game consoles and digital music players. Whether the programming is downloaded via iTunes software or over a cellular network, the trend is changing where—and how—TV watchers are tuning in.

—Meg James, *Los Angeles Times*[10]

The digital revolution produced two types of consequences for television: interoperability and efficiency. These capabilities adjusted viewers' experience as the common language of ones and zeros shared in the digital transmission, reception, and home recording of television advanced the medium considerably. It provided the technological opportunity to converge televisions, computers, and other home technologies, and also allowed more efficient signal transmission and storage. Digital transmission further expanded choice, as broadcasters and cable providers were able to relay more information in their broadcast spectrum and cable wire by using a digital signal. Digital technologies enabled broadcasters to offer three or four "channels" in the six megahertz of spectrum previously required to transmit one analog channel—and the number of channels continued to grow with better compression technologies. Likewise, cable providers expanded channel offerings and added on-demand services once they were able to more efficiently compress their signals. The compression technologies allowed digital cable to increase channel offerings with additional niche channels that sought increasingly precise tastes, such as The Golf Channel and Gospel Music Television. The consequences of choice were widely experienced by the early 2000s and receive limited examination here, where I focus instead on the newer developments of convenience, mobility, and theatricality.

The State of Technology Adoption

Viewers' use of television expanded considerably as they adopted the technologies developed and deployed throughout the multi-channel transition. Many of the technological shifts introduced incremental change to the industry in a manner that did not substantially challenge existing industrial practices, while other technologies instituted such considerable modifications that they contributed to adjustments throughout the production process. The technologies launched during the multi-channel transition were neither uniform in character nor deployed in an organized or coherent manner. Rather, many different sectors, such as computer and consumer electronics industries, governmental regulators, cable

TABLE 2
A Snapshot of Television Technology Diffusion by Spring 2005

Homes with Television	99%
Homes with a Large (30+ in.) Screen	45%
Homes with 3 or More Sets	53%
Homes with Cable	59%
Homes with Digital Satellite	24%
Homes with Only Over-the Air Reception	17%
Homes Receiving 40 or More Channels	74%
Homes Receiving 100 or More Channels	41%
Homes with a VCR	89%
Homes with a DVD Player	66%
Homes with a Videogame System	39%
Homes with High-Definition TV	9%
Homes with a Digital Video Recorder	7%
Homes with a Computer	67%
Homes On-line	59%
Homes with Broadband Connection	28%
Homes with a Mobile Phone	72%
Homes with Two Mobile Phones	41%

All data from Knowledge Networks/SRI, *The Home Technology Monitor: Spring 2005 Ownership and Trend Report* (New York: SRI, 2005). The survey uses a telephone sampling method, so the data is figured off of a base of telephone households with one or more working television sets.

providers, broadcasters, etc., had varied stakes and visions for the role of these technologies in the future of the U.S. television industry.

All of the technologies explored here were widely available by mid-2005, although penetration rates were still low for some of the more significant devices such as DVRs and high-definition (HD). A snapshot of technological diffusion and use collected in spring 2005 revealed the varied emergent and integrated status of different technologies.

In the spring of 2005, 82 percent of homes with a television reported owning two or more sets and nearly half (45 percent) owned a television with a screen larger than thirty inches.[11] Ten percent of homes owned a set larger than fifty inches—a figure growing about 4 percent per year—while 26 percent reported having a home theater or Surround Sound audio system.[12] Such audio technology reached this rate in 2000 and maintained considerable consistency, suggesting a likely adoption plateau.[13] By 2005, only 9 percent of homes owned a high-definition set, although that was nearly twice as many as two years earlier.[14] (Importantly, not all homes that owned HD sets received HD content because of the varying availability of HD packages from cable and satellite services and general confusion on the part of set owners.)

Eighty-three percent of television households reported receiving signals from a non-over-the-air source, with 59 percent subscribing to cable and 24 percent to satellite.[15] Only 19 percent of television households subscribed to digital cable, although it was available to 85 percent of wired cable homes.[16] Seventy-four percent of television homes received more than forty channels and 41 percent received more than one hundred.[17]

VCR ownership continued to decline in 2005, and was down to 89 percent.[18] By contrast, and unsurprisingly, ownership of DVD players continued to increase, with 66 percent of homes owning a DVD player in 2005—a 10 percent jump from the previous year.[19] Despite the omnipresence of DVRs in industry discussions, only 7 percent of homes had DVRs in 2005, which marked an increase from 4 percent in 2004.[20] Twenty-six percent of homes reported they had access to video on demand (VOD) services, but only 11 percent reported viewing a free or pay VOD program in the previous month.[21] Thirty-nine percent of television households owned a videogame system that attached to the television—a distribution level that had been steady since 2000.[22]

In terms of the broader home technology space at the time, 67 percent of homes had a computer, while 23 percent owned two or more, and patterns of growth in home computer ownership suggested that demand had nearly reached equilibrium.[23] Eighty-eight percent of computer households (59 percent of all households) used the computer to go online, a use level that remained steady since 2001. Fifty-two percent of online households connected through a regular telephone line, while nearly half (28 percent of all households) used a broadband high-speed method, with nearly even distribution between cable modems and DSL service (broadband had grown 7 percent each year since 2003).[24] Seventy-two percent of homes owned a mobile phone by 2005, and 41 percent owned two or more.[25] Thirty-one percent of households had an Internet-capable mobile phone or personal data assistant (PDA), although only 11 percent used this application.[26] Just 5 percent of mobile phone homes owned phones capable of receiving television-like video, and even fewer used this feature.[27]

In general, these data illustrate that some, but not all, of the technologies introduced during the multi-channel transition had reached saturation levels by 2005. Particularly, technologies that might be viewed as ancillary to the redefinition of television—ownership of home computers, mobile phones, and home Internet access—all had disseminated as widely as forecasters expected to be likely based on conditions of the time.[28] Similarly, choice—measured by subscription to non-over-the-air providers and the number of channels available—seemed to have reached useful capacity. There always might be room for more, but the average number of channels viewed suggested little interest in the expansion of linear channels. Nielsen estimated that despite exponential growth in availability, the number of channels viewed by a household tended to increase only slightly. A household with thirty-one to forty channels viewed an average of 10.2, while those with fifty-one to ninety viewed just over 15. Even households with 121 or more channels viewed an average of only 19.2, although which 19.2 varied tremendously by household.[29] The call for à la carte cable packaging that would allow viewers to select only the channels they desired affirmed the degree to which viewers had greater interest in both reasonable pricing and specific channels than in more unbridled choice. Most homes did not yet have or use the level of control provided by DVRs and VOD.

In sum, as of early 2005, technology distribution data suggested that about 10 percent of television households made use of post-network technologies and had begun maximizing their television experience in the ways these devices allowed. Many of the advertising agencies and financial services that evaluate the earnings potential of different segments of the industry forecast continued growth in DVRs and VOD; MAGNA Global's forecast suggested that nearly 31 percent of television households would have DVRs by 2010 and more than 90 percent of cable subscribers would have access to VOD.[30]

Digital Control Yields Convenience

Viewers first gained the convenience of defying networks' schedules with the VCR, which established a modest beginning that since has been expanded by DVRs and digital devices that integrate Internet and television to vastly expand consumer control. The DVR initially appeared to offer little additional capability than the VCR, yet its efficiency and ease of use made its contribution significant. While programming a VCR was perceived as so difficult that a joke about the flashing 12:00 VCR clock became ubiquitous, DVRs featured one-step recording capabilities from their introduction in 1999. DVR users found that time-shifting became the default mode of viewing for most programming—particularly in prime time—a difference suggestive of a shift from mere control to convenience.[31] Even early generation devices featured on-screen menus and programming schedules far easier to navigate and quicker to load than those offered by digital cable systems nearly a decade later. The remote capabilities available with some machines that enabled viewers to program the DVR from out of the home by accessing it via computer or mobile phone further illustrated the convergence of digital technologies and expanded control.

The ease of recording common to DVRs and their clutter-free, tapeless option made them a significant threat to the conventional practices of the television industry. VCR users could "zip" through commercials in recorded material—and unquestionably did—but VCR use tended to be restricted to more isolated occasions of particular shows; based on Nielsen data, MAGNA Global estimated that VCR recording accounted for 6 percent of the average prime-time audience in 2005 (notably, that is recording only, as Nielsen was technologically incapable of measuring how many of the 6 percent of viewers ever actually viewed their tapes).[32] Homes with DVRs watched substantially less television live, and the technology introduced viewers to a non-linear programming experience.[33] Industry analysts marveled at the level of satisfaction earned by DVR technologies, as adopters recounted that their DVR "changed their lives" and professed "love" for the machine. Like many skeptics, I saw the DVR as an insubstantial advance from the VCR, until I used one. I quickly joined the converted as my whole approach to viewing television changed radically once I could easily control so many aspects of the experience. Many perceived DVRs as a significant threat to the conventional advertising model of thirty-second commercials embedded in programming, and fear of this technology led to adjustments in advertising strategies and program financing models.

Video on demand—with viewer control embedded in its name—also expanded viewers' control over their television experience and is a technology characteristic of the industry's shift beyond a mere multi-channel transition toward a more full-fledged, post-network era. VOD technologies provide a range of services akin to DVRs—both devices enable viewers to pause, stop, and rewind programs. But the key distinction between them lies in where the technologies store content. DVRs pull content from the twenty-four-hour linear stream of programming networks transmit and store the recordings on a device in the home. VOD technologies store content on a server maintained by cable providers, and viewers access this programming bank at will, choosing among the offerings of the provider. The development of VOD required extensive negotiation between content creators and cable providers in order to identify a financial model that would serve both entities and still be desirable to viewers.[34] Cable providers rebuilt their infrastructure and offered VOD as part of digital subscription packages, which by 2005, primarily allowed subscribers to only access an on-demand version of content already available in linear distribution, and often included only "extras" and "bonus footage" rather than full episodes. Some cable services experimented with subscription video on demand (SVOD), but the model of paying specifically for the on-demand capability was less popular (unsurprisingly) than the "free" access, which cable services included as a "value added" perquisite to encourage digital cable subscription.

Convenience technologies—including the DVR, VOD, DVD, the Internet, and mobile applications such as phones and iPods—enabled viewers to more easily seek out specific content and view it in individualized patterns.[35] These technologies increased viewers' ability to select not only when to watch (DVR, VOD, DVD), but also where (DVD, Internet, mobile phone, iPod, TiVo ToGo), and provided the most expansive and varied adjustments in the technological capability of the medium. Convenience technologies encourage active selection, rather than passively viewing the linear flow of whatever "comes on next" or "is on," and consequently lead viewers to focus much more on programs than on networks—all of which contribute to eroding conventional production practices in significant ways. The viewing behaviors these technologies enabled, in tandem with the vast choice among outlets viewers could now access, were vital to the shift of television from what Miege theorized as a "flow" industry to that more like a "publishing" industry. Convenience technologies also increased the deliberateness in viewers' use of television that allowed for adjustments in how programs were created, funded, paid for, and distributed.[36]

The Convenience of Portable Television Devices

DVRs and VOD allowed viewers to capture television from the networks' linear dictates, but on their own, these technologies still confined viewers to conventional "living room" viewing. Freeing viewers to watch content anywhere they desired required another set of technologies that allowed portability. Viewers first experimented with this possibility by watching television series sold on disks on portable DVD players, but rapid technological diffusion quickly made portable viewing much easier. Soon viewers could record their own DVDs; then technology enabled the more elegant solution of downloading programs to iPod players and devices also used for gaming, such as the PSP (PlayStation Portable). TiVo-brand DVRs also expanded the convenience of the device through the TiVo ToGo application that offered easy transfer of programs recorded on the device to laptops and portable media devices, as well as facilitating DVD burning.

Arguably, two distinctive capabilities emerged from the transportable television technologies introduced in the early 2000s, so I differentiate between technologies that allow *portable* versus *mobile* television use. Viewers use mobile television when they access *live* television out of the home, as opposed to the time-and-place-shifting characteristic of portable television. The mobility of live video on phones and portability of programs loaded onto iPods both enable out-of-home viewing, but the uses and motivations of each vary enough to warrant differentiation. Portability fits clearly within the realm of expanding convenient uses of television, while the desire for immediacy characterizes mobile television. In sum, mobile television technologies allow out-of-the-home live viewing, while portable technologies expand viewers' control by enabling them to take once domestic-bound content anywhere to view at anytime.

Understanding portable television depends substantially on what the viewer chooses to watch in this application and why—with many possible variations. In some cases the motivation to watch television on a portable device may have little to do with a desire to see specific content but result more from the need to fill time with some sort of entertainment, as during a layover in an airport. In other cases, viewers might use a portable device to keep abreast of certain shows that they do not have time to view or are unable to watch at home, such as watching a soap opera or talk show on a daily train commute.

Convenience technologies have supported emergent modes of television such as its use as a subcultural forum and self-determined gated communities, rather than network-era modes that relied on a mass audience sharing homogenous programming. Opportunities to take television out of the home have enabled viewers to watch more television and particularly programming that matches specific tastes. But it also requires pre-planning in the selection of content, unlike the related live application of mobile television that enables surfing. While the need for such pre-planning may make it less likely that viewers use portable television to sample new content, portable television allows users to expand the physical locations in which they view established favorites. Portable television devices provided a visual dimension to a technology such as the Walkman —with all the attendant anti-social and silo-izing concerns that social commentators noted as Walkman culture became common in the 1980s.[37] Use of portable television is highly personalized, and it became easy to imagine a train car with twenty different people using portable television and none watching the same thing.

Convenience technologies have expanded the audience fragmentation and social polarization that choice and control technologies had already enabled by increasing asynchronous viewing. Whether they be DVR owners who reschedule viewing on their own terms or viewers who wait several months to purchase or rent full-season DVDs, users of convenience technologies have come to select their own viewing conditions, including the crucial one of time. The resulting temporal fragmentation may seem comparably insignificant relative to other adjustments—such as the fragmentation of viewers among a multiplicity of channels—but it has had important implications in disabling the coterminous circulation of ideas within the culture. Beginning in 2004, feature articles in the popular press recounted the trend of audience members waiting until a full season of a series was available on DVD and then watching the full season at a self-determined pace.[38] One DVD owner, Rachel Rebibo, who prefers viewing television on DVD explained, "With a DVD player, I can set my schedule and turn it off anytime. It's my choice."[39] Another DVD viewer, Gord Lacy, offered, "I loved *West Wing*. I watched eight episodes in one night. I had only ever seen the pilot, and I'm Canadian watching a show about a U.S. President."[40] Those who turned to DVDs for control began changing the television viewing experience.

Some who waited to view complete seasons on DVD suggested the primary benefit resulted from the elimination of commercials and the tedium of week-long waits between plot developments.[41] Willingness to engage television in this manner also indicated a very active selection process and the planning of viewing uncharacteristic of the network era. As this behavior emerged, full seasons of DVDs typically were not available until a year after the original airing; many studios timed the DVD release to provide a promotional function and to refresh viewers before the start of a new season. This substantially disrupted the immediacy once common to television and the capacity for its stories to function as the source of "water cooler" discussion for all viewers the next day at work. Those who waited for a DVD release might find it difficult to avoid hearing about key plot developments from those who viewed original airings, which also suggested that viewers who elected to wait for DVD release had a very particular relationship with the medium and its content. The unexpected death of a central character in the series *Six Feet Under* provides an illustrative case. The surprise and significance of that creative development, which many television critics discussed and which therefore made this plot twist difficult to avoid, led to a discussion of the propriety of including "spoilers" in reviews because so many audience members deferred their viewing and learning this key piece of information prematurely changed the nature of their viewing experience.[42]

The availability of subscription cable series particularly contributed to encouraging television viewing on DVD, as DVD release provided an opportunity for non-subscribers to view shows that had already achieved substantial cultural buzz. The viability of highly serialized programming such as 24 and *Alias* also was enabled by this behavior as viewers who preferred not to wait a week between each suspense-filled installment chose to purchase DVDs instead. The opportunity to compress viewing allowed better memory of meaningful details that might be forgotten if viewing was stretched over months and suggested the new potential viewing pleasures that might develop from the possibility of condensed viewing.

While convenience technologies expanded asynchronicity in a manner that further eroded the network-era cultural forum function of television, new digital technologies have also enabled viewers to archive, share, and review content in a far more active manner and in ways that suggest other emergent uses of television. Desire to participate in online fan communities, for example, encourages synchronous viewing because discussion of plot points is immediate. Convenience technologies have also allowed viewers greater ability to circulate and redistribute content, although not always legally. Even before the Internet became an efficient source of viewing, many sent links and traded files in a manner impossible in the network era and cumbersome with the analog technologies of the multichannel transition. For example, although an estimated three million people viewed a contentious verbal exchange between Jon Stewart and Tucker Carlson in October 2004 on Carlson's cable show *Crossfire*, only

25 percent of viewers saw it during its original airing on CNN. Once news of the exchange circulated among fans and bloggers, they disseminated the clip online and linked it to their commentaries 1,880 times and an estimated 2.2 million people viewed it (this was before the phenomenon of YouTube, where it was viewed more than 200,000 additional times over two years after the exchange).[43] In effect, then, convenience technologies have not uniformly contributed to audience fragmentation; rather, they have produced varied results that are related to the new ways of controlling content.

Navigating Convenience

Those devices that enable viewers to "pull" content from television, as in the case of the Internet, have revised the network-era function of the medium to "push" content, and can also be categorized as convenience technologies. DVRs and VOD have certainly made it easier for viewers to find programming of interest, but one of the most substantial adjustments in the convenient use of television came not from a new technology but from a refinement of an existing application. Negotiating the multi-channel environment became cumbersome as the number of channels expanded. One need only look at the difference in a *TV Guide* circa 1980 versus 2004 to see the enormity of the shift cable introduced in viewing options. In the 1980s, the publication informed audiences of the prime-time offerings of five channels, while by 2004, it compressed listings for some seventy-six different channels into tiny print on small pages. In October 2005, as the explosion of channels, their inconsistent availability nationwide, and the development of more convenient electronic and interactive onscreen program guides eliminated the utility of the publication, *TV Guide* effectively surrendered to change and discontinued program listings and adjusted its format to report about shows and celebrities. Instead, *TV Guide* evolved and launched its own channel in February 1999 that offered a program listing on a screen shared with original programming focused on celebrity and program "news."

The first innovation from the weekly *TV Guide* magazine or local newspaper listing was the electronic program guide (EPG), a dedicated channel featuring a constant scroll of the television schedule. The slow scroll and limited information about only the next two hours of programming restricted the utility of EPGs, especially as channel offerings expanded. Digital technologies from satellite providers, digital cable, and

DVRs enabled the significant advance of the interactive programming guide (IPG), a refinement of the EPG that allows viewers to search among channels in the present and future, provides the convenience of one-click recording (in the case of DVRs), and often includes more information—such as episode title, plot description, and actors in addition to the series' name. IPGs enable viewers to search as far as two weeks in advance and more easily negotiate the growing multiplicity of networks, although different devices feature search functionalities with disparate capabilities. Artificial intelligence within the TiVo device has provided the most widely hailed advancement: it can identify content like that which it has been programmed to record and maintain standing recording requests for content with certain key words. Despite all the capabilities these devices offer —and some are more convenient to use than others—viewers have not so much needed a new gadget to make use of post-network television. What they've needed is the "killer app"—some mechanism to help find and gather content of interest from among the channels and programs already available.

By the mid-2000s, few viewers had access to devices with these more sophisticated search capabilities, slowing the pace at which viewers adopted television viewing behaviors that emphasized precisely searching out content. The ideal IPG seemed something akin to "Google for television," and unsurprisingly viewers' experiences watching and searching for video online created new expectations of greater customization of their conventional television viewing environments. Thus, much of viewers' demand for greater television functionality has derived from their use of and acculturation with computers. The shift from EPGs to IPGs illustrates a fundamentally different conception of how to use television that developed between the network era and the computer age. The availability of devices that enable viewer-determined, convenient uses of television has been unquestionably critical to establishing the post-network-era characteristic of non-linear television viewing. Vast choice among channels and the ability to record them, typical of the multi-channel transition, meant little to viewers without devices to help manage these options.

Televisions and computers have become integrated at the industry level as well. As Internet giants Yahoo!, Google, and AOL experimented with television, they quickly introduced peer and buddy rating mechanisms characteristic of search engines to help viewers find the content they sought. Paradoxically, these interfaces were simultaneously user-customized and utilized community-building, maximizing the social networking functions of the web to make connections among those with similar tastes. Such interfaces have vastly expanded functionality for viewers, but the industry soon sought to identify a way to earn revenue from viewers' desire for an even more convenient experience—either by charging a subscription or through advertising.

Although convenience technologies may not have caused changes in specific programs, they have substantially contributed to creating a realm in which the viewer, rather than the network, controls the viewing experience. Moreover, even as industry entities such as networks and studios still determine what programs are produced, many of these convenience technologies have come to support new forms of distribution that allow studios to profit from shows that offered only limited revenues in the network era (serials and cult favorites). Whereas the conditions of production during the network era necessitated a narrow range of cultural goods, the post-network conditions of non-linear use and multifaceted cultural processes have enabled the more varied production and use of television.

Mobile Television: Immediacy Unshackled from the Home

Television's ability to transmit live images distinguished it from other media in the network era. Many of the media events that persist in our cultural memory—the days after the Kennedy assassination, the wedding of Prince Charles and Lady Diana—are connected to viewing primarily done on our domestic-bound sets. Mobile television devices defy network-era norms by untethering live television from a specific physical space and enabling it to function much like a hybrid of many existing technologies. The capability of mobile television reasserted the significance of television's immediacy—as moments in which viewers have desired live images have long transcended the times they were at home. Images of people flocked around television sets in offices and restaurants were common on September 11, 2001, particularly for those living in the eastern half of the country who were already at or on the way to work when the disaster began. Such images are likely to become uncommon in the future as events requiring immediate viewing will be watched on individual workplace computers, while coffee shops and other public venues may fill with people watching pocket-sized screen devices such as phones and PDAs.

Mobile uses of television have existed since the 1960s, but the ability to watch "live" television on a mobile phone or a laptop computer significantly expanded previous versions of this largely unused television attribute. Whereas portable devices expand the functions of television in a manner similar to that of the Walkman, mobile television is more comparable to the contemporary radio, adding a visual dimension to a medium that became ubiquitously accessible after television took its place as the primary means for domestic entertainment. By the mid-2000s, mobile phones offered the main opportunity for mobile television. The Slingbox device, which enables viewers to transmit the content currently airing on their home television to a remote location, has also reconfigured television's previous place-based limitations.

Certainly the ability to view television outside of the home is by no means new, and some technologies perpetuate uses of television similar to those most dominant in the medium's earliest days.[44] Mobile television—as delivered to mobile phone and computer screens—freed television from its domestic confines in the same manner as the earliest portable sets from the 1960s, but the cultural meaning and motivation of this mobility differs significantly forty years later. Lynn Spigel notes that the portable televisions of the 1960s "opened up a whole new set of cultural fantasies about television and the pleasure to be derived from watching TV—fantasies based on the imaginary possibilities of leaving, rather than staying, home."[45] But these sets had limited use, due to their size and need to access broadcast signals. In enabling viewers to take live television with them anywhere they can receive a broadcast transmission, mobile phone signal, or access a wireless Internet environment, the new technologies erase nearly all spatial limitations of television as a medium.

Shortly after mobile phone providers began making television available on phones, the Slingbox further disrupted place-based limitations of television. This shoebox size device plugs into the home cable or satellite feed and Ethernet line and enables the viewer to watch the content currently available on the home television screen or stored on the home DVR on any broadband-connected computer, PDA, or smartphone. Eliminating many of the negative features of viewing on a mobile phone screen, Slingbox technology vastly enhances the convenience of mobile television use. It also challenges the geographic specificity central to a network system that has relied on local affiliates. Slingboxes offer viewers a technological solution to sporting event blackouts—such as when local games are unavailable from local broadcasters because they did not sell out.

They also compromise affiliates' promises to advertisers of "local" audiences. As a result, the industry has begun erecting electronic fences in an attempt to restrict video content to certain geographic areas—what the industry terms "geofiltering."[46]

Various industries—consumer electronics, mobile phone service providers, and the television industry—have all eagerly considered how mobile television might yield new revenue. In the early 2000s, various proposals for countless ways to utilize this expanded capability emerged: streaming live shows, producing original vignettes for this smallest screen, and creating a wide array of other programming such as interactive gambling shows. Innovation was less a question of what could be done technologically and more one of coordinating technological capability with existing needs and uses desired by viewers. Even though one might be able to watch a live episode of the cinematically detailed 24 on a screen the size of a postage stamp, did anyone really want to? The industry pursued multiple possibilities in hopes of being involved in whatever might emerge as the "killer app" of this new media form. Lucy Hood, president of Fox Mobile Entertainment, explained the perspective of those pushing these services, "What are the three things that you always have with you? Your money, your keys, and your cellphone. If we can deliver a fun entertainment experience on this device, that will make it a very powerful medium."[47]

Even the most optimistic industry executive suspected the mobile phone would prove better suited to "snack TV," short-form snippets of programming, rather than the thirty- and sixty-minute programs that had long dominated regular television screens.[48] News, sports, and stock tickers seemed ideal for this technology. Unscripted series that featured less detailed cinematography also matched the technical capabilities of these small screens, as did the talking heads characteristic of many news programs that also benefited from more immediate access. Many were skeptical that this use of mobile phones would catch on, but the ubiquity of mobile phones—found in the purses and pockets of more than 217 million Americans—has increased the likelihood that they would be an important part of post-network television. Cyriac Roeding, vice president of wireless at CBS, noted in 2005 that "Anything above 10 million cellphone users is a big success"—a number that suggests the limited audience required to become an important part of the fragmented media environment.[49] Clint Stinchcomb, senior vice president of new media for Discovery Communications, also noted the widespread use of advanced mobile phone functions in other countries as further evidence of the likely future for the United States.[50]

Mobile telephone-based television fits well with the future technology vision of the consumer electronics industry that imagines a "three-screen" world. By 2006, the industry sought to aid viewers in easily moving content among a thirty-two-plus-inch "living room" screen, a seventeen to twenty inch "computer" screen, and a two to four inch screen carried with one at all times—the already omnipresent phone serving as a ready candidate. Some also forecast a fourth screen that would be portable but not as ubiquitous—more in line with my distinction between portable than mobile use, such as the portable DVD player or portable gaming devices. The developing capability of technologies to provide both mobile (live) and portable (stored) television content is likely to determine the necessity of the fourth screen. Further, Van Baker, an analyst with Gartner Inc. noted, "The notion of a particular screen being tied to a particular kind of content is breaking down. It's what kind of screen is available to me right now, and that's what I'll use."[51]

It is important to look beyond technical capability in explaining the surge in interest in mobile uses of television that has emerged recently. Other technologies have profoundly contributed to acculturating viewers to desire more from their televisions. The Internet has particularly led viewers to expect that they can "do" something with screens, including extracting content of interest from them. Likewise, the commonality of mobile phone use and the growing familiarity with portable digital devices such as PDAs and iPods has accustomed users to portable entertainment in a manner that informs their expectations of mobile television. However, emphasizing mobility in some ways misrepresents effects of many of the post-network technologies, which tether us to locations such as the home and office at the same time that they free us from them. Technologies such as mobile phones, wireless PDAs, and laptops that the industry proclaims to be liberators also shackle us to work and family responsibilities. The widespread use of these technologies creates a context for the introduction of mobile television that differs from the 1960s, when the devices Spigel considers were introduced, or the 1980s, when Sony made available the Watchman. Understanding the cultural significance of mobile television as a component of the post-network era requires looking to the deployment of mobile phones and other person-to-person mobile devices.

Cultural Considerations of Post-Network Mobile Television

A late 1990s television advertisement for AT&T illustrates the initial rationale used by manufacturers to sell mobile technologies. The commercial shows the young daughters of a female executive—and it is notable that she is female—imploring her to stay home with them. One child pleads, "When can I be a client?" suggesting the value of this status in her mother's relationships. The commercial later cuts to a scene showing the woman on the beach with her children. When the phone rings with what we presume is a work-related call, one daughter asks gleefully, "Is it time for a meeting?" Mobile devices, the industry urged us, alleviated the need to make those difficult choices between work and family and better enabled us to have it all.

The dark side of the mobile technologies emerged a few years later after they became widely distributed—particularly among the executive corps. Instead of providing freedom, the devices eliminated workday boundaries, infiltrated all aspects of life, and became used so extensively as to diminish the convenience they were meant to enable. For example, cautionary tales about "crackberries"—a term used to note the addictive nature of BlackBerry wireless PDAs—appeared in multiple publications in the United States, Britain, and Canada in the summer of 2005.[52] The crackberry moniker acknowledges the obsessive and controlling force these devices exude over their users as workers feel the need to compulsively check messages before and after the workday as well as in every spare minute. The obsession was not all in the behavior of the user, as clients and coworkers likewise came to expect the ability to reach others at all times.

There is reasonable cause to suspect that the experience with a one-directional communication technology such as television will not precisely reproduce that of such two-directional mobile communication. Yet, contemporary versions of mobile television must be understood as evolving in a post-mobile phone era in which mobile devices provided constant connections to which users have grown accustomed and that are disconcerting if lost. Two-way portable communication devices such as mobile phones and wireless PDAs have acculturated us to desire other communication devices that we can carry with us at all times and that can perform entertainment and information functions on demand.

Current concepts of home, work, technology, and leisure differ significantly from those of the 1960s, when mobile television was first introduced. Whereas, as Spigel observes, the marketing of portable sets then related to the New Frontier rhetoric of the time, the 1980s saw a return to the home that was encouraged by the adoption of cable and early home theater systems, which many trend and marketing specialists identified as "cocooning."[53] Contemporary users accepted and desired technological tethering as a part of the cocooning impulse, as in the AT&T advertisement, in which the woman uses her mobile phone to work from the beach, surrounded by her children. In another important shift, the "corporation" came to be perceived as an increasingly malevolent entity, which, in turn, brought workers to reevaluate the personal sacrifices required by their jobs and gave rise to a desire to manage the intrusion of work into personal time through technology.

In this context, tethering technologies could provide a compromise between the demands of executive work, occupations that significantly were now available to those women who longed to leave the house in the 1960s, and family or personal life since they enable workers to work more efficiently outside the office. The reality of use comes later when work becomes integrated into all aspects of life. Once these technologies become integral to work functions, users desire ways to employ them for entertainment. Instead of growing from a fantasy of leaving the home as was the case in the 1960s, contemporary mobile technologies provide a way to keep home, work, and entertainment constantly with oneself.

Enormous distinctions related to different types of work and socio-economic class distinguished who was likely and able to use and afford these mobile television devices. Technological tethering functioned particularly acutely for the managerial class. Mobile phones had been disseminated across socio-economic divides by 2005, but the use of wireless PDAs remained limited to less than 10 percent of the population, many of whom received the device from employers as a necessary tool of the job (and in many cases employers subsidized their monthly fees). Likewise, early adopters of the Slingbox were business travelers seeking links to their home communities and broader options than hotel room televisions provide.[54] The narrow use of these devices by a specific socio-economic class has yielded a particular relationship with and dominant discourse about these technologies.[55]

Another effect of these applications has been a resurgence in the ubiquity of television. Small mobile screens, which expand the uses of television outside of the home, serve substantially different cultural functions than the domesticated or even just place-based version of television.[56] Mobile television technologies expanded the contexts, meanings, and uses of viewing and troubled public/private dichotomies. Moreover, while the dominant use of television as a domestic technology continues to structure cultural ways of knowing television, emergent uses, particularly by younger viewers, have begun challenging this framework.

Theatrical Television: Enhancing Television's Aesthetics

At the same time that television screens have become infinitesimally small and portable, domestic screens have expanded and offered unprecedented and compelling visual images. A curious dichotomy has developed between television desired for its out-of-home immediacy, regardless of image quality, and television that is sought for its visual richness and is homebound. This bifurcation is not entirely new; Spigel identified varied discourses of theatricality and mobility in the promotion of television sets as early as the 1960s.[57] Yet technologies in the twenty-first century make both applications far more compelling than in television's early years.

Calling technologies that enhance television's visual and audio fidelity "theatrical" may trouble some readers, and indeed the term is not completely satisfying to me either. Whereas it can call up the notion of the stage, what it refers to is the cinema. Because cinema predated television as a screen technology, its norms and capabilities have long served as the standard against which television has been measured—and consistently found inferior. In her book exploring the rise of the "home theater craze" on the film industry and film consumption, Barbara Klinger notes that the "Holy Grail" of home-based visual media has been achieving the "replication of theatrical cinema."[58] A number of the technological advances that she considers, such as high-fidelity audio systems, VCRs, and the DVD, were central to developing enhanced home theater environments throughout the multi-channel transition. But the single most important advance in the enhancement of television quality—high-definition (HD)—did not begin to enter significant numbers of homes until later.

In the late 1990s and early 2000s, industry workers and the trade press did not treat enhancement technologies such as high definition as being likely to introduce extensive change to television. High-definition sets increase the number of scan lines on the screen from 480, the previous standard to either 720 in cheaper, substandard high-definition sets or 1080 in what became the U.S. industry standard—although both are "technically" considered high-definition. (The consumer electronics industry continues to manufacture standard-definition sets with 480 lines.) In 1996, when the government mandated that broadcasters begin switching to digital signal transmission, providing HD service was not similarly required. It did, however, become technologically feasible as a result of the greater efficiency of digital signals. HD consequently developed in a highly haphazard way, mainly as a competitive strategy and point of differentiation. Some programs were produced only with 720 lines of resolution, while others produced the full 1080. The consumer electronics industry also made both 720 and 1080 sets available. To add further confusion, there is also the variation of whether the signal is "interlaced" (720i, 1080i) or "progressive" (720p, 1080p), with progressive scan providing the better image.

Perhaps the easiest way to understand the issue of HD resolution is to know that there is a clear and, I'd argue, stunning difference between 480 and 720. The difference in picture quality within HD—say the difference between 720p and 1080i—is much more in the eye of the beholder, and most likely to be noticed primarily on larger screen sizes and at closer distances.[59] More apparent is that almost all HD sets feature the rectangular 16:9 ratio common to film screens instead of the more square 4:3 ratio previously standard to television. These adjustments, which have produced markedly more vivid and lifelike images, have required shifts in production techniques and technologies. High-definition has evened the playing field between television and film, which has long been considered superior for its finer image resolution, and some film producers have even begun switching to digital video production.

Many prospective television buyers confuse digital and HD because of the simultaneity of their introduction and the coterminous availability of flat screen technology. Digitally transmitted images have better quality than analog, but do not provide nearly the enhancement of HD. While HD and digital are linked in the sense that the size of the HD signal requires digital transmission, the confusion for many viewers arises from the fact that all digital sets are not necessarily HD, nor do emerging flat screen technologies necessarily correlate with digital reception or HD capability.[60] Even by August 2006, industry research reported that only 36 percent of HD set owners had made the transition to the HD service that would allow them to receive HD signals on their sets.[61]

To some degree, HD operated as afterthought and an also-ran for many in the industry after Congress legislated the digital transition in the mid-1990s. The digital transition proceeded because of regulatory fiat, and the industry consequently did not experience a process of negotiation in this transition in the same manner as other technologies that required adjustments throughout multiple production components prior to their implementation. Legislating the transition timetable from analog to digital occupied many in Washington, and the shift certainly proved costly and cumbersome for broadcast station owners. Yet, by 2006, journalists had spilled far more ink on how the DVR and new forms of distribution such as iTunes revolutionized television than on HD. As a result, limited viewer understanding of and interest in HD has persisted into the mid-2000s, slowing adoption, preventing HD from substantially affecting other aspects of production, and making it difficult to determine the likely scope of its consequences.[62]

Because it seems that HD can operate within many conventional production norms, many in the industry have worried far more about other technological developments and their consequences for production. While HD increases production costs with little opportunity for correspondingly higher advertising rates, it does not do so to an extent that has caused existing economic models to collapse. Also, the dominant role regulators played in mandating the transition to digital independently of the market fundamentally divorced the attendant technological development of HD from others. The possibility of a better image standard originally contributed to the necessary regulatory push to embark on the digital transition, but once broadcasters were forced into the digital realm, they became far more eager to explore the expanded revenue possibilities of "multiplexing" their signals—the term for using the spectrum to broadcast three or four standard definition "channels"—or leasing their unneeded spectrum to others than implementing HD.[63]

But to those who own HD sets in the United States, there has been a radical adjustment in the visual experience of television. High-definition provides such an improvement in image quality that whether or not a program is available in this format can become a determinant in selecting what to view. Indeed, one night, while visiting my parents, I selected to watch *CSI: New York* instead of *Law & Order* because the NBC affiliate where they live did not broadcast in HD. Although I would normally choose to watch *Law & Order* based on my preference for the types of stories it tells and its process of telling them, the grainy look of standard definition was so unpleasant that after spending the evening enjoying the rich and sharp HD image I chose to watch a show in which I wasn't particularly interested. Technophiles with HD have reported similar patterns of use and decision-making. If the general populace follows suit, then HD will change the competitive terrain and force substantial adjustments in many components of production.

Theatrical technologies affect how we think about the conditions in which viewers watch television and how and why they view. Technologies that enhance the visual quality of the television experience are distinctive from the ubiquity enabled by devices that make viewing more mobile or convenient. With some audiences constructing home theater environments that more precisely reproduce the cinematic experience, theories reserved for cinematic viewing have become increasingly relevant to examining television. The comparatively inferior quality of network-era television images led few to consider more formal characteristics of the television image—just as the substandard audio capabilities of early sets resulted in few assessments of the role of sound in television storytelling —but HD has opened up new aesthetic discussions concerning television.

Other production components have responded to the enhanced technological capability of the home theater environment to support the new possibilities in image and sound quality. For example, subscription services such as HBO and Showtime have cultivated a production culture that prioritizes aesthetic excellence and originality in a manner that distinguishes their shows from those of conventional television. This effort is best appreciated with HD and high-fidelity sound. Emphasizing modes of production that seek to maximize the artistic potential of television, these channels have created content with budgets and production values once common only to films produced by major studios. Even advertiser-supported broadcast and cable networks have begun to include some "prestige" programming at costs they are unable to amortize though advertiser support alone and that likewise takes advantage of the enhanced viewing experience new technologies offer. The networks need to differentiate their content to standout from the vast competitive field and providing such "boutique" content offers one strategy for doing so.[64] Thus, it is not just new technological capabilities that have led to programming of increasingly sophisticated visual and aural quality, but a nexus of industrial, cultural, and technological forces.

Another consequence of theatricality, when merged with convenience technologies, is the production of a new variation of event television. In the network era, event television meant the televising of "media events," or what Daniel Dayan and Elihu Katz distinguish as "mostly occasions of state—that are televised as they take place and transfix a nation or the world."[65] By this definition, media events derived their status from their vast reach and the attention they commanded—common attributes of television in the past. After the network era, such regular, planned media events became increasingly rare. While the Super Bowl does continue to be an annual event of this order, other sporting events such as the Olympics fragmented among multiple channels in a manner that decreased the status of any single competition—although the opening and closing ceremonies may provide exceptions. In the meantime, events such as the annual Academy Awards Oscar telecast dwindled in significance.[66] Instead media events have become more private, as viewers have come to confer "event" status on programs that they themselves make special, often with the aid of technology. Using control devices, they can separate event television into a distinctive space—possibly both temporal and physical—in which they can watch undisturbed, perhaps on the best set available. A viewer might also distinguish event television by gathering an audience of friends or family to see a program that has been recorded or is shown live, or use the phone or the Internet to chat about a show while it airs; this has become a component of the popularity of unscripted series—particularly *American Idol* and *Survivor.*

For the most part though, theatrical technologies have evolved from established devices and have not dramatically affected how the majority uses television—particularly in comparison with convenience and mobile technologies. Enabling viewers to further enhance their experience in the home, theatrical technologies have perpetuated the trend toward cocooning that was already well established before the arrival of HD television in the U.S. market. Indeed, the most significant implications of theatrical technologies so far may be shifts in commerce, as those able to afford high-end home entertainment decreasingly spend money in traditional public venues—although the advent of the video rental market in the 1980s had already given rise this shift in behavior and commerce early in the multi-channel transition. Expanded services such as NetFlix, VOD, and the DVD sell-through market then continue this trend. But with the number of households able to pay upward of two hundred dollars a month in service fees for new theatrical technologies being limited, access to those technologies is limited as well. So far, it seems unlikely that the theatrical, convenient, and mobile television experiences, separately or together, will become as universal as the conventional mode of viewing of the network era.

While high-definition provided the technological capability for the creation of visually excellent television, the changed competitive environment caused adjustments in other production components to support the costs associated with HD. Most network-era programming did little to stretch the aesthetic boundaries of the medium. Much was, and still is, produced on tight schedules that make its creation more akin to a factory process than an artistic endeavor—and there was little justification to change, given the technological limitations of network-era sets. In contrast, viewers' new ability to purchase sets capable of transmitting visual and aural excellence has provided one reason for supporting exceptional production quality, but commercial considerations have probably been more compelling. Networks sought opportunities to break through the gross abundance of content in the cluttered programming environment that became characteristic after the network era, and high production values have provided one such measure—a strategy perhaps best deployed by HBO.[67] Early adopters of HD televisions have also been disproportionately affluent. A 2006 study found that the average household income of HD set owners was $89,500, which is 42 percent above the national average.[68] Catering to viewers with enhanced television environments, networks can reach the viewers advertisers find particularly attractive and who were previously difficult to isolate.[69]

Those who can afford to face the distinction of high-definition versus standard definition as one more choice in a television environment that already consists of increasingly different ways to use and pay for television programming—regardless of the incomprehensibly vast variety of programming available. With less than 10 percent of homes owning HD sets and the range of available HD networks barely reaching double digits by the mid-2000s, only a cursory suggestion of its implications for programming have emerged. Media industry maverick and HDNet owner Mark Cuban has repeatedly argued that once a viewer buys an HD set and accesses HD channels, those will be the first place the viewer turns in seeking programming and will become the default favorites that the viewer first considers, which has significant implications for competition and program development. To be sure, many naysayers have downplayed the consequences of HD. Others, however, have argued that it is as significant an industry-changer as the DVR in terms of its effect on how and what people view.[70] Leaving aside such sweeping generalizations, we can say that even with its limited availability, by 2005, high-definition had proven particularly effective in enhancing the experience of viewing sports and film and had begun infiltrating more visually mundane genres such as news and game shows.

Many have presumed that the theatricality of HD and the small screens of portable and mobile devices create contradictory aesthetic experiences. Although there are important distinctions, in truth, the small screens are also compelling—viewers just need to hold them much closer to their faces. Those who wanted live television on the go did initially have to sacrifice visual quality, but this resulted from download speeds more than screen size. In any event, as the post-network era takes shape, convenience, mobility, and theatricality will not develop as mutually exclusive qualities. Rather, the growing availability of each has not only come to redefine the experience of television, but also to force more varied and differentiated understandings of the fundamental characteristics of the medium.

Conclusion

Throughout the network era, viewers primarily watched television in the home and were acculturated to passively accept the limited programming choices and schedule mandates offered by a few networks. Where "watching television" meant selecting among the limited range of programs currently streaming through the set, a certain vernacular accompanied this mode of use—people queried, "what is on television?" expecting an answer of a finite set of selections already in progress. New technologies slightly disrupted this "conventional" mode of viewing throughout the multi-channel transition, and dominant viewer behavior adjusted accordingly. Channel surfing, for example, became a common behavior as the array of channels became broader and remote control devices made shifting from one channel to another much easier.

In the network era, the conventional use of television was so uniform and unexceptional that it was not widely contemplated. Because such conditions as choosing among predetermined options came first, they appeared natural, and many theories of television unreflectively assumed them to be inherently characteristic of the medium. Developments during the multi-channel transition diminished the value of such theories. As adjustments in the technological attributes of television freed the experience of viewing from its confinement to an irrepressible flow of externally scheduled programming and resulted in new and varied ways of using the medium, these dynamic changes required similarly dynamic changes in identifying and framing the issues at hand, as well as theorizing about them. As the multifaceted technologies and uses of television continue to burgeon, and television itself acquires disparate and unfamiliar attributes, we need to think of the medium not as "Television" but as televisions.

Returning to practical matters, we might note that uses and ways of viewing identifiable by the early years of the twenty-first century may well persist, while others may be added as the medium converges with other digital broadband technologies. But here, too, these developments can be related to broader cultural concerns, even though industrial and technological formations may be in transition.[71] The selective adoption of new television technologies and ways to use them not only contribute to adjustments in other production components, but also affect the entire process of production, as well as the role of television in society.

New ways to use and view television provide bountiful opportunities for audience research. Existing studies of audience use provide little information about how viewers might use convenient, mobile, or theatrical television, although some research in the uses and gratifications tradition suggests preliminary parameters. Is mobile or portable viewing dominantly a solitary activity or is it shared, and what types of content or locations of viewing encourage variant behaviors? Do people tend to guard their viewing when they use personal screens in public spaces—wary of the cultural capital it might expose—or do they openly flaunt that they can view in non-domestic spaces and expose their viewing selection as a valued marker of their tastes and preferences? Is there etiquette for both users and bystanders of portable television—I wonder as my airplane seatmate chuckles at an image on his iPod screen, while I edit this text? And what content is most often watched outside the home? Industry workers hoping to profit from new technologies seek answers to these questions while scholars try to understand the cultural implications of such changes in media use. Emergent technologies require research in order to understand the broader media field as well as future demarcations of the boundaries of "television."

And yet the old, conventional set and its uses linger. We must remember how entrenched related viewing behaviors may be and not lose sight of them. A network-era "default mode" of watching television will remain part of experiencing the medium, yet even this conventional mode will not be static. Just as the introduction of the remote control and the

VCR altered the conventional use of television during the multi-channel transition, so, too, is the gradual penetration of DVRs having an effect. Even DVR users do not behave consistently; they record far more prime-time programming and are more likely to view morning shows, news, and sports live.[72] Likewise, data revealed that the multiple sets that became more common in the home after the network era mainly provided families with more convenience by allowing them to watch in varied rooms and that roughly 80 percent of homes have only one set turned on during prime time, suggesting far more co-viewing than many assumed.[73]

Various anecdotes inform my understanding of technologically facilitated changes in use explored throughout the chapter and illustrate changing behaviors associated with technologies and their consequences. I do not suggest that these anecdotes represent larger behavior patterns or can replace detailed and rigorous empirical study of these phenomena. At this preliminary point in the distribution of many of these technologies, when only the initial uses of an unrepresentative group have emerged, comprehensive analysis and understanding cannot yet be achieved. Anecdotal information and perspectives, nevertheless, provide clues about coming uses and behavior.

At the same time that new technologies have enabled vastly augmented uses of television, the adoption of devices that enhance theatricality, mobility, and convenience have also made conventional behaviors strange, disorienting, and unpleasant. Once adopted, their use can become so encompassing and natural that it is challenging for even the most critical mind to step outside his or her own habitual practices and meaningfully evaluate the role the technologies have come to play in daily life. Some have adopted new technologies so quickly that it is difficult to "make them strange" or to realize that others may use the devices differently. In the midst of this research I spent two weeks in a hotel room that was not equipped with a DVR, had very limited channel selection, and lacked an interactive program guide. I learned a great deal about how much my television behavior had changed since I had adopted the newer technologies, and during those two weeks I was surprised by what I adapted to, what most frustrated me, and how much less television I watched as a result of the comparative inconvenience of the experience. Likewise, my students complain that an acute lack of pleasure results when they view television without remote control devices[74]—or that, in fact, after a life with the targeted viewing a DVR enables, they would rather turn the television off than surf among linear channel options.

While reading an essay by Norwegian media scholar Jostein Gripsrud that considers the implications of the DVR, it occurred to me that his dismissal of the device seemed that of someone who did not own a DVR.[75] I had the same reaction before purchasing a DVR and experiencing television in such a different way.

It is difficult to consistently name developments and "a medium" in the midst of such substantial redefinition. Even as the author, I can identify tensions and contradictions in the way I write of television as a medium when one of the central arguments of this chapter and the book is that we can no longer conceive of the technology with such singularity. As the transition in use continues, new words and terms will emerge or be reallocated in order to make sense of television and its multiplicity that might ease the tensions still in evidence here.

Devices that allow viewers to enjoy a movie-like experience in their homes or take their television on the go should be considered as a part of a portfolio of products that complement rather than compete with each other in a multifaceted technological televisual field. Over a decade ago, Nicholas Negroponte argued that the technological distinction of real significance was that between analog and digital, and the technological connections enabled by the digital transition have indeed proven to be profound.[76] The convergence among technologies uncertainly connected other than by their digital language raises ambiguity about whether something like YouTube is best categorized as "television," "video," "computer," or perhaps even just as a "screen" technology. Certainly, the ability to deliver video unites television, computers, and mobile devices, but our residual acculturation may lead us to approach screens that feature familiar programs as television for some time—regardless of the technology we use to receive and view it. In the same way that "broadcasting," the "airing" of shows, and "tuning in" have remained part of the industrial and cultural vernacular, even though they precisely describe only a small part of television use, "television" continues to function as a meaningful term. As in other production components examined in subsequent chapters, the adjustments of the multichannel transition and post-network era created multiple and competing uses rather than replacing one monolithic norm with another. We must now think about television as a highly diversified medium; even as "watching television" has continued to signify a set of widely recognizable behaviors, the singularity and coherence of this experience has come to be fleeting.

3

Making Television
Changes in the Practices
of Creating Television

> The business has changed so massively. . . . You will never have the
> market forces again that, how do I put this, that allow people to get
> rich. . . . The reality is you will never have the licensing fees negoti-
> ated again that resulted in *ER* getting [millions of dollars] an
> episode, and that's where a lot of people made what many would
> probably insist is an unconscionable amount of money. . . . The up-
> side home runs for shows have been sort of flattened out by the
> new economic models of how shows are produced.
> —Dick Wolf, Producer[1]

The barrage of new technologies marketed to us in the early years of the
twenty-first century has indicated much about the changing nature of
television—so much so that even non-technophiles have realized that
changes are at hand. Yet, even as television streams into our homes daily,
the process of creating shows remains well hidden from most viewers. To
be sure, by the late 1990s, the casual viewer could notice adjustments in
types of shows and how networks organized them in their schedules.
What most viewers may not have realized was how these shifts related to
the broader structural changes that were revolutionizing the production
of television.

This chapter's epigraph captures the perspective of Dick Wolf, arguably one of the most powerful (and richest) television producers of the
last two decades due to the phenomenal success of the *Law & Order*
brand he created. Here, Wolf replies to a question of whether he could be
as successful if he were entering the businesses today, and his response indicates the consequences of the changes in how television programs are
made that this chapter explores. The "flattening out" of profits changes

the type of programs the industry is likely to produce in significant ways and allows a much broader array of programming to exist and succeed than was the case in the network era.

One of the biggest changes in the making of television resulted from a regulation introduced in the early 1970s and then eliminated in the 1990s. This set of rules—the financial interest and syndication (fin-syn) rules—altered who was allowed to make television programs, adjusted the relations of networks and studios, and affected who profited most substantially. The competitive environment that resulted from the elimination of these rules and many other deregulatory policies allowed expanded conglomeration and necessitated that those who create television devise new methods of funding. It also led to the erosion of the more monolithic norms of the network era, including the division of labor established between networks and studios, as well as the financial model according to which they operated. These adjustments and those of other production components also not only affected the storytelling possibilities of the industry, but also led networks and studios to revise long standard programming practices related to schedules, reruns, and program lengths and formats, and did so in a manner that increased the scope of commercial storytelling. In treating these matters, this chapter also explores the increased need for innovative promotion techniques that networks have adopted in order to reach the splintering audience.

Deficit Financing and the Creation of the Fin-Syn Rules

Developing programs is one of the most difficult, uncertain, and therefore risky aspects of television production. In the early days of television, networks produced their own programming—or received it from sponsors —as they had when they operated as radio networks, but television shows were far more costly than those of radio because of the added labor and complexity of visual recording. As the television era began, the networks sought to decrease the risks involved in creating programs by licensing them from film studios. This strategy was economically prudent: the film industry already had established facilities and structures for visual media. Consequently, a key practice of creating television involved dividing the process between two different entities: the studios that create the programs and the networks that organize and distribute them. Although these are distinctive tasks, the networks still maintain "creative" activities such as selecting programs and often directly shape the creative direction of their shows, especially since the elimination of the fin-syn rules allowed networks greater involvement in production.

Splitting the roles of studios and networks necessitated a means for financing television series appropriate to the varied risks and rewards inherent in the separation. A practice known as "deficit financing" consequently developed—an arrangement in which the network pays the studio that makes a show a license fee in exchange for the right to air the show. The license fee typically allows the network to air an episode a few times (a first and rerun episode), but the studio retains ownership of the show; in effect, then, the license fee just allows the network to borrow it. This is important because the license fee does not fully cover the costs of production—hence the "deficit" of deficit financing. The studio absorbs the difference between the cost of production and the license fee, which can now amount to as much as millions of dollars for each season. If the network orders enough episodes, the studio can then resell the series in various other markets.

This reselling of shows is often called "syndication." Syndication can involve selling programming to individual local stations, to cable channels, or to networks in other countries. Studios sell shows originally produced for broadcast networks to a combination of local stations and international markets (often referred to as different distribution "windows"), a process discussed in greater detail in the next chapter on distribution. Importantly, the "unconscionable" amount of money to which Wolf refers in the epigraph resulted from syndication revenues, not the original license fees, despite the importance associated with the initial broadcast airing.

Deficit financing minimized the substantial risks and costs of developing programs for the networks while initially affording the studios considerable benefits as well. In the case of successful series, the studio receives a large return on its investment when it sells the show in a combination of syndication windows because the sales provide nearly pure profit: no additional work typically goes into the show and the network receives none of the payment.[2] However, if the show is unsuccessful and does not produce enough episodes to be syndicated, or if no buyers want the show, the production company must absorb the difference between the cost of production and the original license fee. This financial imperative of creating shows likely to succeed in syndication thus leads studios to produce certain types of series—typically those with an established record, such as law, police, or hospital shows—and decreases the likelihood of producing less conventional fare. At the same time, though, a production company can counterbalance many series that perform poorly with just one success because syndication provides such substantial financial rewards.

For example, in the late 1990s, an hour-long broadcast-network drama typically cost approximately $1.2 million per episode to produce, with broadcast networks paying $800,000 to $1 million per episode in licensing fees.[3] Assuming the standard twenty-two episode season, a production studio might lose anywhere from $4.4 to $8.8 million on a season of episodes. If the ratio of license fees to production costs remained constant—which is unlikely because producers usually renegotiate license fees after a few years—the production company would assume $22 to $44 million of debt by the fifth season, at which time the series would reach the one hundred episodes commonly necessary for syndication. At that point, however, the studio could sell the series in multiple locations to recoup its costs. According to this scenario, a typical late-1990s drama would likely be sold both to a cable channel and to international buyers, in addition, perhaps, to local stations for once-a-week airing, typically on weekends. *CSI* was the last series CBS added to its schedule in 2000, and although the network expected little from it, *CSI* quickly became the season's breakout hit and regularly ranked among the most watched shows each season.[4] The series was co-produced by Alliance Atlantis and CBS Productions. CBS Productions (through commonly-owned distribution company King World) sold the first domestic syndication run of the series to cable network Spike for $1.6 million per episode and then sold the series to individual stations throughout the United States, while Alliance Atlantis sold the series in 177 different international markets for at least $1 million per episode in each major market.[5] The series also developed into a franchise—adding *CSI: Miami* and *CSI: NY*—and although the original *CSI* remained the most popular of the three in the United States, by 2006, *CSI: Miami* was the top U.S. show around the globe and had earned $6.4 million from DVD sales.[6]

In the case of comedy, the riches that can be earned from the domestic market are typically even greater because local stations have preferred the scheduling flexibility of half-hour shows. While the comedy *Friends* accumulated similar deficits during its initial production for NBC, it generated $4 million per episode (the series library consists of 220 episodes) for its first cycle of domestic syndication on local stations, $2.4 million an episode for its second cycle, and $1 million per episode for its subsequent first cable sale.[7] Earning $1.63 billion in just these distribution windows, the series also sold well internationally and marketed DVDs to earn additional revenue. In its final seasons, NBC paid $10 million per episode for *Friends,* which made it the most expensive half-hour show in television history—but Warner Bros., the show's production company, still produced the show at a deficit because the high salaries of the stars led to uncommon costs.[8] By 2006, the studios that produced *Friends* and *Seinfeld* had earned $3 billion from each show and were likely to earn even more.[9]

Network-Era Practices Lead to the Fin-Syn Rules

Deficit financing provides a balance of risk and reward in principle, but the power the networks derived from their status as the only program buyers during the network era enabled them to tip the balance in their favor.[10] Before the fin-syn rules, the networks attained greater control and less risk by forcing production companies to deficit finance their programs while also demanding a percentage of the syndication revenues. This "profit participation" by the networks caused many production companies to struggle financially, especially independent producers, or those not aligned with a major studio, because they needed all of the revenue from successes to offset both the cost of failures and the substantial overhead expenses of production. Networks had obtained profit participation in as much as 91 percent of programming by the mid-1960s, which led the government to intervene with the fin-syn rules at the beginning of the 1970s.[11]

The rules prohibited networks from holding a stake in program ownership and having a financial stake in the syndicated programming they aired, as well as limiting the number of hours of programming per week that they could produce. Much of the power that the networks developed before the rules did not result from any formal collusion, but from their status as the only three potential buyers for series. The control of distribution by the three networks defined the relationship between studios and networks and significantly disadvantaged production companies that had little recourse against network strong-arming. The realignment of power between producers and distributors—the networks—in September of 1971 by the FCC-mandated fin-syn rules and the consent decrees put forth by the U.S. district court might be considered the first disruption of

dominant network-era production processes. Many regard the years subsequent to the rules' enactment as a golden era of independent production, marked by the heyday of MTM Enterprises (producers of *The Mary
Tyler Moore Show, Lou Grant, Bob Newhart*) and Norman Lear's Tandem Productions (*All in the Family, Good Times, The Jeffersons*), among
others. The practice of deficit financing continued with few exceptions as
a dominant practice for financing series during the network era and
throughout the multi-channel transition despite the adjustments that the
fin-syn rules introduced in the balance of industrial power between networks and studios.

Changes to Fin-Syn and the Practices of the Multi-Channel Transition

The fin-syn rules ruptured some network-era norms for creating programming well before multi-channel transition adjustments occurred in
any other production process. Beginning in the early 1970s and lasting
through the mid-1990s, the rules substantially upset the established
power relation of the networks over the studios and created a fluid competitive environment, but this situation did not last. While threats to eliminate the rules surfaced as early as 1983, the threat materialized in 1991,
when the FCC began eroding the rules, which were completely eliminated
by 1995.[12] Policymakers pursued the deregulation based on the theory
that the availability of cable and new broadcast networks had diminished
the distribution control once exerted by the Big Three. Like the earlier
regulation, this deregulation substantially affected the central practices of
making television and forced a negotiation of new conditions that developed more "naturally" in other production processes.

The rules created two distinct periods of industrial practice that might
be considered characteristic of the multi-channel transition. First, the rise
of the independent studios under the fin-syn rules provided a vibrant and
competitive environment in which networks made programming decisions based more purely on content because the rules removed most
financial considerations. Because the rules eliminated the network's stake
in the revenue that a series might earn in syndication, the networks were
less likely to select to schedule shows in which they had a high stake or
keep them on the air over those that were independently produced or produced by a competing studio. Second, after the rules, various media companies (Disney, Viacom, News Corp., Time Warner) made purchases that

conglomerated studios and networks to create new kinds of corporate entities. The conglomeration created by these deals expanded the practices of profit participation or co-production that networks had abused in the 1960s to bring the production and distribution of many television series within the auspices of a single conglomerate.

As soon as regulators eliminated the rules, the networks began populating their schedules with new shows purchased nearly exclusively from studios owned by the network or from within the conglomerate owning the network—what I will refer to as "common ownership." This preponderance of common ownership, which is also called "vertical integration," radically redefined relationships between studios and networks and adjusted financing norms. Networks prioritized content generated by commonly owned studios and again demanded a share of syndication revenues in order for a show to receive a place on the schedule if it was produced by a non-commonly-owned studio. These were often called "co-production" deals—a misleading term because the commonly-owned studio that was added to "co-produce" often supplied minimal, if any, support, but still earned the rights to syndication profits. Such profit participation was a nuisance for major studios, while it substantially disadvantaged independent producers because they depended upon all possible syndication revenue.

The key reason the networks contracted with commonly owned studios was out of a desire to accrue syndication profits, but fear of top shows demanding exorbitant license fee increases after their original three- or five-year license fee agreements expired also played a role. High profile cases emerged at NBC with its license negotiations for the Warner Bros.–produced shows *Friends* and *ER*. As Wolf notes in this chapter's epigraph, the license fee for *ER* increased to $12 million per episode at one point, ten times the original fee, while NBC paid $10 million per episode to keep *Friends* on its network. These shows could have been purchased by another network if Warner Bros.' license fee demands were not met, as happened in the case of *Buffy the Vampire Slayer* moving from The WB to UPN in 2001.[13] Although few cases of shows moving to a different network actually occurred, the threat was significant enough that networks sought a share in as much programming as possible in order to maintain greater control.

Common ownership among studios and networks created a mutual interest in success, but the performance of both the network and the studio were evaluated separately within the conglomerate, and each had to meet unit budget goals. Consequently, even intra-conglomerate deals remained competitive. For instance, Warner Bros. studio could not absorb a substantial loss on a show just to help The WB decrease license fee expenses. Some advantage might be offered—as in the case of 20th Century Fox studio selling a syndication run of *The X-Files* to commonly owned FX for less than market value. Such uncompetitive practices were often revealed—as occurred in this case—in which actor David Duchovny successfully settled a suit against the studio because the cheaper sale of the program decreased his residual earnings.[14] Common ownership among a studio and a network did not provide either entity with carte blanche. Various aspects of the industrial and organizational structures of television production—whether the independent evaluation of different divisions within the conglomerate or the separate stakes in production profits often held by actors and producers—curtailed the unrestrained provision of advantage that could develop.

The advantage of deals among commonly owned entities results from the increased likelihood that they would negotiate with a sense of equity although not necessarily discount. Paying $10 million per episode of *Friends* was detrimental to NBC, and Warner Bros. may not have pushed for such unprecedented payment had it been negotiating with a commonly owned network.[15] Abuses certainly could and did occur, but many counter examples in which commonly owned networks lost out in bidding or commonly owned networks beat competitive offers also emerged. Such varied evidence made it difficult to sustain claims about the uniform behavior of conglomerates found in the work of scholars such as McChesney and Bagdikian.[16] Still, the alignment of common ownership provided a considerable shift in practice and created a competitive advantage for commonly owned studios that made the financial model of scripted series creation untenable for independent producers.[17]

The shifting norms within other production components also gradually affected program creation and required the development of lower-cost genres. With more choices and control over entertainment options segmenting the audience, networks were pressured to offer fewer reruns to keep viewers' attention. This required networks to create more programming, which, in turn, necessitated expanding programming budgets at the same time that advertisers began to resist paying more for fewer viewers. The unanticipated success of unscripted or "reality" programming, with its lower production costs, blockbuster audiences (in some cases), and unconventional and flexible season lengths and schedules, provided one solution. In the early, experimental phase of prime-time broadcast unscripted programs, a new independent production sector emerged and thrived. The difference between the budgets, schedules, and opportunities for syndication of unscripted programs led the industry to recognize that there were other feasible practices available for financing and creating programs than were common of scripted programming.

Deficit financing was one of the most entrenched production practices throughout the network era and multi-channel transition—and this system of financing necessitated many of the distribution practices explored in the next chapter. The lack of syndication value initially perceived as characteristic of reality programming led these shows to rely on funding structures other than deficit financing. Other methods of financing programs had always existed, and U.S. television producers began to experiment with financing norms common in other industrial contexts, such as Britain's "cost plus" system.[18] In this model, networks pay producers complete costs and often a 10 percent profit at the time of production. The studio effectively sells the program in exchange, so that the network then holds the rights to all profits in any subsequent syndication—reducing both risk and reward for the producer. A cost-plus framework provides a valuable model for negotiating the increasing uncertainty of distribution practices characteristic of the post-network era and may be particularly appropriate for the situation of commonly owned networks and studios that has begun to dominate industrial relations. Another program financing option harkens to the pre-network era in which agencies or advertisers bore production costs. Experiments with this method occurred in the early 2000s, with media-buying companies bearing the burden of production costs for both unscripted (*The Restaurant*) and scripted shows (*The Days*).

At the 2004 National Association of Television Program Executives (NATPE) conference, Caryn Mandabach proclaimed "deficit financing is dead." Mandabach was a partner of the once legendary, but now defunct independent production company Carsey-Warner-Mandabach that created *The Cosby Show, Roseanne,* and *That 70's Show* among others, so her opinion on the matter earned consideration, and it was echoed by a number of executives speaking at the conference that year. Nonetheless, deficit financing has lived on through 2006. The financing and production models of unscripted television did, however, steadily alter the perception that deficit financing provided the only viable model for show funding and made it decreasingly likely that a standard production and financing model will remain common among prime-time programming. The erosion of deficit financing as a dominant model—even if it is by no means dead—involves a significant adjustment in the economics of the industry and perhaps may point to a nascent post-network-era norm.

Many of the changes in the practices of program creation noted here have resulted from external forces such as regulatory changes and shifts in distribution capabilities and norms. Regardless of their origins, though, the development of multiple financing options, including deficit financing, cost plus, and single sponsorship, and the creation of programming with varied cost structures and syndication values, ranging from conventional scripted to short-run unscripted, suggested an emerging multiplicity of possibilities for program creation in the post-network era.

But structures of financing and relationships with distributors are not the only practices involved in creating programs. This process also encompasses matters such as network schedules, rerun policies, and program lengths and formats. These, however, did not deviate from network-era norms until much later than the shifts linked to the establishment and elimination of the fin-syn rules.

Post-Fin-Syn Studio-Network Relations

From 1995 to 2002, the networks gorged themselves on commonly owned or co-produced series. The consequences soon caught up with them, though, as favoring business over creativity contributed to a glut of unpopular programming that studios were unable to sell in syndication: consider, for example, many of the shows that were produced by NBC Studios and scheduled in NBC's Thursday 8:30 time slot—*Union Square, Cursed, Inside Schwartz.* However, after some excesses in decision-making that favored business over creative considerations, by 2005 a new post-regulatory equilibrium gradually developed, and the networks achieved a more balanced approach to buying commonly owned series. Most notably, after falling from first to fourth place in reaching the key 18–49-year-old demographic in a single season, NBC used external purchases in an attempt to reinvigorate its 2005–2006 schedule, for which the network purchased only two of six new shows from NBC Universal Television Studio, and required no co-production deals.[19] The competitive situation of a network—i.e., its level of desperation—contributes to how it prioritizes creative and economic factors in determining programming.

The initial step in the process of program creation—the selection of shows for the schedule—embodies all of the contradictory and contested tendencies inherent to the combination of art and commerce characteristic of cultural industries. A highly rational business process guides networks to make certain decisions about shows; however, the fickle behavior of audiences and the particular features of producing creative goods often defy rationality. Industry decision makers also must weigh competing factors with unclear outcomes. Shows that are commonly owned or co-produced are potentially more profitable than shows in which the network has no profit participation. Likewise, a show with a lower license fee costs the network less than a show with a higher fee, yet an unpopular co-owned or cheap show is less valuable than a popular show with no network interest because it harms the network both in the present by decreasing ratings and potentially in the future by eroding audience and reputation. Determining the best creative content and what viewers might desire involves a decidedly less rational process than many other business decisions, and ultimately, creative needs can trump all other aspects of common and co-ownership. The conflicting artistic and economic forces and the variable competitive situations of the networks complicate assessments of the effects of the elimination of the fin-syn rules on the creative process.

But networks' selection of shows for their schedules is not the only way that they might show favor to a commonly owned series. As networks have come to purchase more and more from commonly owned studios and fewer and fewer independent production studios have continued to survive, many in the creative community have called for a re-enactment of the fin-syn rules or some similar type of regulation. The challenge in making the case that common ownership is detrimental to the industry comes from the often complicated and conflicting array of factors that could explain the success or failure of specific shows. Networks do play a key role in determining the fate of many shows, as scheduling position could influence a show's success as much as its content—consider the difference between airing a show after *American Idol*, which guaranteed a ratings peak as audiences left sets tuned to FOX, and scheduling a show against the ratings powerhouse on another network. With so many networks to watch and viewing spread so disparately, the amount of time and money a network spends promoting a new show also significantly contributes to success. Given limited resources in both ideal schedule positions and promotional dollars, networks can readily stack the odds in favor of shows in which they share financial interest. But this can also prove unwise. If a network too frequently wastes ideal schedule positions and promotion on shows viewers may sample but not return to because of lacking creative quality, the network risks placing itself in a position of not developing new hits to replace aging shows (as was the case of NBC's 8:30 Thursday shows for much of the late 1990s).

Further, one of the consequences of audience fragmentation has been the creation of a vast middle range of programming that was neither clear success nor failure. In annual decisions about which of these mid-range shows to cancel or renew, the networks decide among series with little ratings deviation. Many series balance precariously "on the bubble" at the end of the season because although they had not performed as highly as expected or needed, they may have reached a certain valuable audience, or their poor ratings may have resulted from their placement in a particularly competitive time slot. Renewal decisions for mid-performing series tend to be made on the basis of various considerations, and whether a commonly owned studio produced the show easily could be one. For example, did the renewal of ABC's *Once and Again* for 2001–2002—a series that regularly ranked between fifty and sixty in weekly ratings and often ranked third among the Big Three in its time slot—result from its production by commonly owned Touchstone? Or was it renewed because of the critical attention garnered by lead actor Sela Ward's Emmy award? Did *TV Guide*'s cover story featuring the series as "The Best Show You're Not Watching" turn the tide in the series' favor? Or did its return arise from the fact that it drew an audience with a median age of 41.8 years, considerably below its competitors?[20]

With networks facing such a range of complicated and competing factors in making many of their renewal decisions, it is difficult for those outside of the decision process to ever know in what cases common ownership might prevail over other considerations. And even if common ownership is the deciding factor, is this necessarily problematic? Independent producers may never earn this extra consideration, but unconventional and boundary-expanding content is not limited to the studios of independent producers. A better way to assess the significance of self-interest in renewal decisions on the medium's creativity is to begin by determining whether unconventional programming uniformly benefits or suffers in unclear renewal decisions, and then identifying whether a correlation with common ownership exists. It is certainly the case that financial concerns have been more instrumental in decision-making after the fin-syn era because of the networks' interest in syndication profits—but these remain complicated by less tangible factors of artistry, creative innovation, and audience whimsy.

Freed from fin-syn restrictions and operating as part of expanding conglomerations seeking "synergy," the networks also developed practices other than buying from commonly owned studios to reassert their dominance in program creation in the late 1990s. Adjustments as simple as writing longer-term deals, such as those establishing license fees for five or more years rather than three, provided some control, but most changes were more substantial. In addition to licensing most of their new shows from commonly owned studios—as in the case of NBC buying from NBC Universal Television Studio—the networks also demanded co-production status in a manner reminiscent of the 1960s. While "co-production" did not often require the network to add any creative talent, it did entitle the network to syndication revenue and provided it with more influence in the creative process. Co-production ensured the network a stake in the long-term revenues of programs and enhanced the self-interest likely to arise in situations in which networks purchased series from commonly owned studios.

Networks have often forced co-production upon studios as a condition of scheduling their shows, and often only those studios or producers with some sort of clout can resist these demands. For example, in preparing its 2005–2006 schedule, CBS demanded a co-producer role for its CBS Paramount Studio on two series, *Ghost Whisperer* and *Criminal Minds*, which were developed by Touchstone, in order for the shows to be included on the fall schedule; Touchstone eventually conceded.[21] Such is not always the case, though. Networks may not be able make demands for co-production of shows that a studio might easily sell to another network.[22] For example, at this time, no network could likely force co-production on a show created by Jerry Bruckheimer—the executive producer of the *CSIs, Cold Case, The Amazing Race,* and *Without a Trace*—because his record of success created such high demand for his work.

In theory, the expanded competitive environment suggested by the arrival of hundreds of cable networks should have diminished the degree of control that the networks exercised in the network era, when they functioned as an oligopsony, or industry with a limited number of buyers. The expansion of cable channels did, indeed, create new buyers, but because they operated with greater economic restrictions, these channels did not have program budgets comparable to those of broadcasters and were unable to operate as equal competitors for scripted programming.

In the rare occasions that networks do not purchase shows in which they have a stake, they often purchase them from a studio owned by one of the other major conglomerates. Mandabach describes this as "horse trading" and notes that one part of the competitive environment requires maintaining good relations with competitors—which can be accomplished by buying each other's shows.[23] The conglomerate-owned studios feature an organizational scale that makes it possible to keep talent under contract and amortize overhead expenses in a manner infeasible for independents. Independents consequently struggled to compete with major studios as production costs and license fees increased incommensurately in the late 1990s and early 2000s. Because independents operate on a much smaller scale than the studios, they have less opportunity to spread risk and profits across varied productions, and allowing networks co-production interests cuts into the potential profits of successful series.

A panel of studio and network executives at the 2007 NATPE conference agreed that common ownership of studios and networks had contributed to rapidly escalating programming costs, as they noted it was easier to approve incremental cost increases for productions when one entity had a stake in production and distribution.[24] The common-ownership model allows the conglomerate the opportunity for immediate revenue from production expenditures—in the form advertising revenue—as well as the later revenue available from syndication, increasing the incentive for incremental spending that may make the difference between success and failure. Some on the panel noted that escalating production costs are also likely to have contributed to the troubled status of independent producers, who are less able to afford such incremental spending. Conglomerate-owned studios do not exclusively produce for the commonly owned network, however, and common ownership can lead to complications when a studio such as NBC Universal Television Studio (NUTS) attempts to sell a program to a non-commonly-owned network. Marc Graboff, who is president of NBC Universal, West Coast, and is responsible for both NBC network and NUTS, noted that being on both sides of deals also means that the studio has to give in to the same concessions when producing for other networks as he demands of the non-NBCU studios that license their shows to NBC. For example, if he insists on obtaining rights to stream a Touchstone-produced show aired by NBC on the NBC website, then NUTS would have to be willing to give ABC those rights if it licensed a show to ABC.

Common ownership and co-production have particularly disadvantaged independent producers—so much so that by the end of 2005 the production of prime-time scripted series was no longer a viable possibility for independent producers.[25] Although the competitive demands of the environment required major studios to produce increasingly innovative programming, the loss of independents remains a significant sacrifice in the emerging configurations of the post-network era. Just as competitive conditions forced Touchstone to allow CBS's Paramount to co-produce *Ghost Whisperer* and *Criminal Minds,* network executives can more effectively mandate creative decisions when commonly owned or co-producing studios make series in a manner that undermines the creative autonomy of the producer. For example, Marcy Carsey attributes the ability to resist network demands to adjust a show that ultimately became one of the most successful in television history to her studio's independent status. In the early 1980s, her production company, Carsey-Werner, had difficulty finding a network interested in a family comedy built around comedian Bill Cosby. One network suggested that perhaps they could reconceptualize the show to make Cosby a Vegas performer.[26] The independence of the creators enabled them to take the series to another network and maintain their creative vision, which involved telling a story about an affluent and professional black family in a manner historic for television of the time. Successful producer Stephen J. Cannell recounts similar stories about his series *The Rockford Files* and *The Commish,* in which "wrong-headed network script and casting demands" led him to move the shows to rival networks where he could maintain his creative vision.[27] These examples illustrate the creative pressures that are part of television's business dealings. Had these creators been working under conditions of common ownership, they may not have been able to resist network interventions.

After the elimination of the fin-syn rules, some name-brand producers —such as Steven Bochco and David E. Kelley—have taken the opportunity to establish "alignment" deals with particular studios and sometimes their commonly owned networks, rather than maintaining complete independence. These deals usually link the producer and studio for a set number of years or series and typically require the producers to allow the network the first chance to buy any shows they develop—if not including some "put pilots" in the deal, which are effectively guaranteed to make the schedule or else the networks suffer substantial financial penalties. In return, studios help support the producers with major overhead expenses and ensure a steady income—aspects of financial security that can lead to greater innovation and willingness to take risks in some cases. The necessity of these deals for top talent indicates a key shift from the fin-syn era, when the studios of top producers succeeded while maintaining independence from the major studios.[28]

Another indication of the changing economics, distribution of power, and relationships of networks and studios appeared when studios began declining to produce series accepted by networks if they did not think they could recoup production costs. The highest profile case occurred when Touchstone backed out of producing *CSI* for CBS. Touchstone estimated that *CSI* would cost $2.4 million per episode, while CBS offered only $1.1 million in licensing fees. In a substantial miscalculation, Touchstone did not think that international and domestic broadcast and cable syndication would compensate for the substantial deficit.[29] Again, the slippage in trying to rationalize creative decisions through economic logic emerges. Touchstone based its decision on perceptions of the syndication marketplace, but this marketplace is not static and tastes shift: *CSI* earned $1.6 million per episode in its first round of cable syndication, while different versions of the show became some of the most popular U.S. series in other countries.[30] As the economics of the industry change, the potential viability of a show in international sales has come to be an important consideration in whether it is produced for the U.S. market in the first place.

The refusal of studios to produce programs with an episode order from a network offers contradictory evidence about the consequences of the competitive environment and common ownership of networks and studios. Series creators whose ideas survive the gauntlet of being selected for a network schedule achieve an extraordinary success, but the subsequent evaluation process by studios can negatively affect unconventional or innovative shows that lack a track record in syndication markets. This concern about international syndication has particularly affected programming with non-white casts due to the perception that African-American cast shows have less syndication value or that only a certain type of blackness can be depicted.[31] Further, the relationships networks have with commonly owned studios may be important in creating a show that the network supports but is deemed too risky by other studios. The late 1990s drama *Any Day Now* faced this challenge when Lifetime desired to schedule this show about the interracial friendship of two women. Even with a series commitment from Lifetime in hand, producers Gary Randall and Nancy Miller struggled to find a studio to produce the series because of the limited syndication value perceived for an original cable series and story about race relations. Ultimately, dealings among agents led Spelling Television to produce the show, but this difficulty could have been avoided if Lifetime had a commonly owned studio.[32] This case contradicts the assertion that common ownership has uniformly negative consequences for creativity and producer autonomy.

The studios and networks negotiated a shifting regulatory environment throughout the multi-channel transition as they sought a workable balance of creative and financial considerations in creating television series. Despite vociferous calls from the creative community for a return to fin-syn or similar re-regulation, such intervention remains unlikely. Many, for example, have championed a mandate of 25 percent non-studio content similar to regulations instituted in Britain. Adjustments in other production components—particularly those in distribution explored in the next chapter—have also introduced new complexity into the post-fin-syn relationships of networks and studios. As the next chapter illustrates, common ownership has become imperative in initiating certain post-network distribution experiments. Initially, new distribution practices replicated the networks' exuberant pursuit of commonly owned content in the same manner as the immediate post-fin-syn years. Yet it is likely that creative concerns will again reassert their status in these decisions as other production components respond to adjustments throughout the production process.

Labored Relations

Many activities are involved in the creation of television programming. Practices such as deficit financing and federal regulation such as the fin-syn rules operate at a macro level and exist as given norms of operation for those who work in the industry on a day-to-day basis. There are also many other important aspects of making television that are not as externally structuring, one of which encompasses the working conditions and standard labor practices of the industry. By the end of the multi-channel transition, the Hollywood creative community at the center of U.S. television production featured many norms increasingly atypical of U.S.

labor relations. Hollywood continued to operate with an unusual level of unionization, with almost all work in the mainstream creative industries relying upon a collectivized agency to negotiate basic fee scales for work and residual payments on content. While the maintenance of union and guild centrality in Hollywood might be almost inexplicable relative to the union-busting and destabilization of workers' collectives throughout the United States, it does support the notion suggested by many who study creative industries and argue that this work involves features fundamentally distinct from most others.[33]

Despite the centrality of Hollywood's collectivized workforce, major labor disputes emerged throughout the multi-channel transition as studios and networks tried to save money by decreasing labor costs. Media scholar Chad Raphael notes that in the 1980s and early 1990s, five creative industry unions went on strike once (the National Association of Broadcast Employees and Technicians, the Directors Guild of America, the American Federation of Musicians, the Screen Extras Guild, and the American Federation of Television and Radio Artists); and the powerful Screen Actors Guild went on strike twice and the Writers Guild of America three times.[34] The 1988 Writers Guild strike lasted twenty-two weeks, delayed the premiere of the 1988 season, and cost the industry an estimated $500 million.[35] Indeed, the costs of this strike for both sides continued to weigh particularly heavily as new contracts created patchwork agreements for much of the multi-channel transition.

New technologies and distribution windows threatened to lead the guilds to strike again in the mid-2000s. One issue arose from a deal agreed upon in the mid-1980s that established the residuals creative talent would earn on VHS sales and that remained in effect through 2006— by which point DVD distribution had become a $4 billion industry, and various online distribution formats were exploding.[36] The key contention for creative talent resulted from the categorization of new technologies as "home video," rather than as "pay tv," which earned four times as much.[37] Likewise, deals for cable production crafted in the 1990s remained in effect despite the substantial change in the type of programming and budgets of these networks. Studios and networks began experimenting with allowing viewers unconventional access to programs, such as enabling them to download shows with and without commercials, in hopes of adding new revenue to their financial models. They also began creating other forms of content such as "webisodes" and "mobisodes" (for web and mobile phone viewing, respectively), and it was unclear how the labor involved with these efforts should be remunerated. The guilds, however, wanted compensation appropriate to their contribution to these new ventures, which threatened studio and network shares of the new bounty.

The new technologies and distribution formats that threaten contracts due to expire in 2007 and 2008 indicate just one point of tension for the television industry's uncertain labor market. Some television producers had evaded the cost of union production by fleeing Hollywood in a practice known as "runaway production" and led many to worry about the future of work in this "industry town"—although it was already diminished film industry production that was primarily responsible for reducing the available work in the immediate Los Angeles area. Television work began climbing slowly in the early 1990s in response to new broadcast and cable needs and reached a peak in 2002—the year it bested feature films as the area's primary production activity.[38] During this time, much television was also produced outside of the city; while 75 percent of prime-time series were shot in Los Angeles in 2005, only 44 percent of surveyed cable programs were filmed there. One way cable has been able to afford original programming has been by moving production to Canada where producers avoid union rates and benefit from a weaker Canadian dollar. Some dramas that aired on The WB and UPN were also shot outside Los Angeles in response to the efforts of various cities and states throughout the United States that offer tax incentives to encourage the financial boost of production spending; most of the shift has been to New York.

The labor conditions at the heart of runaway production and the union and guild strikes affected the creation of programming in various ways. Although some people may associate fame and stardom with working in television, the percentage of workers who achieve household name recognition is infinitesimally small relative to the number of people required throughout the production process. The guilds and unions have functioned primarily to secure basic rights and suitable working conditions for those paid at base level—as the irregularity of production and the high demand for jobs have created ample opportunities to exploit this particularly unstable labor force. As the economic conditions of the industry changed in relation to the adjustments examined here, networks and studios sought cost savings wherever possible, and, with wages forming a large component of production budgets, these savings often came at workers' expense.

Raphael argues that early in the multi-channel transition the economic conditions and practices of the newly acquired broadcast networks contributed greatly to labor unrest, and that skyrocketing star salaries drove production costs so high that the networks had to begin including some low cost programming. Such programming was first evident in shows like *America's Funniest Home Videos,* then in the surplus of newsmagazines through much of the 1990s, and finally in the unscripted shows that did away with the need for many unionized employees—particularly actors and writers.[39] Cost savings was an important factor in the surge in reality programming in the early 2000s, but the novelty of reality shows, as well as the fact that they drew larger young audiences than other lower budget programs, were also part of their appeal. Nonetheless, by the end of the multi-channel transition, the industry had begun running out of the stopgap solutions that had allowed it to continue operating by subtly modifying the network-era model.

In 2005, a massive reorganization of economic practices began in response to shifts in distribution inaugurated by the ABC-iTunes deal that subsequently affected the creation of television. While the influence of adjustments in other production components—particularly technology and distribution— required negotiation of existing practices, by 2006, a number of labor disputes also emerged, many in response to network and studio efforts to profit from new forms of television. The renegotiation of major union and guild contracts due to occur in the late 2000s has been widely acknowledged as likely to be particularly contentious—although this is not the only source of conflict. For example, the writers of the unscripted series *America's Next Top Model* went on strike in the summer of 2006 because the production company for the show would not recognize their vote to join the Writers Guild of America (WGA) or the compensation to which they were consequently entitled. Such unionization and controversy suggests that the savings unscripted series have achieved at the expense of low labor payments might be short lived. That same summer, as the WGA began its campaign to bring labor agreements in line with the new era of technology and distribution, the organization asked the showrunners—those who oversee production—on *The Office, Heroes, Crossing Jordan,* and *Battlestar Galactica* to refuse to provide materials for webisodes or other web content in order to draw attention to the new, uncompensated work networks were demanding.

One of the consequences of adjustments in program financing models has been a significant disruption in the norms of industry compensation.

Certainly many eagerly eyed the new revenue streams available from DVD sales and seemingly endless distribution possibilities, but determining how those funds would be shared has proven to be difficult for the industry. By the beginning of 2007, the only certainty was that the adjustments in other production components would force significant revisions of labor arrangements and that establishing post-network norms would be highly contentious.

Transitions in Programming

Many of the features of television programming that we have long taken for granted—that shows should last thirty or sixty minutes and have commercials embedded throughout, that they should air at the same time every week, that sometimes a network will air an episode that we've already seen—result from network-era norms of program creation established by the broadcast networks. Many of these practices resulted from a negotiation of economic considerations in a manner that again underscores the intricate connection among artistic and commercial components of cultural production. For example, once it became technologically possible, the "rerun" was a key strategy of broadcast economics as it decreased the number of weeks that the networks needed to pay for new programming. Likewise, conventional program lengths developed to facilitate the constant flow of programming and included the use of commercial messages embedded at anticipatable intervals which became characteristic of U.S. commercial television. These norms differ from those of other countries in which networks might allow periods of blank screens to air because of irregular program lengths.

The television "season" provides a quintessential example of an industrial ritual with commercial and artistic ramifications. No external force mandated this practice, but once developed, it proved difficult to suspend. In the early 1960s the Big Three networks established the concept of the "television season" that mirrored the U.S. school year (more on this in Chapter 5). Spanning September through May, the season remained dominant for four decades and then began declining in the early 2000s as a result of a number of competitive pressures. NBC, FOX, and The WB all announced variations in January 2003, while FOX made changes in its development calendar to enable the "fifty-two week" season many suggested should become the new industrial norm.

The television season was a prototypical network-era concept fundamental to a linear viewing environment and emerged from factors of competition, audience research, and program acquisition and financing. Networks commonly purchased the licensing rights for twenty-one or twenty-two episodes per season throughout much of the network era and multi-channel transition; these rights allowed the networks an initial and at least one rerun airing to fill a time slot for roughly forty-three weeks of the year. Remaining weeks were left for specials, films, sports, and holiday programming.

The three networks did not establish this practice through formalized collusion; rather they developed and maintained the practice as an unofficial industrial norm of mutual benefit that freed them from the need and expense of purchasing new programming for the fifty-two weeks of the year. When upstart network FOX sought entry to what seemed a zero-sum industry in the late 1980s, it achieved some success by launching new series during the summer—thereby counter-programming the reruns of the Big Three with original shows. Competition from FOX initially was not significant enough for the Big Three to adjust their conventional practices, but in the late 1990s, cable networks launched original narrative series during the summer such as *Any Day Now, Sex and the City,* and *Witchblade*. The increasing loss of audience members to cable during summer months began to jeopardize the network-era model of the television season. Although broadcasters' abdication of summer competition had been supported by industry beliefs in sizable programming drops during these months, such drops had become insubstantial by the early 2000s. Whereas in the 1950s, the HUT level (homes using television) dropped 28 percent during summer months, average summer use in 2003 measured just 5 percent lower than during the regular season.[40]

Apart from the tendency for television use to lessen in the summer, another rationale for the "television season" was maintaining optimal audiences during the key "sweeps" months of November, February, May, and July, in which Nielsen collected national audience data. The Big Three networks consequently organized their schedules to debut programs in mid-September in order to acquaint viewers with new programs before the November measurement. They then scheduled new and rerun episodes throughout the year so that the season concluded with highly viewed finale episodes during the May measurement. By 1987, however, Nielsen had refined its technology to allow it to measure viewing practices on a nightly basis; the People Meter could sample enough homes nationwide to produce nightly ratings that were accurate nationally, but not in individual markets.[41] This made sweeps periods unimportant to the networks' national advertisers, but the networks continued sweeps-schedule "stunting" both because the period remained crucial for their local affiliates and because the networks earned most of their revenue from the affiliates that they owned and operated. In 2004, Nielsen began implementing Local People Meter (LPM) technology in the largest markets, which enabled it to produce accurate local data nightly as well. Sweeps became irrelevant to LPM markets, which included most of the networks' owned and operated stations, and further diminished the need to maintain the network-era television season.

Adjustments to the television season affected other aspects of the process of programming, including the corresponding cycle of program development. In the network era, the broadcast networks all began to develop new series in the late summer months, known as "pilot season" to some, during which time program executives scheduled countless meetings with hopeful producers who "pitched" new ideas. Based on their interest in the ideas and their needs, the networks committed to pilot scripts and even pilot productions during the winter, so that by early spring they would have a variety of pilot episodes or presentations to consider for the fall schedule they announced at the upfront presentation in May. (The upfront presentation immediately precedes the upfront advertising sales process during which broadcast networks have historically sold 75 to 90 percent of the advertising time in their schedules for the upcoming season.)

The broadcast networks' shared schedule for program development affected the creative process itself, as well as power relations within the industry. On the one hand, the shared calendar afforded creative talent a level of power, as networks wary of the scarcity of certain ideas sought to lock talent and ideas in place so as to not risk losing them to another network. On the other hand, operating on an industry-wide schedule constricted talent availability, placing actors and other workers in the dubious position of committing to certain projects and "passing" on others, while having little assurance that the project they committed to would be chosen for the network schedule. In fact, talent working on a series in production were often eliminated from consideration for new series because they believed their series would continue when they faced the real likelihood of show cancellation and minimal job security. This system created difficulties for networks, too, as when they signed "holding" deals with actors and creative staff to ensure that they would be available to the network—and to prevent them from working for others. This practice created inefficiencies when networks paid talent they did not use or if ideas sat on a shelf because a network would rather pay for a concept they might develop than risk losing an idea to a competitor. The use of holding deals also led networks to prioritize series that made use of the actors they were "holding," creating a dynamic in some ways reminiscent of the Hollywood studio era.

The decreased observation of the television season forced adjustments in the norms of the yearly development cycle. At least one network, FOX, could claim to utilize a year-round development process by 2005, and the irregular schedules of cable channels also led to the emergence of alternative development cycles. Other networks claimed to program year-round, but primarily achieved this by maintaining the September through May norm and airing short-run unscripted series during the summer months. Maintaining the network-era convention of the television season benefited the networks because it eliminated the financial burden of year-round original programming. The financial losses networks faced as audiences not only switched to cable programming during the summer but also decreasingly returned in the fall provided the impetus to adjust strategies. NBC's experiment with new, non-narrative programming during the summer months of 2003 led it to lose fewer audience members than it had in previous summers, and it was successful in drawing the largest audiences among broadcast networks.

Adjustments in these cycles has reallocated power within the television industry. Freeing specific parts of the series development process from certain calendar periods could create more opportunities for creative workers. Writers and producers might be willing to present more unconventional ideas to networks if they do not need to fear that pursuing the project might lead them to be locked out of the job market until the following development season. Yet networks have continued to create countermeasures—such as holding deals—to reassert their control of this process. The interrelations among the convention of the television schedule, the upfront advertising buying process, and the annual cycle of development illustrate how an adjustment of one component of the production process substantially affects others and contributes to the reallocation of control in significant ways. While new norms can (re)establish power relations among the various entities involved in the program creation process, change as significant as the erosion of the dominance of the television season is rare and can have widespread, substantive effects.

This erosion has also been due to the distinctive economics and programming organization of cable channels, which forced them to defy the dominant programming and scheduling practices of broadcasters as they began to produce original scripted series. As the competitive environment adjusted, however, broadcasters increasingly borrowed from cable channels' experiments. The cable channels had greater difficulty establishing audiences and particularly risked losing viewers if they broke the audience's habit of viewing a series every week because viewers sampled cable channels less frequently compared with broadcast networks. In response to concerns that weekly viewing times for cable programs were more likely to be forgotten, cable channels airing original series sought to establish a regular viewer commitment by forgoing reruns and airing new episodes in consecutive weeks.

At the same time, though, cable channels produced much less original programming than broadcasters—a practice that both facilitated the creation of their varied scheduling practices and season norms and increased the challenge of helping viewers find their programs. For example, premium cable network HBO defied broadcast norms by airing consecutive new episodes of a program over twelve to eighteen weeks and then left audiences without new episodes for as long as twenty-one months—as was the case of *The Sopranos*' hiatus from June 2004 through March 2006. The ability of HBO's shows to reassemble their audience despite the long absences, which defied conventional wisdom about audience behavior, resulted from the exceptional differentiation in the quality of its shows, as well as from the subscription payments that created a monetary investment in consuming content. Ultimately, a key component of HBO's strategy required developing enough series to air new programs on one night year-round in order to maintain a constant habit of viewing. Basic cable channels followed suit, often airing consecutive new episodes after a substantial promotional campaign, with long gaps between seasons, although airing new episodes in the same time slot year-round. FX, for example, reproduced the HBO strategy to the letter on Tuesday nights. The flexibility in season length offers series' creators latitude in how and what kinds of stories they tell in a manner that—in addition to the differentiation provided by their narrowcast focus—makes the cable channels a distinctive storytelling venue. The flexible season length also altered production schedules, which provided more leeway for writers and actors who also wished to pursue film and stage work, as well as making the production calendar less chaotic.

Drawing from such developments in cable, some broadcasters decreased or eliminated their rerun load in order to aid lagging ratings for highly serialized shows. The WB first tried this strategy when it split the same time slot in 2000–2001 between *Felicity* and *Jack & Jill*. Although this provided viewers with few reruns and more content, such a scheduling tactic was costly for the network as it essentially paid twice the license fee normally required for one time slot. A more efficient use of this practice evolved in 2004–2005 when ABC and FOX delayed new episodes of returning series *Alias* and *24* until January in order to run them consecutively through the end of the season in May. At this time, many episodic dramas—shows that confine their stories to single episodes, such as *Law & Order* and *CSI*—drew large audiences for repeat episodes and dominated network schedules while repeat episodes of such highly serialized shows as *24* performed poorly, and too many weeks of reruns led to dwindling audiences for new episodes.[42] The willingness and ability of networks to pursue unconventional scheduling strategies has aided the resurgence of serial drama and diversified the range of stories the medium offers. Importantly, the use of lower cost unscripted shows figured prominently in networks' ability to balance the costs of forgoing the rerun episode of many of the serials, as does the newer practice of charging for purchase of the episodes online.

Viewers' experience with cable channels' unconventional scheduling and season organization contributed to their changing expectations of broadcast programming and broadcasters' willingness to deviate from network-era practices. Although shorter and more irregular seasons meant there would be less new programming than during the twenty-two-episode seasons common throughout the multi-channel transition—and twenty-two was a reduction from earlier norms—the variation in scheduling and season lengths expanded the types of stories that could be profitably produced for U.S. television. Before this, the production conditions that offered advantage to narrative series that provided ongoing stories limited the types of stories that could be and have been told. The demand for successful series to endlessly perpetuate themselves resulted in many stale hours of U.S. television and made it difficult for the medium to explore stories that have a more finite narrative range, as is common in other national television contexts.

The changing competitive environment has reinvigorated interest in the short-run or limited series that had been quite successful in the 1970s (*Roots, Winds of War*) and standard in many other countries. In many cases, networks—both broadcast and cable—have produced limited-run series to test program ideas that seemed to defy conventional boundaries (NBC's *Kingpin, Revelations, Book of Daniel*; Showtime's *Sleeper Cell*; USA's *The 4400*; FX's *Thief*). Of these examples, only *The 4400* and *Sleeper Cell*, notably both cable series, proved to have the necessary viewer interest to warrant subsequent seasons of production, but even the others expanded the storytelling world for a few weeks. If not for the limited-run option, networks are less likely to commit programming budgets and schedules to such risky programming endeavors and consequently might avoid them altogether. Another advantage of the closed-ended nature of these series is that they can attract creative talent unlikely to work in television otherwise—the director Steven Spielberg, who served as executive producer of the SciFi mini-series *Taken*, is a case in point. To be sure, the limited series has not replaced ongoing series; rather, the fracturing of the competitive environment allowed the return of programming forms that had become infeasible and indicated an important expansion in the storytelling U.S. commercial television could encompass.

Although I argue that the multiplicity of practices emerging by the end of the multi-channel transition provided important new opportunities for television, it is also true that the variation in scheduling practices and season organization confused many viewers accustomed to network-era norms. As scheduling practices grew increasingly uneven and shows did not appear at regular and expected times, viewers often became uncertain about what shows might have been cancelled—for instance, when 24 did not appear with other new fall programs. Likewise, where the cable networks used no apparent logic in determining when to present new episodes of shows, casual viewers who did not regularly watch those networks had difficulty learning when new seasons would begin. Maintaining network-era practices, as did The WB with its heavy rerun load, also became confusing amidst so many other varied scheduling and season organization strategies. This inconsistency in scheduling norms contributed to networks' enhanced efforts in promoting their shows.

New Challenges in Promotional Practices

Program promotion has tended to exceed the regular activities of making television, but the central role of the network in this process warrants consideration. Few commented on networks' self-promotional activities for much of television history. Networks commonly included clips from upcoming programs within their commercial blocks and, for the most part, limited their promotional activities to using network airtime. There were a few exceptions, especially with respect to particularly important markets: in this case, you could determine the value of your home television market by noting the number of billboards and other out-of-home advertisements on which networks considered it worthwhile to spend portions of their promotional budgets. Otherwise, the few viewing options of the network era made on-network promotion particularly efficient. Adjustments throughout television production processes required new promotional techniques and increased the importance of this already essential practice.

In the course of the multi-channel transition, broadcasters responded to expanding competition by increasing their on-network promotions; for example, a study of NBC and ABC found that an hour of each network's programming contained five more minutes of promotional content in 1999 than 1989, and another study estimated that the U.S. broadcast networks collectively aired 30,000 promos per year.[43] If the networks had sold that time to advertisers, they could have earned an estimated $4 billion—lost revenue that further suggests the economic significance of promotion.[44]

Broadcasters' reliance on their own network as their primary promotional venue meant that the emergence of cable competition produced twice the consequences. Cable programming lured broadcast audiences away from broadcast series and also removed them from the audience for promotions; the latter effect became particularly problematic as audiences missed promotion for the fall season during their summer cable viewing. As a result, broadcasters suffered decreased ratings for new shows and had fewer opportunities to pitch upcoming content to their target audiences. The diffusion of audiences into niche venues, which also diminished the utility of on-network promotion, required more varied and precise practices.

As the post-network era began to emerge and most programming no longer attracted a large and heterogeneous audience, networks began experimenting with new promotional strategies to find the audience members who were eluding their traditional techniques. First, they made use of "sister" networks joined through common conglomerate ownership to reach a broader audience with conventional strategies. These endeavors often illustrated the "synergy" the vast media mergers were intended to create—as in the case of MTV airing a special about the new season of *Survivor* just before its launch on CBS, when both networks were part of the Viacom conglomerate. A telling indication of the extent of sibling promotion emerged in 2002 with the news that the largest advertiser on AOL Time Warner media was AOL Time Warner. The conglomerate contributed 5.5 percent of the $8.5 billion AOL Time Warner reported in advertising and commercial revenue that year.[45]

In addition to leveraging cross-ownership, the networks also maintained conventional promotional strategies or enhanced efforts in established venues such as through television critics. The networks staged elaborate press tour events for critics in hopes that they would draw attention to new shows, as critics' columns provided a way to reach viewers who may not be watching the network. Critics became increasingly important as their reviews and "tonight on" recommendations provided promotional venues to alert viewers of programming on networks and cable channels they did not regularly view and as legitimate, unbiased sources within the cluttered programming field.

Irregular and infrequent viewing, which was an acute difficulty for cable channels from their launch, complicated their promotional efforts. Like broadcasters, the cable channels were their own primary venue for promotion of their content, but few cable channels could rely on regular and consistent viewing in the manner that broadcasters maintained. (There were exceptions such as MTV and ESPN, which cultivated regular viewing in their niche audiences.) Thus, cable channels would have to commit substantial budgets to off-channel promotion if they hoped to reach an audience broader than their few million regular viewers—a significant expense not incurred by most broadcast programs. Under the circumstances, common ownership proved particularly valuable for cross-promotion, and this provided one of the few places where conglomerates achieved their goals of synergy.

Although broadcast networks had the advantage of regularly attracting more viewers than cable channels, as audience segmentation expanded, they found it increasingly difficult to maintain their audience status in a promotional environment valuing niche appeal. For example, in some weeks of the 2005–2006 season, over half of the CBS schedule featured episodic crime dramas. Although these series greatly contributed to CBS's status as the most viewed network at the time, the consistent success with a specific genre gradually decreased the diversity of the audience likely to "stop by" CBS where they could be reached with promotions for other shows. In that same season, CBS launched an innovative series called *Love Monkey,* starring the established actor Tom Cavanaugh, yet poor ratings for the series in its first three airings led the network to pull the remaining episodes and cancel the show. *Love Monkey* was very different from most CBS programming at the time and was therefore likely to reach an audience distinctive from the one that viewed the CBS criminal dramas —viewers who liked crime drama were more likely to switch to NBC to watch *Law and Order: Special Victims Unit* during the hour when *Love Monkey* aired. Consequently, not only was much of the promotion for this show, which appeared in crime dramas, wasted, but also the lack of similar programs on CBS's schedule made it difficult to marshal an audience for a series different from those already airing on the network. Apart from illustrating the challenges of promotion in a more fragmented media environment, this incident also indicates the importance to networks of mass events such as *American Idol,* the Olympics, and many sports broadcasts, which collect a more heterogeneous audience. In addition to garnering high ratings through them, networks can recoup the value of costly league license fees and exploit the value of such events for promotion.

These possibilities notwithstanding, by 2004, the networks had begun experimenting with less conventional promotional strategies off the air. ABC is widely regarded as the instigator of this trend with its promotion of *Desperate Housewives* through dry cleaner bags printed with "Everyone has a little dirty laundry" in 2004 and its promotion of *Lost* through the distribution of messages in bottles with details about the show to beach locations. Of course the success of these creatively exceptional shows might have been entirely unrelated to these unconventional promotional campaigns, but many networks followed the strategy regardless. Significantly, these uncommon strategies also yielded substantial public relations buzz, enhancing the effectiveness of the campaign without additional cost. Experiments grew more varied in the subsequent season: NBC strapped portable television screens showing previews of *My Name is Earl* to young women in bars; The WB installed special mirrors with a paranormal effect in two hundred nightclubs in three cities to promote *Supernatural.*[46]

Although these gimmicks garnered public relations attention, some networks have developed promotions that better enable them to achieve their primary goal: getting viewers to just watch the show. Here, a key strategy involves expanding opportunities for audiences to sample content, which, in turn, involves experimenting with alternative distribution methods for it. In fact, the first experiment emerged over a year before the explosion in distribution platforms and possibilities that began in October 2005. In September 2004, The WB made available the pilot of *Jack & Bobby* for free to AOL's 3.5 million broadband subscribers. Audience members viewed the episode more than 700,000 times in the eight days before the series' launch.[47] Although *Jack & Bobby* did not survive the season, alternative distribution proved a valuable promotional technique in helping the new series break out of the cluttered environment at the beginning of the season. The WB tried again the next season, offering *Supernatural* in an un-gated Internet space free to anyone on Yahoo!; meanwhile a captive audience numbering over four million had the opportunity to view the pilot of UPN's *Everybody Hates Chris* aboard American Airlines flights. In other cases, networks included DVDs of pilots in copies of *Entertainment Weekly* or gave them away in other promotional venues, while the studios' practice of releasing the previous season on DVD just before the launch of the new season also made use of new distribution possibilities to aid series promotion. The networks' promotional efforts were estimated to cost them as much as $200 million for the 2005 season.[48]

Digital promotion began in earnest as the networks introduced new shows in 2006. Many pilots were "leaked" to popular sites such as YouTube or peer-to-peer sharing networks such as TVtorrents. In the case of ABC's *The Nine*, the series was downloaded 36,000 times in just a month.[49] Networks also use legitimate digital means to promote their new shows in an increasingly broad range of venues. The SciFi network loaded a special recap episode of *Battlestar Galactica* onto the online gaming service for Microsoft's Xbox, while NBC reran the pilot episodes of its new series on the various cable networks owned by NBC Universal and allowed free iTunes downloads.[50] CBS embraced cutting-edge technology with billboards advertising shows that allowed commuters with Bluetooth-enabled mobile devices to download a thirty-second clip of the show to their device.[51] In addition, the networks began to make available many episodes of new series on their websites—in some cases for months after original episodes debuted. For example, NBC offered all of the episodes of its critically hailed, but low rated *Friday Night Lights* during the otherwise rerun-heavy holiday season. This online availability, which offered viewers a second chance to catch up with the series outside of the fall programming blitz, came after the network had committed to producing a full season of episodes, effectively assuaging viewers' concerns

that they would become involved in a series otherwise liable to be cancelled at any time. The non-linear opportunity to view programming offered a valuable tool for exposing audiences to shows in a way that could
encourage them to join the linear audience. For all these new approaches,
though, the networks have also maintained traditional practices, typically
including 100–120 spots, or nearly an hour of promotion time, for each
series.[52]

These strategies may have been new to broadcasters, but most have
simply taken pages from the book HBO has been writing on successful
promotion for the last eight years. In addition to the challenge of airing
on a subscription network—and therefore being unavailable in the majority of homes—the unconventional and irregular seasons of HBO series
have required that the network engage in a major promotional blitz to re-
mind existing subscribers of new episodes and lure new ones to subscribe.
HBO used out-of-home and DVD previews years before broadcasters'
seemingly invented these strategies. The differentiation of the HBO product from that of other networks has also enhanced its marketing options.
Significantly, the style of HBO promotions tends to replicate the network's value proposition of offering something of exceptional quality and
clearly distinct from the rest of the televisual field. Despite the fact that
HBO reaches only a third of television households, buzz about HBO programming has frequently dominated the popular culture space, as was
vividly illustrated by a front-page article in *USA Today*'s Weekend issue
about the long anticipated sixth season of *The Sopranos*.[53]

Following HBO's effectiveness at achieving word of mouth about its
programming, network marketers have also sought to make use of
"viral" marketing strategies emerging on the web as competition among
broadcast networks has grown more intense. The networks have thus designed campaigns to reach "super fans," those peer-influencing viewers
who might talk up a series in offices and chat rooms. Where the common
viewing of the network era once led viewers to discuss the previous
night's viewing around the apocryphal water cooler, the conditions of the
waning years of the multi-channel transition and the opening years of the
post-network era have required networks to utilize pop-culture opinion
leaders to lead viewers back to their sets.

Promotion has also become more integrated into the basic processes of
series creation. Many shows have developed additional content that networks make available on their websites to better serve viewers' desire for
"more" of their favorite shows. Some series also utilize blogs written by

a member of the series' writing staff as a way to communicate and engage their fans. In some cases the blogs present "extra-textual" content—storylines and information related to, but independent of, the actual series narrative. In other cases, series' staff use the blogs in the same manner as many fan forums that predated the blogs, treating the space as a means for talking about the show and joining in fan discussion.[54] In some cases, networks have seen immediate results from their online promotions. Viewership of the CBS comedy *How I Met Your Mother* increased by one million viewers, an 11 percent increase, the week after showrunners posted a music video supposedly made by one of the characters on MySpace, while the *Late Show with David Letterman* increased its viewers by 5 percent in the month after a promotional deal between CBS and YouTube began.[55] Even the public auditions for unscripted series can provide promotional value. Although the series cast few "characters" in these venues, local press about them, as well as publicized casting calls, encourage existing fans to increase their stake in such shows.[56]

In stressing such innovations in promotion at the beginning of the post-network era, as well as the challenging conditions that gave rise to them, I do not mean to suggest that establishing successful shows in the network era was easy. Fred Silverman, the renowned programmer of that era, was once quoted as saying, "Fifty percent of success is the program and fifty percent is how the program is promoted."[57] But the new conditions of the multichannel transition and emerging post-network era have certainly required adjustments in how programs are made, scheduled, and promoted, and here it is important to note that promotion does more than draw audiences to programming; it also prepares them to have certain expectations of the show and thus contributes to how they understand it.[58] For example, in its promotion of its 2002–2005 series *American Dreams,* NBC often emphasized nostalgia and conventional characteristics of family drama, despite the series' regular engagement with deeper conflicts and darker aspects of its 1960s setting. Not only did this promotion repel audiences uninterested in the saccharine stories that are common to family dramas, but not characteristic of *American Dreams,* it also contributed to how viewers who did watch the series approached and defined the show.

Even though programmers' promotional efforts illustrate new levels of creativity, as of 2006, the networks had not yet used their digital tools to develop effective recommendations in the manner offered by a retailer such as Amazon.com or a service such as NetFlix, whose use of "because you bought/rented X, you might like Z" formulations have proven to be particularly effective in cultivating sales and loyal customers. Data from Net-Flix shows that viewers who selected rentals based on the recommendations that matched both their rental histories and their ratings of those earlier rentals had far higher satisfaction rates than viewers who selected rentals based on blockbuster promotion.[59] Although networks have not yet taken this next step for television promotion, variations on it have begun to emerge in online venues for video viewing. For example, YouTube provides opportunities to rate videos and organizes links so viewers can easily find similar videos. The peer recommendations available on various social networking sites, the recommendation intelligence gathered by TiVo, and the increasingly sophisticated web interfaces of the networks make it easy to imagine that networks will find ways to provide personalized promotions that will help attract the likeliest viewers to new series in those early chaotic weeks of the season or to non-linear trials, although they have yet to do so.

The current challenges to promoting series—apparent even on broadcast networks by the mid-2000s—are related to the programming bounty emerging with the post-network era and, paradoxically, to the limitations that come with this bounty. Much of the unconventional and uncompromising programming that circulated in the early years of the twenty-first century did so beyond the awareness of most viewers. In 2005, the ultra niche cable network Discovery Times (available to only 37.3 million homes) aired *Off to War,* a remarkably frank docudrama about National Guard soldiers deployed to Iraq and the hardships that resulted for their families, while a similar series, *American Soldier,* aired on the Country Music Television network. Despite their important contributions to the cultural discussion of the war—or to the lack thereof—neither network had the promotional budget or status to help many viewers find these series. For all of the new potential the fragmented television space provides for the circulation of ideas and stories far beyond the limited mainstream of the network era, many series air as though they are trees falling in unoccupied forests.

Unlike the case of the production components considered in the chapters before and after this one (technology and distribution), where preliminary post-network-era practices were coming to be established by the time I completed this book, the practices of making and promoting television series remains at the present time more characteristic of the multichannel transition. Adjustments in the distribution and financing of television programs will surely continue to alter the process of show creation in significant ways, and the collapse of the network season and schedule certainly suggested further steps toward the erosion of linear viewing norms. The freedom from the constraints of only telling stories that could be confined to thirty- or sixty-minute episodes, in twenty-two episodes per season, and in an ongoing narrative began to illustrate the expanded programming possibilities of this environment. The diversifying financial models explored in subsequent chapters disrupted norms for program creation even further.

The displacement of linear viewing also posed substantial consequences in program promotion. This environment shifted emphasis from promoting when a program will air and suggestions of "this week's" story, to promotion more akin to film trailers designed to rouse viewer interest in core aspects of the story.[60] Given the changes in technology and distribution, it has become increasingly possible to imagine a future in which broadcast networks exist as advertising-supported venues for free initial program sampling that viewers could then subscribe to and view at a self-determined pace. Such a situation would disrupt many norms of program creation even more than they have been thus far. Programming decisions would no longer be subject to the need to find shows to fit an established schedule, and new financial models would develop. Indeed, the very place of networks, both broadcast and cable, could become uncertain in such an environment, where studios could become less dependent on the distribution capabilities networks once controlled.

Conclusion

> It used to be that the hits paid for the failures. But now, as the margins get smaller and your upside is cut in half, the economics of doing business become much more challenging. We're extremely sober about being an independent in this climate but being independent may have also enabled us to weather this downturn better than some of the competition.
> —David Kissinger, President, Studios USA, 2001[61]

Here Kissinger reflects on how being an independent studio helped Studios USA survive the changing industrial environment for program creation in the late 1990s. Importantly, Studios USA's independence was short-lived; the studio became part of Vivendi-Universal less than two months after these comments and is now part of NBC Universal.

Moreover, in the years following Kissinger's comments, there has been little to indicate that independents have had any competitive advantage.[62]

The relationship between the dominant financing structure used to create programming and the content produced is neither direct nor absolute. It is not the case that deficit financing yields only one type of programming, while cost-plus categorically results in another. Rather, factors relating to who assumes risk and opportunities for different levels of compensation contribute to making certain types of programming more or less likely. Consequently, the increased variation in financing models that emerged late in the multi-channel transition will most likely yield greater variation in programming. As the next chapter suggests, the vertical integration that occurred during the multi-channel transition bore important effects beyond the network-studio relationship, especially since the relative value of various productions changed when a conglomeration controlled more aspects of the production and distribution process.

If industry prognosticators predicting the declining importance of networks in organizing viewing are correct, then this central defining feature of the network era and the multi-channel transition among studios and networks may become devoid of significance in the post-network era. Nearly fifty years of television have indicated the importance of network schedule construction to the success of an individual program, and as long as U.S. television maintains the network-era construction of a linear schedule, networks are likely to continue to control the schedule and have great power in the selection of programming. Even so, it is already possible to imagine a period in the not-too-distant future when linear schedules recede as a dominant structuring frame for television. At the same time, though, while the adoption of on-demand technologies and increasing viewer interest in self-selecting content diminishes the function of the network-as-distributor, these developments renew the importance of the entity that controls the production purse strings—namely, the studio.

By early 2007, too many practices throughout the production process were navigating residual and emergent norms to offer much indication about the conventions of series creation in the future. Many of the lower-cost program formats appear destined to remain part of television, contrary to the wishes of those who seek an end to "reality" television. The increasing adoption of on-demand and non-linear viewing also posed another kind of looming threat as networks have begun to reconsider the need to program twenty-four hours a day, seven days a week. As Oxygen executive Geraldine Laybourne noted to an audience of industry workers at the 2006 National Cable Show, the demands of the twenty-four-hour schedule have led networks to air at least some content that was not their best. But the conditions of the emerging post-network era may well eliminate the mandate to provide programs at all times and instead encourage the production of programming of distinction, rather than the inevitable inclusion of some marginal content to fill out the daily schedule. Importantly, it is not audience size that determines what constitutes marginal content, but the relative levels of audience attraction to various shows, and here it is the programming people watch because their favorite show is airing a repeat that is the type of marginal content most threatened. Niche programming, consequently, should not be perceived as being in danger. Still, any adjustments in how much television the studios produce annually or the development of substantial variations in budgets will introduce consequences throughout existing practices for making television.

By the mid-2000s, new programming entities began seeking carriage on cable systems as non-linear channels. One of the earliest examples, Fearnet, a "channel" featuring horror films from the Sony/MGM library, debuted on Comcast cable systems on Halloween 2006, although it was available online nearly a year earlier. Rather than scheduling programs throughout the day, the channel makes available horror-themed programming for viewers to watch on their own schedule. Thus, although this represents an innovation, the continued importance of a network brand also remains clear: even though the "channel" does not operate an outlet that streams predetermined content at certain times, it does function as a branded folder in which viewers can look for programs with particular characteristics. A truly post-network environment is precisely that, television without networks—or at least without networks in their current configuration. Program aggregators—as in those entities or locations in which viewers can find programming of a certain sensibility or about a certain topic—will remain crucial, but the future of networks as aggregators that schedule the delivery of programming at certain times appears dubious. Post-network practices in which the viewer's pursuit of content dominates the process of selecting what to view increases the value of studio or producer reputation and diminishes the centrality of networks (depending on the mechanism for distribution). It also affords a competitive advantage to the types of programming that viewers particularly want to watch, instead of what they've watched simply because it's been "on." These new conditions, which can enhance the status and reach of what have previously been "cult" hits, should encourage studios to shift support from broad slates that include some mediocre programs to smaller line-ups with programs that all offer some distinction. Whether this will mean an increase in programs that are creative and innovative or in those that tap into broad-based tastes, or perhaps both, is not clear. What is clear is that post-network television programs will not succeed simply because a network makes them available to the viewers at particular times.

4

Revolutionizing Distribution
Breaking Open the Network Bottleneck

The future is about whatever I want, wherever and whenever I
want it. . . . and the more ways you do that, the more revenue there
is for everybody in the business.
                              —Josh Bernoff, Forrester Research[1]

An age-old debate within the television industry concerns whether content or distribution is "king." Your position on this question depends
greatly on what sector of the business you work in, with favor going to
your own role as either a creator of content or a controller of the means
by which content reaches viewers—i.e., a distributor. This debate was
somewhat less complicated in the network era, when ways to distribute
television were scarce. Producers sold series either to networks or to local
stations—a situation that created a significant bottleneck that allowed
only a limited amount of programming to get through to viewers. After
programs had an "original run" on a network, producers typically resold
the episodes in international markets, to independent stations, and to
broadcast affiliates to recoup the costs of deficit financing. These opportunities to sell content after and even during the original network run are
called "distribution windows."[2] The limited number of distribution windows in the network era greatly contributed to the ephemeral nature of
television programming at the time, for without personal recording capabilities and few alternative ways to receive programming, viewers had
hardly any opportunities to re-screen content and never on their own
terms.

The limited ability to reach viewers was such a fundamental aspect of
the network era that few realized how considerably it defined the basic
functioning of the medium. As the post-network era develops, however,
the distribution bottleneck is being eliminated. Previously unimagined

possibilities for television have developed as new ways for video story-telling to reach audiences have emerged, including easy distribution of amateur and non-commercial content. New distribution methods ranging from the DVD to the myriad Internet video services that exploded throughout 2006 have changed the nature of television: no longer a linear trickle of programming dictated by network executives, it has come to be a wide ocean of content into which viewers can dip at will. New forms of distribution have also created new revenue streams for studios and adjusted the types of programming they develop. The growing variety of ways to reach viewers has decreased some of the risk of unconventional programs because new distribution routes provide opportunities to make money on shows that fail to achieve high ratings during network runs. Internet distribution also provides a venue for additional and supplemental programming, as well as circumventing the gatekeepers of cable systems and satellite providers.

The expansion of standard network-era distribution windowing—in which shows were sold first to broadcast networks, then local affiliates, international markets, cable, and so on—and new developments in bringing content to viewers have thus affected all the other components of production, from business models, which have altered the type and range of content that can be profitable, to creative processes, which have responded to new opportunities in the industry. Changing the nature of television as a cultural institution, these new distribution methods have contributed significantly to inaugurating a post-network era of U.S. television.

To be sure, ways to distribute television were already expanding appreciably throughout the multi-channel transition. Cable networks rapidly proliferated and hungered insatiably for programming. Broadcast stations increased from 1,011 to 1,442 between 1980 and 1990—some of which remained independent or established affiliation with non-full-service networks (FOX, The WB). Video tapes initiated an affordable way for viewers to purchase programs—called "sell-through" in the industry—and such media became particularly viable and significant a decade later with the creation of the DVD.[3] Cable systems then began offering programming on demand, and soon after, the possibility of distributing video on the Internet gave viewers even more ready and varied access to programming, as did new technologies such as portable and mobile devices. All of these developments opened new distribution windows and created new markets for producers to sell programs.

Importantly, "distribution" describes a broad range of activities—some of which are interrelated, others of which are fairly independent. Changes in distribution after the network era are best understood in terms of those relating to new "distribution windows" and to new forms of "distribution to the home." Distribution windows include the different locations producers sell programs after their original run on a network. In the network era, the only options were international markets and local stations. During the multi-channel transition these windows expanded to include cable networks, direct sale on VCR tapes, and then DVD and VOD; more recently they have also come to encompass Internet sites, where episodes can be downloaded or streamed. Distribution to the home, though related, involves another perspective that takes into account how television content reaches the home and the convergence or competition among communication and entertainment technologies once it arrives there. While television once came into the home only through signals broadcast over the air, an increasing range of possibilities developed during the multi-channel transition. Cable and satellite became common mechanisms of delivery, and companies traditionally limited to telephony such as at&t and Verizon prepared to join the competition by the mid-2000s. Even more significantly, broadband Internet distribution of video exploded in 2006, diminishing the domination of cable and satellite as the only pipeline for most channels into the home—although cable services continue to provide the broadband connection for many viewers. Indeed, not only can Internet distribution seem to eliminate any scarcity by allowing an exponential expansion in content capabilities—including that not produced by a commercial media system—but also wireless Internet can eliminate the place-based viewing that tethers audiences of cable channels.

Conventions of Distribution during the Network Era and the Multi-Channel Transition

Like the film industry, which releases films in theaters, then to pay-per-view, VHS/DVD, premium cable, and broadcast or basic cable, the television industry has also utilized similar standardized, time-delayed distribution windows with tiered pricing that makes content cheaper in later windows.[4] In this way, the network paying the license fee could enjoy a period of exclusivity in which viewers could find the program only on the network supporting the original run. Viewers typically could not watch syndicated episodes until a show had been on the air for about five years, and the buyer of that first syndication run enjoyed exclusivity in the syndication market.

To understand how the process works, consider the example of the comedy *Friends,* which the Warner Bros. studio produced for NBC beginning in 1994. Although syndicated episodes could not begin airing until September 1998 in order to have produced enough episodes, the series was sold for its first syndication run in 1995. This first-run of syndication went to individual stations in each market—the major metropolitan areas with television stations.[5] Often the stations in a market bid against each other for multi-year rights to a series, because being the exclusive provider of a popular show is important for stations' schedules. Consequently, syndicated episodes of *Friends* might air in the early evening on the FOX station in your area, while new episodes would continue to be found nationwide during prime time on NBC. After selling the series exclusively to local stations two or three times, Warner Bros. then sold syndication runs of the hit show to cable, with the result that there could be old *Friends* episodes on your local FOX station and on cable channel TBS and still new episodes weekly in prime time on NBC.

Such practices were highly standardized in the network era and much of the multi-channel transition. Series did not begin airing in syndication until one hundred episodes had been produced; stations paid cash for the episodes and had exclusive rights to the show in their market.[6] Subsequently, however, what windows a show was distributed through, in what order, and how much money a show made have come to vary greatly. Studios can sell shows and begin syndication runs before a series reaches one hundred episodes; stations can purchase the shows with various cash and barter agreements—meaning they trade advertising time to the distributor in exchange for a lower cash payment—and they rarely maintain exclusivity as most series become available on DVD and even through online distribution before beginning syndication.

Unquestionably, cable channels provided the first significant shift in distribution and marked the beginning of practices characteristic of the multi-channel transition. Budgets for original cable programs were diminutive relative to those in broadcast television, but the rapid proliferation of cable networks meant the creation of new buyers to which studios could sell syndicated programming, as well as cheaply produced original content. The average one hundred channels received in homes by 2003 created many opportunities for studios to sell both old and new programming.

Although the advent of cable seemed to revolutionize distribution, these developments appear quite subtle now that digital technologies have radically expanded viewers' opportunities to access video. First, direct sale of full seasons of shows on DVD began to change distribution practices in a way that eroded the exclusivity and ephemerality of programming, and then, in a few chaotic months in late 2005, industry workers threw out all the old rules. New technologies ranging from VOD and broadband delivery to devices such as the newly video-enabled iPod are eliminating the need for viewers to rely solely on networks to transport programs to them. Viewers can now pay directly for episodes, introducing a fairly unprecedented "transactional" model to television. In the process, decades-old practices that derived their value from exclusivity and delay among windows have been tossed aside overnight, with regret and uncertainty, but new technologies and viewers' embrace of them has made it impossible to cling to network-era practices any longer. To be sure, many feared the consequence of immediate transactional purchase on later windows, but with the very real possibility that programs could illegally circulate online within hours of airing, studios and networks have had no choice but to experiment—recalling the consequences of the recording industry's unwillingness to alter distribution practices a few years earlier. Banking on the notion that the best defense against piracy has been to make content legally available for purchase, networks have made shows available within hours of their original airing. Thus the television industry has jumped into new norms of distribution that allow viewers their desired access to content anytime and anywhere, but often at a price.

Close a Window, Open a Door: Shifting Norms of Video Distribution Windows

The proliferation of networks throughout the multi-channel transition created many new buyers for original and syndicated programming, but until the whirlwind of new viewing devices and platforms, networks and studios did not experiment extensively with varying distribution practices. As they have come to do so, many in the studios have feared that new distribution methods would destroy old models of revenue that the industry relies upon, but, in the course of developing and adopting distribution experiments, they have also found unanticipated benefits. The opening of myriad distribution windows has provided networks with new promotional tools to reach audience members, as well as creating revenue-producing opportunities for both studios and networks to amortize failures. For their part, studios have found new opportunities to profit from their libraries. Many of the new distribution windows were just emerging in 2006, but they have already become significant and suggestive of substantive long-term consequences for creative possibilities for the industry.

Changes in distribution shifted production economics enough to allow audiences that were too small or specific to be commercially viable for broadcast or cable to be able to support niche content through some of the new distribution methods—particularly those featuring transactional financial models. Just as cable had radically expanded the array of content that could be found on television, the new distribution windows promise to again rewrite the possibilities for what can be found on television. Fearing added competition, networks did at first try to quash some of the new distribution opportunities. The true push to change came from other industries and viewer behavior. Cable providers wanted to offer VOD because it differentiated their service from satellite competitors, and an eager consumer electronics industry hoped to expand product lines by adding to the technologies used by most viewers. Early adopters then used new technologies and technical savvy to redistribute content on various online peer-to-peer services without network clearance. With technology available and viewers clamoring to use it, the networks realized they could no longer slow the evolution and began openly experimenting with new models of distribution and financing.

Repurposing and Reallocation

The practice of original run repurposing that began in 1999 marked the first significant adjustment to distribution practices after the industry adapted to cable.[7] "Repurposing" refers to a practice in which content providers crafted deals that allowed a series to earn additional revenue during its original run either by airing multiple times on the broadcast network licensing the series (more than a typical rerun) or by airing concurrently on a cable network. Repurposing consequently shortened the previous window between original run and syndication to as little as a matter of days.[8]

In the case of one of the earliest examples, NBC and the USA cable channel arranged a financing deal giving USA rights to air *Law & Order:*

Special Victims Unit (SVU) within two weeks of its broadcast airing (Studios USA produced *SVU* for NBC).⁹ In the same season, Lifetime aired the new series *Once and Again* the same week it appeared on ABC. Industry journalist Deborah McAdams credited the vertical integration of the entities involved—Disney's Touchstone produced *Once and Again*, the series first aired on Disney's ABC, and was repurposed on Lifetime, half-owned by Disney—with the deal's rapid resolution.¹⁰ But the role of conglomerated ownership caused concern as networks announced repurposing arrangements that appeared to favor products from commonly owned studios. Not only did commonly owned broadcast and cable networks frequently develop these pacts, but repurposed series were often produced by studios also owned by the broadcast network or its conglomerate. To many in the industry, it seemed repurposing developed from the deregulatory policies of allowing conglomeration and eliminating the fin-syn rules. Nonetheless, the practice expanded in 2001–2002 as networks and production studios established repurposing deals for The WB series *Charmed* on TNT, NBC's *Law & Order: Criminal Intent* on USA, and FOX's *24* on FX.¹¹ Subsequently, repurposing has been a conventional, although not particularly widely used, practice. By fall of 2001, broadcast networks officially began "double runs" of series on their own network by airing the same episode twice in one week, a practice common on cable channels but a significant change in the established procedures of broadcasters.¹² FOX first offered this as part of its announced upfront schedule for 2001 as the "FOX Comedy Wheel" in which it aired encore episodes of comedies in a Friday timeslot.

The utility of these deals depends on one's perspective. For production companies, the increase in license payments decreased initial risk, thus making more expensive productions possible and helping to finance rising production costs—as in the case of *Once and Again* noted in the previous chapter. At the same time, however, conventional wisdom suggested that over-exposing a series in its original run would be likely to diminish profits from more traditional syndication opportunities, particularly before norms of exclusivity were eroded by other distribution changes. Broadcast networks that first aired the series argued that the second airing would bring viewers to their networks for the original run, although media analysts produced data indicating that the availability of a show in any form of syndication negatively affected the audience size of the original run airing.¹³ Nevertheless, repurposing continued as cable programmers hoped the cachet of top network series would increase audiences' awareness of the cable channel and its brand. This strategy seems to have been particular to the multi-channel transition; as non-linear programming norms emerge, cable channels' reliance on broadcast network content becomes less beneficial.[14]

The late multi-channel transition strategy of reallocating content between broadcast and cable networks also related to repurposing and the conglomerated ownership of broadcast and cable networks. "Reallocation" involves shifting shows that were developed for broadcast networks but that found insufficient audiences there to cable networks, where they might reach niche audiences and be considered more successful. In rare occasions, programming developed for cable has aired as a special event on broadcast networks or during otherwise rerun-heavy summer schedules, as in the case of special episodes of Bravo's *Queer Eye for the Straight Guy* aired by NBC and the reallocation of USA's *Psych* on NBC in summer 2006. The opportunity to shift programming to a commonly owned cable network allows the conglomerate to amortize development and production costs that it would otherwise have to absorb and provides an important distribution option. Reallocation consequently decreases the risk inherent to program development; it also encourages programmers to pursue shows that would otherwise be deemed too uncertain by offering an additional opportunity to recoup production expenditures.

Common ownership among production studios, broadcast networks, and cable channels facilitates the reallocation of programming, but is not a requirement for the practice. Cable channels owned by conglomerates also owning broadcast networks often operate in a manner similar to baseball's farm team system, as a space to test boundary-pushing or niche-focused content (*Significant Others*) or as a venue for demoting struggling programs to amortize their costs (*Boomtown*). In other cases, networks use reallocation to provide additional promotion for underperforming content (*Veronica Mars*) or to recover the cost of particularly expensive productions (*The Court*).

In the case *Significant Others,* this unconventional improvisational comedy was initially developed for NBC and produced by NBC Studios, but the series aired instead on Bravo in 2004 and 2005.[15] The creators may have originally targeted the broadcast network, but NBC shifted the show to the commonly owned cable network as its uncommon nature and tone emerged. The show aired at the same time many pronounced the death of the television comedy because of the years of consistent failure of conventionally formatted comedies on the broadcast networks.

Significant Others drew small audiences, yet was critically-lauded and "successful" enough to earn a second season of episodes.[16] ABC subsequently tried an improvisational comedy, *Sons & Daughters,* in 2006, indicating how successful cable experiments such as *Significant Others,* HBO's *Curb Your Enthusiasm,* and Comedy Central's *Reno 911* could affect broadcast programming.[17] Many media analysts have been critical of inter-conglomerate reallocations because such opportunities are rarely afforded to independent productions. Without such a distribution option, however, this show would probably never have aired at all, prohibiting it from either pushing generic boundaries on a niche network or influencing programming beyond.

By 2005, countless examples existed of series cancelled by broadcast networks whose unaired episodes were shipped over to cable channels and aired with little promotion. Common ownership can be a factor in this practice—as in the case of the critically lauded *Boomtown,* which was produced by NBC Studios and originally licensed by the NBC network, but was then reallocated to the commonly owned cable network Bravo. But common ownership is not always essential, as the example of *Pasadena* demonstrates. In 2001, FOX cancelled this show after just four episodes; four years later, SoapNet, a channel owned by Disney, resurrected the Columbia TriStar production for an airing of all thirteen existing episodes, presumably basing its decision to do so on the quality of the show, its fit with the network's brand, and the intervening success of similar shows (*The OC, Veronica Mars, Desperate Housewives*). After the success of *Pasadena,* SoapNet subsequently aired *Skin,* a 2003 FOX series produced by Warner Bros., which had suffered a similar early cancellation.

A broadcaster can reallocate original content to a cable channel for reasons unrelated to cancellation. Take, for example, the case of *Veronica Mars,* a show produced by Silver Pictures (part of Warner Bros.) and licensed by Viacom-owned UPN and later The CW. When the network began a weekly repurposing of the show on Viacom-owned MTV, it did so in an attempt to expose more of the target audience to the critically hailed but comparatively under-viewed series.[18] Here, the network primarily sought to nurture a potential hit—a strategy that could serve both UPN and the producer who desired longevity for the show. Viacom-owned CBS also aired episodes of *Veronica Mars* during summer months in an additional effort to reach more viewers. Other repurposing deals may arise from more direct economic considerations, as when ABC developed a repurposing deal with ABC Family cable channel to help cover the high production costs of the 2002 series *The Court.* The Warner Bros.–produced show was particularly expensive because ABC was eager to have John Wells—creator of *ER* and *The West Wing*—take over the project. Here, the advantage of the repurposing deal was that it required no deficit financing by Warner Bros.: ABC paid $1.65 million per episode for both the ABC and ABC Family airing. If this deal, which included a six-year license, was especially complex, its outcome was particularly ironic, given that *The Court* produced just six episodes—and aired only three—because of the lack of sizable audience interest in the series.[19]

The practices of original run repurposing and reallocating programming among networks reveal the importance of conglomeration to many emergent distribution practices, especially since it is mainly, if not exclusively, the commonly owned entities that tend to experiment. Both repurposing and reallocation developed in response to shifting industry economics introduced by audience fragmentation among cable channels during the multi-channel transition—a development that decreased broadcasters' dominance and profit margins. As audience size diminished, the networks required multiple revenue streams to maintain budgets and remain competitive. Adjustments in distribution practices such as repurposing and reallocation have provided substantial cost savings, produced new revenue, and enabled studios to take greater risks.

DVD: Own All the Episodes of Your Favorite Series

The next industrial development that adjusted conventional distribution windowing and revolutionized the possibilities for profiting from content resulted from the DVD sell-through market. In the early 2000s, the success of full seasons of shows packaged on DVD surprised many in the industry. By 2005, DVD sales of television shows reached $2.6 billion and accounted for nearly 20 percent of the overall DVD sales market.[20] For a popular television-on-DVD series such as *24*, the nearly three million DVDs of the series purchased by 2006 was equivalent to the DVD sales of a movie that earned $50 million from ticket sales; in terms of revenue, *24* generated $72.1 million from its first three seasons of DVD sales.[21] High sales have even characterized less popular series, such as *Buffy the Vampire Slayer,* which was never a top Nielsen performer during its network run; but by the end of 2004, the sale of six seasons of episodes on DVD earned $123.3 million.[22] DVDs conveniently aggregate multiple episodes—unlike VCR tapes that can include only two or three episodes—and are commonly sold in complete seasons that require limited shelf space, making them attractive to fans who want to create libraries, to new viewers who seek to catch-up on previous episodes, and to anyone who wishes to avoid television conventions such as commercials and one-week gaps between episodes.[23]

From an industry standpoint, DVD sales have provided a new revenue window for successful shows as well as new economic support for boundary-defying ones that did not succeed in their original airing. Thus, DVD distribution also enables studios to recoup production costs on shows that may or may not also be reallocated to cable channels or broadcast stations. This was the case with the creative and innovative 2003 FOX series *Wonderfalls*, which failed to find an audience quickly; the network cancelled the show after four airings, leaving nine episodes unaired. The series' studio, 20th Century Fox, later released a DVD set of the thirteen episodes in February 2005 and sold 25,000 copies in two weeks, rewarding fans with some narrative closure and the studio with added revenue.[24] Similarly, fan favorite *Firefly* had sold 500,000 copies of the complete series of fourteen episodes less than two years after its release. FOX cancelled the series after just eleven episodes in 2002.[25]

The bigger DVD story for FOX/20th Century Fox was the case of *Family Guy*, a series the network aired from April 1999 through April 2002. FOX decided to take the series back into production and began airing new episodes in 2005 after the unexpected performance of the DVD, which ranked as the number-two single-season television DVD release as of May 2005, and the sizable audiences drawn by the show's syndication on Cartoon Network.[26] After receiving the request for new episodes, *Family Guy* creator Seth MacFarlane noted, "The DVD market barely existed when we were cancelled. But now, fans can protest the cancellation of a show with their wallets, buying DVDs, rather than just writing letters to the network. . . . It's completely changed the economic model."[27] And, as Jeff Zucker, chief executive officer of the NBC Universal Television Group, acknowledged in 2004, "The numbers are already affecting how some shows are developed."[28] DVD revenues have, in fact, become an enormous boost to the industry. DVD earnings for the early seasons of HBO's *The Sopranos* were significant enough that the studio recouped the entire cost of producing those seasons through DVD sales alone.[29]

Studios have also sought to make the DVD purchase an additionally attractive proposition for audience members by making special features that are available only on the disks. The series *24* filmed a brief sequence that occurred between seasons three and four for the season three DVD set, and the DVDs were the only place fans could see this bit of narrative. Lisa Silfen, senior vice president of program enterprises at MTV Networks, has noted the value of special features and extra content: "It's a great opportunity to give the viewer that added value—what got left on the cutting-room floor, what we didn't have time to put on the air, extra photos, contests, games—all different things to create that package for them."[30]

Top sales of DVDs often do not mirror the top performers in original airing. The CBS series *CSI* spent much of the early 2000s as the most watched scripted show and drew large audiences and fees in syndication, but produced lackluster DVD sales; this was also the case for shows in the *Law & Order* series.[31] The profits available in DVD sell-through can consequently support the production of more varied types of programs and provide a revenue opportunity for unsuccessful programming—thus reducing risk and increasing the likelihood of more innovative products being created. *Wonderfalls* and *Family Guy* were a bit exceptional in both their content and distribution histories, but the sale of television series on DVD had important implications. In addition to providing a way to amortize the production costs of failures, as in the case of *Wonderfalls*, DVD release provided economic support for program forms such as serials (*Alias*) and cult hits (*Buffy the Vampire Slayer*) that were often marginalized by standard syndication practices in which episodic programs earned premium rates because they drew more substantial audiences and offered scheduling flexibility to stations. Experiments with DVD release also allowed the networks and studios an initial, comparatively controlled experiment in selling programming directly to the viewer before the possibility of the sale of individual episodes revolutionized distribution practices.

Content On Demand: VOD, Downloading, and Broadband Channels

In the mid-2000s, myriad opportunities to distribute content electronically on demand seemingly developed overnight, revolutionizing distribution practices and pushing them into the post-network era. How networks and studios deliver content to viewers—over the air or through a wire connected to a television or a computer—has quickly become unimportant relative to viewers' ability to access what, when, and where they want, even at a cost. A key characteristic of advances in distribution such as VOD, downloading, and broadband channels resulted from their intangibility—the viewer never accesses a disk or hard copy of the content. These distribution windows consequently reduce production and distribution costs, which are, of course, critical concerns in the industry's economic models.

Another benefit arising from on-demand distribution is that it allows studios to profit from content that may be pretty obscure or fairly far down what *Wired* magazine editor Chris Anderson has identified as the "long tail" of digital distribution for cultural products.[32] Some of these on-demand distribution windows are seemingly limitless in terms of how much different content can be pushed through them, especially in comparison with the severe limitations created by the network schedule. Studies of creative industries whose distribution practices already had experienced disruptions resulting from online and digital retail, such as books and music, revealed that their ability to provide a multiplicity of relatively obscure content contributed as much to their profits as the plurality of purchases characteristic of blockbuster successes. In 2004, Anderson reported that whereas an average Barnes & Noble store could hold only 130,000 titles, more than half of Amazon.com's monthly book sales came from outside its top 130,000 titles.[33] Likewise, in 2006, between 70 and 80 percent of NetFlix rentals drew from the service's back catalog of 38,000 DVDs rather than from recent releases.[34] Anderson notes that the "back catalog" distribution capability of e-retailers who maintain goods in a warehouse or those who sell digital downloads gives these venues infinite shelf space and near zero marginal cost and thereby radically shifts much of the operational logic of commercial creative industries. Moreover, even though consumers have enjoyed a three-hundred channel universe for years, their interest in and support for niche goods suggests even more desire for narrowly targeted content.[35]

The video-on-demand (VOD) capabilities introduced by cable providers arguably marked the first step into the content-on-demand world. Cable systems identified VOD as a strategic enhancement that offered added value to their subscribers and provided the cable systems themselves with a competitive advantage over their satellite challengers. Cable VOD services experienced a significant increase in 2005 in both use and frequency of use, as 88 percent of homes with the service used it in 2005, an increase from 65 percent in 2004, while 53 percent of those viewers used VOD at least once a week, compared with 24 percent in

2004.[36] But even by 2006 the content available for free VOD remained limited. Cable systems have primarily offered short-form versions of content available on existing networks, such as extra footage and cast interviews, although in some cases, cable systems (particularly Comcast) have also aggressively pursued original, low-budget content including fitness, education, and niche interest fare—such as the Fearnet horror "channel" noted in the last chapter. By and large, though, viewers wishing to use on-demand capabilities to catch up on current series have been forced to pay per-episode fees in the limited cases such content has become available, although cable providers have gradually come to secure deals with networks to supply limited full programs supported by advertising, but with far fewer commercials than typical of linear airing.

Subscription services such as HBO and Showtime identified one of the more consumer-friendly video propositions with their on-demand channels that required no separate fee. The on-demand capability reduced the frequency with which viewers had the experience of finding there was nothing on when they tuned in to the service, which had been a perennial complaint and cause of "churn"—the industry's term for the canceling of subscriptions. On-demand channels allow access to a constantly rotating slate of films and original series that enable viewers to time-shift their viewing of these networks. Such a model, which provides an ideal way for viewing all programming, in principle eliminates the need for DVRs. Of course, advertiser-supported networks remain wary of risking the commercial skipping likely to result from making their programs available on demand, and all were aware that such a system would introduce even greater complications to the already challenging task of Nielsen measurement of time-shifting homes. Nonetheless, as VOD adoption and use grew, networks approached licensing deals with attention to enabling some on-demand distribution—particularly as a promotional tool that might lead more viewers to regularly airing programming. Negotiations involving commonly owned content again proved most flexible in many cases.

Once Internet distribution became viable, the opportunities to make programs available on demand expanded exponentially. A wide variation of experiments with Internet distribution emerged throughout 2005. Viacom properties MTV and Comedy Central expanded video streaming availability with their respective Overdrive and Motherload sites; these enable on-demand access to short-form video such as outtakes and other content very similar to that provided to cable VOD systems and as extras on DVDs. Such "broadband television channels" have effectively created another access point for the networks' viewers, and have done so in an entirely on-demand, often advertiser-supported environment that enhances the television experience, even as they provide content that differs significantly from traditional thirty- or sixty-minute fare. Other established television brands have also pushed unutilized video onto the Internet—as in the case of broadcast networks that substantially expand their news offerings by providing online distribution of content such as regular correspondent reports not included in the limited twenty-two minute television broadcast. In addition, other networks have experimented with subscription financing, such as CNN's short-lived fee-based Pipeline service, which required a three-dollar monthly fee for unlimited access to video stories.

The launch of the cable network Current TV in 2005 points toward another version of the video-on-demand future. This network predominantly features viewer-created content and uses both Internet and cable distribution, first airing videos submitted by viewers on the website and then allowing the audience to vote on what should air on the cable network. The fact that the Current cable channel reached only twenty million television homes six months after its launch increased the importance of the web distribution. Using this means, the network can introduce content completely unlike that which has previously been available, and even content that does not achieve enough support to air on the cable network can find an audience online. To the surprise of many, Current's prescient embrace of online video set it up as model emulated by many others.

Outlets that possessed an existing television branding like MTV and CNN were the first to dominate the Internet distribution of video. The barrier to others was not inherent to the distribution mechanism, but a matter of promotion and acculturation; these were the sources viewers expected to look to first. At the same time traditional television brands moved into broadband distribution, traditional computer brands such as Google, Yahoo!, and AOL began to compete and collaborate. Many in the broadcast sector fear that in the post-network era, Google, Yahoo!, and AOL could come to play the role CBS, NBC, and ABC had in the network era. Such a revision of broadcasting is not impossible: at the end of 2005, Yahoo! reported 411 million unique users, 191 million of whom were registered and known to the company, and therefore capable of receiving targeted advertising.[37] These few Internet portals have, in fact, achieved a vaster audience reach than those of most broadcast networks or cable channels; they are also often able to precisely report information about their users to advertisers, who, in turn, can target advertisements more effectively. Both attributes provide an immense advantage for competing in a world of integrated digital technologies and offer advertisers the tools they desire.

But new competitors emerged before any of these established Internet entities could implement a successful broadband video strategy. Within four months of its late 2005 launch, newcomer YouTube streamed about thirty-five million videos a day and drew an audience of more than nine million people per month and has continued to grow.[38] Unlike the mainly professionally produced and commercial content considered here, much of YouTube's initial popularity resulted from its amateur content and non-intrusive commercials, but the success of YouTube quickly drew interest as its most popular videos reached audiences larger than broadcast hits. As entertainment columnist Scott Kirsner has noted, "It's a stunning shift when a single low-budget viral video can reach roughly the same number of people as an episode of *Seinfeld* used to."[39]

Yet another expansion in on-demand content available online arrived in early 2006 with the launch of AOL's In2TV. As part of AOL's strategy for shifting from a walled-garden environment accessible only to paying members, to an open, advertiser-supported one, the In2TV platform provides six channels featuring hundreds of television series from the Time Warner library. Making 14,000 episodes of 300 series including *Wonder Woman* and *Welcome Back Kotter* available at launch, this distribution outlet marks a particularly significant shift from short-form to full-length content.[40] AOL uses a conventional advertising model to support the service, which has no cost for viewers. As far as advertising is concerned, the service features a less cluttered environment, with one advertisement before and after the program and one at each established commercial break. Viewers are able to fast-forward through the shows, but not the commercials. Another advantage is that advertising distributed via broadband can be sold based on census audience measurement, counting only those who actually click and view advertisements and with fairly specific demographic information that allows for more precisely targeted advertisements. Another broadband distributor, iWatchNow, provided older films and television for ninety-nine cents each. Even as early as January 2006, iWatchNow reported an average of 6,337 viewers per hour.[41]

Although applications such as In2TV and iWatchNow provide content that tends to be fairly far down the "long tail" like *Eight is Enough* or *The Rifleman*, in many cases they do allow viewers to watch television shows that have not been available since their original airing. Providing audiences with access to a previously inaccessible back catalog, these distributors also give studios a way to profit from unutilized libraries. And, of course, their on-demand capability offers viewers more control than they have when they view shows sold to a linear platform, such as Viacom's TV Land cable channel. Emerging just as DVD sales of television shows began to slow, these online services begin to suggest the potential of a distribution route with lower costs and unlimited "shelf" space.

While the back-catalog availability of full-length shows involves an enhancement of distribution capabilities, the more widely hailed development has been viewers' increasing ability to download or stream A-level content from very high up on the long tail from the Apple iTunes store, Yahoo!, and eventually directly from the television networks to computers and mobile video devices. A flurry of announcements followed the revolutionary deal between iPod and ABC in October 2005 that allows download of certain current shows immediately after they air. This deal established a transaction model in which viewers could directly purchase content and an initial industry standard price of $1.99.[42] Broadband video distribution began in earnest in 2005 as compression capabilities and broadband access reached a critical mass. The release of content for a fee immediately after its airing introduces a new revenue stream for studios and networks, while using the Internet to deliver video to consumers circumvents intermediaries such as retailers—although the networks initially allowed Apple middleman status. Networks quickly began to experiment with distributing content on their own websites to eliminate revenue sharing with intermediaries.

The Internet has thus provided revolutionary access to viewers in a way that potentially threatens the future of many previous distribution entities such as affiliate stations and even networks and cable channels. Ryan Magnussen, chief executive of Ripe TV, a company that produces video content for the web noted, "The value of NBC in the past was their [sic] distribution platform, which was incredibly powerful. But now that's starting to break down."[43] Similarly, in 2006, former WB CEO Jordan Levin noted, "Production and distribution are the barriers to entry that have kept studios and networks in power, but those barriers are continuing to come down."[44] Although much of the industry has focused on how established television entities make use of new distribution methods, the changes in distribution possibilities also enable new companies to become part of the "television" industry in their own right.

Internet content aggregators such as Yahoo! and YouTube have redefined the role of the network by amassing and organizing available content with varied models of economic support including advertising and transaction fees, as well as free access. And the web has also assembled commercial content different from that traditionally found on television. Adam Berry, vice president of marketing and strategy at Brightcove, an online video distribution company, noted that web distribution "is not just another way to watch *South Park*. It's a way to watch a whole bunch of stuff you were never able to watch before."[45]

Broadcasters have approached the opportunity of broadband content distribution in varied ways. Some broadcasters have offered free streams of new shows as a preliminary promotional technique, while others have used broadband distribution to promote shows struggling to find an audience or those in a particularly competitive time slot, like The WB's premiere of *Jack & Bobby* on AOL in 2004, CBS's *Threshold* in 2005, and many more cases by 2006. At the other end of the success spectrum, the earliest deals enabling viewers to purchase downloads of current broadcast shows have primarily featured established hits produced by studios commonly owned with the network, including *Lost, Desperate Housewives,* and *Survivor.* In the case of particularly serialized shows such as *Lost,* this mode of distribution allows new audience members to catch up on back-story or regular viewers who may have missed an episode to stay current with the narrative. In other cases, the first shows available for download have simply been those co-owned within the conglomerate, with companies within it being willing and able to craft a quick deal to enter this preliminary marketplace. ABC has established itself as a leader in experimenting with broadband availability, and after the success of the initial iTunes sales, it made some shows including commercial messages available on its website for free streaming. In the first two weeks, viewers streamed the four available shows more than two million times.[46] The streaming trial outperformed the iTunes experiment within just a month: the commercial-supported shows were streamed eleven million times versus the six million downloads sold over eight months.[47]

Some content has become not only more accessible, but even only exclusively available on the Internet. In the summer of 2005, AOL's webcast of the Live 8 concert drew raves because it offered comparatively unedited access, while MTV's limited cable coverage garnered criticism and paltry ratings. The online version of Live 8 drew audiences in 160 countries, and there were ninety million video streams of the concert in the forty-five days after the event.[48] As this case suggests, while the Internet's lack of national boundaries makes previous practices of exclusivity difficult to maintain, it also presents new opportunities for global distribution. Indeed, by early 2006, the U.S. Public Broadcast System (PBS) found that more than 25 percent of its online audience came from outside of North America.[49]

Experimenting with distribution has yielded unanticipated outcomes and often defied the conventional wisdom that governed industrial practices. In the winter of 2006, when NBC decided to move its marginally successful show *The Office* to a new time slot, the network put past episodes for sale on iTunes as part of a strategy to promote the schedule change. Although scheduling shifts often erode established audiences, this show not only quickly became the most downloaded program, but also expanded its on-air audience.[50] Network executives' main fear of download availability was that it would cannibalize the broadcast audience and thereby lead to diminished advertising rates, but consecutive trials have illustrated no audience loss. In an experiment involving streaming forty-eight games of the NCAA basketball tournament live in March 2006, CBS found that even as the online games drew four million visitors, there was no erosion in their conventional broadcast viewing.[51] Such data underscores the manner in which the technologies and distribution methods that make television more convenient also allow networks to expand their audiences.

Video on demand, downloading, and broadband channels offer similar capabilities, albeit from different service providers. The key differences involve the nature of the available content, how it is paid for, and the type of screen likely to be used for viewing. As the industry has come to experiment with the rapidly changing distribution environment, there has been great variation both in the kinds of shows available in different on-demand venues and in the financial models used. All of these new distribution opportunities violate the established spacing between distribution windows that has enabled value-enhancing exclusivity. If the variety in the initial experiments makes it difficult to discern how these new distribution methods might change the economics and distribution models for the average show, it is nonetheless apparent that the industry has become willing to experiment with revolutionary possibilities.

Consequences of New Distribution
Windows and Practices for Television

> I view YouTube as a glimpse into the future of video distribution, completely untethered from media companies and linear distribution models based on schedules. I don't think it's a flash in the pan as a concept, but rather it opens the door to a landscape that allows consumers to be content providers, creating a new form of community particularly of common interest.
>
> —John Lansing, President, Scripps Networks[52]

Changes to the network-era distribution window structure radically disrupted established norms of how studios and networks profited from their content and required similarly radical shifts in the economics of the industry. The speed with which the industry accepted new distribution practices, particularly in the aftermath of the announcement of the first Apple-Disney deal, led many to venture into single-show, immediate, transactional distribution simply because they could not risk being left behind. Few had any certainty about the economic consequences of making individual episodes available for viewers to purchase, and many deals were structured as short-term, limited-availability trial experiments. While conventional wisdom forecast certain likely outcomes, such as a decrease in the value of later distribution windows from the use of these new early ones or a cannibalizing of the linear audience, such concerns have not been borne out. For example, one unanticipated result of DVR deployments was that the homes that used them actually watched more television, not only because of time saved through commercial skipping, but also because viewers could more easily and effectively access content of interest. The innovation posed by these new distribution windows was unprecedented enough that they too were likely to produce unexpected results—as early evidence suggested. Just as some industry discussion posed mobile, theatrical, and convenient television use as opponents in a zero-sum competition for viewers, another outcome was expanded use of television across all of these technologies—so long as desirable content existed—limiting the threat of cannibalization and supporting a high value for content in multiple windows.

The availability of on-demand distribution has been affecting the rules of financing and distribution that dominated the industry for more than fifty years. In testing new distribution methods, the networks have been uncertain about the consequences for subsequent traditional windows such as syndication, but then syndication as it was known in the network era and the multi-channel transition could well become irrelevant in a post-network era in which viewers can access programs on demand without the limitation of a network or its scheduling imperatives. In an environment in which networks and channels do not need to "fill" a twenty-four-hour schedule, they are likely to have less need for programming readily associated with another entity such as the network that first licensed it (USA as the place to go to watch *Monk* instead of *Law and Order: SVU*). Cable channels would derive greater competitive advantage by focusing funds on distinctive, original programming than through paying high license fees for shows already associated with a broadcast network. Likewise, local stations might be more willing to use their budgets for producing original local fare instead of purchasing off-net sitcoms, and studios might distribute their content directly to viewers—as evident in channels built around U.S. studio content available outside of the country. For example, the Warner Channel in Latin America features *Friends, Everwood, Third Watch, Angel,* and *The West Wing*—all series that were produced by Warner Bros. Studio, but that aired on various networks in the United States. Such a radical adjustment to distribution norms would have significant implications for economic models. The relationship between studios and networks and the practices of license fees and deficit financing rely on maintaining existing syndication revenue. As these new practices emerged, it was not clear whether profits from new distribution methods could counterbalance the likely decreases in revenue from other windows.

Although the initial deployments of on-demand distribution used a transactional, pay-per-show financial model, many others can be employed, and each will create its own ramifications. Thus, for example, using advertising or an all-you-can-watch subscription is more likely to encourage sampling than a transactional model. The transactional model emerged first because it was the easiest to implement amidst a complicated array of rights and royalty agreements. Indeed, at first all of the shows available on iTunes or for online streaming were produced by studios that shared common ownership with the network to which they were licensed. The industry was unlikely initially to try an advertising model because the networks needed to first illustrate value for advertisers, and a subscription model would have required far more complicated rights negotiations. But ABC's success with advertiser-supported online streaming suggests that conventional commercial models could also be used to finance new distribution practices.

Curiously, it was the networks—as licensers of programming—that executed the early distribution experiments that made A-level content available in 2005 and 2006, rather than the studios that owned the programs and traditionally had profited from subsequent distribution windows—although both network and studio were often commonly owned. So it was NBC that set up the deal with iTunes to distribute *The Office* and *Scrubs,* rather than NBC Universal Television Studio or Touchstone —the shows' respective studios. Certainly the networks could not make these deals without agreement from the studios, but tying this secondary distribution to the original-run license was an unprecedented and significant change. By the beginning of the 2006 season, a new model emerged in an agreement between Warner Bros. studio and NBC. This deal gave the network the rights to revenues from advertising sold in streaming series near the air-date, but reserved revenues from downloading shows from sites such as iTunes for the studio. Networks used the immediacy of availability in their defense and argued that the substantial promotional effort that they conducted on the network was crucial to the transactional success and that viewer payments should consequently reward the network and not the studio. Little information about the profit-sharing involved in the transactional deals has been made public, so it remains difficult to assess how distributors, networks, and studios have fared. What is certain is that had the fin-syn rules still been in place, these initial deals and the relative power they give to producers and distributors would have developed much differently.

Although use of many of the new distribution windows has been experimental, these preliminary forays have forced adjustments throughout the production process. For instance, one effect of the immediate availability of programming online has been to exacerbate the already strained relations between networks and their affiliates. These relations had been increasingly complicated since networks began repurposing content on cable in the late 1990s and decreased the compensation paid to affiliates. Although the networks still earned money from the iTunes purchases, in most cases, non-owned-and-operated affiliates initially received no compensation, and many feared their audiences would diminish. NBC and FOX were able to craft deals to share revenues in a manner that sated some of the affiliates concerns—and FOX even made programs available on affiliates' web sites to allow local advertising—but many of these network-affiliate conflicts foreshadowed coming discord. The new distribution methods are not only eroding the network-affiliate structure that characterized the network era and multi-channel transition, but also leading some to suggest that there may be little need for local affiliates in a post-network era since a near national audience can be reached by cable or satellite, and perhaps someday, the Internet. This is not to say that local stations are irrelevant now—but their role as distributors of content produced by a national network is becoming increasingly redundant.

Complicated profit-sharing arrangements and intellectual-rights issues create the biggest impediment to making more programming available in new distribution windows—particularly in the case of programming created and contracted before the early 2000s, when the expansion in distribution outlets became evident.[53] Common ownership of the producer and studio can help to overcome these rights concerns and enabled many of the initial deals, but the arrangements remain complex.[54] A CBS executive reported that the deal between UPN and Google to air the pilot of the new 2005 series *Everybody Hates Chris* required more than two months of work, while at NBC fifty people needed six weeks to clear the rights for a handful of NBC Universal shows on iTunes—and both deals involved commonly owned studios and networks.[55] The protracted negotiations, cost, and labor required when these agreements were not inter-conglomerate negotiations initially slowed the participation of non-commonly-owned shows in new distribution windows, preventing them from taking advantage of the opportunities on-demand distribution offered in expanding audiences or the extra revenue that might lead to more generous network evaluation of series' performance.

Shifts in distribution have also contributed to substantial adjustments in the programming the industry is likely to produce. Commercial broadcasters now have more of a reason to create programming that closely matches the specific tastes of discreet audience groups because audience members are more likely to pay for programs they are fans of, rather than programs they watch just to pass time. Moving beyond the limitations of network-era schedules and seasons, programming has come to be more varied in length and to have other unconventional features. Indeed, the elimination of the distribution bottleneck has made it easier for even more narrowly targeted programming to be profitable, as well as making it possible for independent and amateur producers to access an international audience.

The case of *Nobody's Watching* in 2006 indicates yet another effect of new distribution windows on programming. *Nobody's Watching* was created by *Scrubs* producer Bill Lawrence for The WB in 2005, but after funding a pilot, the network chose not to schedule the series. The pilot was loaded onto YouTube by an unknown source in June 2006, and within a week nearly 100,000 viewers had streamed the show.[56] In less than a month, that audience grew to 300,000, and buzz about the show led NBC to schedule a meeting with the creators and order six scripts of the project; during subsequent months, various short videos with the cast continued to appear on YouTube.[57] A number of other failed pilots also appeared in Internet forums, but in other cases, networks demanded they be removed. The WB was scheduled to cease operations within three months of the YouTube leak and consequently had no reason to demand its removal. Apart from this particular circumstance, though, the case of *Nobody's Watching* suggests more generally how new forms of distribution might allow audiences more input in what the industry produces and provide the industry with new tools to decrease the uncertainty of its program development.

As distribution windows such as iTunes, Motherload, Overdrive, and In2TV are changing television because of the new access to programming they provide, these early competitors in the market are also playing an important role in changing viewers' experience with and expectations of content. Negotiating the chicken/egg conundrum of what comes first—content or viewer adoption—slows or thwarts the dissemination of many industrial innovations. For example, little HD programming was available for quite a long time because so few homes owned HD sets, but viewers had little motivation to buy HD sets as long as there was so little content available. Early forays into broadband video such as those noted here provided an experience that helped viewers realize that such video need not be limited to small, grainy, slowly loading images, but that it could compete with, and even exceed, their existing living-room television experience. Although the early experiments evident by 2007 may not characterize dominant distribution patterns to come, they played an important role in leading viewers to watch in new places and in new ways.

All of these new distribution windows upset the long-existing norms that derived value from time delay and exclusivity. If the number of windows and the patterns content took through them became increasingly varied during the multi-channel transition, such variety has become even greater at the beginning of the post-network era. What windows a show would pass through and how much money it might earn depends upon the nature of the content (serial or episodic), the type of audience attracted (niche or mass), and the status of the producer relative to the multinational conglomerates dominating the television industry—with great diversity possible.[58]

Changes in Distribution to the Home

The changes in distribution to the home that occurred late in the multi-channel transition also adjusted the industry's norms of operations at the structural level. The arrival of cable inaugurated the multi-channel transition and the establishment of a competitor to cable—namely, satellite—marked the maturing of this competitive environment. A decade after the Telecommunications Act of 1996 enabled telephone companies to compete in providing video, as well as allowing cable to offer telephony, traditional telephone companies finally began to experiment with video service offerings. This additional competitor—and the integrated phone, video, and data services all seek to provide—marks a new stage in distribution to the home, although in early 2007, it remains unclear how quickly telcos such as Verizon and at&t will make their product available or how significantly the added competition might affect the industry.

"Internet protocol television," or IPTV, is the term associated with the technologies Verizon and at&t (formerly SBC, which was formerly AT&T) use to provide video service, although "cable" has also begun using Internet protocol technologies. Without descending into too much techno-jargon, I'll note here that — "IP" denotes a specific way of sending messages that involves breaking them down into packages that can then be conveyed separately—as is the case on the Internet. Where television is concerned, IP distribution is significant because it enables providers to transmit only the signal for the television channel that you want at that particular minute, in contrast to the method of sending all the channels to your home all the time that cable providers have used. So if you receive your multi-channel service from Verizon, and at 5 p.m. on May 3rd, you wanted to watch CNN, then CNN would be the only signal coming through the wire into that television. If you had conventional cable service, all the channels in your package would be coming through the wire, even though you could only watch one at a time. Although the difference may be imperceptible to the user, IP technology is more efficient and makes possible distribution beyond the bandwidth limitations that restricted cable systems to roughly three hundred channels. As the new telco competitors develop systems that use IP technologies, many cable systems are also updating their infrastructures with similar systems, but at the nascent stage of this technological development in 2007, it remains unclear whether IP will particularly advantage the telcos or if it might become the industry-standard method of signal delivery. Because the term IPTV has given rise to some confusion, it is important to note that IP technologies differ from "broadband channels," such as Motherload and In2TV, which are sites that give access to video on the Internet. IPTV distinguishes the technical means for the distribution of a signal, which differs from "television" being distributed on the "Internet."

The preliminary availability of IPTV has led to much concern about the future of video distribution, particularly among the cable providers which still dominate in bringing services into the home. In addition to fearing new competitors, cable systems worry about "disintermediation," or separating the content and the delivery system in a manner that could allow programmers to bypass cable operators and even broadcast networks and go straight to the consumer through the open access of the web. Viewers have always turned to cable to watch certain channels, but if those channels became available on the web, cable's status could be threatened. Take the case of the Trio cable channel, which was owned by NBC but became redundant after NBC merged with Universal and obtained the similar, more popular channel Bravo; in 2006, NBC Universal made Trio a broadband-only channel, following what appears to be a trend for the most niche networks that struggle for commercial viability as linear channels. But the problems facing the cable industry as a whole are more like those of affiliate stations in a post-network era in which broadcast networks might just as easily distribute their content through cable supported VOD. Cable systems may be similarly vulnerable where other avenues for distribution to the home, such as broadband and telcos, become competitive means for allowing viewers access to the content they desire. And there are other competitors, such as services that deliver video to mobile phones, that also circumvent conventional ways to reach viewers.

The arrival of IPTV competitors has introduced many new questions for telecommunication policy. As broadband Internet access emerged as a critical part of most homes' information and entertainment expenditures, a debate began as broadband service providers—cable services and the telcos—sought to ensure their relevance and increase their profits. In order to prevent disintermediation, the services want to make more money by "intermediating" and making deals that would give certain content providers preference on their distribution systems. Comcast broadband subscribers, for example, might not be able to access web portals and content in Time Warner's Road Runner application, or might have access only at slower rates. Although this issue goes far beyond the television industry, it does particularly affect the industry because online video distribution requires broadband lines, and many expect video access to be a central part of future Internet use. The debate surrounding the issue has been framed in terms of "network neutrality" and the question of whether cable systems and telcos can seek competitive advantage by pairing with content providers. For instance, some worry that without regulation ensuring network neutrality, agreements reached between broadband service providers and content creators would determine download speeds and site access. Without deals for content exclusivity, the providers could really compete only on price—this, when the services enviously see the massive growth in advertising revenue being earned by Internet content providers such as Google. The service providers, after all, built the costly infrastructure from which content providers such as Google and Yahoo! profit. Broadband services can only squeeze so much money from subscribers and view advertising revenue as the source of the real riches. While complete blocking of Internet sites seemed likely to draw FCC intervention, the chairman of the commission, Kevin Martin, noted early in the debate that adjusting access by allowing users to pay for different speeds might not draw regulatory action.

Widely publicized in 2006, the network neutrality debate has occupied substantial legislative time, but the deep pockets of industries on either side means that for the time being there will be no easy resolution. What is clear from the past is that the freedom of use and open content availability that characterize new technologies in the early years of adoption tend to be subsequently constrained by the imposition of commercial structures and the establishment of practices that favor dominant industrial entities. If the pattern holds in the case of these new distribution technologies and the potential inherent in them, then it is probable that once they become widely used and profitable, the balance of power will shift back to entrenched commercial interests. Certainly, viewers might maintain some of the expanded capabilities enabled by new distribution methods even after commercial forces become more integrated, but the most likely scenario is a negotiated outcome that will depend greatly on action on the part of informed viewers, consumers, and citizens.

Consequences of Changes in Distribution

Although IPTV, network neutrality, and changing competition in television delivery to the home are clearly significant, at this time, in 2007, it is too early to determine what their impact is likely to be. Nonetheless, as the effects of these developments become more perceptible, it becomes possible to begin to imagine a significantly different television world in the future.

Niche programming is one component of this scenario, which might be illustrated through the example of *Arrested Development*. As cancellation of the critically lauded niche favorite loomed in the fall of 2005, at the same time Apple and ABC announced alternative distribution deals, many quickly identified the possibility such distribution methods might provide for cult favorites like this series.[59] A key part of the niche-hit equation is not only the smaller audience, but also the intensity of feeling for a show, which, in turn, makes viewers more willing to pay directly for content. Niche hits have an advantage over general interest successes that draw audiences who are seated in front of the television at the right time, but take little notice of missing an episode. Although *Arrested Development* did not find extended life in another distribution system, the very existence of new distribution methods make it possible to imagine how broadcast networks might evolve into primarily promotional sources, exposing audiences to content to which they would then subscribe. Such a development would introduce a very different economic model with substantial ramifications throughout the production process and have considerable implications for television's cultural role as well.[60] *Arrested Development* faced cancellation once its audience diminished to an estimated 4.3 million each week. Assuming standard production costs of $1.8 million per episode, an audience of just 1.25 million paying $2 per episode could finance production costs, even after an approximately 20 percent payment to the distribution service—Apple's estimated cut of the early iTunes deals.

In the months immediately following the first introduction of downloading and streaming A-level content, industry insiders were tightlipped

about the economic specifics of the deals. Networks reported the experiments as successes, but released few figures of total sales, revenues, and
how those revenues were shared with studios and distributors. Business
analysts offered informed but inexact estimations, as in a *Business Week*
article that explained that *Desperate Housewives* generated $11.3 million
per episode in advertising revenue, which when divided by the show's audience, afforded each viewer a value of 45 cents per episode.[61] In comparison, the network initially sold episodes by download for a fee of
$1.99, of which analysts expected ABC would receive at least $1.20, although others estimated the content provider's cut to be closer to $1.60.[62]
Given these economic outcomes, the value of the transactional model to
the industry is apparent: a viewer who leaves the broadcast audience and
opts for the direct-pay download more than repays the network for the
loss—at least insofar as assumptions concerning audience behavior hold;
in fact, there is a fair amount of evidence already suggesting that effects
on audience behavior are far more complicated. A widespread change in
viewer behavior would affect the economics of the situation significantly.
The value of advertising time on a show correlates with the value advertisers afford to the size and composition of the audience, so the valuation
could change greatly in either direction as advertisers reassess their spending based on the future value of the comparatively mass audience and
other opportunities to reach audiences.

The emergent nature of many of the new distribution windows makes
it difficult to predict the role they will play in evolving economic models
for creative content distribution in the post-network era. It remains unclear which fee structure is more likely to become dominant—whether it
will involve added value for an existing service, pay-per-use, or an all-
you-can-view subscription. It seems most likely that a multiplicity of revenue streams will coexist, even as each introduces different considerations in other components of the production process. Each of these options affect the content likely to be produced, and the resulting variety
will give viewers an even greater range of options.

What is clear at this point is that the standard practice of distribution
windowing featuring exclusivity and tiered pricing that supported the
dominant economic practice of deficit financing has eroded and that it is
unlikely to dominate industrial practice again. Norms such as windowing
and deficit financing were fundamental to the operation of the television
industry and established thinking about its economics. Their diminished
importance consequently suggested the arrival of a very different era of

industrial operation and moneymaking. Changes as pronounced as those that occurred in distribution in late 2005 and 2006 have arguably generated significant opportunities for the reallocation of power within the system. Although entrenched commercial interests have the greatest assets through which to reassert themselves, the scope of change may well create new relationships among cable and satellite systems, telecommunication providers, and technology manufacturers.

The increased profitability of tiny audiences and the multiplicity of financing mechanisms that enable the production of a greater variety of content are significant and enduring consequences of the adjustments in distribution. Such gains first became evident during the multi-channel transition as the distribution mechanism of cable enabled the creation of content directed to more specific audiences and afforded value to niche audiences that would always be underserved by the network-era competitive environment. Following this development, many of the newer distribution windows conferred value on audiences even smaller than those required by cable. In prompting changes in economic models involved in financing content production, the multiple uses of television and the variety of devices upon which it can be viewed have also increased the array of content feasible in a commercial media system.

Although I want to avoid the "blue skies" rhetoric that early on forecast cable as a democratizing force, it is nonetheless important to consider some of the implications of broadband, which has dismantled the bottleneck of distribution that afforded substantial cultural power to the gatekeepers and agenda-setters of the network era. As of 2007, broadband distribution offers previously unimagined opportunities to distribute video—including those beyond the confines of commercial profitability. To be sure, the gross surplus of content has made finding messages, videos, or stories of interest increasingly difficult. In response, companies such as Yahoo!, Google, and AOL, as well as Internet video specialists such as YouTube and Video Bomb, continue to busily refine search and distribution applications that aggregate content and decrease the difficulty of sorting. In the process, though, they may well offer advantage to certain content and providers and thereby contribute to reestablishing commercial media control.

Perhaps the biggest change new distribution windows have introduced to television as a cultural institution is the creation of new means for independent or amateur productions to find audiences. Of all the art and storytelling forms, television was under the tightest commercial grip due to the stranglehold of the networks on distribution. For decades, public television provided the most viable outlet for unconventional or non-commercial content, but its lack of independence from state funding manipulation and general under-funding ultimately afforded it limited additional breadth. Local cable access provided another alternative to commercial television and the networks' stranglehold over distribution but was geographically, technologically, and financially limited. By contrast, broadband distribution enables a radical disruption in television's norm as a medium limited to commercially created content.

Another substantial adjustment that has resulted from the dismantling of network-era distribution practices is the displacement of the "network schedule" as the dominant means of content organization. As we have seen, this schedule, and the conventions of other production components related to it, restricted variation in program length, with thirty, sixty, and one hundred and twenty minutes being the only options in most venues and mainly just MTV's video flow and sports programming providing variations in length. But as commercial content providers tested new distribution platforms such as video on demand and broadband channels, many offered shorts, outtakes, and other programming outside the bounds of conventional program length. The growing variety of distribution methods and the schedule-free structure of on demand has now also enabled the further diversification in content forms considered in the previous chapter. DVD distribution has created an additional market for limited-run series, as has video on demand. Some content created for Internet distribution has even come to be redistributed on cable networks (Bravo's *Outrageous and Contagious: Viral Video*) or on DVD (*Happy Tree Friends*).

As suggested in the previous chapter as well as the next, the increasing multiplicity of ways of paying for and circulating programs have substantially expanded the range of programming that can be produced within the dictates of a commercial media system. Multiple opportunities for producers to recoup production costs allow a much greater variety of forms than the standard windowing process that demanded consistent program lengths and at least one hundred episodes. In the network era, international syndication provided the only way to recover production costs on miniseries—a circumstance that contributed to the telling of only certain types of stories in this format.[63] The possibility of DVD release has added another revenue stream, as have some forms of on-demand distribution. Morgan Hertzan, chief creative officer of Code.TV, an online network that features short video clips on New York shopping, nightlife, food, arts, and other categories, notes the advantage of Internet video distribution: "You can service a niche audience and only deliver a couple hours, well-focused and well-produced."[64] The expansion of his company to additional cities indicates the potential for local commercial and informational content which were largely absent throughout the network era and multi-channel transition.

As the post-network era continues to become established, most of the distinctions such as VOD versus broadband channels and streaming versus download that I make here with painstaking deliberateness will erode. Broadband channels and cable channels will simply be "television" in the viewer's common experience. Who will wear the crown in the post-network era: content or distribution? Speaking at the Annual Livery Lecture at the Worshipful Company of Stationers and Newspaper Makers in March 2006, News Corp. magnate Rupert Murdoch proclaimed, "Power is moving away from those who own and manage the media to a new and demanding generation of consumers—consumers who are better educated, unwilling to be led, and who know that in a competitive world they can get what they want, when they want it. The challenge for us in the traditional media is how to engage with this new audience. There is only one way," he continued. "That is by using our skills to create and distribute dynamic, exciting content. King Content, *The Economist* called it recently."[65] But the multiplicity of post-network technologies and distribution windows that have enabled an expanded diversity of content have also suggested a new competitor for status as king. Indeed, much of the more revelatory rhetoric about changes in the television industry asserts that viewers will be sovereign in the post-network era as industries compete to provide them with the content they desire on their own preferred terms. Comcast CEO Brian Roberts declared as much at the 2006 National Cable Show, while a few weeks earlier Disney CEO Robert Iger announced, "We've concluded the consumer is king. Remaining a slave to fixed consumption would be a huge mistake and at Disney we're refusing to do that."[66]

Viewers do, indeed, appear likely to benefit to some degree as the cultural institution of television evolves and the status distributors have long held as the few and limited gatekeepers of content diminishes. New distribution methods allow more viewer choice, so that they can watch commercials or not, pay directly for programming or not, view content at self-determined times and locations, and have more ready access to content outside of that created by commercial conglomerates.

Yet Roberts' fellow panelist, Time Warner CEO Richard Parsons tempered the "consumer is king" assertion, recalling the words of Gerald Levin, who had orchestrated the once heralded but by then negatively regarded merger of AOL and Time Warner. Levin posited that content might be king, but distribution was the power behind the throne, a maxim that again left the viewer out of the equation. Although expanded viewer sovereignty still seems possible in this nascent stage of the post-network era, the history of distribution tells a different story. All too frequently emergent technologies provided multiplicity and diversity in their infancy, only to be subsumed by dominant and controlling commercial interests as they became more established. The contradictory interests of various industries may create room for viewers to win some victories. Stay tuned: a battle royal has just begun.

5

Advertising after the Network Era
The New Economics of Television

Madison Avenue is stuck in a 1950s time warp. While the era of
mass media has long since departed—just glance at the hundreds of
cable channels and thousands of special-interest magazines if you require proof—most ad agencies still operate the same way they did
during the Eisenhower administration: Toss a single TV spot at millions of random viewers in the hope that a small fraction might be
interested in that new Chevrolet or life insurance from Prudential.
—Paul Keegan, "The Man Who Can Save Advertising"[1]

The advertising business has not matured in the past thirty or forty
years. I wouldn't blame the current need for change on TiVo. It's an
evolutionary process that has stagnated because advertisers and networks have been slow to recognize and adapt to changes in the consumer marketplace.
—Lee Gabler, Creative Artists Agency[2]

From its establishment in the mid-1960s, the commercial model supporting U.S. television remained stable for a long time. As many have criticized,
the lack of innovation and change in the relationship among television networks and their Madison Avenue supporters indicated a stunning lack of
dynamism. Certainly, shifts occurred as audience measurement systems
grew increasingly sophisticated and cable networks introduced new options throughout the multi-channel transition. For the most part, however,
dominant practices remained in place until the late 1990s, when it became
apparent that changes of prodigious proportions were approaching. Most
tried to ignore them. Others attempted to halt them or hoped for some sort
of intervention that would offer reprieve. A few boldly looked forward.
    An unusual confluence of immediate economic crisis, programming in-
novation, and cultural uncertainty combined with the established conse-

quences of expanded viewer choice and control to prepare the variety of responses attempted by advertisers in the early years of the twenty-first century. Historically, U.S. commercial television was dominated by certain advertising norms—such as the thirty-second commercial. But this convention resulted from particular industrial organizations and competitive strategies of the network era and multi-channel transition, and was no more inevitable than the emerging post-network norm in which multiple advertising strategies, including product placement and sponsorship, coexist with the thirty-second ad. Such a multiplicity of strategies corresponds with the increasingly diverse practices and diffuse industrial organization characteristic of the post-network era. The multiple television advertising strategies explored here—product placement, integration, branded entertainment, and sponsorship—did not "kill" the thirty-second ad, as so many trade articles suggested. Rather, they reflected the increasing variety of practices common throughout the production process —although, again, the transformation was not instant.

The scope of coming changes was clear to all by the late 1990s, but advertisers had the greatest interest in identifying new models and norms because they paid for the system. Certainly all of the relevant players observed the data that trickled in during the multi-channel transition. Broadcasters, with their diminishing audiences and successful demands for higher rates, were not going to suggest a change in the status quo. Cable channels had much to gain and regularly agitated for more support from advertisers. Despite cable's multi-year existence, the channels did not develop compelling, word-of-mouth-generating narrative series programming until the late 1990s—particularly in the key prime-time period —which helped perpetuate broadcasters' dominance. The cable networks offered advertisers a new multiplicity of advertising sites, but the expanded choice of the multi-channel transition alone was not significant enough to cause a reevaluation of the commercial funding practices of U.S. television.

Ultimately, it was one of those boxes viewers connected to their sets that brought about the most hand-wringing and finally moved the industry to action. As the epigraph suggests, it was less the DVR box itself, but the fear of the DVR box and the empowered consumers who owned them that finally shifted Madison Avenue out of fifty years of complacency. Over a decade before the first DVRs entered the home, the technology's analog predecessor, the VCR, sparked the industry to a similar panic.[3] Yet the end of the world of commercial advertising predicted in the early 1980s never transpired, which made it all the more curious that advertising agencies and networks so quickly forgot their unfounded fears when the DVR debuted. Despite the fact that the DVR, like the VCR, enables viewers to record and later playback programming, DVR early adopters—many of whom worked in the industry—knew something was different. The technology was too easy to use, its digital capabilities involved too substantial a leap, and its ready program guide was far more likely to entice viewers to actually view the shows that they recorded and thus become a default mode of viewing. Industry experts also knew that video-on-demand technology was maturing. Viewers were no longer going to be satisfied with a mere range of options; once allowed to sample the new technologies, they would demand control over when and how they would watch, and they were no longer going to be captive for commercial breaks. Instead of the 300-channel universe, the control technologies and distribution adjustments provided a 10,000-hour universe of instantly available programming.

Blaming the DVR for the sizable shifts in advertising techniques and program financing norms makes for an elegant argument, but it is a grand overstatement of the impact of the device. Certainly the reassessment of dominant advertising models was overdue long before TiVo promoted its advertisement-skipping features. The future uncertainty fueled by the DVR only helped the industry toward the "tipping point" at which the risk of trying something new appeared less dangerous than blindly maintaining the status quo.[4] By mid-2000, other factors including the dot-com crash and the economic downturn also had substantial consequences for the advertising market. Heading into the fall of 2001, local television advertising was down 14.7 percent from the first half of 2000. When the attacks of September 11th then occurred, they further called into question the status of the economy and introduced substantial uncertainty about whether the national psyche might embrace or reject entertainment and other commercial fare.[5] After the attacks, analysts revised forecasts to predict even greater declines in advertising spending, and advertisers feared for the future of their industry.[6] But before things became too dismal, the networks pursued cheaper programming to shore up their failing economic model and found a programming form that interested audiences and achieved surprising success with prime-time game shows (*Who Wants to Be a Millionaire?*) and competitive reality shows (*Survivor*). Advertisers then began to rethink old strategies and try new opportunities. Although initially wary of viewers' potential reaction to integrating products into programs, companies such as AT&T and Pringles paid to have their brand names and products used in shows such as these and experienced no viewer backlash in response. At the same time, the industry developed tools for gathering and analyzing increasing amounts of market data that enabled advertisers to target fragmented populations and tailor messages to psychographic specificities rather than demographic generalities. This, too, contributed to coming changes.

The industry also was well aware that network-era audience estimations offered only a suggestion of those who might, or might not, view a commercial—trips to the bathroom and the refrigerator had long stolen audiences. VCRs and remote controls had a similar effect. While introducing a panel discussion of new advertising practices in 2004, industry commentator Jack Myers described the content of a trade advertisement hanging in his office. The ad reminds its audience—that is, advertisers— that only through "creative ingenuity" will they reach the "disappearing America," such as those fleeing to the kitchen or elsewhere at commercial breaks. Myers' punch line: the ad was created in 1953. The problem of reaching the right viewers with the right advertising messages was thus by no means new, but by the early years of the twenty-first century, advertisers had more tools to aid them in this task than ever before. At the same time, though, the lean, post-Fordist corporations supporting the industry would not tolerate any economic inefficiency or uncertainty and sought guarantees that no advertising dollar would be wasted.[7] This concern about the efficiency of money spent on advertising drove an obsession with return on investment at the same time that the industry experienced unprecedented change in its advertising techniques and consumer research methods.

The industry press often framed the redefinition of advertising practices as a question of the life or death of the thirty-second spot, but the relevant questions were far more substantial and nuanced. The advertising industry responded to the challenges of an increasingly fragmented and polarized audience empowered with control devices that enabled them to avoid commercial messages in a variety of ways. An assortment of new and old strategies emerged or reemerged haphazardly during the waning years of the multi-channel transition. Although advertisers experimented with a distinct range of strategies, little consensus existed within the industry about what to call them: anything other than a thirty-second spot was often labeled "product placement" despite the significant variation in the strategies used. This chapter consequently distinguishes among different practices and notes their ramifications for the advertising industry and beyond. Shifts in dominant advertising practices can substantially affect television programming and, consequently, the stories the medium provides. As in the other production components considered throughout the book, the adjustments in the operation of the advertising industry have significant implications for television as a cultural institution. Advertisers' desire to reach young, upscale demographic groups enabled the production of content defying previous norms, while the multiplicity of financing strategies likewise diversified the range of programming commercial models could support.

Advertising Practices during the Network Era and the Multi-Channel Transition

The norms of radio determined the commercial basis of the U.S. broadcasting system while television was still just an imagined technology in the hopes of inventors. As a result, many of the key debates about and experiments with possibilities for financing broadcasting were established before television functionally existed. In television's early years, however, the inherent differences between the two media required some adjustment of practices inherited from radio. Primarily, the cost of television production relative to radio introduced complications to the established system of commercial funding.

The dominant commercial model of radio utilized a single sponsorship system in which a corporation paid all of the production costs of a show and was the only product or corporate entity associated with it. While initially this system carried over to television, it soon became apparent that a single sponsor could not feasibly pay for the many facets of visual production on a continuing basis. Some genres with lower production costs, such as game shows, still enabled single sponsorship, although that contributed to other difficulties—as became apparent in the quiz show scandals of the late 1950s, when it was revealed that advertisers rigged the shows to support popular contestants and used other disingenuous strategies to maintain viewers. Reaction to these scandals, as well as the networks' desire to control their schedules, further contributed to the development of a new advertising model using a "participation" or "magazine" format; the latter term refers to the way television shows came to be supported in the same way as magazines, with advertisements for many different products mixed in with the programming.

By contrast, the sponsorship system of the 1940s and 1950s afforded advertising agencies and their clients considerable command over program content and even networks' schedules.[8] From the beginning of television, the networks objected to this arrangement, but they could not institute an alternative quickly enough to prevent it from migrating to the new medium in the early 1950s.[9] As they identified that a deliberate and strategic schedule was as important as the quality of the programming placed in that schedule, the networks became eager to displace advertising agencies' centrality in program development and to gain control over their schedule—which included ending the norm of "time franchises" that allowed agencies to control specific slots in the networks' schedules. William Boddy's research recounts clear evidence of network pressure to end single sponsorship by the mid-1950s, although multiple sponsor shows did not become dominant until 1962–63, when 55 percent of the ninety-four shows on the air used this commercial format.[10]

The shift away from single sponsorship increased the network's control of its programming content and schedule and diminished the sponsor's role in both. Advertisers became less invested in specific content issues once they became one of many companies with commercial messages in a program. As networks assumed authority over their schedules and show selection, the change also had advantages for advertisers, including spreading their risk across a number of shows each week, while still providing agencies with substantial revenue opportunities.

Participation provided a far more beneficial advertising system for all involved, except perhaps, for the viewers. Although it responded to the problem of the cost of producing television, which was substantially higher than that of radio, a number of other forces contributed to the transition. As Boddy notes, shifting corporate strategies regarding the nature of television advertising messages and the type of corporation likely to advertise occurred concurrently with the move away from sponsorship.[11] Whereas large manufacturing corporations had dominated sponsorship and used this as an opportunity to promote their corporate image, they themselves began to rethink this "corporate angle" or "company voice" strategy at the same time that networks started to want to have a broader blend of advertisers less likely to be uniformly affected by periods of recession.[12] Increasingly, television became a medium more desired by packaged-goods companies that used advertisements to explicitly sell the attributes of a product or to sell the lifestyle they wanted consumers to attribute to the product. Although a large packaged-goods advertiser such as Proctor & Gamble could easily afford sponsorship, such an arrangement, which privileged the P&G name, would not provide name recognition for the substantial variety of products it sought to promote, such as Tide, Crest, and Palmolive.

The networks' identification of the competitive importance of schedule control enabled the establishment of many network-era norms, including the creation of programming that rendered television more than a haphazard assortment of disconnected programs. The motivation of sponsoring programs to further a certain corporate image or angle led to the production of a different type of programming than characteristic of most of the network era. Single sponsorship encouraged distinctive programming that expressed prestige. However, this, too, began to change as the networks began to seek out much cheaper programming, such as the kind Christopher Anderson examines in his study of Warner Bros. film studios' efforts to produce for television.[13] The studios mainly wanted to monetize old background footage and more efficiently use their back lots and attempted to recycle old and promotional content as television programming. The shift from sponsorship to participation also contributed to the networks' pursuit of profit participation (discussed in Chapter 3) that made the environment difficult for independent producers and resulted in the fin-syn regulations. A weak program aesthetic dominated much of the 1960s as FCC Chairman Newton Minow noted at the time and television historians have since affirmed. This programming resulted from characteristics of production practices of the era that overemphasized cost saving and led the networks to pursue only modest programming achievement.[14]

Various norms of the "television season" and the timing for selling advertising time developed once magazine-format advertising established its dominance. The annual September debut of programs led to the related annual process of securing advertising commitments in the spring in what came to be known as the "upfront" market. During this period, which once lasted eight weeks but may now span only a week or two, broadcast networks sell 75 to 90 percent of the advertising time in the upcoming season on tentative, but fairly reliable commitments.[15] Networks sell the remaining advertising inventory throughout the year in the "scatter" and "opportunistic" markets. The upfront market is advantageous for networks because it affords them committed advertising spending before they begin producing programming. In exchange for the reduction of risk, the networks offer "discounted" rates on advertising purchased upfront.

The upfront functions as a speculative market, as later scatter prices may be significantly higher depending on advertising demand.[16] Most advertisers purchase time upfront because the limited supply of programming in certain programs and on particular networks makes some buys available only during the upfront. The later scarcity traditionally has led to scatter rates that average roughly fifteen percent higher.[17]

The upfront process generally benefits the networks, although they have developed some practices in response to advertisers' more substantial concerns about the uncertainty and potential inequity of the process. The networks decreased the uncertainty of the upfront purchase—a key concern for advertisers—and received higher rates in return when they initiated "guarantees" beginning in 1967.[18] Under this arrangement networks began guaranteeing a certain audience size for the advertisers' purchase and providing "make-goods" or supplementary advertising slots if they failed to achieve the guaranteed audience reach with the initial purchase. According to veteran media buyer Erwin Ephron, this led to a shift from advertisers buying specific shows to their purchasing "CPMs," an acronym for cost per thousand, or cost for one exposure to one thousand viewers of a certain demographic type. The CPM became a standard industry currency, which operates as follows: if an advertiser wishes to reach 50,000,000 viewers and had established a CPM of $15, or $15 per thousand viewers, a network would put together a package of advertisements that would reach the 50,000,000 viewers for $750,000.[19] Networks usually only guarantee audience delivery if advertisers purchase CPMs in the upfront. The networks benefit from this method of purchase because they distribute advertiser support between both popular and less established programs.[20]

The dominance of the upfront as the means by which advertisers allocate their spending is important because this in turn affects network practices. If networks sold individual commercials instead of the exposure to a certain number of viewers spread across multiple programs they would likely make different programming decisions. The upfront allows the networks to package their new or weaker shows with their established hits —a practice not entirely dissimilar from the film industry's practice of block booking in which studios required theaters to show lower budget films in order to get the high-profile films they most desired. Although advertisements in hit shows might command even higher prices if sold individually, this would weaken the networks' ability to nurture new shows and could further discourage the pursuit of unconventional stories or for-

mats. The process of upfront selling garnered significant critique and debate from its inception, but regardless of perennial declarations of its
death, and despite the substantial adjustments in other production components throughout the multi-channel transition, the practice has proven
remarkably resilient.

Major shifts in advertising and the economic support of television
more broadly began early in the multi-channel transition and then
shifted again at the beginning of the post-network era. The arrival of
subscription financed television marked the first major rupture from the
network-era model of monolithic advertiser support through thirty-second ads. It required two decades for subscription network HBO to produce a successful "television series," but the subscription experience prepared viewers for the transactional distribution opportunities that subsequently became available. Subscription television also established a
content creation environment very different from that pervading advertiser-supported content. The financial mandate of drawing and maintaining subscribers led subscription networks to create programming of
such distinction that viewers were willing to pay for it—if not in subscription, then perhaps in the various subsequent markets such as DVD
sales.[21] Again, norms of who pays for programming and through what
financial model bears substantial effects throughout the production
process.

Challenges for Advertising at the Beginning of the Post-Network Era

In addition to various direct-pay opportunities, the later years of the
multi-channel transition featured an uncommon variety of advertising
practices that suggested the multiplicity in this production component
likely to characterize the post-network era. Crises resulting from frag-
menting audiences, rising production costs, and commercial skipping behaviors enabled by control technologies compounded until advertisers
could no longer rely on the presence of an audience during commercials.
Consequently, they began experimenting with product placement and integration, branded entertainment, and sponsorship, along with continuing to support the thirty-second commercial. Calls for the end of the upfront system continued throughout the multi-channel transition, yet remained unheeded despite the sizable adjustments in nearly every other

industrial practice. The only real threat to this buying practice emerged once advertisers began shifting money out of thirty-second advertisements because strategies such as placement and sponsorship could not be developed and sold in this way.

Advertisers also made greater demands for accountability and return on investment information as they faced a variety of new platforms on which they could reach consumers. Agencies dealt with clients who made increasingly contradictory demands as advances in marketing research and new media venues allowed the more creative and precise messaging that clients' marketing divisions prized, while their procurement divisions —those who allocate the clients' advertising budget—demanded definite information that remained elusive about how advertising spending correlated with sales. Advertisers' interest in alternative data—such as measures of viewer loyalty and engagement—indicated the rising disillusionment with continuing network-era advertising practices in a dynamic and cluttered media environment.

As the post-network era emerges, conglomeration has come to play a role in many different ways. Although few have explored the conglomeration that has occurred within the advertising industry, this process has developed alongside the concentration of media ownership in the content and delivery businesses. By the mid-2000s, four holding companies (Omnicom Group, WPP Group, Interpublic Group, and Publicis Groupe) came to control most of the industry's business, own forty of the top fifty U.S. agencies, and earn over $31 billion in revenue in 2005 from their various advertising and media, public relations, marketing communications, and specialty firms.[22] Since the consolidation, some agencies have unbundled different components and created separate independent media departments. As part of the trend toward "communications planning," agencies have eliminated segmentation by media, or the use of separate teams for television, magazine, and point-of-purchase, and instead combined all media for more integrated planning.[23] More recently, agencies have created product placement divisions particularly charged to develop ideas for clients and networks and to expand this growing practice in a manner similar to the early years of television.[24]

By the early 2000s advertising agencies provided a range of services including creative development, strategic planning, media buying and planning, and account management. Sometimes a single agency supplies a client with all four types of service, while in other cases the work might be spread throughout different arms of consolidated holding companies

TABLE 3
Top Marketing Organizations and Their Holdings

OMNICOM GROUP ($10.48B)	WPP GROUP ($10.03B)	INTERPUBLIC GROUP OF COS. ($6.27B)	PUBLICIS GROUPE ($5.11B)
Core Agencies—Int'l	*Core Agencies—Int'l*	*Core Agencies—Int'l*	*Core Agencies—Int'l*
BBDO Worldwide	Grey Worldwide	FCB Worldwide	Leo Burnett
DDB Worldwide	JWT	Lowe Worldwide	Worldwide
Communications	Ogilvy & Mather	McCann Erickson	Publicis Worldwide
TBWA Worldwide	Worldwide	Worldwide	Saatchi & Saatchi
	Y&R Advertising		
Media Specialists		*Media Specialists*	*Media Specialists*
OMD Worldwide	*Media Specialists*	Initiative Media	Starcom MediaVest
PHD	MediaCom	Worldwide	Group
	Mediaedge:cia	Universal McCann	ZenithOptimedia
Mainly U.S.	MindShare		
Bernard Hodes	Worldwide	*Mainly U.S.*	*Mainly U.S.*
Group		Campbell-Ewald	Bromley
Dieste, Harmel Part-	*Mainly U.S.*	Campbell Mithun	Burrell Communica-
ners	Bravo Group	Carmichael Lynch	tions Group
Doremus & Co.	JWT Specialized	Dailey & Associates	Fallon Worldwide
Element 79 Partners	Communications	Deutsch	Kaplan Thaler
Goodby, Silverstein		GlobalHue	Group
& Partners	*Mainly Non-U.S.*	Gotham	Team One
GSD&M	Asatsu-DK	Hill, Holliday,	Advertising
Martin/Williams	Bates Asia	Connors,	
Merkley & Partners	Chime Communica-	Cosmopulos	*Mainly Non-U.S.*
Zimmerman & Part-	tions	Martin Agency	Bartle Bogle Hegarty
ners	Communications	Mullen	Beacon Communica-
	Group	TM Advertising	tions
Mainly Non-U.S.	Diamond Ad		Publicis-Graphics
Proximity	FullSix	*Marketing Services*	
	G2R	Draft	*Marketing Services*
Marketing Services	HighCo	FCBi	Arc Worldwide
Agency.com	STW Group	Jack Morton	Publicis Dialog
Alcone Marketing	Team/Y&R	Marketing Drive	Saatchi & Saatchi X
Group		Worldwide	
AtmosphereBBDO	*Marketing Services*	Momentum	
BBDO Detroit	Grey Direct	Worldwide	
Critical Mass	Grey Interactive	MRM	
Grizzard Communi-	Worldwide	R/GA	
cations Group	OgilvyInteractive		
Integer Group	OgilvyOne		
Ketchum Directory	Worldwide		
Advertising	141 Worldwide		
Marketing Arm	RMG:Connect		
Organic	VML		
Rapp Collins World-	Wunderman		
wide			
Targetbase			
Tequila			
TracyLocke			
Tribal DDB			

Source: *Advertising Age*, 30 April 2006.

or among entirely different companies.[25] The creative staff develops advertisements and the content of point-of-purchase or other brand communication within the mandate of a carefully researched and tested brand strategy, typically developed by the strategic planning staff that researches consumer behaviors and attitudes about the product. Media planners develop strategies for reaching particular consumers through targeted media buys—often across multiple media—and media buyers negotiate the purchase with the networks. Television buyers develop and purchase the best plan in the upfront and scatter markets and then monitor those buys throughout the year, tracking make-goods and overseeing the buys as networks adjust their schedules. As ratings data have grown increasingly sophisticated and the number of networks has expanded, media buyers have collected and sorted through much more information in order to predict likely series performance prior to the upfront to determine the best purchase to reach the client's target consumer. The account management component of the agency deals directly with the advertiser and facilitates communication among the other units, particularly in the increasingly common case that a single agency does not house the media and creative development divisions.

Even before agencies began creating separate product placement specialists, Jack Myers noted that industrial shifts caused by new media and challenges to the status quo operation of television resulted in a shift of power within agencies from creative divisions to media buying and planning.[26] Such developments repositioned this facet of the industry from what one executive described as an "assembly-line factory" business to one more craft-oriented. He added that the additional "creative" role now common for planning and buying divisions suggested a need for a compensation model based on outcome, which entailed a significant adjustment in the financial underpinnings of the existing, but eroding, norm in which the agency collected a fee based on a percentage of an advertiser's buy.[27]

The conglomeration of the advertising industry has created a complicated environment because a client typically will not allow its agency to represent another company in its competitive sector—for instance, Wendy's will not allow its agency to also house the account for McDonalds, Burger King, Subway, etc. In addition, the conglomeration of the corporations that support the commercial television industry—such as the purchase of Gillette by Proctor & Gamble or the merger of Sears and Kmart—has also affected the industry, making opportunities for new business for agencies increasingly limited and decreasing the clients available to agencies as the merged companies integrate their advertising.

Increased cost efficiencies have been a key outcome of the consolidation of all disciplines of advertising into a handful of holding groups, and the agencies also benefit from the expanded information about the health of the market they gain from aggregating so many clients within one holding company. This bottom line, tight fiscal management, has become apparent in the broader U.S. economic environment in this period as well, as market maturity has resulted in few opportunities for expansion and required corporations to manage costs precisely. Accountability to budget and attention to performance measures have come to be tightly observed throughout the economy in general, but these developments have had specific consequences for the particular economies of advertising and a television industry in the midst of substantial redefinition.[28]

Adjustments in the industrial organization and norms of practice in advertising affect television production and network operations in many ways, especially since advertising dollars support much of the industry. These changes in advertising are among the most substantial explored in this book. Unsurprisingly, advertising agencies have been particularly vocal prognosticators of the significance of the changes occurring and have been among those most willing to accept and embrace changes in economic models and technological possibility. This became increasingly necessary as advertisers received decreasing returns on their commercial dollars throughout the multi-channel transition. As a result, they were in a position to adopt and to benefit more from new commercial practices than other areas of the industry—like broadcasters—for which a network-era status quo remained preferable.

Throughout the multi-channel transition, advertisers faced the loss of a mass audience, which was caused by the steady increase in choice of new networks and leisure devices. Expanding viewer control technologies such as DVRs and VOD applications also diminished the viability of decades-old practices, including the thirty-second commercial. But even as these factors provided particular impetus for adjusting norms, they should not be viewed as the only causes of the paradigmatic shifts that began to occur early in the twenty-first century.

Since then, advertising possibilities unimaginable in the 1940s— graphically inserted ads on sports fields and stadium backgrounds, digitally created promotions of products placed in shows produced decades ago, tags added to the bottom of personal correspondence such as emails, sponsorship of every substantial cultural event and even component parts—have become routine and, although annoying and disconcerting to many, commonly accepted. The increasingly precise data about viewers and their behavior has offered advertisers and media planners ever-clearer pictures of whom they reached and how, while experiences with Internet advertising have provided new models for creating alternatives to legacy practices. Media buyers also began to choose among a much greater range of media than in the network era, as the Internet in particular introduced a new venue to reach potential consumers in a very targeted and often participatory way. Finally, a significant shift in cultural sentiment toward commercials and commercialism has occurred in the twenty-first century with the unprecedented expansion in the venues in which we tolerate commercial messages. Indeed, advertising researcher James Twitchell estimated that even by the mid-1990s Americans observed three thousand commercial messages each day—a figure that also points to the cluttered nature of the advertising space.[29] Advertisers long had reason to explore alternative television advertising strategies, but risk aversion prevented the allocation of substantial funds to methods other than the legacy model of the thirty-second advertisement. DVR diffusion and audience dispersal helped push advertisers to the tipping point, but there were other important factors at work. The influx of new and old advertising strategies—haphazardly and inconsistently identified as product placement, sponsorship, "advertainment," and branding—date to the early months of the twenty-first century, during which other socio-economic factors contributed to advertisers' willingness to embrace change. Each of these advertising strategies introduced ripples of adjustment throughout the production process as they enabled commercial support of a greater variety of storytelling and both facilitated and constrained a range of distribution methods.

Distinguishing Post-Network Advertising Strategies: Old Methods, New Names

Following the quiz show scandals and the decline of sponsorship arrangements, networks and producers avoided including brand name goods in television shows during much of the network era. This avoidance helped to prevent conflict among those buying commercials in the show—whether during the original run on broadcast or later in syndication—but it also arose from a sense of social unacceptability, and in some cases, government regulation.[30] Many shows of the network era consequently featured families with kitchens stocked with generic "cola" and "beer." In contrast, the high-profile appearance of the Aston Martin in 1960s James Bond films and, in what many note as the great success story of product placement, Reese's Pieces in *E.T,* illustrate the use of this strategy in film. In television, the practice of including named goods in both scripted and unscripted series reemerged at the end of the multi-channel transition, when it came to involve several distinct forms such as placement, integration, branded entertainment, and sponsorship.[31]

In much 1950s programming, advertisers made no distinction between the practices that we now differentiate as product placement and sponsorship. Reference to the sponsors' goods may or may not have been included in the content of a series, and the titles of series did not consistently name the sponsor. After magazine-style thirty-second advertisements became the norm, the differences between the two became more distinguishable, although trade publications and even the books that have explored the emergence and reemergence of alternative advertising strategies have not been consistent in defining them.[32] As I do so in the following sections, I draw on actual practices that developed in the early 2000s and attempt to delimit distinctions through a more precise vocabulary. However, at the time of this writing, the lexicon I use here is not necessarily shared more broadly. For example, while trade publications might often refer to a number of practices as product placement, the financial underpinnings of these deals vary significantly.

Placement

"Product" or "brand placement" refers to situations in which television shows use name brand products or present them on the screen within the context of the show, yet, even within this simple advertising strategy there have been significant variations.[33] Placement can be either paid or unpaid, a distinction that highlights how two different aspects of business drove growth in this practice. In the case of unpaid placement, or what Twitchell refers to as "product subventions," companies donate products needed on the set for reasons of verisimilitude—if a scene takes place in the kitchen, that set needs to be dressed with products that make it recognizable as a kitchen.[34] While set dressers developed relationships with the prop companies that supplied them with their needs, during the multi-channel transition many of these prop companies moved into the product placement business as they found manufacturers willing to donate the needed product in exchange for making the brand name apparent.[35] In contrast, paid product placement commonly originated in a deal created by an entity representing the advertiser and developed through negotiations with a network or studio. These deals could involve arrangements to feature a sponsor's product or name across the network or a night of programming, but most often they focused on a particular episode or show. In some cases, these deals evolved as part of "added value" to a purchase of commercial time: instead of sponsors paying a fee specifically for it, the network supplied the placement in return for another transaction. A network might offer "added value" opportunities in exchange for an advertiser increasing its annual upfront spending or just in recognition of a regular large spending commitment to the network.

In addition to paid and unpaid placement, there is another level of distinction which I term "basic" versus "advanced" placement. In the case of basic placement, set dressings make the logo or brand of products clearly apparent, but the narrative or dialogue does not call attention to the product or brand. In contrast, an advanced use of placement mentions the product or good by name. In an episode of the NBC comedy *Scrubs*, for example, the doctors played the game Operation, while in *The Office* restaurants such as Chili's and Benihana have been used for staff lunches and parties, and not simply as identifiable settings: significantly, the restaurants are explicitly named and discussed on the show.[36]

To be sure, such distinctions are not ironclad. Thus, it may be difficult to determine the point at which a placement might be considered advanced or precisely when placement becomes integration (see below). Furthermore, in some cases placement can result from an advertiser's sponsorship of a show, which, in turn, can also create variations in the practice. For example, Coca-Cola and Ford used both placement and sponsorship in their support of the FOX talent-competition show *American Idol*. Large cups of Coca-Cola sat in front of each of the three judges, and the couch shared by the competitors featured the trademark swirl of the company's logo, but it was this subtle placement in tandem with the video shot in the "Coca-Cola Red Room" that particularly highlighted the brand relative to the program. No contestants requested a sip of Coke before going on stage in a manner more characteristic of advanced placement, but Coke's presence on the show seemed more than that of basic placement because of the blending of placement and sponsorship. Identifying these kinds of variations allows for more precise analysis of the increasing range of advertiser participation in programming.

By 2005, many examples of paid, unpaid, basic, and advanced placement appeared across the networks. Among them, basic placement has become an especially common practice, although not necessarily most effective. For instance, whereas industry analysts hailed the arrangement between the advertising agency OMD and the SciFi miniseries production *5 Days to Midnight,* which included ten OMD clients in the series, as a success story of placement based on the show's increase in audience over the same time period a year earlier, as a viewer—who watched the series closely—I had no recollection of even seeing any of the brands in the narrative.[37] By the end of the network era, advertisers and social scientists both had expansive research about how to maximize recall and effectiveness of thirty-second advertisements, but less data existed to explain the need for recall in placement situations or to otherwise evaluate the efficiency and outcome of placement strategies.[38]

The key attribute repeated by advertisers, production executives, and networks regarding the viability of placement—and the related strategy of integration that is explained below—is that the product must be "organic," meaning the product must not be too obvious, call too much attention to itself, or seem out of place. Of course, all of the things that make placement organic also make it less noticeable to audiences accustomed to encountering thousands of brand messages everyday. By contrast, an "inorganic" placement calls attention to itself and does so in a way that not only exposes the constructed nature of placement but also breaks the viewer's submersion in the narrative. Even here, though, differences between organic and inorganic may not be clear cut. Take, for instance, a 2004 episode of the spy drama *Alias,* in which an early scene featured the heroine and her partner running from the bad guy du jour. From off-screen, the audience heard protagonist Sydney Bristow shout to her partner, "quick, to the F-150," and a car chase scene featuring the named vehicle with its logo prominently displayed in its grill ensued. This use was jarring and disruptive, although there was nothing that made this use particularly "inorganic"—by definition, car chases require vehicles. The step of including the brand name in the dialogue and the fact the character was off-screen when she used the line—which suggests it was edited in during post-production—caused the break in narrative that drew attention to the placement. Importantly, it was because this placement failed to be organic that I, for one, noticed it and could recall it over a year later—in fact, it might be the only truck I know by name. A more successful example of placement within *Alias* involved the spy's use of a Nokia phone: while much of the country was adopting personalized ring tones, Sydney continued to program her phone with the Nokia-brand ring that functioned unobtrusively within the narrative while nonetheless remaining identifiable.

New digital technologies also allow advertisers to rewrite the television past as companies such as Princeton Video place contemporary products and brands into existing series. Products can be placed in the kitchen settings of old situation comedies using the same technology that imposes the first-down line on television broadcasts of football games or brand logos onto the field of soccer matches.[39] The capability of adding and deleting products provides an important level of control, given the sometimes unanticipated subsequent markets for television series.[40] Likewise, this capability provides a response to concerns about placement deals for original run programming. Many have wondered what happens to the good in subsequent markets and how its presence could produce additional revenue. Digital technologies enable studios to create new placement revenues in syndication by reselling the placement opportunity in these secondary markets.

The particularly noteworthy aspect of placement is the speed with which it became a common practice. Although articles in trade press and panels at industry meetings were exploring the strategy by the mid-2000s, the topic—as related to television—was largely absent from industry discourse until 2001.[41] Despite the seeming omnipresence of placement by the end of 2005, this advertising strategy still represents a tiny, albeit growing, piece of most advertisers' budgets. A PQ Media study estimated that spending on television product placement amounted to only $1.88 billion, out of an estimated $60 billion in annual total television advertising spending, while another study estimated that networks or studios received payment for only about 29 percent of the placements seen in 2004.[42] Placement has nonetheless reemerged as a strategy that advertisers are willing to pursue, and there is little evidence that the trend will diminish.

Integration

"Product" or "brand integration" is an additional category of advertiser support in the post-network commercial economy. In cases of integration, the product or company name becomes part of the show in such a way that it contributes to the narrative and creates an environment of brand awareness beyond that produced by advanced placement. Because of their generic attributes, unscripted series have been more successful in integrating products than scripted series. For example, beginning in its second season *The Apprentice* challenged contestants to develop an advertising campaign or a similar activity for a known and real product. Thus, the series utilized the organic marketing potential that it effectively wasted during the first season's use of unbranded activities such as selling lemonade. In addition to selling commercial time within the series, *The Apprentice*'s producers added millions to their budget by selling advertisers the opportunity to be featured within the storyline of the show.[43]

The development of both placement and integration has thus provided unscripted series with important financing, especially in view of the escalation of production costs arising from competition in the form. According to conventional industry wisdom, most unscripted shows have little potential to recoup production deficits through syndication and consequently require producers to fully fund production through license fees or placement. Integration and placement revenues enable shows to afford impressive concepts or hire the limited skilled editing and production talent in this area of the industry, despite lower license fees and lack of deficit financing. Notably, each of the main unscripted shows for the Big Four networks in the mid-2000s (NBC, *The Apprentice*; CBS, *Survivor*; ABC, *Extreme Home Makeover*; FOX, *American Idol*) features a format that allows for organic placement or integration.

Organic integration is unquestionably easier to achieve in unscripted formats, but notable examples of integration in scripted series exist as well—although rarely in prime-time series. The daytime soap operas *All My Children* and *Passions* have both featured plot lines including a real cosmetic company. In 2002 *All My Children* used Revlon as the competitor to the company run by character Erica Kane (Susan Lucci) and featured Kane's daughter gaining employment at Revlon and working as a corporate spy.[44] *Passions'* deal with Mark, an Avon sub-brand, featured one of the central characters becoming a salesperson for the line at the same time that the company was launching Mark and seeking young women to join its independent sales force.[45] As of 2006, there have been fewer examples of successful integrations in prime-time scripted series—particularly on broadcast networks. The 2004 USA film *The Last Ride* drew substantial criticism for its emphasis on a new Pontiac sports car, which many felt to be detrimental to the narrative, and failed to draw audiences. In another case, Campbell's Soup had better success integrating its essay contest into the 1960s-based family drama *American Dreams*.[46]

Advertisers desperate to reach customers have continued to push boundaries between narrative and commercial messaging in hopes of finding an integration that succeeds. Many viewers may recall a high profile deal between the series *Friends* and Diet Coke that dated to 1996. Although Coke paid an estimated $30 million for the campaign centered on the show and its characters, the deal was predominantly focused on the right to use the cast in promotion. Actual integration of Diet Coke within the series played a much smaller role. Nonetheless, commercials during episodes of the series functioned crucially in the sweepstakes promotion that awarded the winner with a trip to a taping of *Friends*.[47]

Industrial discussions of the growing practice of integration have focused on creative workers' fears that they could be forced to construct storylines to include brands. Such fears are justified, although to date, both the advertising and network sides of the business generally have shown restraint, aware that producing bad television diminishes the reputation of all involved. Still, some producers have accepted placement as a necessary compromise that can expand budgets in valuable ways. Peter Berg, executive producer of *Friday Night Lights,* acknowledged that "anything that gives a little financial relief, you can't ignore . . . it's all about giving them [the network] what they need in a way that doesn't violate the integrity or offend the audience."[48] His show frequently sets meals at Applebee's among other placements, and the extra revenue from placements allowed the series to renovate the dilapidated Texas stadium in which it films. Yet, the challenge of successfully negotiating advertiser desires and the sensibility of savvy audiences makes it likely that integration will remain a tool of unscripted programming that coexists with conventionally supported scripted shows.

Branded Entertainment

"Branded entertainment" is a third advertising strategy that has grown increasingly commonplace from the beginning of the post-network era.[49] In this case, the advertiser creates the content of the show, which then itself serves as a promotional vehicle—somewhat akin to a long-form commercial or infomercial. Branded entertainment shifts more toward a sponsorship model and has taken a number of forms. *The Victoria's Secret Fashion Show,* aired by ABC in 2001 and in subsequent years by CBS, provides one example. The "entertainment" of the hour-long show served the promotional function of revealing the attributes of Victoria's Secret lingerie.[50] Here, the financial model featured ABC and Intimate Brands splitting the advertising time in the hour, and Intimate Brands paying for production fees—estimated at $9–10 million by the time the show aired on CBS—so that the event had no cost for ABC.[51] Although this deal may make the show appear to be little more than a long advertisement, Andrea Wong, ABC vice president of alternative series and specials, defended the program by noting, "Clearly this is more than an infomercial. You will see Victoria Secret product but also entertainment in the show," which also included popular musical performers.[52]

Because of the economics of television production, branded entertainment has not found a central a place on television—at least as its initial market. BMW's support of major filmmakers' production of eight, five-minute mini-films featuring the vehicle in 2001 and 2002 was acknowledged as one of the most successful branded entertainment ventures at the time, yet initially audiences could view the films only on the Internet or in theaters before feature presentations. The Internet has become an important distribution force in building word-of-mouth and interest in branded entertainment campaigns. The 2004 "Seinfeld and Superman" ad series for American Express first drew audiences through web viewing, but ultimately aired on broadcast television. The web spot garnered an average of 20,000 daily visits in the week following its debut; subsequently, Jerry Seinfeld embarked on a press tour including the *Today Show* and Jon Stewart's *The Daily Show* in support of the campaign.[53]

Branded entertainment marks a fundamental shift from intrusive advertisements pushed at audiences who are engaged in other content to advertising of such merit or interest that the audience actively seeks it out. Given that branded entertainment involves very different viewer behavior and perception of content than thirty-second magazine-format advertising, the genre may well require a wholly different understanding of the psychological processes involved, as well as new terms for assessing market effectiveness. As far as advertisers are concerned, branded entertainment also requires a massive shift in where they commit their money.[54] *Advertising Age*'s Scott Donaton explains that in traditional advertising, the advertiser allocates 90 percent of the budget to distribution—or buying time or space—and 10 percent to content production.[55]

To develop content of such interest that audiences seek it out requires that advertisers spend 90 percent on production, leaving only 10 percent for distribution.[56] The economics of television will likely need to shift more significantly for branded entertainment to become more common on the medium—particularly on broadcast networks and during prime time.

Single Sponsorship

Finally, the long established practice of single sponsorship has also become more common than it had been since the establishment of the network era. Sponsorship involves a single corporation financing the costs normally recouped through selling advertising time. Sponsored shows often include no in-text commercials, but feature "a word from the sponsor" before or after the show. By the end of the multi-channel transition, sponsorship did not take a uniform pattern, and it may or may not have included product placement or integration in the narrative. In most cases, a company sponsored a single episode rather than an entire series. But even here, episode sponsorship was rare enough that it could create a distinct promotional attribute for the series, as well as providing the sponsor with a comparatively uncluttered environment for its message. Many of the sponsored episodes were for cable series, which involved a lower cost to the corporation than sponsoring a broadcast episode. For example, FX featured "commercial-free" first episodes for each of its original dramas in the summer of 2004 (XM: *Nip/Tuck*; Miller Brewing: *Rescue Me*). Likewise, Ford sponsored the season opener of 24 in 2003 and episodes of *American Dreams* in 2005. Significantly, Ford blended branded entertainment in the 24 sponsorship by wrapping the episode with a six-minute film which began before and concluded after the episode and presented a 24-like plot that utilized a Ford vehicle. The sponsored episode of the 1960s-era drama *American Dreams* featured the iconic 1960s Ford Mustang at the same time Ford launched a new model of the vehicle in 2005. Sponsorship may not always be effective, though. For example, when Pepsi entered into its deal with The WB to be the title sponsor of the *Pepsi Play for a Billion* game show event and the summer concert series *Pepsi Smash,* neither the series nor the event drew audiences or the type of word of mouth sought by the sponsor.[57] (Almost every sporting event—and every aspect of their broadcasts—might also be counted as sponsored programming.)

Importantly, sponsorship situations in which the advertiser chooses not to disrupt the show for brand messages allow for the creation of narratives of some distinction. Magazine-format advertising requires story construction that can be interrupted, and the practicalities of maintaining audiences require writers to manufacture plots with points of climax before the prescribed commercial breaks. Sponsorship, by contrast, can eliminate the need for such interventions. As Tom Fontana, writer and executive producer of the HBO series *Oz*, explains, "When you don't have to bring people back from a commercial, you don't have to manufacture an 'out.' You can make your episode at a length and with a rhythm that's true to the story you want to tell."[58] Many identified the freedom from content restriction and advertiser meddling as key causes of subscription cable networks' success in garnering a lion's share of accolades for the quality and aesthetic form of their series. Such institutional factors are significant, but the freedom from the tired narrative structures that require plot climaxes before commercial breaks also contributed fundamentally to their distinction. No scripted series has yet been produced with a regular sponsor, but such an opportunity could yield dynamic possibilities for storytelling unavailable to writers constrained by the narrative plotting required by commercial pods.

In early 2007, experiments in sponsored "channels" began developing —mainly using broadband for entertainment video distribution. Perhaps the most widely noted such venture emerged from Anheuser-Busch, which launched bud.tv in February 2007. The company planned to feature "new humorous webisodes, sporting events, consumer-generated content, field news reports, celebrity interviews, music downloads and comedian vignettes" on a web-based video network; however, rumors that the site would be shut down circulated less than six months after its launch, and bud.tv appeared to be a $30–40 million failure.[59] Although such sponsored outlet experiments were still in development as I completed the book, they have captured the attention of many in the advertising industry, who expect the likelihood of considerable growth in this type of sponsored programming.[60]

The renewed use of placement, integration, sponsorship, and branded entertainment has affected advertising companies and the networks in various ways. For one thing, agencies have redeveloped in-house divisions focused on creating integrated deals for branded entertainment beyond the standard thirty-second advertisement. The advantage of locating such divisions inside conventional advertising agencies is that it provides coherence with other ongoing strategies and also creates more continuity in the relationships between clients and their agencies. Another effect has more to do with technique and style. Many in the agencies quickly identified the need to integrate and place products in such a way as to not repel consumers and worked to scale back the commercial messaging requested by overly eager clients. Francis Page, principal, strategy and business affairs for MAGNA Global Entertainment, argued that the best uses of integration and placement include subtle penetration into the entertainment narrative, but also noted the need to utilize other public relations venues to maximize the exposure of the placement.[61] This strategy fits well with the "360-degree communications planning" that the consolidated holding companies seek to provide.

For example, in 2004 Tylenol constructed a placement deal with CBS's *Survivor* in which viewers voted for the *Survivor* contestant who exemplified the Tylenol "Push through the Pain" ethic and had an opportunity to enter a sweepstakes that awarded a trip to the *Survivor* location. The process of voting sent viewers to a Tylenol website where they registered for the sweepstakes. In addition to creating the website, Tylenol's agency, purchased advertisements in *USA Today*, in magazines (co-branded with the *Survivor* logo), and on radio encouraging viewers to watch *Survivor* and join the sweepstakes. The campaign included in-store promotional displays, commercials in each *Survivor* episode, and a thirty-second vignette at the end of the episode in which the series' announcer revealed the winner of previous week's vote. In this campaign, then, not only did the product fit "organically" in the show, but also the client spent extensively in other media to support the value that could accrue from the integration deal. Ideally, a well-deployed promotion garners free publicity as well.

New challenges have emerged as these advertising strategies become more central to the industry. Key concerns include establishing norms of pricing and standards of measurement, as well as determining the effectiveness of the various strategies. Even as these experiments began, however, much about the value and effectiveness of new advertising strategies remained uncertain. Substantial change in advertising practices was deterred by advertising clients unwilling to pursue new strategies without proof of their value, while networks and agencies could not offer such certainty without clients willing to engage in the trial and error of initial experiments. Ms. Page suggested that in this transitional environment, clients might place 70 percent of their budget in established and traditional media, 20 percent in more unconventional but still tested media, and allow 10 percent to boldly experiment with new venues and possibilities. This informal 70/20/10 rule indicates the pace of change at which wary clients will finance alternatives to legacy models, particularly when little data exists to indicate the effectiveness of their efforts.

Efforts to Save the Thirty-Second Advertisement

At the same time that the industry has been attempting new strategies in response to the changing technological and economic environment, it has also been pursuing efforts to save or shore up the thirty-second spot. The growth in alternative strategies of advertising should not suggest that any group within the industry sought the elimination of the thirty-second ad. On the contrary, although newly developed control technologies form one of the most substantial threats to it, different groups in the U.S. and Britain have sought to keep it viable by using emergent technologies. For example, the British Sky Broadcasting satellite service owned by News Corp. developed interactive applications to motivate viewers to stay with content during commercial breaks. In one case, the company enabled viewers to play along with game show contestants while using interactive features to keep track of the viewer's score. The viewer had to keep the set tuned to that channel for the duration of the program in order for the device to remember the score, which decreased the likelihood of channel changing. Similarly, in 2005 U.S. cable provider Time Warner introduced a digital capability on a trial basis which it marketed as "Start-Over." This function allows a viewer to restart a program already in progress from the beginning; however, it does not allow for commercial skipping. Another Sky initiative included the distribution of "loyalty cards" that viewers inserted in their set-top box. The device could monitor the viewer's behavior, and the willingness to stay tuned during commercials yielded rewards for the viewer at area retailers or enabled them to purchase other video content.[62] Significantly, while each of these endeavors offered viewers a service or reward for keeping their sets tuned to channels displaying commercials, none could actually confirm viewership: the messages might have played to empty rooms or to viewers engaged by other media. Still, many have seen the introduction of an added-value proposition for the viewer/consumer as a likely trend for the future, especially as new applications and services create new fees.

Advertisers have also pursued more minor adjustments to the conventional ad, such as experimenting with ten- and ninety-second formats. The ninety-second spot, which allows for narrative development, requires an approach similar to branded entertainment in order to maintain the audience; in turn, the longer form also aids brand building. Advertisers use ten-second ads for different types of messages, such as those that reinforce name recognition.[63] Advertising companies estimated ten-second advertisements to be 75 percent as effective as thirty-second ads, but they cost only 25 percent of the thirty-second rate, which further underscores their attractiveness.[64] In November of 2005, AOL even experimented with five-second "pod puncher" commercials that were positioned at the end of the commercial break.[65]

New technologies outside of the home also figure in supporting the continuation of the thirty-second advertisement. In the fragmented and niche environment of the multi-channel transition, viewers increasingly expected personalization and targeting of content, and new servers and switchers allowed cable systems to similarly target viewers with commercials. By 2005, advertisements already could be customized to particular cable systems and neighborhoods; potentially, they might be even more narrowly targeted. Using the Comcast Spotlight service, 1-800-Flowers.com targeted affluent neighborhoods with floral arrangements costing over one hundred dollars, while viewers located in more economically modest neighborhoods saw advertisements for arrangements costing less than twenty dollars.[66] Likewise, in 2006, targeting technologies allowed fast-food retailer Wendy's to run commercials for chili when the local temperature was less than 60 degrees and commercials for Frosty desserts in warmer temperatures. A late 2006 *New York Times* article reported that "targeted commercials delivered through digital cable systems could have more than 100,000 versions, as advertisers use different songs, punch lines and actors to reach different customers."[67] Tracey Scheppach, vice president and video innovations director at Starcom USA, explained, "It's down to the individual household. It will look much more like direct mail." Targeting both solves the problem of wasting money to reach unlikely consumers and aids the effectiveness of the message by allowing the advertiser to offer more consumer-specific appeals. Advertisers believe consumers are more likely to watch and engage with advertisements particularly relevant to their needs and preferences; thus, they might send dog food commercials only to dog owners or otherwise reach consumers with price-appropriate goods and psychographic appeals.[68]

When combined with interactivity, this kind of personalization allows viewers in the market for particular goods to seek out relevant advertising. An established feature of the TiVo-brand DVR allows advertisers to place long-form advertisements on the box for viewers to access according to their interest, and many digital cable services also include such offerings in their on demand menus. Other technology has offered more interactivity. A system tested by Time Warner allows viewers to request that an agent contact them with a click of the remote following a State Farm Insurance advertisement; it can also enable them to order a pizza from Pizza Hut. Some cable systems offered targeting as early as 2004, but major impact on the advertising sales market was still negligible in 2006. Although cable companies can target as narrowly as the household level, cable systems have traditionally held very little advertising inventory— only about ninety seconds per hour—which greatly limits the number of spots they can sell. Moreover, spots sold by cable systems tend to be populated with cheaply produced local advertisements and thus have been considered undesirable to national advertisers. Cable has had the early lead in adopting targeting technology, but many hope that "channel agnostic" targeting systems can be developed for a variety of applications, including cable wires, broadcast airwaves, satellite, and broadband Internet connection.[69]

Despite the technological ability to target more narrowly defined demographic groups, much remained uncertain about whether privacy laws would be adjusted to allow narrower targeting. Hank Oster, senior vice president of Comcast Spotlight, noted that "Privacy laws are very specific—we are not able to take that list of subscribers and target them by name."[70] Likewise, Forrester analyst Eric Schmitt expected subscriber resistance to targeting and that cable systems would be unwilling to risk losing consumers for what he perceived as a negligible increase in advertising revenue.[71] Many of the emerging technologies have indeed raised privacy concerns, but any substantial legal reconsideration of the effects has yet to begin. Still, advertisers' growing demand for more accountability from the media they purchase suggests that targeting possibilities will continue to be attractive. Forrester Research predicted an estimated 75 percent of national advertisers would cut spending on television commercials by at least 20 percent by 2009 as the availability of advertisement-skipping devices increased.[72] As a result,

Rishad Tobaccowala, executive vice president of Starcom Media Vest Group, predicted "an increased merging of two worlds: the performance-based world of Internet protocol networks with the engaging world of TV and gaming."[73] Such forecasts, which support the notion that thirty-second advertisements will remain viable, also suggest that they will come to be used in new ways.

In effect then, none of the many advertising strategies in use by the end of the multi-channel transition has replaced the thirty-second advertisement; nor is any likely to become the singular advertising strategy of the post-network era. Instead, the proliferation of strategies at the end of the multi-channel transition suggests that a mix of placement, integration, branded entertainment, sponsorship, and the thirty-second spot will continue to exist in a post-network era in which television encompasses a range of conventional, on-demand, and subscription services.

Cultural Consequences of Post-Network Advertising

At the same time television advertising strategies began to diversify and multiply, a variety of new perspectives in critical thinking about the relationship of culture and consumption emerged. Some scholars construed consumption as an empowering activity expressive of agency. Others, pointing to the construction of the "consumer" in industrialized and post-industrialized countries, questioned the nature of such an identity and whether it could be experienced in meaningful ways.[74] Still others explored issues arising from the increasingly niche quality of contemporary media and looked at the consequences of de-emphasizing mass culture in the advertising of goods.[75] While all register the complexity of consumerism in post-Fordist and postmodernist cultures, the redefinition of television at the beginning of the post-network era poses further challenges for the critical evaluation of emergent advertising strategies. Experimentation with placement and integration in texts that maintain thirty-second advertisements clearly suggests an increasing commercialization of television, but with marketing strategies shifting substantially, their specific cultural effects remain uncertain.

The programming created in service of the industry's commercial goals provides the link between television as a commercial enterprise and television as a social force. The expansion in strategies used to finance programming affected other production components, just as the shift from sponsorship to magazine-format advertising affected the types of programming supported by those models. My focus here is on the implications of alternative advertising strategies for the creative output of this resolutely commercial medium. Thus, I am specifically concerned with the ways they have affected the transition from mass to niche audience norms, disrupted long-held industry practices, and created new textual possibilities.

Becoming a Niche Medium

Television's transition from broadcasting to narrowcasting has enormous implications for advertising. Narrowcasting enables advertisers to direct their messages to much more specific demographic and psychographic groups, and as a result, design creative messages that are different from those that would be used in broadcast forums. Studies examining advertising in fragmented media spaces have reached disparate conclusions about the socio-cultural consequences of this shift. Two of these, quite different in approach, are worth singling out: Joseph Turow's treatment of the historical development of fragmentation across advertising media and the transition from mass to target marketing in various media, and Arlene Davila's exploration of the creation of a differentiated Hispanic marketing sector.[76] In emphasizing the consequences of fragmentation on dominant white society, Turow finds the "gated communities" of taste and image culture that result to be a particularly negative development for democratic society.[77] Davila examines the issue from the perspective of Latinos, perhaps the most underrepresented cultural group in U.S. media, and emphasizes the constitutive role of advertising in culture. Instead of viewing Latino-targeted advertising as a means for marginalizing their status in society, she asserts that "the reconstitution of individuals into consumers and populations into markets are central fields of cultural production that reverberate within public understanding of people's place, and hence of their rights and entitlements in a given society."[78] This approach echoes that of Nestor Garcia Canclini, whose work likewise deconstructs the dichotomy between consumers and citizens as an essential aspect of understanding the circulation of culture and capital in a post-Fordist, globalized context.[79]

Many exploring advertising and culture as television transitioned from a mass to niche medium have examined changes in the content of commercial messages. However, advertisements were not the only creative content affected by these adjustments. The transition to niche target marketing bore significant, if subtle, implications for the programming television networks created to collect that audience, as advertisers embraced programs directed to narrower and specific audiences. Target marketing provides economic support for ways of constructing and viewing television that are emerging in the post-network era, including those that render television a subcultural forum.

Opportunities Arising from the Disruption of the Status Quo

The growing threat to established norms of commercial funding and viewer behavior in the early years of the twenty-first century has forced a long-complacent advertising industry to break from conventional practices to a degree absent in the network era and much of the multi-channel transition and created the opportunity to experiment with new strategies—many of which have been chronicled in the preceding pages. Inevitably, some endeavors failed. Nonetheless, advertisers' support of unconventional programming content and their willingness to explore different strategies to reach audiences have in themselves had an effect on perceptions of what might be possible and viable. Here, too, successful cases create opportunities for programming that is unlikely to be produced under the once-dominant thirty-second advertisement model.

Drawing from the study of organizations and innovation, Turow considers how periods of industrial transition can be linked with the creation of unconventional programming.[80] Such transitory periods, which create "cracks" in established organizational operations, disrupt hegemonic relationships and allow new norms to be established.[81] To be sure, this is not always the case. Those with more power can maintain their status, especially when the hierarchies that privilege them continue to seem natural and a matter of "how it has always been." But the scope of change throughout the production process of commercial television at the beginning of the post-network era has been so substantial that new practices have had to emerge and to do so in a manner that allows an uncommon degree of power redistribution.

For example, while the new viability of product placement as an advertising strategy has consequences for programming, it is also shifting power relations behind the scenes. Producers who bring scripts to the networks with advertisers already attached to placement deals not only challenge network sales divisions, but also threaten to usurp their authority and management of advertising dollars. Advertising agencies also gain more control, especially when they develop in-house divisions specifically charged with creating programming into which clients can be integrated. As these new brand integration divisions take on expanded creative roles, previously ancillary jobs such as set dressing also compete for a place in developing shows.

In the post-network environment, advertisers have had the least at stake in continuing to pursue dominant network-era practices, particularly as they steadily came to pay more for less. Frustrated with the status quo and aware of the coming changes resultant from widespread adoption of DVR technologies, advertisers willing to commit part of their budgets to non-traditional strategies have pushed the business out of its complacency. Advertisers reasserted their status as the economic lifeblood of a commercial media system, but shifts in their behavior enabled significant adjustment throughout many other industrial relationships.

Advantages of Multiple Advertising Strategies

In addition to the experimentation and industrial reconfiguration occurring during the recent period of transition, new opportunities have also arisen with advertisers' and networks' willingness to accept a situation in which multiple advertising strategies coexist. It is too early to know how long this environment will continue or what might ensue, but in the near term, a multiplicity of possible financing models is indeed available, and each one creates more possibilities for variation than could develop in the long-dominant singular system.

To illustrate how the co-existence of multiple advertising strategies might lead to a broader diversity of programming, we might begin by looking at the ways that the differences in programming on broadcast, basic cable, and subscription cable can be linked to their different financing structures. In many cases, the differing financial models of subscription and basic cable have enabled the profitable production of series with new ideas or a capacity to speak to particular demographic groups. Whether one focuses on the edgy content of FX's dramas or on the low concept, character-driven shows such as HBO's *Six Feet Under* or *Big Love,* it is clear that such series could not be profitably offered by broadcasters. By 2005, successful subscription cable, basic cable, and prime-time broadcast series exhibited clear distinctions that marked them as characteristic of their distribution outlet. The business model of subscription services mandates that they provide programming of such distinction—whether by measures of quality or value of niche address—that viewers are willing to pay directly for the content, thereby negating the need for advertiser support. Basic cable networks operate on a dual-revenue stream, receiving some financing from subscription fees, while also earning revenue from commercial sales. The subscription income helps offset the lower CPMs they earn and the generally lower advertising fees that result from smaller audiences. Cable networks have consequently sought to develop programming that establishes their narrowly focused brands and allows them to deliver high indexes of particular demographic and psychographic groups of consumers. By contrast, broadcasters are supported only by advertising revenue, so their ability to earn more money depends upon delivering larger audiences. This aspect of their economic model prevented broadcasters from adopting a competitive strategy of too narrowly addressing audiences.

For all the derisive commentary it has garnered, unscripted programming has instigated some valuable innovation in conventional business operations. Since many of these shows incorporate sponsorship or placement fees, they do not require deficit financing. As experiments that originated in unscripted programming come to be repeated in scripted programs, networks are increasingly able to realize value from new and diverse advertising strategies.

Product placement has provided cable networks with additional dollars for production costs that in turn have helped them compete with broadcasters' textual attributes. For cable networks, high-profile programming events have derived value beyond the ratings they achieved. Thus, a miniseries such as SciFi's *5 Days Until Midnight* also raised audience awareness of the network, which was exceptionally valuable in the highly cluttered programming environment. Indeed, by 2005, one breakout-hit series could move a cable network from the tier of relative obscurity to high-profile awareness, as *Trading Spaces* did for TLC, *Queer Eye for the Straight Guy* did for Bravo, and *The Shield* did for FX. And once a cable network achieves substantial cultural awareness, it is much easier to secure the advertising dollars necessary to maximize its niche status through additional programming.

Importantly, the highly competitive leisure environment that characterizes twenty-first century U.S. homes has created a measured negotiation between content and commercialism in television. Here, the situation differs considerably from that of the 1960s. At that time, when television was still the next big thing in home leisure technology, and there were no competitors such as computers, gaming devices, and home video technologies to draw away viewers, these conditions helped enable the resolutely commercial practices of cheap and often uninspired telefilm production of the era. After twenty-five years of audience erosion, broadcast networks were far less cavalier in their attitude toward the audience and recognized that while cheap programming might aid the short-term bottom line, they could not take their viewership for granted.

Two series and one television event that aired in the transitional period of the early twenty-first century indicate how the competitive environment and related shifts in advertising have affected programming. Here, in terms of advertising, the series *The Shield* and *The Days* offer important counterpoints to dominant network-era practices, while Super Bowl XXXVIII illustrates the confusing situation of programming for, and advertising on, a medium in transition.

Cases of Note: The Shield, The Days, and Super Bowl XXXVIII

The Shield debuted on the FX cable network in March 2002. The series provided the network's most high-profile attempt at original series production, and the network supported its premiere with an extensive promotional campaign. Textually, *The Shield* reinvigorated the police drama genre by centering its narrative on a rogue police detective clearly playing outside the bounds of proper procedure. Visually sophisticated and highly stylized, the look of the series matched the unconventionality of its narrative, and critics appropriately hailed the series as the most HBO-influenced show to air outside of a subscription network. *The Shield* pushed the boundaries of established norms of acceptable use of violence and coarse language. Although basic cable networks were not prohibited from airing such content, no network had aired such graphic material in a series.

It was consequently unsurprising that *The Shield* immediately became a target of public advocacy groups concerned about violence and adult themes on television. Trade magazine articles recounted the increasing number of advertisers who withdrew from the series as early episodes of *The Shield* aired. To be sure, the series' location on FX and its post–10:00 p.m. time slot reasonably freed it from fears that it would come under government regulation, but advocacy groups such as the Parent's Television Council pursued a successful strategy of exerting pressure on advertisers through threats of boycotts and negative publicity in order to starve the series of the commercial support necessary for survival. Thus, many advertisers did exit during early weeks of the series, but as FX continued to air new episodes and audience numbers not only remained steady but continued to grow, this trend was reversed. FX Networks' president of ad sales, Bruce Lefkowitz, explained that despite the polarizing tendency of shows such as *The Shield,* they also delivered a "demographic that is often MIA. With *The Shield, Nip/Tuck* and *Rescue Me,* we can reach an underserved audience that isn't generally catered to by the mass market. Advertisers see that FX has those early adopters, the trendsetters—people with spending power who tend to get drawn to our authentic, unique programming."[82] The series proved successful in drawing otherwise difficult-to-reach upscale male audiences, and by the end of the season new advertisers stepped in to replace those who had exited. *The Shield* and other FX shows did remain on many advertisers' "do not buy" lists; still, the network was able to fully sell its inventory despite the unabashedly mature content of its original series.[83] *The Shield* was not the first or only series that violated norms of acceptable content, but it is meaningful in the degree to which it did so and survived—and even thrived.

The Shield thus indicated some advertisers' desire to be associated with distinctive content, as well as their willingness to support programming that willfully offended some viewers. Like much of the programming produced in a niche-focused media environment, *The Shield* exhibited a substantial amount of "edge," meaning that it clearly defined the boundaries of its intended audiences and deliberately excluded some tastes and sensibilities.[84] Such a strategy is clearly the opposite of that which seeks the broadest possible audience through the least objectionable programming, as was characteristic of the network era. The commercial viability of the newer strategy—in such an extreme case—is a significant indicator of the changing dynamics of advertising at the beginning of the post-network era. Whereas conventional wisdom suggested that the protest of advocacy groups would result not only in advertisers pulling support from the series but also the end for the show, as had been the case in the network era, the old rules have been rewritten. In the new environment consisting of fragmented audiences and niche-programming strategies, edgy programming produced in clear affront to some viewers can more than succeed: it can become particularly attractive to certain advertisers and accrues value from distinguishing itself so clearly in the cluttered and intensely competitive programming field.

If *The Shield* indicated shifting norms related to the transition from broadcasting to narrowcasting, then *The Days* offered a case of programming that emerged from non-network-era industrial practices and advertising strategies. *The Days* was a limited-run, six episode series aired on ABC during the summer of 2004. Named for the family at the center of the hour-long drama, the series involved an experiment with a new— or rather revisited—economic model for scripted television. MindShare North America, a media agency owned by the WPP group, created and funded the series that was produced by Tollin/Robbins Productions. ABC paid nothing for the series, and ABC and MindShare equally split the advertising inventory in the program. MindShare, which represents Unilever and other major advertisers, placed the products of some clients within the show, but primarily viewed the series as an opportunity to create the type of program in which its clients sought to include commercial messages. MindShare clients also received advertising exclusivity in the show—meaning no products that compete with those of the MindShare clients could advertise in it.[85]

Here, again, long-standing assumptions—this time about the effects of such an arrangement on content—were overturned. According to those assumptions, such a situation wherein an advertising agency developed a family drama in which its clients would be comfortable placing commercials could only result in a banal narrative both devoid of controversy and wholly supportive of dominant ideology and traditional "family values."[86] This, however, was not at all the case. The six hours of *The Days* chronicled a family challenged by the crisis of teen pregnancy; by a father's lack of fulfillment in the corporate world, his decision to quit his job, and his subsequent unemployment; by a working mother's questioning of her life's path, including having had children at all, and then her struggle with a late-in-life pregnancy; by an unsociable son experiencing the traumas of being a teen; and by an exceptionally bright—and similarly misfit—adolescent son who experiences panic attacks. The series suffered some from its attempt to tell a normal season's worth of stories in just six episodes, but the narrative certainly featured complexly drawn characters and a compelling story.

The Days thus indicates that the type of content advertisers seek is not necessarily limited to tried-and-true formulas. Although perceptions of family-friendly programming may continue to be dominated by the saccharine 1960s-era conceptions, by 1999, major television advertisers had become so frustrated with broadcasters' inability to create compelling programming that could be shared by parents and children that they created the Family Friendly Programming Forum initiative, which provides development money for pilot scripts.[87] Significantly, by 2006, The WB's *Gilmore Girls* was the most successful series to come out of the initiative. Based on the relationship between a teen mother and her now teenaged daughter, the series hardly suggests that a conservative interpretation of family values resides at the core of advertisers' thinking.

The *Days*, like *The Shield*, indicates how a paradigmatic transformation of business models and the introduction of alternative advertising strategies can enable the production of narratives that have been hitherto absent from television. To date, *The Days* remains the only prime-time scripted example of both a barter arrangement—in which the network trades advertising time for content—and a situation in which a media agency produces a series, although another is in production (*October Road*), and similar arrangements have become increasingly common in unscripted production (*The Restaurant, Blow-Out*). Importantly, the distinctive financing and product placement of *The Days* remained unobtrusive and likely went unnoticed by those unfamiliar with industry matters. A full-scale shift to a dominant model of agency funding might provide cause for concern, but it was more likely that the competitive environment would support a multiplicity of financing models rather than replace a monolithic network-era process with a new monolith. Here, too, a competitive environment that supported multiple financing models allowed for greater programming innovation.

Advertiser-initiated programming may help disrupt the tendency of networks and production companies to be overly conservative in anticipating the content many advertisers will support, and such programming was consequently particularly valuable in the period of redefinition suggested by the case of *The Shield*. Networks and producers had long been accustomed to developing "planed" programming—that is, programs without edge—and were still more likely to self-censor on the side of pleasing broad audiences than attempting to reach more narrowly targeted ones. The creation of series such as *The Days* from outside of conventional programming and funding models has allowed networks to expand their perception of the range of alternatives in existence.

Importantly, viewers' willingness to pay for programming such as that produced by HBO and Showtime has similarly informed the industry about the degree to which the opportunity to view well-executed and compelling narratives devoid of commercials presents an attractive proposition. Veronis Suhler Stevenson's annual 2004 Communication Industry Forecast and Report found that for the first time, consumers spent more money accessing media content directly than advertisers did on ad-supported media.[88] Industry journalist Joe Mandese reported that while the difference was relatively small, it suggested a "highly symbolic tipping point for the ad industry because it indicates that the fundamental economic model for the U.S. media industry has shifted from Madison Avenue to consumers themselves."[89] Such a shift in financing has important implications for what types of stories are produced; it also suggests that viewers' attitudes toward media content is undergoing a fundamental change.

Few televised events continue to reach a mass audience, except perhaps the Super Bowl. As much a high-profile advertising event as it is a championship game for the football league, the Super Bowl remains the one night each year when U.S. television revisits its network-era composition. Yet, the cultural meltdown following the 2004 Super Bowl indicated the complexity of programming for a medium that shifted between niche and mass tastes. The AOL Super Bowl XXXVIII Half-time Show, produced by MTV Productions, adhered to a niche era aesthetic and included a sexually charged performance from Janet Jackson and Justin Timberlake. The now infamous "wardrobe malfunction" that resulted in the momentary broadcast of Janet Jackson's nipple to an audience of eighty-some million potential viewers led to a multi-year campaign against broadcast indecency that coincided with a particularly contested American presidential election. The inclusion of advertisements for erectile dysfunction medications, with their mandated graphic warnings, and a number of ads featuring crass humor also added to the sentiment that the evening's presentation was inappropriate.

Although the half-time incident led to introspection about a range of television and radio content—much of which was targeted only to adults —the particular misstep of the Super Bowl show resulted from coordinators' forgetting the family audience and broad appeal of the event. By 2004, the Super Bowl arguably remained the only scheduled such event of the television year, and the incident illustrated how extensively television embodied the new norms of niche media. Advertisers, networks, and even the audience were well aware of the significant number of viewers the event drew, but those same advertisers and network planners disregarded the fact that such moments demanded a different aesthetic from that which characterized their more niche-focused appeals. The postmortem discussions of the 2005 Super Bowl telecast, which included a much more subdued half-time show featuring aging rocker Paul McCartney and commercials devoid of the sophomoric humor that characterized those of the previous year, noted the marked change in the tone of the event. Many even complained that the response of planners was too extreme and that they erred in being overly cautious. Regardless of the merits of such judgments, what these complaints failed to acknowledge was the dilemma such occasions present in their requirement to entertain a diverse audience accustomed to a medium that now ordinarily targets particular tastes and sensibilities. Broadcast networks—which are supported only by advertisers—suffer most acutely from the schizophrenia of attempting to bridge the chasm between the mass and niche possibilities of the medium. Although many cable channels are nearly as widely available as broadcast networks, the programming mission that derives from their financial structure does not require them to produce programming likely to encounter a broad audience.

Conclusion

An old advertising industry bromide attributed to both Lord Leverhulme of Lever Brothers and department store magnate John Wanamaker claims the men said that they knew they wasted half of their advertising budget, they just didn't know which half. The quip acknowledges that advertisers long have been aware of the inefficiency of their promotional endeavors, and yet, history illustrates that they have pursued them nonetheless. The increasing use of product placement and integration, as well as new experiments with advertiser-created programming, all suggest that the existing model was failing. Advertisers' willingness to devote some of their budgets to strategies other than the thirty-second advertisement indicated the level of crisis they perceived in existing models and the sense that this was not a passing fad, but the beginning of changes that could not be avoided.

Despite the similarity of current strategies such as placement and sponsorship to those that were dominant before the network era, the renewed use of these methods does not require a return to the power relations that characterized the earlier period. As existing practices eroded, a realignment of power occurred, privileging those best positioned to compete given the composition of the industry at that moment. Advertisers' willingness to explore new financing structures offered an initial salvo to which other players responded. The negotiation of the interrelationships among and the duties of network sales divisions, advertising agency media divisions, and talent/product placement firms illustrate the degree to which the industry was in flux. Various groups rushed to stake a claim in product placement and integration as the lucrative nature of these practices became evident. Network sales divisions, previously the gate-keepers who determined whose commercial message got on the air and when, saw their role threatened when producers such as *Survivor* creator Mark Burnett came to networks with programs already integrated with support and financing. Network sales divisions began competing to maintain their status of delivering the golden goose as producers and various agencies attempted to usurp the power afforded to those who control the advertising dollars. Likewise, advertising agencies developed placement specialists, old prop companies morphed into placement contractors, and talent agencies attempted to leverage their existing position in this area of the industry.

Situations such as this represent key moments of crisis when conventional industrial practices and power roles can be challenged. Different workers rarely had the opportunity to redefine their task within the broader production process, as entrenched entities and status quo operations normally prevent change because of the threat of lost power that change poses. As in other sectors of the U.S. television industry, the erosion of norms and practices during the multi-channel transition created a situation in which the dominant processes faltered and created the opportunity for a reallocation of power among entities related to advertising and advertising strategies. Toward the end of the multi-channel transition, such opportunities were particularly important to those whose roles and relative power within the system of production were enhanced or diminished, but these adjustments also affected programming by creating new gatekeepers and allowing for a reallocation of content and audience priorities. The extent to which status quo industrial relationships were disrupted by this environment of innovation should not be underestimated. Where the conventional power relations that had so long stood as barriers to change had come down, fear of being shut out of the newly redefined industry motivated further innovation.

Very little critical scholarship has explored the cultural implications of differences among media that consumers pay for directly versus those that are advertiser supported—particularly within a single medium. As financing models diversify and co-exist, we need a much more comprehensive understanding of the significance of different payment methods to viewers' use and enjoyment of programming. Subscription television— a leading application of the direct-pay model—has defied many foundational assumptions of television's defining attributes. Indeed, it is in some ways more like media such as magazines or even mobile phones than advertiser-supported television, and the video-on demand-environment offers viewers even more opportunities to escape advertising through transactional payment. The availability of such options and patterns of viewer use—what types of viewers choose to pay for what types of content—are important factors to consider in studying the nature and effects of transactional television.

Exploring the differences between television that audiences are willing to pay for and television supported by some advertising means is but one of many new research areas resulting from developments of the multichannel transition. Many of these developments require substantial research into viewer uses, behaviors, and preferences. They also give rise to many questions which have yet to be answered about the consequences of the erosion of mass audience advertising opportunities, the social implications of narrowly targeted advertising, and the effects of expansion in placement and branding on consumption. The continued process of transition allows only for conjecture about how the erosion of mass media affects Fordist models of consumption. It is also too soon to know the full range of textual consequences that results from eliminating the thirty-second advertisement norm and the social ramifications of narrowly defining consumer groups not only in programming, but in advertising as well. What we do know is that changes in program financing and in assumptions about the audience scale necessary for commercial viability have played key roles in determining the kind of programming that can be produced.

The diversity in advertising practices that emerged at the beginning of the twenty-first century indicates the extensive changes the television industry was undergoing. While network-era advertising practices had provided advertisers with decreasing returns for a long time, the continued supply of capital from this sector discouraged change. Advertisers' willingness to finance experiments with different advertising strategies was the first domino to·fall in the chain of events advancing transformation, and it influenced many subsequent aspects of production and financing. Different advertising strategies led to different business models; different business models led to different funding possibilities; different funding possibilities led to different programming; different programming redefined the medium's relationship with viewers and the culture at large. Changing advertising strategies consequently indicated a vital development in the broader process of redefining television.

6

Recounting the Audience
Integrating New Measurement Techniques and Technologies

> Finding out whether *C.S.I.* beats *Desperate Housewives* is just the beginning. Change the way you count, for instance, and you can change where the advertising dollars go, which in turn determines what shows are made and what shows are then renewed. Change the way you count, and potentially you change the comparative value of entire genres (news versus sports, drama versus comedies) as well as entire demographic segments (young versus old, men versus women, Hispanic versus black) . . . Change the way you measure America's culture consumption, in other words, and you change America's culture business. And maybe even the culture itself.
> —Jon Gertner, *The New York Times Magazine*[1]

For most of U.S. television history, Nielsen Media Research provided the common currency supporting the entire economic framework of the U.S. commercial television industry. The industry trusted Nielsen as an independent player—and remunerated it well for supplying the agreed-upon standard audience measurement values upon which the industry allocated millions, and eventually billions, of advertising dollars each year. At first glance, audience measurement may seem a secondary and insignificant business relative to what is commonly thought of as the "television industry," but as Gertner's remarks in the epigraph suggest, adjustments in audience measurement and research norms have the potential to significantly reconfigure a commercial media system. Audience measurement is also increasingly important during periods of industrial change, and so it is particularly vital for forming an understanding of the emerging post-network era.

The role of audience measurement in television production became particularly controversial in the late years of the multi-channel transition as industry leader Nielsen Media Research endeavored to introduce technological upgrades that contributed to the reallocation of advertising dollars at the same time that new distribution methods and advertising strategies required impartial measurement for validation. The existing paradigm of audience measurement proved increasingly inadequate to the variation characteristic of post-network television. This chapter consequently considers the crucial role of audience measurement and developments in this area during the tumultuous early 2000s, as well as the effects that adjustments in this sector have had on the production of television. In a statement that underscores the uncertainty and sense of transition gripping the long-dominant measurement service as well as the industry, Nielsen CEO Susan Whiting commented in 2005 that the next three to five years would bring more substantial change to the television industry than had taken place in the previous fifty years.[2]

Network-Era Audience Measurement

The shift to magazine-format advertising generated a need for audience measurement and spurred the development of the related yet independent audience measurement business. As advertising agencies became less involved in program production and more involved in determining ideal locations for a sponsor's message early in the network era, they carefully evaluated the increasingly sophisticated audience data to determine whether they achieved value in their purchases.

U.S. television history features a range of systems, companies, and methods that provided increased precision as technological tools and the viable approaches to measurement expanded. From the advent of audience measurement in the 1920s, when announcers requested that audience members send letters and postcards, through Hooperatings, Audimeters, and People Meters, the techniques have grown increasingly sophisticated and yielded ever more information about the habits, behaviors, and characteristics of the viewers at home. U.S. television audience measurement has relied mainly on sampling in order to derive the audience size estimates upon which advertisers base the value of their purchases. During the 1960s and 1970s, Nielsen introduced the Storage Instantaneous Audimeter, a device that daily sent viewing information to the company's computers using phone lines and made national daily ratings available by 1973.[3] At this point, audimeters offered no information about the demographic attributes of the audience, but Nielsen could triangulate the audimeter's information about the stations sets were tuned to with diary reports that provided some sense of the audience composition. By the early 1980s the Nielsen sample included approximately 1,700 audimeter homes and a rotating panel of approximately 850 diary respondents.[4] Nielsen introduced its Nielsen Homevideo Index (NHI) in 1980 to provide measurement of cable, pay cable, and VCRs, and the NHI began offering daily cable ratings in 1982. Nielsen dominated the measurement of national network television and competed with Arbitron in measuring local markets at the beginning of the multi-channel transition.

Nielsen made a substantial technological advance before network-era norms entered crisis with its transition to the national People Meter sample in 1987. The initiative was a competitive move required by the entry of Audits of Great Britain (AGB) into the U.S. market and its implementation of a similar technology. AGB helped create a competitive environment that allowed for innovation, but the industry was unwilling to pay for two sets of numbers, and AGB's competitive efforts were short lived. People Meters represented significant advancement over the preceding technique, but no adjustment in audience measurement norms occurs without substantial controversy. Any change in method—with its attendant change in results—dearly costs those whose audience had been overestimated. This reality leads to protest even if the new data provide more precise results. The nearly constant changes in technology and distribution that characterize the end of the multi-channel transition were thus especially troubling for Nielsen, as they required onerous adjustments in measurement techniques. At the same time, though, the industry's uncertainty about emerging advertising strategies, distribution windows, and ways people were using television increased Nielsen's centrality, because all sectors of the industry were eager for information about audience behavior in the new context.

The implementation of the People Meter at the start of the multi-channel transition resulted in growing pains as the networks and advertisers knew such a significant methodological shift would likely indicate some disparity from the established system. The networks did not offer audience guarantees on advertising purchased in the upfront for the 1987–88 season because of the uncertainty of the new measurement system, and CBS in particular experienced significant audience loss because the previous methods tended to over-count older viewers who disproportionately favored CBS.[5] The People Meters indicated that fewer audience members were watching broadcast networks, but did not find these audience members to be watching something else instead. People Meters reported a 5 percent drop in the number of female daytime viewers, a 3.7 percent decrease in broadcasters' prime-time viewing, significantly smaller audiences for many popular programs such as *The Cosby Show* (10 percent in the case of *Cosby*), and higher ratings for some late-night shows.[6]

Most of the industry-shifting features characteristic of the multi-channel transition were fairly rudimentary at the time of the introduction of the People Meter, and audience erosion due to cable and VCR penetration had not yet significantly reconfigured audience distribution norms. The People Meters arrived the year after advertising spending dropped for the first time in fifteen years, which compounded anxiety about the measurement switch. Broadcasters were generally nonplussed about the results, but there was little recourse available. CBS dropped Nielsen and briefly opted for the meter service of competitor AGB, which did not show as significant audience decreases; ABC and NBC threatened to do the same, and ABC signed only monthly contracts with Nielsen instead of year-long commitments during the People Meter implementation.[7]

The backlash against the introduction of the People Meter was minimal compared to the industry response to measurement adjustments once the multi-channel transition was more definitively established. The resulting audience fragmentation created a competitive environment in which fractions of ratings points meant the difference between a network ranking first or fourth and affected the allocation of millions of dollars in advertising. According to an estimate produced by the Broadcast Cable Financial Management Association, by 2005 a prime-time rating point on a Big Three network was worth $400 million per year.[8] By the beginning of the twenty-first century, researchers simply could not test new methods and implement them quickly enough to keep up with industrial changes.

The influx of new technologies such as DVRs complicated established in-home measurement systems and required the development of entirely new protocols in order for DVR owning households to be included among sample homes. Historically, the Nielsen box derived its measurement by registering the frequency of the television signal in order to determine the channel being viewed. This technology does not work in an era of DVRs because even when a viewer watches content live, the signal still goes through the DVR, which constantly emits the same frequency.

Nielsen consequently needed to develop an entirely new device, the A/P (active/passive) meter, which reads a code embedded in the audio track of programming rather than the tuning frequency.

One of the most challenging aspects of audience measurement during the multi-channel transition resulted from the intermediary nature of new technologies and distribution systems. The sampling techniques that most audience research relied upon were based on a fairly uniform nationwide availability of technologies and programming, and thus reflected a network-era experience with television. The arrival of varied programming tiers of cable channels challenged this system as U.S. television homes began having highly discrepant access to technology and programming and consequently began using television in significantly different ways. Although the A/P meter solved the problem of DVR use, programming on video-on-demand systems initially did not include the "audio watermark" used by the device. The nation's many cable providers also limited access to the proprietary data recorded by their set top boxes, which reduced the informational gain offered by this new technology. Video on demand desperately needed to establish measurement matrices to prove its economic viability, but the lack of shared and consistent information further confounded knowledge about use. Likewise, the erosion of the thirty-second advertisement's dominance and the new advertising strategies that became increasingly common required the creation of new methods and matrices to determine value and pricing.

Despite these challenges to sampling, more information about second-by-second viewing have become accessible as more homes subscribed to digital cable systems and used DVRs. Some of these new technologies and services make available census data of use or a record of all actual use, rather than relying on a sample. This is a substantial adjustment from the long-dominant norm, although the initial census measurements did not offer as precise and robust demographic information as Nielsen's sampling systems and were limited to those early adopters of technologies such as DVRs and digital cable. In addition to changes within the traditional television industry, the continued growth of Internet advertising has concerned networks and led them to demand more of audience measurement services. According to Jon Mandel, chairman of MediaCom US, in 2006, "The research has finally gotten to the point where we can do deals that are based on the advertising actually working. The television industry has woken up to 'the way to beat [new media] is you prove it works as well if not better than other media.' We have finally been able to hit a new level of advertising measurement."[9] Although changes in audience measurement have occurred throughout television history and the data supplied by measurement services have often been disputed, by the early 2000s, the scope of changes within the television industry and throughout the broader media environment earned audience measurement an even more central and contested status in the industry's evolution.

Any one change in the measurement environment represents an enormous challenge to audience research norms and requires exceptional resources in response. But as these challenges confounded research firms' current plans, more threatening forces have gathered on the horizon with the emergence of the post-network era. The arrival of cross-platform media delivery, or "television" content delivered via the Internet, by mobile phone, etc, would render television-only measurement technologies obsolete, especially once audiences embraced the platform "agnosticism" many predicted. Data about use of these new technologies and the effectiveness of commercial messages transmitted through them was vital to engender the confidence of advertisers to leave legacy models of commercial message delivery. As the measurement incumbent and monopolist, Nielsen was set to play a pivotal role in charting the future of television.

A Lesson in the Politics of Measurement: Introducing the Local People Meter

Many accused Nielsen of complacency as adjustments in the industry compounded in the mid-2000s, but Nielsen had been making steady changes since the beginning of the decade. Nielsen changed counting methods and began weighting their sample in the fall of 2003 in response to census shifts and requests from some sectors of the industry. But then the industry responded with a torrent of criticism when it appeared young men had all but disappeared from the television audience that autumn and quickly blamed Nielsen. While the networks cried foul, media buyers noted the season featured few new programs likely to attract men and that the count might address the suspected move of the demographic to cable and video games. Eventually the young men were found—after many new programs in 2004 distinctly targeted the demographic—but this public attention to Nielsen was just the beginning of the firestorm that continued as Nielsen implemented its automated Local People Meter (LPM) technology in New York and Los Angeles in 2003.[10]

Nielsen introduced the Local People Meter as evidence of the fracturing network-era business model became widely apparent and anxiety about the future of the industry raged in all sectors. The LPM marked the shift from active, diary-based local measurement to more passive, meter-monitored measurement of local markets. Technologically, the LPM is similar to the People Meter Nielsen had used for their national sample since the late 1980s. The key advance of the LPM is that, in contrast to the People Meter, which dealt with a sample that was representative nationally, the new device provides accurate measurements of particular local markets. The mechanized LPM system has also pushed the industry further toward year-round measurement, as opposed to focusing on the quarterly "sweeps" periods used in diary-based surveys of local markets. Nielsen began a test of the technology in Boston in 2002 and completed the measure in 2003, at which point it announced plans to rollout the technology in the top ten Designated Market Areas (DMAs) over the next two years.[11]

The initial rollout, particularly in New York, garnered substantial negative publicity and even congressional inquiry as a result of differences in audience behavior reported by the LPMs. Much of the concern centered on the discrepancy between diaries and LPMs in reporting minority viewing (African American and Hispanic) as broadcasters that traditionally dominated in reaching these audiences, such as FOX and UPN, earned substantially lower ratings. In response, some industry players, specifically News Corp., engaged in a particularly belligerent public relations campaign aimed at discrediting Nielsen. The creation of the News Corp.–funded "Don't Count Us Out" coalition made the new measurement technology a hot-button political issue by framing it in terms of racial disenfranchisement. Nielsen also received substantial complaints and faced a lawsuit from Univision for adjustments in its procedures for counting Hispanic households in Los Angeles.

Such developments make it very apparent that advances in measurement can be politically precarious. Nonetheless, researchers believed that in comparison with the diary method it replaced, LPMs more accurately reported the full range of programming viewers watched, including that observed while channel-surfing. Many speculated that diary-writers underestimated the viewing done while surfing and were more likely to remember to write down well-known shows that were more commonly found on broadcast networks—thereby increasing the audience estimates of broadcast shows and decreasing those of cable.[12] The new methods generally indicated greater viewing of cable and decreased viewing of broadcast—results broadcasters were neither interested in knowing about or funding. For example, while LPMs found fewer African American audience members watching FOX than the diaries had, the LPMs also reported a 180 percent increase in total day viewing of BET and reported more than 100 percent increases in the number of African Americans viewing cable networks ESPN, LMN, Telefutura, and Starz.[13]

Despite the increased precision of LPMs, it is unlikely that Nielsen will utilize them beyond the top twenty-five or fifty markets—out of 210 nationwide—because of the cost of this measurement system and the inability of smaller market stations to afford the resulting expense of a LPM-based report. Although Nielsen introduced LPMs in New York, Los Angeles, Boston, Chicago, and San Francisco by October of 2004, it pushed back implementation goals for the entire top ten until 2006; this goal was achieved in June of that year, by which point Philadelphia, Washington, Detroit, Dallas, and Atlanta also offered LPM measurement.[14] The Media Ratings Council (MRC), an independent oversight organization, initially withheld support for the LPM technology, but granted conditional approval of the New York and Los Angeles samples on July 30, 2004.[15] The conditional approval marked a turning point as detractors began to accept the inevitability of the LPM implementation. News Corp. and its coalition shifted their focus and resources toward encouraging a new competitor to join the field, and in early 2005 the Media Ratings Council advocated for the formation of an industry consortium charged with finding better measurement techniques.[16]

For the most part, members of the Madison Avenue advertising community have remained out of the political fray and focused more on measurement issues arising from DVR adoption and the potential of the Portable People Meter.[17] Advertisers have allocated their most substantial budgets to national buys guaranteed on national audiences, so the shift in measuring local markets has not been as pressing an issue as for other sectors of the industry. Yet, this adjustment at the local level has significant implications for the networks because, although "national," they derive much of their income from their locally owned and operated affiliates—most of which are located in the large markets shifting to the LPM.

Other Measurement Innovations

The amount of public criticism Nielsen endured as a result of the LPM seems curious, considering how small an improvement it represented relative to more radical developments in measurement technology. In effect, the LPM involved a linear advancement from norms established during the network era. In other words, the LPM allowed Nielsen to maintain established measurement practices, but to do them better. At the same time that Nielsen pushed ahead with the LPM in a way that did little to account for the chaos increasingly challenging the television business model, it and other companies also attempted to account for various technological and programming developments that were transforming the industry. From 1998 through 2006, Nielsen was involved in an endeavor instigated by Arbitron to develop a Portable People Meter that would better measure the broad range of media that viewers encounter in and out of the home—a much more revolutionary development in measurement norms.

Portable People Meters (PPM) are the size of a beeper. Those being measured wear them on their belt throughout the day and then dock the device at night in a unit that relays usage information back to central servers. Arbitron engineers developed a system that allows the company to embed inaudible codes in the audio portion of media and entertainment content, and the PPM registers these codes as an indication of the content participants hear and, by extrapolation, see.[18] This allows the device to record in a variety of out-of-home contexts, such as cars, elevators, and other public locations, ranging from taverns to movie theaters, as well as including friends' homes. The limitation of Nielsen's methods to in-home viewing always had been a problem, but the ubiquity and variety of contemporary out-of-home media devices has exacerbated it and increased the need for measures of the whole media field users encounter everyday. A study of adult television viewing conducted in 2005 by the Total TV Audience Monitor revealed that forty-four million adults watched television in unmeasured, out-of-home locations each week—a figure that suggests the sizable audience missed by domestic-based measurement technologies.[19]

Although Nielsen continues in its efforts to account for this out-of-home audience, it dropped out of the partnership with Arbitron in March 2006, choosing not to be part of a joint venture to deploy the PPM technology commercially.[20] Instead, Nielsen suggested it may license the technology as part of the "portfolio strategy" it announced in early 2006 as it began identifying core principles for measuring television in its increasingly multifaceted forms and spaces.[21] Later that year, Nielsen also announced its Anytime Anywhere Media Measurement plan (A2/M2), which endeavors to "follow the video." The plan charted Nielsen's intended future with a number of bold initiatives: to create a panel of four hundred video iPod users to track the programs they download and watch; to integrate the company's television data with its NetRatings unit that measures Internet use and viewing; to track video usage on mobile phones and portable devices; to switch to LPM measurement in the top twenty-five markets; to develop cost-effective meters for midsize markets; to add digital set-top box data to its measurement arsenal; and to completely eliminate hand-written diaries.[22] The bold innovation of the A2/M2 plan has been desperately needed, and thus far it has been well-received by the industry. But announcing the plan was much easier than developing and implementing its many facets—a process that was initially scheduled to take place over the coming five years.

But even before the A2/M2 plan, others in the measurement industry —often in conjunction with Nielsen—imagined a research nirvana such as that embodied by "Project Apollo." Apollo, a joint venture undertaken by Procter & Gamble, Arbitron, and the Nielsen Company (of which Nielsen Media Research is a subsidiary), expanded the potential of PPMs by having PPM users correlate their media consumption data with records of their purchases.[23] The involvement of Procter & Gamble, the nation's biggest mass marketer, reflected the increasing desire for return on investment data among advertisers and their recognition that the media environment had changed substantially enough that advertisers needed to know more about actual consumption practices rather than simply finding out whether audiences saw advertisements. Announced in November 2004, Apollo was not without precedent. ScanAmerica, a joint venture of Arbitron and Sales Area Marketing Inc. developed a meter in the mid-1980s that merged television-viewing data with household purchases, but the meter was discontinued in the early 1990s.[24] Although the costs and level of participation required by Apollo make it unlikely that it will ever serve as the industry measurement standard, a successful version of the system could still provide advertisers with information about buyer behavior that would substantially reconfigure how they use media to deploy their messages. Commenting on the Apollo initiative, Wharton marketing professor David Reibstein reflected,

"There will be some people who—correctly—will say, 'Let's not panic. The sky has not fallen down.' The answer is they are right; it hasn't. But all the signs are there that this is the beginning of a time when we will have to do things a lot differently than before."[25]

The technological and industrial shifts of the multi-channel transition led to substantial adjustments in both the type of audience research available and the role of such information in the economic transactions of the industry. Changes in the advertising business, including the conglomeration of its players, resulted in an increase of proprietary research and created greater economies of scale that enabled media research divisions to spread their costs across more clients, and thus fund increasingly detailed research in-house or through commission. Joe Uva, president of media buying agency Omnicom explains, "We're developing more customized and proprietary measures on a client-by-client, case-by-case, and even medium-by-medium basis. We're less focused on comparing media choices than ever before and more interested in understanding what consumers are doing and how we can use proprietary insights to help drive our clients' business."[26] Reflecting on the changing environment in 2004, former FCC commissioner Dennis Patrick acknowledged that television programs might reach fewer audience members, but that advertisers and marketers knew more about those viewers than ever before, and that that knowledge increased the value of those audiences.[27] Less optimistic about the expanding availability of research, veteran market researcher Leo Bogart countered that "More research data and more complex ways of manipulating them on the computer will make media buyers better informed but won't necessarily make them more intelligent."[28]

In addition to Nielsen's measurement of audience size and buying agencies' proprietary studies for specific clients, a third type of research has also grown increasingly sophisticated. Companies such as Mediamark Research Inc. (MRI) and Simmons Market Research Bureau have produced broad surveys of psychographic and attitudinal measures biannually that media agencies can cross-tabulate to learn ever more intricate information about their intended buyers.[29] The computer age has enabled agencies to look far deeper than the demographic features such as age, gender, and income that were long standard in evaluating audiences. For example, a Simmons study released in 2003 provided an index of the average weight of the audience members of various prime-time programs— data perhaps relevant to packaged-food advertisers and those selling diet products—while other research firms have sought to establish new matrices such as levels of viewer engagement, involvement, and loyalty.[30]

Such studies may indicate the truth of both Patrick's and Bogart's claims, but none has yet attained the gold standard envisioned by Project Apollo. Advertisers have spent billions of dollars each year despite the fact that there has been little definitive data to explain why and how advertising influences buying behavior. The existing system of evaluating advertising based on the number of people watching the show in which it was embedded developed because of technological possibilities of the network era. Since then, new technologies enabled more direct and precise measurements, such as that of audience size and composition during commercials, but advertisers have continued to seek measurements that directly link their dollars with the number of goods moved off the shelf. Such a desire is by no means new or particular to the arrival of a post-network era, but changes throughout the production process increase the likelihood of attaining its fulfillment.

Adjustments in Existing Practices

In addition to prompting innovation in measurement technologies and methodologies, the challenges of fragmentation forced audience researchers to further refine their techniques. As audience members spread to a greater variety of television channels, sample-based audience studies required increases in sample size and the inclusion of audience members who had not been represented before for various reasons. As advertisers sought more particularized data, refinements in methodology could help reduce margins of error and make findings more precise and were important because smaller and smaller differentials separated ratings winners and losers. Nielsen increased its sample size beginning early in the multichannel transition in order to provide more reliable information for networks with smaller distribution and audiences as well as greater detail about the composition of that audience.

Another endeavor to better measure more of the viewing done by its sample included what Nielsen termed "extended home viewing." This initiative sought to incorporate viewing that occurred in domestic settings not currently measured by the service. One component of the initiative measured the viewing of college-age members of Nielsen families who resided in college housing during much of the year. As of 2003, census figures estimated that 7 percent of the 18–24-year-old population lived in dormitories, and Nielsen had never included this viewing in its sample.[31] The outcome of the preliminary study found significantly higher viewing among this group than expected, with an average of 221 minutes per day, and notably, this group often viewed with visitors. Additionally, the college students watched ad-supported cable over broadcast networks by nearly a two-to-one margin.[32] Although college students had been counted in the Nielsen sample previously, no viewing was attributed to them when away from the family home, which depressed the usage levels of this particularly advertiser-coveted group. Nielsen began regularly including college students living away from home in February 2007.[33]

Another part of extended home viewing involved measuring viewing that took place in a family's second home. In 2003, Nielsen confirmed that 11 percent of its national viewer sample maintained such homes—homes where it had never measured viewing.[34] Nielsen's pilot study found very different habits among this group with 48.6 percent of viewing spent on broadcast, 34.1 percent on cable, and a notable 11.6 percent on PBS.[35] Amount of time spent viewing was low among this sample, and since the median age of sixty of heads of these households made it less likely that advertisers would be as interested in maintaining this survey, Nielsen announced no plans for continuation. Much other relevant viewing—such as that done in hotels—remained unmeasured by the home-based People Meters.

Due to its domination of U.S. ratings, Nielsen was a frequent whipping post for networks and advertisers whenever the economics of their businesses shifted in negative ways. Towards the end of the multi-channel transition, the further changes facing the industry and their consequences for media measurement services were difficult to anticipate, but it is likely that the monopolization of U.S. ratings by a single company contributed to its lack of preparedness at the dawn of a new age of television. The lack of competition within the field of audience measurement discouraged innovation until innovation became imperative, and the clients who fund audience research did not want to face the additional costs of experimental new services. Nielsen had no reason to develop additional services until absolutely necessary because no competitor threatened to provide a better method, a more precise report of in- and out-of-home viewing, or an inclusion of DVR and VOD audiences.

The challenges in audience measurement faced by the television industry during the shift to the post-network era are not so much the result of Nielsen's decisions as they are a consequence of the industry's historic willingness to accept a ratings service monopoly. But Nielsen's status is even more complicated. At times it has seemed to exist as joint-industry committee—or a collaboratively developed body tasked with industry oversight—an option preferred in European media markets and enabled by their different approach to anti-trust and collusion laws.[36] This awkward status of the company contributed to the politicization of the LPM controversy and to heightening agency and network frustration with not being able to keep up with changing audience uses of television that resulted from the technologies and distribution possibilities by the mid-2000s.

Challenges to Research Methodologies in the Post-Network Transition

The methodological issues that resulted from audience fragmentation during the multi-channel transition offered only a slight suggestion of the scale of difficulties yet to come. As noted already, DVRs have affected a wide-range of industry norms—and audience measurement is among them. The devices have required new practices for reporting audience viewership, and their capabilities for commercial skipping diminish the significance of series viewership to the economics of television.

Over the decades, as U.S. homes added new technologies, Nielsen reconfigured its electronic measurement systems in order to adapt them to the hundreds of different models of televisions and then VCRs that became available. Nielsen disqualified DVR homes from their sample for the first eight years that the technology came into use. (The DVR's arrival at the same time that the company struggled with the LPM introduction compounded the new technical challenge.) DVRs and VCRs may appear to offer similar technological functionality, but Nielsen's preliminary DVR use studies found that DVR households recorded a daily average of 30 percent of programming and 46 percent of prime-time viewing.[37] By contrast, viewers used VCRs in more extraordinary circumstances, such as when they needed to be out at the time of a particularly favored program—as in the case of regular time-shifting of soap operas—or for the creation of archives. Upon the widespread adoption of the VCR, Nielsen reporting practices changed little largely because it lacked a way to measure if viewers played back the content they recorded. But the situation changed with DVRs. Including DVR use in its sample required Nielsen to create multiple reports in response to different requests from clients. Advertisers wanted to negotiate pricing based on live viewing or at most that done the same day. Networks requested reports that gave viewers a longer opportunity to view, such as that done within a week of the recording.[38] Nielsen offered various reports as the advertisers and networks negotiated their way toward standards on which they could agree.

Such reports do provide more information about viewer behavior, yet the utility of their figures remains questionable given the tendency of those viewing DVR recordings to skip through commercial blocks. Under the circumstances, it remains up to advertisers to determine whether they will "count" DVR viewers in the same way as those watching live. Industry analyst Jack Myers opined in 2005 that "It will realistically be another three to ten years before new technologies such as the DVR have sufficient penetration to upset traditional viewing behavior and before new metrics are fully developed, tested, successfully modeled, and syndicated."[39]

The slow adoption of DVRs has aided measurement services struggling to keep up with the pace of technology. However, the lack of audience information has also slowed the adoption of video on demand (VOD), much to the chagrin of the cable providers who invested extensively in the infrastructure and technical capacity required to make the service available. The problem is compounded by an uncertain financial model that in some ways depends on the creation of a greater amount of information about who uses VOD and how they use it. And it is further complicated by the difficulties of aggregating and sharing such information. VOD availability varies not only by cable provider, but also according to whether cable homes subscribe to digital or analog programming tiers. Early on, when cable providers thought of VOD as a pay-per-view distribution method for films, they reported how many times "streams" began, but as more innovative networks have made content available in non-subscription VOD applications, advertisers have sought information about whether viewers watch entire programs and whether they fast-forward through commercials.

Getting such information requires accessing information stored in cable providers' proprietary set-top devices but allows census rather than sampling data. Advertisers might consequently allocate money for VOD advertising differently because cable providers can report how many homes actually remain tuned during commercials. Recent research shows that commercial viewing in ad-supported VOD content tends to be only 10 percent lower than that which normally occurs during live commercial viewing (which is nonetheless higher than DVR commercial viewing).[40] Further, VOD viewership differs from national households in general because of the different demographic profile of digital cable households and requires active behavior of seeking content out, which might suggest that viewers have a different relationship to the content than those who view in a live, linear stream. Industry analysts have speculated that because VOD requires the active behavior of seeking out content, VOD viewers might be more willing to engage an embedded commercial message and that commercials could be more precisely targeted than possible in mass live viewing.

The increase in product placement and integration has also led advertisers to call for the establishment of a viable matrix for measuring and valuing these deals, even though the lack of a standard way to value, measure, and price placement expenditures has held back the explosion of these agreements only slightly. Industry veteran Nielsen has competed with many start-up services that have sought to provide advertisers with data about placement, yet a standard matrix is difficult to develop because product integration takes so many different forms. Various services have measured factors such as number of brand mentions and time on screen relative to the size of the audience in an effort to create a standard currency comparable to the gross rating point used in comparisons of thirty-second advertisements.[41] While quantifying such mentions and appearances has required new labor from measurement agencies, gathering data has been far less challenging than determining the relative value of placement in terms of audience recall and recognition.

By 2006, the need to incorporate DVR viewing posed the most immediate challenge, but research services can see the new ones taking shape on the horizon. One arises from cross-platform media distribution, which became a reality when Verizon and Sprint launched services that delivered television content to mobile phones in 2005. Additionally, the development of new compression standards has led to expanded access to content via broadband channels and Internet download as networks increase viewers' opportunities to stream programs online. Efforts by TiVo and Microsoft enabled users to transfer content recorded via conventional TiVo systems to Microsoft's Portable Media Center, and many other ways of moving content are continuing to develop. For advertisers to support these new delivery technologies, the technologies need to be measured, especially since it has become apparent that audiences might view content with at least some advertiser support on conventional linear television, VOD, video delivered to mobile phones, and online.

Such cross-platform capabilities have threatened to further fragment audiences, as well as affecting measurement techniques of "old" delivery methods. Measurement companies have been challenged by the fact that the user characteristics of each of these delivery systems differ, as does the blend of advertiser and subscriber support. Such variation requires audience measurement mechanisms for each form of delivery, and each faces the lag between invention, adoption, and refinement of measurement methodology that the industry has experienced with the DVR. Many of these delivery systems achieved technological capability by 2005, but deployment and wide-scale adoption depends on viewers' willingness to try them. The delivery systems also depend on the development of adequate models to finance them, which, in turn, depends significantly on audience research and measurement—which, once again, suggests the centrality of measurement to an industry in a period of transition.

Even as new technologies create new challenges for audience measurement and research, they also provide new tools. All of the technologies and devices that have been introduced in the digital era are significantly "smarter" than those they replaced. Digital cable boxes and DVRs not only keep track of what viewers do but are also linked to communication systems through which activity is reported to central servers. The possibility of replacing the sample-based data-gathering methods that had figured audience behavior since radio with actual data of real set use represents the most significant advance in audience measurement to result from the introduction of digital technologies. Importantly, deployment of new digital technologies did not occur so quickly that such an advance was imaginable right away—at least not without some significant limitations. But for the audience researcher looking out upon the sea of "smart" delivery systems coming available, it seemed time to stop repairing the sampling boat and to begin working on a measurement system that would be aided rather than thwarted by coming technologies.

Competitors seeking to develop a non-sampling method of measurement were already emerging by 2005. For example, a company called erinMedia drew data from digital set-top boxes in a manner that reduced many of the limits of the Nielsen methods while introducing new ones. ErinMedia's system eliminated recruitment bias, human error, and technology installation and servicing costs by using devices already in viewers' homes.[42] Additionally, the system provided a census of all digital cable homes, not a sample, in an approach that substantially increased the number of homes about which real data became available. Because of its passive nature and privacy regulations, set-top box data did not include demographic information other than the zip code of the home using the box. To address this problem, erinMedia added a demographic component through a complicated mathematical process called the Inverse Demographic Matrix (IDM) technique, which was far less transparent to non-mathematicians than Nielsen's sampling techniques, but drew from U.S. census data, set-top box data, and a description of the program to determine who was watching the show. Such census-based measurements were particularly valuable to new cable channels that barely registered in a sample.

For all such advances, though, the only certainty in audience measurement at the beginning of the post-network era seems to be that the days of a single measurement service with a standard currency are over. Much of the need for a plurality of measurement protocols has resulted from the adoption of the plurality of advertising strategies, technologies, and means of distribution explored in preceding chapters. As in other sectors of the industry, the multi-channel transition led to a fracturing of a single dominant standard that had been characteristic of the network era and the creation of a more diverse and complicated industrial field. Developing measurement capabilities for new technologies such as VOD has been crucial to attracting advertiser support, yet measurement services for unproven technologies have been slow to develop, creating a classic Catch 22 situation that has slowed innovation. Still, the ability to measure audiences and gauge the effectiveness of new advertising strategies for television plays a critical role in determining the forms and content of television in the post-network era.

The Significance of Measurement during Periods of Transformation and Challenges of the Next Era

Audience measurement and research services expanded their techniques and technologies throughout the multi-channel transition because there was an economic imperative for them to do so. Advertisers would willingly underwrite endeavors to know more about the viewing and purchasing behavior of the audience members that they paid so dearly to reach. Yet, these refinements in audience research had broader consequences than the bottom-line of advertising agencies and ad-supported networks. They also substantially affected the speed at which further changes in television could occur. Advertisers' interest in placement techniques, and their shifting of budget allocations from thirty-second spots to placements, encouraged the rapid development of new measurement protocols. Measurement techniques for other delivery systems developed more slowly because advertisers were less eager to invest in these areas. Cable providers certainly desired a faster adoption of VOD use, but they could only make this form of distribution possible—they could not also finance all of the programming available on demand. Consequently, this use developed more slowly.

One way to understand the role of research in industry innovation is to imagine where U.S. television might be had AGB not threatened Nielsen and led the corporation to substantially enhance its service with the People Meter. In the late 1980s, at the same time People Meters launched, cable approached the 50 percent penetration rate and the average number of channels received in U.S. households had already risen to 18.8.[43] Previous measurement techniques undercounted cable viewing, which made it more difficult for these networks to secure the advertising support they needed to finance innovative and distinctive programming. If Nielsen had not updated its methodology in a manner more likely to accurately value cable viewing, the development of cable might have been much slower. Likewise, fifteen years after the introduction of People Meters, the introduction of the LPM provided a similarly instructive lesson. Here too, a reallocation of viewing occurred alongside a refinement in research technology. Again, it was the emergent segment of the industry (still cable) that the old method undercounted. The more precise data helped cable networks continue to argue their worth to advertisers, and consequently, expand programming budgets and the range of new content included on their schedules.

Nielsen's independence and lack of corporate affiliation with any of the buyers or sellers of television programming have been key advantages for the company throughout television history. By contrast, research derived from digital set-top boxes, mobile phones, or Internet streaming data will probably be proprietary and involve conflict-of-interest situations that Nielsen has avoided. Verizon may report that sixty thousand users watched a sponsored clip last month, but what guarantee do advertisers have that Verizon properly represents the data which is available only to the corporation? The revolution in technology has solved some of the problems inherent in existing research protocols, but it has also introduced new challenges and dilemmas.

One way the industry has used the increasingly detailed research about audiences is to target them more precisely with persuasive advertising appeals. Another is to create entertainment programming most likely to appeal to the target audience. New capabilities in this second type of research pose profound implications for the medium. Network programmers have long sought formulaic recreations of "successful" shows— often with inconsistent results—and so television's creative workers have come to fear that enhancements in research could expand formulaic tendencies as networks seek to "engineer" programming based on research. Most broadcasters already carefully test show concepts and completed shows in front of focus groups in order to more precisely predict performance and to fine-tune casting, characterizations, plots, and so on. For example, producer Tom Werner reported that network tests of his new 2006 show *Happy Hour* indicated that "The test audiences really liked the character Amanda . . . so the networks asked us to give her more to do. So, you'll see her character play a bigger role this fall."[44] New measurement technologies and capabilities encourage even more extensive testing and, accordingly, adjustment of the original creative vision.

Hollywood's creative voices and network executive suites have therefore regarded the potential of new research tools very differently. The network executives who receive training in business schools identified the ability to know how audiences behave minute by minute—if not second by second—as a tremendous advantage. But telling a good story differs significantly from building a better a widget, and the industry's storytellers have argued that too much data threatens to numb the creativity of those who already work within narrow parameters. Some of the television programming most valued for its creativity has emerged from networks that either opted against extensive testing, such as HBO, or could not afford it, as has been the case for many basic cable networks. The technological possibility may exist to use refined viewer data for content creation, but executives will be wise to open this Pandora's box carefully.

Another aspect of the new measurement and research capabilities that has extensive implications is the increased surveillance of viewers inherent in research such as census data collection. Although news stories regarding the use of the data maintained by services such as TiVo or Google circulate on occasion, viewers do not seem to be concerned about the amount of information media services gather about their preferences and behaviors. This general indifference may be particularly surprising in light of the post–September 11th "anti-terrorism" efforts that made library records and book store purchases available to government agency investigations as well as subsequent news of unprecedented government wiretapping of citizens. But the contemporary reaction to such developments has not been like that which gave rise to Orwell's *1984*. Rather, the forces of consumerism and experience of audience and market construction have led viewers to accept and even support surveillance. Joseph Turow identifies the acceptance of surveillance as an outcome of multiple shifts in U.S. consumer society and the development of interactive and digital technologies such as those discussed here.[45] Tracing the growth of target marketing in the post–World War II era, he notes how it contributed to creating a contemporary society composed of individuals who understand their role and power as those of consumers more than as citizens. Turow even acknowledges the degree to which audience members support surveillance if it can aid them in receiving access to products with increased customization or allow them to use services at a decreased price. Services such as TiVo that use artificial intelligence applications to suggest programming based on what a viewer previously had selected illustrate this application and to some degree, its advantages: we are not so much in Bruce Springsteen's world of "fifty-seven channels and nothin' on" than we are in one of three hundred channels and no hope of finding what we want to watch. Viewers can and do accept monitoring as the means to the end of the greater availability of desirable products.

Despite such acceptance, the transformation of television from a window on the world to a two-way mirror deserves more interrogation and critique—especially insofar as television-related surveillance has not been a topic of much concern. Viewers may willingly allow aggregation and individuation of their data, but most are probably unaware of the type of information that is gathered or what is done with it: service-provider disclosures tend to be exceedingly long documents of fine print. Acceptance of surveillance is effectively a condition of participation in digital societies. Concern or outrage is not likely to be marshaled until a situation widely acknowledged as an abuse of information-gathering becomes well known—perhaps a newspaper report of a public official's pay-per-view porn habits? For the time being, though, viewers appear unaware of disadvantages to sharing information, which makes their revolt unlikely.

Although audience research has rarely been part of the discussion of the monumental revolution in television underway in the mid-2000s, the stealth status of this topic should not belie its importance. The outcome of endeavors to develop viable and accurate research will ultimately determine the winners and losers of coming struggles over technologies, distribution platforms, and programming. Media executives and the advertisers that support them have not forgotten the lessons of the dot-com boom in the 1990s in which millions were lost as a result of money spent without understanding the fundamental attributes of a new technology. Now, with so many more new media technologies, advertisers have become increasingly suspicious of the value of their existing ways of doing business and have sought for networks to prove the value of their audience delivery in thirty-second commercials as well as in the new developing advertising strategies. All of the distribution applications and technologies that rely on advertiser support require tools for counting and valuing audience members. The network-era norm of a singular ratings service and standard exchange of advertising dollars for gross ratings points might remain part of the business, but many other advertising techniques and currencies will coexist as a result of the increasing ways to use and pay for television.

As Gertner notes in the epigraph that begins this chapter, changing the way the industry measures audiences will change the business and the culture. However, changes in audience behavior will precede many of the other adjustments. Different segments of the television industry have invested billions of dollars hoping to identify the technology or use of television that will be central to the new era. Those at home, and those who have begun taking television on the go, will determine the winners and losers—that is, if the measurement services can find a way to count them.

7

Television Storytelling Possibilities at the Beginning of the Post-Network Era

Five Cases

At the summer 2003 Television Critics Association tour, CBS researcher David Poltrack presented data reporting the comparatively miniscule amount of attention paid to CBS series by the nation's journalists relative to the network's substantial audiences. The shows, including *JAG, The Guardian,* and *Judging Amy,* were among the most watched each week, yet Poltrack bemoaned that the critics insisted on devoting expansive column space to relatively obscure shows on The WB and HBO. What Poltrack's research did not address, however, was the fact that there just wasn't much to say about many of his network's programs. CBS had successfully decreased the median age of its audience and moved into first place for household viewing, but there was minimal innovation in much of its programming—although exceptions existed such as *Survivor* and early seasons of *CSI.* CBS became the most watched network by developing formulaic crime and forensic dramas that were only exceptional in their focus on the most uncommon scenarios for death and mayhem. For critics, who watch much more television than the average viewer, many of these successful shows were tried, trite, and predictable—notwithstanding their popularity.

So then, perhaps much to the chagrin of broadcasters like Poltrack, I do not focus exclusively on the biggest blockbuster hits in this chapter. My selection of case studies does not result from how many people watched these shows, but from the lessons these shows provide about the industry's changes. Each of the five cases explored here—presented chronologically—tells a distinctive tale about production on the cusp of the post-network era. I include them here at the end of the book instead of locating one in each of the preceding chapters because of how they illustrate the interconnections among changes in multiple production components. The cases include various genres (comedy, drama, and unscripted) and address shows on major and minor broadcast networks and on basic and premium cable channels. Despite the variety of shows and their distinctive economic situations, some aspects of their development, production, and distribution stories repeat in important ways. None of these series could have existed on network-era television; each not only illustrates changes in the production process, but also how these changes have created opportunities for stories much different from those of the network era.

Sex and the City

HBO's *Sex and the City,* which debuted in June 1998, provided one of the earliest series to feature a production process that substantially differed from network-era norms. The series is important to the questions examined here because of its status as an early original cable success that defied many expectations about the popularity and commercial viability of a show produced by a subscription cable network. *Sex and the City* debuted before *The Sopranos* and was the network's first series to achieve considerable popular awareness. *Sex and the City* told a story unlikely to be found on broadcast networks—or at least unlikely to be told elsewhere in the manner that it was on HBO. Because of the distinctive economic and regulatory context of the network, *Sex and the City* was able to push boundaries even further than its basic cable counterparts, which had likewise begun to produce series differentiated from broadcast by their niche address and unconventional themes; Lifetime's *Any Day Now* serves as the clearest coterminous illustration. Much journalistic attention to the first few seasons of *Sex and the City* focused on the explicit sexual content and frank conversations about sex among its four characters. Although such forthright depictions and expressions were unlikely to be found outside of the premium cable television space, the series also derived significance from its uncommon focus on female friendships and its examination of the negotiations made by a group of women previously absent from television.

Despite its unconventionality as a series produced for an original run on a subscription cable network, *Sex and the City* followed a fairly conventional development history. The series was adapted from a book written by Candace Bushnell and based on her *New York Observer* newspaper column. Bushnell was actually the "sexual anthropologist" who wrote stories about sex in New York City and served as the model for Carrie's character; the series reduced the much larger collection of people inhabiting Bushnell's book to Carrie's three female friends. Executive producer, creator, and occasional series' writer Darren Star (*Beverly Hills, 90210, Melrose Place*) chose to produce the series for HBO despite an offer from ABC.[1] The premium cable channel was necessary in Star's mind in order to maintain elements of "eliteness" in writing and production, as well as a budget—initially $900,000 an episode—on which he could afford independent directors and writers. The series' home on HBO also provided Star with considerable content freedom. This enabled the series to derive its humor from the sexual adventures of the four characters, rather than from the double entendres and hidden discussion about sex typical of broadcast sitcoms.

Many focus on the freedom from advertiser influence when considering the distinction of subscription television networks, but the difference in these networks' economic processes is more fundamental. Broadcast and basic cable networks are primarily concerned with how many people tune in to their programming. Since advertisers evaluate the networks they support in each hour of each day, networks must select programming likely to reach the broadest audience possible and allocate their programming budget accordingly—for example, by creating or purchasing new programs for each hour of almost every day. In contrast, subscription cable services rely on viewers desiring to watch their programming so much that they are willing to pay for it. They do not worry about how advertisers evaluate programming—there are no advertisers. This difference in subscription networks' financing model changes the conditions of production, but more significantly, provides these networks with a mandate for selecting programs that differs vastly from advertiser-supported networks. Subscription networks care much less about who watches and when; rather, they are chiefly concerned with providing subscribers with a service with enough value that they continue to subscribe. Of course, willingness to subscribe is closely related to what the network programs, but this mandate leads the network to construct its schedule and select programming much differently than advertiser-supported networks.

Subscription networks seek to provide as many viewers as possible with adequate reason to keep paying their monthly fees. HBO achieved considerable success by offering a wide range of programming that very specifically targeted the tastes of a broad array of audience members, but did not provide an exceptional amount of programming for any one group. It matters little to the network whether a viewer subscribes because of the networks' films, sports, or original series. Rather, its economic model requires that viewers find some aspect of such value—ideally something unavailable on advertiser-supported networks—so that they maintain their subscription.[2] A show such as *Sex and the City*, with its specific address to young, upscale, professional women, provided an ideal addition to the HBO schedule. No series on television so precisely addressed this group, and much of HBO's other programming, such as original series *Oz*, boxing, and *Inside the NFL*, more emphatically sought to entertain male viewers.

The first season of *Sex and the City* consisted of only twelve episodes, followed by eighteen in each of the subsequent five seasons. This shortened and flexible schedule is characteristic of subscription and even basic cable channels and has significant artistic and economic consequences.[3] Artistically, the shortened season decreases the burden of originating so much new content each year, which is one of the key aspects of television production about which creative personnel often complain. In addition, HBO's flexible and commercial-free schedule allowed creators to develop episodes at a length determined by the story rather than according to the strict twenty-two minute format of broadcast comedies, with narrative climaxes prescribed to occur at regular intervals to allow for commercial breaks.

The substantial syndication success enjoyed by *Sex and the City* could not have been predicted when it began production in 1998. Although the series produced substantial "buzz" within the culture, actual audience size for the original run on HBO was quite small by television standards. At the time the series aired, only about 30 percent of U.S. homes subscribed to HBO, and many of these homes did not view the series. HBO reported an average audience of 6.6 million homes in the series' second season for the premiere play of each episode.[4] This limited audience size in the original run added to the series' syndication value because there remained so many new potential audience members for the series. Those who did not subscribe to HBO first had an initial opportunity to view the show on DVD, which gave viewers an uncut version of the series as it had appeared on HBO. In the first half of 2003, the series earned more than $65 million just from DVD sales.[5] The series also enjoyed immediate revenue from international syndication.

More significantly, the series was among the first original cable series, basic or premium, to earn revenue from other distribution windows.[6] The series was sold for a first-run to cable channel Turner Broadcasting System (TBS) and Tribune-owned stations in deals that involved a combination of cash and advertising time. TBS paid $450,000 for each of the ninety-four episodes. The terms of the Tribune deal were not disclosed, but a month later HBO sold the series to independent San Francisco station KRON for $10.4 million plus advertising time.[7] Unlike most broadcast series that could be sold in the same form in which they aired on the network, *Sex and the City* episodes had to be reedited in order to make them of a conventional length, allow for commercial insertion, and make them acceptable for broadcast content standards. Although this reediting incurred costs, they were not as high as they might have been since the producers had shot additional scenes during the original production to replace scenes that might be troublesome for international syndication. This lengthened original production minimally and proved invaluable once domestic buyers such as TBS and Tribune emerged. HBO also continued to air the series long after it finished production and included it among its offerings on its video-on-demand channel.

This case also indicates the importance of the availability of a programmer such as HBO that operates with a distinctive and differentiated set of production norms. *Sex and the City* eventually defied many conventional norms of distribution and proved surprisingly valuable in many secondary markets, but it could never have been created outside a subscription network. Certainly, the version of the show Star might have produced for ABC would not have had nearly the same tone or storytelling emphasis, as ABC executives would have insisted on making the content more accessible to a broader audience. The programming HBO began producing in the late 1990s was among the most widely hailed by critics and in award competitions, and it indicated previously unimagined possibilities for television as a creative medium. While HBO's particular industrial situation enabled much of its programming, HBO's efforts had effects across the television spectrum—and not just by increasing sexual and violent content.

In another strategy particular to HBO, the channel reports that it accepts no paid product placement despite what many have noted to be an exceptional amount of clearly named commercial goods in shows such as *Sex and the City* and *The Sopranos*.[8] Producers do accept products for use in shows, but HBO has repeatedly denied that any money changes hands for them, including the oft-noted use of Absolut vodka in an episode of *Sex and the City* that required the creation of a fake ad including one of the series' actors as a model.[9] Many in the marketing community are skeptical of HBO's claims of refusing payment, especially considering one marketer estimated that *The Sopranos* could earn $6.8 million per episode if it accepted placement payments.[10] Nonetheless, the channel emphasizes its particular industrial status as a subscription service. As HBO spokesman Jeff Cusson explains, "We're not a network that accepts advertising. And product placement is a form of advertising."[11]

The unusual economic mandate of subscription networks provided an incubator for creative television that expanded program content through their niche address and innovative production techniques. Contrary to its late-1990s slogan—"It's Not TV, It's HBO"—HBO programming was indeed television, and the network's original series had significant implications for both subsequent shows on all television channels and on how others approached, produced, and viewed television.

Survivor

One of the most profound adjustments in programming during the multichannel transition resulted from the unexpected success of unscripted, or reality, programming. Not only did these shows alter expectations about norms of program content, but they also introduced a vast variety of production practices. Just as the original production of *Sex and the City* involved the unique economic arrangements of a subscription network, so, too, do most unscripted series use economic practices fundamentally unlike those common to most scripted television programming. The success of unscripted programming led producers to break from status-quo assumptions about how shows could be financed, and this, in turn, disrupted many residual network-era norms of industrial practice and programming.

Although unscripted television has often been haphazardly amalgamated into a single category of "reality" television, substantial differentiation in both program content and production norms had arisen by the mid-2000s. Indeed, production practices for unscripted series vary significantly—so much so as to support the contention that no single one serves as a norm. This variation makes it difficult to select a meaningful case that might loosely characterize this genre. CBS's 2000 breakout hit,

Survivor, provides an informative case, although its exceptional success made it unlike most other "reality" shows produced in this era. Nonetheless, *Survivor* illustrates how unconventional formats can revolutionize the business and programming of major broadcasters and yield *broad*cast success in an increasingly narrowcast competitive environment.

Debuting in May 2000, *Survivor* was one of the earliest unscripted competition series to disrupt the balance broadcasters had established in the 1990s of schedules filled mostly with scripted programming and some cheaper newsmagazines to help compensate for rising scripted programming costs. The newsmagazines and various early "reality" shows such as *Unsolved Mysteries* and *Cops* had low production costs that could be covered by license fees that were even lower than those for scripted programs.[12] The frugal production expenditures eliminated the need to syndicate this programming, although many shows, including *Unsolved Mysteries, Cops,* and *America's Funniest Home Videos* still earned substantial profits in both international and domestic syndication.

As shows such as *Survivor* entered homes in the early 2000s, many believed that "reality" programming represented something entirely new. These shows developed not so much out of innovation as out of necessity, as integrating low-cost shows simply became an essential part of networks' programming cost equation in the mid-1980s. The development of competitive reality shows such as *Survivor, American Idol,* and *The Amazing Race* made sense for networks that had saturated viewer interest in newsmagazines but needed to maintain some lower cost shows. Despite the sense that "reality" television was taking over in the early 2000s, consistent reports indicated an increase in dramatic programming and only a slight decrease in comedy, which was mainly due to difficulties in developing successful comedies. The "reality" series primarily replaced newsmagazines and theatrical films, and drew larger or at least younger audiences than other lower cost programming forms. "Reality" has never really threatened to take over network schedules—viewers have shown interest in the novelty of the programs, and younger audiences have watched in greater numbers than viewed newsmagazines, but scripted series remain central to network identities and overall strategies. It is the case, however, that some sort of lower cost programming is likely to always play a role in network programming norms as long as a linear system remains in place.

Mark Burnett, a newcomer to television whose reputation was mostly based on the *Eco-Challenge* race he produced for the Discovery Channel, acquired rights to the concept that would become *Survivor* in the mid-1990s, when U.S. "reality" television consisted of *Cops* and *America's Funniest Home Videos*. As he pitched *Survivor* to various networks, he received rejection after rejection in a manner that retrospectively seems inconceivable (although significantly, *American Idol* received similar treatment). Burnett spent years trying to sell a network on *Survivor* and succeeded only when a junior member of the CBS programming department became an advocate for the show and persistently argued his case to upper-level executives.[13]

Few suspected unscripted programming would succeed, and certainly no one believed that these shows would attract blockbuster audiences in the manner that came to be regularly achieved by *Survivor* and *American Idol*. Many did perceive, however, that the contest format of these series would prevent them from performing well as reruns or in syndication of any kind. Without the syndication revenues to support deficit financing, these prime-time "game" shows would have to find an alternative financing system that did not require distributing them through additional windows to recoup costs. Most unscripted series could be produced more cheaply than scripted series because they required no actors or writers who must be paid at guild rates—a considerable advantage at a time when actors' fees were particularly blamed for the "skyrocketing" costs of scripted series and when networks were casting major stars to help distinguish their programs in the increasingly competitive environment.[14] Yet some of these shows, such as those produced by Mark Burnett, were known for "putting money on the screen" rather than in the producer's pocket, and had production costs similar to those of scripted series. Such shows faced the dilemma of lacking syndication value, which made deficit financing a poor option, yet were unable to finance production from license fees alone. *Survivor* was one of these series.

Mark Burnett and CBS executive Les Moonves tell somewhat different stories about the arrangement negotiated to get *Survivor* on the air. According to Burnett, the network was uncertain about the completely untested nature of the series and was wary of losing money. CBS consequently entrusted Burnett with the responsibility of selling the advertising time in the series and agreed to split the profits 50-50 if the show actually succeeded.[15] CBS, wary that any producer think it would agree to such a deal, has denied Burnett's claim repeatedly and asserted that Burnett received only 50 percent of the advertising revenue earned from expanding the *Survivor* finale—which drew an unthinkable fifty-one million viewers

—from one hour to two. Regardless of where the precise truth of this deal might be found, Burnett's unconventional approach to selling advertising time is not disputed. Rather than trying to convince advertisers to simply buy thirty-second commercials, Burnett sought for companies to buy in to the show through what he termed "associative marketing," but has since come to be known as product placement or integration. The fees paid by the eight sponsors Burnett attracted covered the show's production costs, and many received both placement in the program and a package of thirty-second commercials.

The reason the truth of the agreement between Burnett and CBS is so elusive is because the stakes are so high. The 50-50 split, or even sharing any revenue with a producer, would involve an unfathomable reallocation of economic norms that could wreak havoc for the networks. If highly sought after producers thought they might negotiate for a share of the profits from programs, the networks would relinquish additional control and revenues in a way that would further require massive adjustments throughout all their financial arrangements. For his part, Burnett became an instant sensation, and networks quickly began bidding for him to develop subsequent projects. It served him well for the other networks to believe CBS had been willing to offer such a grand deal.

Regardless of what CBS paid, few could argue that they overcompensated given the key role *Survivor* played in bringing more viewers to the network, decreasing the network's average audience age, and wresting control of the lucrative Thursday night from NBC's long-held dominance. Thursday-night advertising is in particular demand due to the night's proximity to the weekend; this makes it especially key for advertising films opening on Friday and for weekend events. Indeed, the viability of the show was not the only expectation that proved faulty. The exceptional popularity of *Survivor* helped fuel DVD sales of the series, and the popularity of other unscripted series led to the creation of windows for subsequent syndication. Many unscripted series have come to be distributed on the FOX Reality Channel launched by News Corp. in May of 2005, which is primarily available to the eighteen million households subscribing to then News Corp.–owned DirecTV.[16] In the case of *Survivor,* Burnett and CBS sold the rights to air seasons one through ten to the Outdoor Life Network (OLN; which changed its name to Versus in September 2006), defying expectations that the show had no subsequent value. CBS also established unconventional distribution deals for new episodes of *Survivor* in various transactional payment markets. The network included *Survivor* in its limited initial on-demand offerings available for purchase in certain local markets with Comcast cable service and experimented as the distributor by making downloadable episodes available for purchase on the CBS website, in both cases for $.99 each. Such sales further upset the notion that unscripted series have no value after their initial airing, particularly those shows with stories or contests confined to specific episodes, such as *Fear Factor,* which earned $250,000 per episode in its syndication sale to FX.[17] Despite these expanding opportunities to earn subsequent revenues, deals for new unscripted series rarely relied on deficit financing.

Another key source of revenue for unscripted programming developed through international format sales. This means that templates of these relatively cheap to produce contests are sold, rather than episodes of U.S. contestants competing; thus, each country can reproduce the show with local contestants and in response to cultural particularities. Such flexibility has proven to be especially advantageous. For example, *Who Wants to Be a Millionaire?* was produced in 130 different territories at one point. *The Weakest Link* sold similarly well, but the brash and rude persona of the female questioner and her winking had to be adjusted—replaced with a male host or the winking eliminated—in some cultures that responded negatively to the initial importation of the style and gender performance of the original British host, Anne Robinson.[18]

The sale of formats was a phenomenal business in the early 2000s and suggested very different global relations than the cultural imperialism thesis in which Western countries, and the United States in particular, were believed to impose their culture around the globe by dominating network-era program exports.[19] Indeed, many of the biggest successes were imported to the United States, and format trade was so vibrant as to lead to the sale of scripted formats, as in the BBC's sale of *Coupling* and *The Office* to NBC. Scripted formats had been sold before and sometimes with considerable success—a case in point is Norman Lear's *All in the Family,* which was based on the British series *'Till Death Us Do Part.* But the format business and especially international format sales of unscripted series helped enable culturally specific production and decreased U.S. dominance in the international market.[20] In fact, few of the unscripted series that succeeded in the United States originated as domestic productions, and the country purchased more formats than it sold. The case of *Survivor* discussed here is one instance: Burnett purchased the series from creators in Sweden.

By 2005, Burnett's *Survivor* continued to perform well, defying much conventional wisdom. The financing arrangements Burnett constructed after *Survivor*'s success indicated what he learned from his early endeavors and the changing nature of the business. Despite the fact that his subsequent series such as *The Contender* and *Rock Star* failed to attain *Survivor*'s blockbuster success, Burnett continued to require unconventional deals with networks and increasingly sought and achieved greater control of international distribution, sponsorship, and product integration.[21] From the beginning of *Survivor*, Burnett rightly insisted that the show's innovation was not in the programming form, but in the business model. Shows such as *Survivor* changed broadcasters' thinking about how shows could be financed and the audience sizes that lower cost formats could attract. Out of sheer necessity, *Survivor* introduced a major shift in advertising norms with its sponsorship funding and skillful integration of products into the story.

Significantly, though, even five years after its launch many executives would look at the chances of a concept like *Survivor* succeeding with great skepticism. The success of the show and its consequences for television's production process illustrate the profound uncertainty that sometimes characterizes this industry as well as the highly haphazard process of change. Burnett's persistence helped CBS assuage its fear of risk, and *Survivor* opened the industry's eyes to the variety of programming and industrial practices available through its success in captivating audiences with its competitive narrative and by deviating from conventional program economics. But for anyone looking at the series at its inception, these were hardly predictable or even imaginable outcomes.

The Shield

As is true of all of the shows discussed in this chapter, *The Shield* is unlike any show created or financed during the network era. The series also achieved a variety of "firsts." As noted in Chapter 5, *The Shield* debuted to great controversy due to its use of graphic violence and vulgar language in depicting a law enforcement unit different from any to have come before. *The Shield*'s central protagonist, Vic Mackey, is neither hero nor anti-hero, and the series' writers artfully compel the audience to be alternately drawn in and repulsed by him. *The Shield* aired for seven seasons on basic cable network FX beginning in March 2002. Although some successful original series had emerged on advertiser-supported cable networks by this point, the extensive promotional campaign FX used to announce the show, cultural debate and discussion about the series' content, and early advertiser defections generated more expansive cultural awareness than other basic cable series had. The series won a Peabody award in 2006, a Golden Globe award for best drama in 2003, and actor Michael Chiklis won both a Golden Globe and an Emmy for his portrayal of Vic Mackey following the show's first season. Not only was Chiklis' Emmy the first won by a basic cable program in a major series category, so, too, was the series' Peabody the first earned by a basic cable live-action original series, and all these awards were significant to establishing the legitimacy of basic cable original series. SciFi's *Battlestar Galactica* and Comedy Central's *South Park* also received Peabody awards in 2006.[22]

The story of how FX came to purchase *The Shield* is as unusual as the series' content and is symptomatic of the uncertainty and unpredictability of production practices at the beginning of the post-network era. Creator Shawn Ryan began his career as an intern on the comedy *My Two Dads* before suffering five years of unemployment and writing comedy spec scripts (scripts for shows already on the air which writers use to find jobs). In 1997, he began writing for the CBS action/buddy show *Nash Bridges* and then moved to the more character-driven WB series *Angel*. Ryan also had been hired to write a sitcom script for Fox TV Studios, but the idea Ryan had at the time was for a dark police drama. The Fox TV executives liked the script, although it was clearly not the comedy they needed. A few months later Kevin Reilly, FX entertainment president, had an idea for a show, but needed a writer. The Fox TV executives sent Ryan's script to Reilly as a sample of his work, and Reilly liked the script so much that he decided to pursue making *The Shield* rather than his original idea.[23]

It is significant that Ryan had not bothered trying to sell the show, as it indicates how strong and pervasive ideas about what shows networks will and won't make may well be. The story also illustrates the chance that sometimes characterizes the operations of this industry. Ryan could have been pitching the series all over town and not have achieved a network deal, simply because he might not have thought to pitch to a small cable network that had not previously produced original drama—up until then, FX had aired only the mildly successful *Son of the Beach,* a parody of *Baywatch* created by Howard Stern. If happenstance had a role in the development of the show, so, too, did conglomeration. The FX cable channel and Fox TV Studios are both owned by News Corp., and Reilly may never have received this particular script were it not for inter-conglomerate awareness that the network was seeking to produce an edgy drama.

The particular circumstance of producing an original police drama for a basic cable network while maintaining "broadcast quality" production values presented other challenges. The risk that production deficits could not be recouped made any single studio hesitant to produce the show, so Fox TV Studios and Sony Pictures Television (formerly Columbia TriStar) agreed to co-produce—thereby reducing risk. They produced the show for $1.3 million per episode—which compared with $1.8–2.2 million for an average broadcast drama at the time—and divided the various syndication rights; Fox Home Video distributed the DVD, while Sony syndicated the show to broadcast and cable networks.[24] To save money, *The Shield* shot each episode in seven days instead of the more standard nine of broadcast series, and the producers were able to pay a lower union-scale rate in the early seasons because the series aired on a basic cable channel.[25] The producers were able to find enough cost savings in these production adjustments to keep production in Los Angeles, unlike many other original cable shows that produced in Canada in order to avoid union costs and take advantage of currency rates, developed international co-production deals to spread costs (such as SciFi's *Battlestar Galactica*), or partnered with a foreign distributor to share costs (as was the case for USA's *The 4400*).

The limited budget of *The Shield* had consequences for how the show looked. The show utilized a lot of handheld steady-camera shooting, which is more time efficient and created a distinctive, frenetic visual style. Budget limitations also probably played a role in the relative inexperience of the writing team Ryan assembled and the series' use of primarily unknown actors. Although the inexperience of the writers could have been regarded as a drawback, it also helped the series in its pursuit of originality. The writers were not burdened with the acculturation of "how things are done" that prevents deviation from established norms. The police drama has an elaborate history, and Ryan sought to tell different stories or at least tell them in a different way than those that had come before. The selection of Chiklis for the role of Mackey initially broke the series' budget, but Chiklis' audition persuaded the network and studios that the actor was worth the cost.[26] The budget flexibility that allowed the hiring of Chiklis arguably paid great dividends as the attention to the series that resulted from his Emmy nomination and win provided invaluable promotion and legitimacy.

The financing of a series has ramifications in terms of both covering costs for the initial production and recovering deficits in secondary sales. Advertising dollars were the most important consideration in terms of the show's profitability for FX. As noted in Chapter 5, *The Shield* faced many advertising cancellations during its first season. But by the beginning of the second season, thirty-second advertisements in the show were selling for 30 to 50 percent more than the median price of $40,000 from season one, which made them among the most expensive in cable.[27] These rates hardly compared with those of broadcast networks, but were significant enough for the series to be an economic success for FX. *The Shield*'s audience was also much smaller than that of most broadcast shows: it averaged only 2.8 million viewers in its fifth season, but then 1.8 million of these were in the key 18–49-year-old demographic.[28] Importantly, the value of a series such as *The Shield* extended well beyond the advertising rates the series earned. When *The Shield* launched, FX lacked a channel brand identity and was not well-known. The publicity *The Shield* garnered in awards and critical praise raised the profile of the channel and probably contributed to adding viewers throughout the programming day. The development of original series such as *The Shield, Nip/Tuck,* and *Rescue Me* was credited with lifting FX from ranking as the number-twelve cable channel in prime time among 18–49-year-olds in 2001 to number five in 2006.[29]

The particular industrial positioning of FX also contributed to the making of *The Shield*. FX launched in June 1994, but had a fairly low subscriber base until the late 1990s. In 2003, an industry analyst noted that the channel had fairly low CPMs (cost-per-thousand advertising rates), but that it benefited from high license fees because it operated as FOX's "ransom channel."[30] Throughout the multi-channel transition, the broadcast networks and cable systems reached a relative détente over the issue of whether cable systems would compensate broadcasters for carrying their networks on cable systems. The broadcasters generally did not require payment from the cable systems—which they had a right to under the must-carry rules—but instead leveraged this non-payment in order to gain better carriage or license fees for commonly owned cable networks. So, for example, instead of ABC negotiating a fee to carry the broadcast network, ABC convinced cable systems to agree to launch ESPN2. Likewise, News Corp. allowed systems to carry FOX for free, but negotiated a license fee for FX estimated to be around $.30 per subscriber, which was three times greater that what its competitors earned.[31] Importantly, these negotiations varied around the country because they were established between each city-based cable system and the channel. However, the conglomeration of cable systems nationwide and common ownership of local stations, broadcast networks, and cable channels often led to large-scale deals.

This particular situation of FX revealed the complexity of production processes that must be considered in assessing the consequences of shifting industrial practices on the types of programming that are produced. Chapter 5 argued that the survival and success of *The Shield* as a boundary defying program relied upon a shift in the tastes of advertisers and that by 2002 there were some willing and eager to be associated with a show otherwise experiencing advertising boycott. The industrial position of FX as a "ransom channel" that earned substantial fees from cable system operators is likely to have played an important role in both financing the license fee for the series and allowing the network to be patient after the initial advertiser defections. These industrial practices also greatly contributed to enabling Ryan to produce a series of exceptional quality and unlike that found on broadcast and other advertiser-supported cable networks. A difference in any one of these industrial practices could have yielded a very different outcome for the series.

The potential syndication life for *The Shield* was highly uncertain when the series began production. At that time, it would have been reasonable to assume the international market would provide the only additional revenue for the series. Many original cable series had successfully sold international syndication rights, but not found buyers in the domestic market. By the time the series finished its first season in the U.S., it had already been sold in forty countries, which helped repay the production deficit.[32]

But the international market proved not to be the only source of potential revenue. *The Shield* premiered just as DVD sales of television shows began to escalate. As was the case for *Sex and the City,* this distribution format was particularly valuable for *The Shield,* a show that aired on a more obscure cable network to a smaller audience. The first season DVD sale enabled new viewers to join the audience before the second season—which was particularly important because many may not have heard about the show until the press coverage related to its awards. Like many broadcast shows that have sold particularly well on DVD, *The*

Shield featured a fairly serialized storyline that made DVD viewing especially attractive and the series sold roughly 250,000 units of every season.[33]

In addition to the DVD distribution, a more surprising secondary revenue window emerged when Sony was able to sell cable syndication rights to Spike. No series produced for a basic cable network had been purchased in syndication by another basic cable network, and the boundary-pushing content of *The Shield* also could have served as a deterrent to buyers because it would require many outlets to reedit it or only air the show at certain times of the day.[34] Cable network Spike actually outbid FX in this first case of a signature series of a basic cable network being syndicated by a competing basic cable network, and Spike paid an estimated $300,000 to $350,000 per episode.[35] Although somewhat odd in terms of cable competition, this purchase made great sense creatively. Spike had been explicitly promoting itself as a network for men since 2003, while FX more successfully established this brand through its original programming. Sony also sold *The Shield* to Tribune and The WB 100+ stations in an all-barter sale that made the series available on local broadcast stations across the country in a deal expected to earn at least $30 million.[36] (An all-barter sale means the stations pay no cash, but give the studios half of the advertising slots to sell to national advertisers.) Significantly, there is no hint of conglomerate self-interest in either deal, as Spike is part of the Viacom conglomerate and has no links to either News Corp. or Sony.

The economic success of *The Shield* beyond its original airing on FX provided an important lesson for the industry about the ability of original cable series to return profits. Although the earnings from *The Shield* may not come close to those of a broadcast success, it has been more profitable than most moderate broadcast hits. And this achievement has had additional consequences. FX entertainment president Kevin Reilly noted that writing submissions to FX increased tenfold in the fifteen months after *The Shield*'s premiere, indicating shifting perceptions about where to sell series, and the network followed *The Shield* with the similarly edgy, critically lauded dramas *Nip/Tuck, Rescue Me, Over There,* and *Thief* that made FX a leader in original cable series production.[37] Just as the differentiated economics of HBO and Showtime allowed the production of unconventional television and radically adjusted notions of television's storytelling capabilities, basic cable networks such as FX, SciFi, and USA also contributed to expanding television storytelling in important ways. Before *The Shield*, producers had good cause to be wary of original cable productions, but cases such as *The Shield* illustrated the different possibilities available to producers willing to forgo the conventions of broadcast production.

Arrested Development

An Emmy would be nice, but I'd settle for an audience.
—Mitch Hurwitz, creator and executive
producer of *Arrested Development*[38]

When *Arrested Development* premiered in fall of 2003, no one could have predicted its fate. On one hand, the series had been the subject of an intense bidding dispute between FOX and NBC that earned it the status of a "put pilot" a year before it was to go on air—that is, it was effectively guaranteed to have a place on the programming schedule. There is often a substantial financial penalty that the network must pay if it chooses not to air put pilots—a high six-figure penalty in the case of *Arrested Development*.[39] It was also being produced by an established studio, Imagine TV, the studio of Brian Grazer and Ron Howard that was aligned with 20th Century Fox TV Studios. Moreover, not only did the show have the support of successful director and producer Ron Howard behind it, but he was actually involved in production, providing the series' voice over. On the other hand, there was no doubt that the series was unconventional. Producers planned to develop an unusual film style, the show used a somewhat sprawling cast, and none of the characters was particularly likable. Yet the early 2000s were dark days for television comedy, with no breakout hits emerging after *Everybody Loves Raymond*'s debut in 1996. There were comedies that lasted many seasons and were sold in syndication (*King of Queens*)—but this was largely a function of the required programming economics of television, and none achieved the riches or cultural currency of *Seinfeld, Friends,* or their many predecessors. Each year the number of comedies rating among the top ten and twenty programs dwindled. Even using a proven comedic formula no longer predicted hits, so networks increasingly considered that being unconventional might provide the key to success.

The paradox of expectations bore out as a paradoxical reality for *Arrested Development*. The series was nominated for an unimaginable seven Emmys in its first season and won five, including best comedy, best writing, and best direction; it also won the Television Critics Award for best new show. But it limped through the first season in the ratings competition, finishing the year as the 120th most viewed show among households and 88th among 18–49-year-olds.[40] Set amongst the other case studies examined here, *Arrested Development* illustrates the situation of a comedy with too niche a tone to succeed on a Big Four network. Although the innovation of *Arrested Development*'s tone and visual style would have been impossible a few years earlier, even consistent and uniform praise and a cult following could not keep the show on the air beyond three seasons.

Arrested Development proved to be too narrow a hit for the original-run distribution possibilities of its time. Its edgy comedy earned it a devoted fan base, but not one large enough to support broadcast economics. Its audience was more comparable to that of basic cable original series, but these channels also struggled with original comedy development and, as of 2006, had yet to produce a successful original narrative comedy series.[41] The uncertainty of televising comedy at the beginning of the post-network era was apparent beyond the circumstances of this particular failing sitcom. Growing acculturation with narrowcast strategies and niche comedy yielded uncomfortable results when audiences with diverse comedic tastes reconvened for what had once been media events—such as the Academy Awards—as it seemed, by the mid 2000s, that no comedian could bridge the country's varied comedic tastes. This was a complicated environment in which to produce any comedy series, especially one needing to attract broadcast-sized audiences.

Arrested Development first marked its difference from other contemporary comedies through its visual style. It did not use the multiple-camera, fixed-set, studio-audience, laugh-track style long dominant in comedy production, but then it also deviated from the emerging single-camera style used in shows such as *Sex and the City* and *Scrubs*. Instead, it blended the two, shooting on location and on film, but with multiple cameras—in a manner similar to some unscripted series.[42] The use of natural light and steady cameras further contributed to its documentary-like effect and helped facilitate the show's rapid pace, which was not primarily the result of economic considerations, as was the case for *The Shield*. On the contrary, the distinct stylistic attributes of *Arrested Development* complemented the particular tone and depiction of family life the comedy sought to offer. In addition to these visual innovations, the use of voice-over also contributed to the series' distinctive style.

Most basically, the series told the story of a wealthy disconnected family that must unite when its patriarch goes to jail. The show presented family as neither an idyllic space nor a dystopia as many previous sitcoms had offered. Rather, much of the comedy developed from the distinct characters and their absurd reactions to absurd situations. Fast-paced, the show also offered jokes that were neither obvious nor particularly complicated (a character named Bob Loblaw, which is pronounced blah, blah, blah) but that rewarded regular viewers, whose familiarity with the characters and their back-stories added a layer of meaning from which much of the comedy evolved. This self-referentiality and use of in-jokes evolved over multiple episodes; old jokes returned unexpectedly and passed by quickly in a manner that added to the pleasure of longtime viewers but made it difficult to begin watching the series after its first season. The show demanded close attention from viewers, but also compensated them—perhaps making its cult fandom the least surprising aspect of its story.

Another somewhat astonishing component of *Arrested Development*'s history is the consistent support FOX gave the series despite its poor ratings performance. The series received a full-season order for season two despite lackluster ratings. The decision to schedule the series for a third season seemed more labored, as the crew did not learn that the show would return until thirty-six hours before it was announced at the network's May upfront presentation. But as ratings continued to falter in the third season—especially after it failed to gain after being scheduled in a prime post-*Simpsons* timeslot during the second season —it seemed FOX had done all it could to support the series. News of cancellation never came despite repeated cut backs in the original order of twenty-two episodes and the network's intermittent airing of remaining episodes in poor positions in the schedule. Unwavering fans held out hope that rumors of another network buying the series would materialize, and in early 2006 the subscription cable network Showtime reportedly offered a deal for twenty-six episodes over two seasons so long as creator and executive producer Mitch Hurwitz remained at the helm. Fans' dreams were dashed in late March when Hurwitz declined the offer, with many speculating that he found the compensation package unacceptable.[43] In any event, he and the writers had clearly anticipated the end on FOX and had produced final episodes that adequately closed the story, allowing the series a creative completion many do not receive.

The story of *Arrested Development* leaves as many questions as answers. Although it is unlikely that viewers would have been able to enjoy this series in a previous era, the competitive environment of the late multichannel transition was ultimately unavailing as well. The series produced only fifty-three episodes, which reduced its opportunity for subsequent distribution. As has become increasingly standard, the series was released on DVD and sold internationally. In addition, while the negligible HDNet cable network—a high-definition network available in only three million homes—purchased a syndication run for undisclosed terms, MSN bought exclusive portal rights to syndicate the show online for three years, and cable network G4 also purchased the basic cable rights for a three year run.[44] This deal marks the first time a show has been simultaneously syndicated on three platforms, but because of its unprecedented nature and the small audiences of each venue, the deal can give little indication of whether it might be successful for any of the distributors or the studio, or what it might mean for subsequent programs with strong fan interest, but small overall audiences.

While the fate of the show illustrates the complicated state of comedy production in a narrowcast competitive field, its failure at the same time as the emergence of iTunes' distribution of television series has led some to imagine how different norms of distribution and economics might make a show like *Arrested Development* viable—as I noted in Chapter 4. In a truly post-network era of all non-linear content in which viewers deliberately select programs and the intensity of feeling for a show characteristic of cult hits creates greater economic value, a series like this one would be more likely to succeed. Yet *Arrested Development* cultivated its loyal fans through "free" viewing on FOX, and how to create initial support for new series remains an uncertain component of such a non-linear and transactional economic system. Will people be willing to pay to sample content? What economic model might introduce new programming? Some forecast a scenario in which broadcast network airtime could serve as a promotional vehicle—FOX might air the first season of a show, but continued production would depend on its gathering enough viewers to support subsequent seasons through some combination of advertising and subscription. Such a transaction model might not produce the billions of dollars in profits some producers have enjoyed over the years, but it could provide a real opportunity for those who seek to use the medium to tell a story regardless of whether it might bring exceptional fame and fortune. With economic models continuing to develop, it may be possible to find ways to support niche hits other than through direct transaction. After all, advertisers very much want to remain part of viewers' television experience—they're just wary of supporting unproven methods of reaching audiences.

Off to War

Of the five cases under consideration here, *Off to War* arguably deviates most significantly from any norm of network-era commercial television. In a stunning piece of documentary, filmmakers Craig and Brent Renaud embedded themselves with the men and families of the 239th National Guard Infantry during the eighteen months of their deployment to Iraq in 2004 and 2005 in order to tell a rich and detailed story about the war and its effects upon the part-time soldiers. One of the filmmakers followed the Guard unit to Iraq, while the other stayed behind in the small town of Clarksville, Arkansas, to record the experiences of their families, thereby allowing viewers to see how war affects both those who go and those who remain at home.

The limited-run series that aired on the Discovery Times channel in 2004 and 2005 began as a documentary with funding from Japanese broadcaster NHK. As the Renauds prepared to join the unit, the Pentagon mandated that they find a U.S. network or channel to support their project as a condition of being embedded. The filmmakers subsequently reached a deal with digital cable channel Discovery Times for three one-hour specials that went inside the world of the unit preparing for deployment and then going to Iraq. The response to the specials, aired in the fall of 2004, led the network to commission another seven hours that aired in the fall of 2005. Significantly, the unit was called up and began training before the insurgency changed the nature of the war. The additional episodes consequently allowed the filmmakers to explore the situation of part-time soldiers with limited preparation and equipment for the task they ultimately faced.

Off to War first aired just before the 2004 U.S. presidential election, although most episodes aired during the period in which support for the president and the war eroded under the mounting evidence of falsehoods circulated by the administration in the run-up to the war. Under the circumstances, the series' honest look at how the war affected the soldiers and their families in profound, unfair, and largely unconsidered ways made it an important contribution to the culture's (re)assessment of the war. The series also featured working-class, rural, Southern Americans—that is, individuals who were most unlikely to appear on television screens, despite the way the 2004 campaign often invoked this population as the heart of the nation.

For all of its cultural centrality, however, *Off to War* existed in comparative obscurity on what might be described as an ultra-niche cable network. Discovery Times launched in March 2003 and reached only 37.3 million homes by November 2005. At the time, Discovery Communications and The New York Times Company jointly owned the network that serves as a prime example of the additional providers made possible by the efficiency of digital cable transmission. Many of the networks launched after 2000 received carriage only on digital cable systems, as by that point, space in analog transmissions systems had become too crowded for new entrants—especially those without some sort of leverage. (ABC, for example, may have gained better distribution for ESPN Classic because of the power of ESPN.) The Discovery Times channel would thus never have existed without digital cable, and its part ownership by an established cable entity also greatly contributed to creating an opportunity for such a niche venture.

New and niche channels such as Discovery Times struggle financially as their limited distribution makes it difficult to draw advertisers, yet without substantial advertiser support their budgets remain inadequate for developing programming that might grow viewership. Rather than purchasing off-network series such as the various iterations of *Law & Order* and *CSI*, as has been the strategy of many cable channels that attempt to use known content to draw viewers to an unknown channel, Discovery Times has developed limited original content that it promotes as extensively as it can afford to outside of the network in hopes of finding viewers. *Off to War* provided a timely project for the channel, and Discovery Times' relative newness enabled it to schedule the series as soon as it was complete—as opposed to established network HBO, which often had its documentary schedule set at least a year in advance.[45] Although the commission Discovery Times could afford was not as substantial as some other networks might have paid, the production costs of the series were limited enough to enable the filmmakers to cover them. (Because the Renauds were embedded, their housing, food, and flights to Iraq were paid by the military.) They also retained the rights for international and DVD distribution in order to profit from the series. Just as a marquee program can be invaluable for establishing the identity of a cable channel, so too can an opportunity that might be small by broadcast network standards be extremely valuable for independent filmmakers. *Off to War* earned the Renauds a nomination for outstanding directorial achievement in documentary from the Directors Guild of America, an Overseas Press Club award, and significant exposure at a number of international film festivals that likewise provided more value than just the tangible revenue from the series.

Discovery Times economized the purchase of the series by replaying it many, many times. A review of the channel in June 2005 noted that it produced approximately thirty hours of new programming each month, filling much of the rest of its schedule with programming from other channels in the Discovery family.[46] The same article asserted that about 75 percent of Discovery Times' content was unique to the channel, which suggests how many times original content such as *Off to War* might be replayed. Due to its small audience size, the network sold its advertising time as a companion to cable news channels, which have a similar demographic composition. At the time *Off to War* aired, the channel targeted men and adults aged 25–54; its viewers had a median age of 47, compared with 57 for the cable news channels.[47]

From the channel's perspective, *Off to War* was a big success and catapulted it to where its staffers hoped it would be in five or six years in just a matter of one or two.[48] In one weekend that aired an *Off to War* marathon, the network ranked among the top ten of cable channels, which is significant relative to the competition, but still negligible compared with broadcast audiences.[49] Despite this success, The New York Times Company announced plans to sell its stake in the channel in April 2006, which makes the channel's future questionable. The rationale is perhaps indicative of the arriving post-network era, in that The New York Times Company reportedly decided to shift the budget that had gone to the channel to developing online video content for the paper's website. In many ways, the Discovery Times channel itself is a prime candidate for such non-linear distribution. Although the new content the *Times* endeavor develops is likely to be much shorter than the documentaries aired by Discovery Times, the decision underscores a perception of the need for content to be available on demand. If this were the case on Discovery Times, viewers might more easily access its limited new programming. Instead, the channel's linear schedule and its heavy reliance on repeats of original content and programming made for other Discovery channels inhibits such access. For example, I initially missed the last episode of *Off to War* and had to wait three months for the network to re-play the entire series before they re-aired the one episode I wanted to see. If the series had been available on demand, new viewers could begin watching at any time instead of at the pace determined by channel schedulers.

Since the series reached only thirty-seven million homes and was buried deep in the expanse of rarely viewed cable channels—channel number 111 in my home—few viewers were likely to just happen upon *Off to War*. Discovery Times promoted the show heavily, but the nature of the channel forced it to focus its effort and money outside of the channel—spending nearly as much on promotion as production in order to draw viewers to the series. Promotion was one of the key assets of the channel's part ownership by The New York Times Company, with full-page color advertisements often appearing in the *Times* in advance of each episode. The filmmakers also appeared on CNN, FOX News, and on radio shows such as *This American Life* and *Weekend Edition*. In terms of more conventional television promotion, the channel also benefited from its co-ownership by Discovery as it could air promotions on the other four Discovery channels available in most digital cable packages. Still, the series garnered little promotion compared with a "broadcast" show and would probably have escaped even my attention were it not for my regular reading of many of the nation's television critics, particularly those who offer less mainstream recommendations.

The story of *Off to War* may well beg an answer to the question, "If an unconventional show airs in obscurity on an ultra niche cable network, what contribution can it make to the culture?" Here, there is room for much speculation, but there are other issues to which the series speaks directly. *Off to War* illustrates that commercial television at the beginning of the post-network era could encompass a once inconceivable range of content. For those who saw the series, this capability mattered a great deal. Indeed, while the other shows considered here derive much of their significance from their unconventional economic and distribution practices, the significance of *Off to War*'s is in its very existence. *Off to War* also reminds critics that the medium encompasses more than the base motives of commercialism. Alongside those willing to tell whatever story will earn the most residuals are those who have a meaningful story to share and a passion for telling it, undeterred by limited economic reward. The production conditions of the multi-channel transition and post-network era create far greater opportunities for such stories than existed in the network era.

Conclusion

In an era of a couple hundred channels I obviously could have selected a group of cases to tell just about any story about the television industry. I could have looked at a stalwart like *Law & Order*, which has been one of the most profitable shows in television history regardless of its adherence to conventional production practices. Or I could have considered one of the many programs that survived the grueling gauntlet of development and pilot selection, only to disappear into network oblivion after a handful of episodes. Another story, admittedly a bit harder to tell, is of the shows that still do not achieve distribution on U.S. television. Many of these are no more unconventional than those I consider; they just lacked the right mix of happenstance and opportunity that intervened in these cases.

Each of the cases I did select tells a different story that brings to life the detailed production practices chronicled in the other chapters. I offer them in hopes that the concrete circumstances of specific shows might help illuminate the behind-the-scenes practices that influence the business of television in crucial ways. Program success and failure may be difficult to anticipate, but a confluence of industrial factors contributes significantly to explaining why audiences now choose among a broader array of televised storytelling than at any previous moment in the medium's history. Likewise, understanding the yet-to-be-established practices hinted at in previous chapters prepares us to assess how television is likely to continue to change in coming months and years.

Of the cases that I present here, it is *Off to War* that gives me the most hope for what the post-network era might mean for television as a cultural institution, but it is also the case that makes me most skeptical of the consequences of what is to come. I could replace *Off to War* with many different series: PBS's *American Family* (2002–2004), Lifetime's *Any Day Now* (1998–2002), even Comedy Central's *The Daily Show with Jon Stewart* (1998–). All offer stories about people or perspectives not usually found on U.S. television and address important social issues. But these shows typically reached a few hundred thousand people on a medium well known for its ability to gather tens of millions.

The variation in the audiences reached by different programs at the beginning of the post-network era suggests the need for multiple ways of thinking about television as a cultural institution. Those shows that are watched by audiences numbering in the multi-millions continue to allow television to operate as an electronic public sphere, as it did in the network era. By and large, these will continue to be shows designed for outlets that require mass audiences, such as the broadcast networks, and will have certain attributes that will aid their broad address. As is the case now, in seeking inclusiveness, they will often "plane" the contentious edges from their programs. With more neutralized and mainstream ideas, these shows for mass audiences will do significant work in reaffirming certain ideas and norms within the culture.

By the late multi-channel transition, other categories of programming supported television's more emergent cultural functions—the significance of which we have yet to fully understand. This programming exists on a continuum. At the extreme are programs that address narrow audiences—whether they be Bill O'Reilly's angry conservatives or Bill Maher's liberal hipsters. Somewhere in between are more niche-specific shows and channels for distinctive audiences—MTV's adolescents, Univision's Spanish speakers, Lifetime's traditional women. These are not nearly as exclusive as programming at the extremes, but they also raise the question of how to understand the contribution of exceptional niche shows relative to the mass hits that remain. While many tell stories about specific groups of people, they were never meant to reach only people who look like those on the screen. After years of living amidst so much niche media, a "performance of the niche" emerged as audiences that could find themselves amply represented on some shows grew uncertain of those that did not feature people who looked like them or whom they might emulate. This situation has fueled a retreat of the audience into enclaves of self-interest, where, despite the medium's enhanced commercial ability to tell a broader range of stories, few of us allow those different from ourselves into our television world —at least those of us who can find ample representations of ourselves.

Changes in production practices enabled new stories to be told on television, but these industrial processes could not overcome the behavior of viewers who perform the demographic and psychographic separation encouraged by advertisers. The new capabilities of the medium to offer diversified stories and perspectives became moot against viewers' inability to find these stories or the disinterest of many in stories not directed to their particularities. Television offers its viewers access to profound and meaningful narratives—admittedly interspersed among ample uninspired and mind-numbing drivel—but few members of the audience venture outside of their like-reflecting silos of self-interest, which keeps this programming more constitutive of television's margins than its core. But it is still out there, and brought to us by television.

Conclusion
Still Watching Television

So this is how we end up alone together. We share a coffee shop, but we are all on wireless laptops. The subway is a symphony of earplugged silence while the family trip has become a time when the kids watch DVDs in the back of the minivan. The water cooler, that nexus of chatter about the show last night, might go silent as we create disparate, customized media environments.
 —David Carr, *The New York Times*[1]

Despite the wide-ranging changes in the norms and experience of this technology we have called television, I feel safe in asserting that the verb "watch," or maybe "view," will remain the primary word most of us will continue to use to describe our experience. Regardless of the screen size or our location, television fundamentally remains a cultural experience valued for the simultaneous visual and aural glimpses it provides of everything from fictional worlds to breaking news. But otherwise, any further commonality in the experience or the use of television is likely to continue to diversify.

We may keep watching television, but the new technologies involve new rituals of use. Few have considered their conventional behavior with regard to network-era television in terms of ritual—probably because there was nothing to compare it to. Television use typically involved walking into a room, turning on the set, and either turning to specific content or commencing the process of channel surfing—notably, true channel surfing is a behavior that developed early in the multi-channel transition. But integration of post-network technologies—such as the DVR—into regular television viewing has inaugurated entirely new television-related behaviors. Specific shows might be set to automatically record weekly, while some devices might be programmed daily. Using a DVR requires a very different and far more deliberate process of content selection than was possible before—as is true of many new television technologies.

Although my particular DVR-setting behavior is probably not widely representative, it nevertheless illustrates the process of adapting to new modes of decision-making regarding television. My DVR is set to automatically record *The Daily Show* Monday through Thursday and keeps two episodes. Typically, I automatically record only cable series (set a Season Pass, in TiVo vernacular), because I often forget when they are on; and I usually take advantage of the late-night replay of episodes so that I can record something on a broadcast network during the prime-time airing. My DVR only has one tuner, so I can record only one show at a time, and it holds only thirty hours of programming on extended record level, which also affects how I use the device. I set the broadcast recordings nightly, usually before preparing dinner. I have a better sense of what broadcast shows are on which nights, but scroll through the interactive programming guide making selections based on what shows might be repeats or new episodes and to keep abreast of network scheduling changes. Then I set the VCR on the other television in cases where two shows air simultaneously. On rare occasions, I'll set something to record far in advance—typically a show on a cable network I don't usually view—because I have read a provoking review or there is a lot of buzz within the culture or among my students. I record almost all shows on the "extended" (poorest) quality level because my hard drive is often nearly full and because this mode allows me to fit the most shows on the recorder. Some exceptional shows—those for which viewing becomes an event in my household—are recorded in high quality, so long as there is space. I neither watch nor record much programming outside of prime-time with the exception of limited sports coverage—which is always viewed live. I'm more likely to go online for breaking news coverage than bother with television, but in some cases, may turn on the television for live updates of a developing story.

This particular set of practices may be unique to me, but it illustrates the deliberate nature of my viewing. I am one of the people who can honestly say that I have not channel surfed since my DVR arrived in my home, and my replaying behavior is equally purposeful. Most nights begin with *The Daily Show*—a nightly dinner ritual. Adopting arbitrary network-era norms, I usually watch comedies first and often intentionally save the "best" offering on the recorder for last, unless it is too action-oriented or gruesome. If I need to multitask while viewing (pay bills, make a grocery list, surf for something online), I'll select programs that do not require watching closely; I save the most involving programs for times when I can devote my full attention. I never watch anything live— except sometimes an HBO show, although I usually watch these on de-mand—largely because my viewing is pretty much contained to prime time. I have found it has become almost unbearable to watch live com-mercial programming: I've become very impatient with the commercial breaks and often occupy myself with something else until the show re-turns. Sometimes I'll start watching something in progress and time it so that I catch up with the live airing by the end. Yes, I skip nearly all com-mercials, but I will go back and watch some if they catch my eye during my thirty-second jumps. On the rare occasion that my hard drive be-comes empty, I typically turn the set off and wait for it to deliver more goodies.[2]

I have been thinking about how I use my DVR a lot lately because I have been contemplating buying a high-definition set. My current DVR does not have the capacity for HD recording, so I'll have to buy a new DVR too. This is a bit of a technological quandary, given that few HD DVRs are available, but after careful consideration I've concluded that I cannot go back to viewing on the network schedule—even if the images are the crisp and stunning ones offered by HD—I'll become a television-on-DVD watcher first. I suspect that if I redrafted this conclusion after living with HD for a while, I'd need more space to explain the added in-tricacies of my viewing behavior.

This description is also simplified by the fact that I am still a "living room" only viewer. In the year that I've owned a video-capable iPod, I've only once downloaded an episode of *Lost*—one I missed due to a glitch with my digital cable box. Even then, I watched it on my laptop because I wasn't the only one viewing in the room. I would probably use the iPod more if I had a longer commute, traveled more, or didn't always have something I needed to read. In the course of researching the book, I have started watching more video online, but mostly just short-form clips as a matter of keeping current with the latest pop culture flash in the pan— but I do find the experience compelling. The ability to search out video and control its beginning and ending adequately compensates for the small screen size—although I'd never want to do all of my viewing this way. Being able to view on a laptop helps me view more comfortably than if I had a desk-bound unit, but if there are delays or jumps in the stream-ing, I quickly move on to something else. I have no television watching capability on my mobile phone, which I rarely use anyway, and I have not become a television-on-DVD watcher, although I do plan to because I missed the beginning of the season of *Battlestar Galactica* and kept forgetting to search out reruns of the episodes I missed. Unlike most of my students, I do not download shows from services such as TVtorrents. I have thought about it, but only to get episodes of favorite shows that I've missed due to technological malfunctions or forgetting to set the recorder —although if I find out it is as easy and of as good a quality as many colleagues and students claim, my whole television use paradigm might shift again.

This is all a very long way of illustrating the complicated, deliberate, and individualized nature of television use for those adopting new technologies and shifting into the post-network era. The technologies have been available for some time, but required studios and networks to release content—or for pirates to beat them to it—in order for us to fully experience their capabilities. As I examine my own behavior, it becomes clear to me how complicated negotiating new uses might be for industry decision-makers. The industry seeks comprehensive new practices and financial models, while each viewer probably values each piece of content, as well as the opportunity to access it, differently. In the past few months, it seems as though a new story has emerged weekly reporting that X percent of viewers prefer free content over paying for it, or Y percent watch the commercials in DVR-recorded content—with the values of X and Y varying considerably depending on the study. The problem with such studies that seek aggregate answers is that they reveal little about the intricacies of individual uses and values—and it is only at the individual level that the viewer finds any of these new capabilities meaningful. For example, if I missed an episode of *Veronica Mars,* I'd think nothing of paying five, maybe even ten dollars to download the missed episode—with or without commercials. My willingness to pay decreases from there. I might pay a few dollars for *Lost* or *Rescue Me,* and I'd make the effort to download or stream a few other shows if there was no cost involved, but I would probably just skip most others and wait until the next episode. Every viewer allocates value differently based on taste, ability to pay, and the technology at hand, all of which makes establishing standard industry pricing very difficult.

This suggests how the experience of television in a post-network era fragments beyond the narrowcasting of the multi-channel transition to personcasting in terms of what is viewed, when, how, and even in how viewers pay for it. Although such variation in what we watch might not entirely disrupt our network-era understandings of television and culture, the disparity in when we watch programs will make asynchronicity a defining feature of the post-network era. When industry journalist Diane Mermigas queried in 2006, "Isn't 'primetime' a misnomer in this new 'anytime' era?" the question itself suggests one of many coming adjustments in the very way we talk about television.[3]

The Five Cs of the Post-Network Era

After becoming accustomed to expanded *choice* and *control* throughout the multi-channel transition, viewers began to require new attributes such as *convenience, customization,* and *community* in order to have their preferred television experience. Both convenience and customization resulted from viewers' experience of choice and control—they indicated a second stage of adjusted use and expectation after network-era norms eroded and conventions of the multi-channel transition vied for dominance. The plethora of programming opportunities is meaningless without a means for viewers to find relevant shows and organize their viewing, which necessitates finding technological and distribution solutions for the problem. Amidst such vast choice and opportunity, viewers can only find the custom content they desire through sophisticated search mechanisms and elaborate recommendation functions determined by real and artificial intelligence mechanisms that redraw social relationships among viewers and content.

The desire for community emerged in user behavior with new digital technologies and, in the case of television, may result from viewer efforts to reestablish some of the shared cultural experience that had once been more typical of the medium. While viewers' ability to customize their experience has become essential, paradoxically, community remains a crucial part of the media experience. Beth Comstock, president of digital media and market development at NBC Universal, acknowledged that "In the digital age, community is all about gathering people with shared interests and giving them a platform to interact with each other, to engage in relevant content and to create something new."[4] Thus, the emerging post-network-era version of community differs greatly from the network-era one, which was created by watching common shows at a common time. The post-network version develops through like interests and connects people who may be geographically disparate. These are not communities in which people share reflections about television at water-coolers or cocktail parties; rather, they are ones in which people communicate their favorites among peers and through online venues and thereby create meaningful relationships. Communities of viewers sharing interests, favorites, and self-produced content have emerged to organize post-network viewing in the manner previously provided by the networks. As a result, the industry has struggled to restructure its profit and production systems in accord with these new conditions. Here, communities may be more mediated, but thinking that mediated communities are less meaningful than unmediated ones indicates our bias toward previous norms. As Chris Anderson explains, the fact that you and I may have both watched *CSI* last night might start a conversation, but this might indicate only slightly more intimacy than talking about the weather. The investment in stories and ideas that lead to the connection people make online provides the tools for the beginning of relationships—what he has identified as the creation of "tribes of affinity."[5]

Although initially resistant to the industrial reconfiguration wrought by viewers' adoption of the enhanced possibilities of the five Cs, by 2005 industry leaders accepted the inevitability of the medium's redefinition. Innovators, established industries, and viewers began a negotiation as each sought to expand their status in the system and the opportunity to determine a television experience most in their interest. Consumers could not maximize their choice and control without new fees, nor could the profit-makers proceed without offering value to audiences in the complicated transactions of the cultural industries. Understanding that one medium or model of practice does not necessarily replace another remains crucial to developing industrial plans for what a post-network era featuring converged technologies might look like.

As I completed work on this book in early 2007, many uncertainties about the future of television remained, but some new practices and norms had solidified enough to allow us to contemplate the dominant features of the emerging post-network era. The changes in the industrial norms and conditions of production chronicled here yield substantial implications for the creative possibilities of cultural industries. As a result, much of the "conventional wisdom" of both industry workers, concerning the type of programs that can be profitably produced, and scholars and analysts, regarding how the industry operates, requires reconsideration. The previous pages illustrate many instances in which monolithic network-era norms have been replaced with a variety of practices that are in turn likely to support a further diversification in the content produced by the industry and available to viewers.

As the new competitive environment began to take shape, many industry assessments compared the situation of the television networks with a perhaps apocryphal story of the railroad industry's response to the advent of passenger air travel.[6] The story goes that the downfall of the passenger train service resulted from the industry's inability to recognize air travel as a competitor—that it narrowly viewed itself as engaged in the railroad business rather than the broader transportation business. The oft-made comparison in the rise of the post-network era of television contemplates whether the television networks and stations will choose to narrowly conceive of themselves as networks in the network-era sense—as entities bound to previous norms of program acquisition, distribution, and scheduling—or whether they will recognize that they are in the content aggregation and distribution business and adjust their competitive practices and business models accordingly. By 2007, some evidence existed that network executives are expanding their paradigms in order to remain relevant industry players—and here, their embrace of free online video availability throughout the 2006–2007 season is notable. The questions now are whether they can adapt their financial models quickly enough to maintain quality production standards, as well as how soon advertisers might reallocate their spending among expanding options.

The changes of the multi-channel transition and post-network era obviously have manifold consequences for the study of media and its role in society, some of which I have raised here and about which I have offered some preliminary ways of thinking. Few have offered detailed considerations of the significance and repercussions of the erosion of mass media, or how audiences exercising choice and control require us to revise fundamental ideas about media and culture.[7] Questions such as how cultures and subcultures come to know themselves and each other without widely shared programming and how this affects perceptions of difference in society require new thinking. Many assumptions of the "mass" nature of media undergird theories postulating the emancipatory potential of media. Even as the new norm of niche audiences eliminates some of these imagined possibilities, it may create others.

As this book went to press, two particularly significant issues loomed over the developing post-network era, and both are likely to have notable consequences. First, the new technologies and distribution possibilities that functionally define the opportunities of the post-network era also come with significant costs for viewers, for whom television requires considerably higher spending than had been the case in the network era. Adoption rates of technologies and services remained too low by the end of 2006 to provide an accurate picture of how the financial requirements of the post-network era would segment viewers' ability to participate in its possibilities, and how the composition of the post-network audience might in turn affect the industry. Second, I completed the book during what many regarded as "the year of online video."[8] Google had just purchased YouTube for a mind-boggling amount, and it was clear that video services were next in the progression of new economy businesses. By early 2007, viewers downloaded one hundred million videos from YouTube each day, and various old and new media companies rapidly expanded the video available on their websites.[9] Heady optimism dominated the moment, but again, it is too early to determine the long-term consequences of amateur video distribution and other emerging online video services. Although there are such uncertainties surrounding online video as well as media costs, these developments are themselves conspicuous enough to warrant some further consideration.

Costs of the Post-Network Era and the Consequences of Online Amateur Video

The unprecedented degree of choice and control viewers now enjoy have come at a price. Throughout the network era and multi-channel transition, advertisers subsidized many costs, but to more or less captive audiences. Forecasts of the end of television as wrought by TiVo reasonably have emphasized how the device empowers viewers to renege on their implied commitment to watch the commercial messages of the companies who bring them their nightly programming.

Once the fear of change subsided, advertisers and networks came to some important realizations. The user revolt of TiVo seemed less an indictment of advertising than an indictment of advertising's excesses. The number of non-program minutes per hour had increased precipitously, particularly since the mid 1980s, with networks and advertisers exploiting the "value proposition" involved in television advertising—we'll pay for the program if you watch the commercials—by adding more advertising and decreasing programming minutes. Control technologies provided viewers with a way to illustrate that the value of that proposition had eroded too significantly for their continued participation. Advertisers and networks have found that commercial skip rates decrease and ratings increase when they use fewer commercials per hour, and some advertisers recognize that new technologies also offer them some controls that might help reinstate the value proposition.[10] Early experiments with commercial support of video on demand, for example, found much lower fast-forwarding rates when only one or two commercials appeared in advertising breaks. Some studies also reported that viewers who fast-forward through advertisements have recall levels equivalent to those who watch the commercials—which also suggests that the thirty-second ad might not be in dire peril. Aware that monthly fees have been compounding for viewers, advertisers have begun to consider how they might offset some of those fees through advertising.

If the agencies have noticed the proliferating fees, viewers most certainly have too: as the Veronis Suhler Stevenson report cited in Chapter 5 found, consumers paid more for media in 2005 than did advertisers. This shift from commercial support indicates a development with significant social consequences, for it seems likely that the expanding range of fees related to television use in the post-network era will create notable social and cultural cleavages. Many have attended to the digital divide, wherein access to computers and the Internet is variable, as well as to the consequences of disparity between lower- and upper-income homes and schools. The issues at stake in the post-network divide are related to these concerns, but also very different. The expense of home entertainment systems introduces significant socio-economic distinctions in who can afford the technologies that enable theatrical viewing or convenient and mobile television, and such economic division further fractures norms of television viewing within the culture.

Network-era television was never really free, but the absence of a per-use cost reduced economic barriers.[11] Throughout the multi-channel transition, the expanding television services and technologies introduced ever-increasing costs to viewers both in technology expenses and monthly service fees. Cable costs vary based on the level of the package, but expanded services such as subscription networks or HD channels require the purchase of digital cable in addition to fees in excess of ten dollars per month *each* for a package of HD networks, premium networks, or DVR service; a NetFlix subscription adds another twenty or so dollars each month.[12] By spring 2005, 74 percent of digital cable homes and 53 percent of digital satellite homes paid more than fifty dollars per month, while 19 percent of digital cable and 6 percent of satellite homes paid monthly fees equal to or greater than one hundred dollars. Expanding packages and new services have certainly driven up the income of cable and satellite providers: by the spring of 2005, the proportion of cable and satellite households paying at least fifty dollars a month had nearly doubled in just four years.[13]

Other integrated technology such as mobile phones also require a monthly fee—typically a minimum of forty-five dollars. Wireless PDA applications double the cost and expanded services on mobile devices such as text messaging or receiving video content add yet other fees. The service that is being adopted most quickly is broadband to the home, with monthly fees that range between thirty and sixty dollars. These monthly costs are particularly substantial when multiplied as yearly rates. Based on Bureau of Labor statistics, the *New York Times* reported in November 2005 that the average American spent more on entertainment than on gasoline, household furnishings, and clothing, while the most affluent quintile, those earning more than $77,000, spent more on entertainment than on health care, utilities, clothing, or food eaten in the home.[14]

Many of the post-network technologies have not been adopted widely enough to know how they may exacerbate class-based differences. One logical expectation is that access will break down on income lines, but past technological dissemination has illustrated that the adoption of entertainment technologies is often more complex. Although cable would be most certainly categorized as a luxury good, many more lower- income homes than predicted subscribed because of the value it offered in terms of leisure spending. A monthly basic cable subscription cost nearly the same as the price of taking a family of four to a film, while providing many more hours of content. In 2004, research by the National Association of Broadcasters estimated that six million of the twenty million homes that did not subscribe to cable or satellite did so because they could not afford the average forty-dollar monthly bill.[15] While that number is significant, it is also notable that for the other fourteen million, the decision not to subscribe was not economically based—a fact that indicates the complexity of factors contributing to technological adoption.

As Juliet Schor notes in *The Overspent American,* however, the monthly fees for entertainment and communication services have multiplied extensively and greatly contributed to the strain on many middle-income families, who are stretched to pay for services that increasingly have come to be perceived as needs rather than luxuries.[16] Phone and cable bills once provided the extent of monthly service fees, but households now pay for any number of mobile phones, for broadband Internet access, for DVRs, and for high-definition programming tiers. Although once again, conventional wisdom would certainly suggest that significant stratification among the haves and have nots will emerge, others have suggested that many will continue to pay the new fees until economic crisis forces reassessment. Cultural critic James Poniewozik has opined that the growing costs won't make television an elite medium, but that "More than likely, we will thoughtlessly suck up the additional expense just as we have every other increment in the entertainment budget"—although it is unclear how broad the "we" he invokes might be taken to be.[17] The situation is complicated by the fact that as new fees emerge, others can be decreased or eliminated—take, for instance, plummeting long-distance calling fees or households that do away with landlines after adopting mobile phones. Shifting uses and pricing of older technologies also contribute to uncertainty about how widely new services might be adopted.

Service providers are certainly aware of the competing demands for discretionary household spending, and the debate about network neutrality that emerged in 2006 illustrated their awareness that consumers alone could not bear the prices required to meet stockholders' expectations. At its core, the debate resulted from Internet service providers' desire—both cable and telephone—to access a share of the rapidly multiplying riches of Internet advertising enjoyed by companies such as Google. No hike in monthly rates could compare with the coffers of online companies and content aggregators, who service providers suspected would pay dearly to maintain the reach and speeds that kept them popular among Internet users. Of course, the network neutrality debates were never publicly framed in these terms, but service providers' concerns about how much of their economic model could depend on consumers' monthly fees illustrates the limited growth expected by the industry. As competitive pressures lead networks to experiment with alternative ways of making their programs available, great uncertainty remains about how many would or could afford to adopt new technologies and ways of using television even once ample content became available.

But questions about profiting from the possibilities of the post-network era are not the only ones on the minds of industry leaders; they also wonder about how the proliferation of amateur video might cut into demand for industry production. By late 2006, it remained unclear whether the flurry of amateur video was merely a passing trend or likely to revolutionize television well beyond the ways addressed here. Although the conditions of the post-network era vastly expand opportunities for amateur production and distribution of television, it is difficult to know how significant this content might become to viewers' daily television consumption. Like so much of the new technological space, existing amateur video was largely confined to the efforts of high school and college-aged students by the end of 2006. But as cultural discussion of YouTube grew, politicians and corporations quickly began adding their videos, creating an odd amalgamation spanning talking-head video of Ted Kennedy, Paris Hilton's music video debut, and cats using human toilets.

Without question, amateur video creation and distribution on the scale achieved by "The Evolution of Dance" troubles the preliminary rethinking of television I've suggested here. While I agree with industry pundits who argue that there always will be a significant and important place for programming produced with the expert talent and budgets available only to commercial productions, the online video phenomenon involves a significant expansion in the revolutionary ways new media allow us to communicate and further indicates the importance of visual media in cultural communication. Much of what circulates on sites such as YouTube involves amateurs making use of professional content—whether through mash-ups, by posting clips, or using unlicensed music. This adds new complications to already fraught intellectual property concerns in ways that have no foreseeable resolution. The amount and diversity of content these outlets provide also exacerbates dilemmas about niche media's reach, the challenge of conveniently navigating the vast content available, and the establishment of communities of like-interested people.

By the beginning of 2007, however, some distinctions in video distributed online have become clear enough that they may be helpful in thinking about the vast array of content that circulates. First, professionally created video—often cut into shorter clips than that which aired originally—provides one type of programming with a distinctive set of production, distribution, and payment requirements. Networks have caught on quickly to viewers' desire to watch their content on demand and in particular segments—whether this be a popular skit from *Saturday Night Live* or David Letterman's nightly monologue. At first viewers had to post such content illegally on sites such as YouTube, but once networks recognized the promotional value of freeing content from conventional distribution, they began to seek to control the video and profit from advertisements on their own sites. A second category of online video is created by amateurs and offered for the sheer joy of exhibition—or, as was the case of many early web video stars, in an effort to get a job in conventional media or to secure a production deal. Creators have not sought to control this content in the same manner as the networks, so it has been free to circulate virally without the concerns of monetization or rights management central to professional content. A third category seemed to be just emerging in early 2007 and has yet different dimensions. In this case, established media professionals have begun to consider web distribution for its potential to offer artistic freedom, even if it does not provide the level of financial reward that may be available from conventional media. For example, in late 2006, Stephen Bochco entered a strategic alliance with MetaCafe in one of the earliest of such instances in which known and established creative talent produced original content for online distribution.[18] Indeed, this situation seems different enough from the others to warrant its own category, even as it in many ways blends the artistic impulse that can motivate amateurs, while placing the camera in the hands of a skilled creator in a manner likely to produce content comparable to that which might be expected of professional media. As the space of web video continues to diversify in 2007, it is clear that very different motivations drive both creators and viewers, and that those differences are likely to require distinct distribution and financing mechanisms for online video content.

A Closing Salvo

The post-network era is introducing immense changes to the medium and its role in society, yet television remains every bit as relevant and vital a site for exploring intersections of media and culture as it has ever been. Some prefer identifying this era as one of "convergence" and specifically object to the way "post-network" might suggest the irrelevance of the entities that have long defined the medium. Others are concerned that the "post-network era" might indicate a newer, more improved version of television that disregards its rich past. There is a certain irony that a post-network era comes to characterize television at the same time as theorists of new technology posit the establishment of a network society—a concept that draws on the networked communication systems characteristic of this era.[19] In this case different notions of networks operate on parallel but distinctive trajectories, so that the shifts in industrial practice that inaugurate the post-network era of television are complementary to developments in the network society.

Let me be clear that in using the term "post-network" I do not mean to suggest the death or complete irrelevance of what we have known as television networks or channels. Rather, the term acknowledges the degree to which the centrality they achieved as controllers of distribution and schedulers of programs has diminished. The post-network era will still include some semblance of "networks" and "channels"; however, their fundamental activities and responsibilities will be adjusted greatly. There still will be a need for program aggregators, like networks, to which viewers attribute a certain identity. The same thing that led you to tune to NBC during the multi-channel transition might lead you to select the NBC folder on your on-demand menu or go to the NBC website to see what programs might be available. Or rather than using a specific brand, an aggregator that offers the easiest and most accurate search function might come to dominate the previous function of networks, as Google did on the web by the mid-2000s. We do need to acknowledge how much of a network's identity also has been bound up in its selection of what programming it would stream into our homes and when, even though the "naturalness" of this activity prevented us from reflecting much upon it previously.[20] The same studios, conglomerates, and distributors that dominated the network era and multi-channel transition remain important at the dawn of the post-network era, but their relationships and control of cultural production require significant renegotiation. Ultimately, the relevance of the networks will depend upon how they adapt to viewers' changing desires and expectations.

By noting the increasing control that viewers achieve over their television experience—in determining when, where, and how they watch and even participating in it increasingly as creators—I do not mean to indicate that power shifts to the viewers. Viewers have come to enjoy a meaningful increase in and expanded diversity of programming as a result of the industrial changes of the multi-channel transition and emerging post-network era, and television has come to be revolutionized in comparison with network-era norms. However, commercial interests still control production, and viewers' choice is still limited as there remains much that cannot be found on television. The new possibilities in programming that have been achieved are significant, but by no means do they indicate that viewers now control the process or that a democratization of the medium has occurred. The conditions of the post-network era allow some steps in that direction, but we still have a long, long way to go.

The ways that new television technologies, uses, and programming both separate us and bring us together provide rich new topics for study and interrogation. Acknowledging the fluidity of the medium's use is crucial—we may switch at any time from the increasingly default mode of "alone together" television use that David Carr describes in the epigraph to turning our collective eyes to same content. Although we have little data or experience to explain how modern societies respond to the loss of common culture, Joseph Turow is probably right in noting that our move into individual silos of entertainment and information is significant. Turow, however, does not allow for viewer-driven efforts to re-establish community through the media they now use, and this is also an important factor to take into consideration in understanding these media and new norms of use. If the lack of interactivity inherent in the one-way transmission of television made it difficult for viewers to recreate viewing communities during much of the multi-channel transition, the web has since created locations for the development of rich fan cultures and communities. As the "viewsing" of television and the Internet continue to converge, audience members will be better able to participate in communities of fanship, view virtually together, and share their viewing tastes and pleasures with friends, family, and others. Many aspects of the industry are very interested in developing empirically based understandings of how viewers use television differently in the post-network era, and this information is important for reassessments of its cultural role as well. We know a lot about how viewers used to watch television, but those old understandings provide little information about current and coming experiences.

This book focuses nearly exclusively on prime-time programming, but other program areas require similar reconsideration. Some of the arguments made here apply to considerations of post-network television news, post-network sports programming, or post-network daytime programming, but each of these areas also has aspects that distinguishes it from prime-time shows—and few have the economic mandate of earning revenue in syndication. These other types of programming further indicate the inadequacy of assuming that "television" exists as a coherent entity. I am uncertain whether we should ever have spoken of "television" in a manner suggesting uniformity and cohesiveness, but we most definitely cannot continue to think of it in this way.

In his 1974 *TV: The Most Popular Art,* Horace Newcomb closed his pioneering critical look at the nation's most derided and engaged media form by proposing characteristics of television aesthetics.[21] Basing his views upon the network-era content and available uses of television in the 1970s, Newcomb argued that intimacy, continuity, and history were the elements that distinguished television and earned its status as popular art. These characteristics particularly differentiated television storytelling from that of cinema, and while he noted that the "smallness of the television screen has always been its most noticeable feature," Newcomb could not have anticipated the two and one-half inch display on my video iPod some thirty years later. The established norms of visual storytelling common to cinema framed the media context through which we initially began to understand television.

Decades later, we no longer need a separate medium to frame our understanding of television because its own historical features and distinctions now serve that function. I have provided scant consideration of television programming or television as an artistic form beyond my attention to the consequences of production on the stories it tells, and I won't start now. But it is worth noting, despite my attention to the changes, adjustments, and disruptions of network-era television, that the same aesthetic elements Newcomb outlines continue to characterize television storytelling—and in some cases are even more pronounced now.

In his 1995 bestseller *Being Digital,* Nicholas Negroponte wrote that "The future of television is to stop thinking of television as television."[22] In many ways the longevity of the multi-channel transition resulted from the slow realization of this fact and efforts to keep thinking about television within the box introduced half a century earlier. Negroponte's words were prescient in 1995 and continue to be relevant over a decade later. Television remains very much alive and an important part of culture, and understanding the variety of production practices and multiple functions of the medium provides a first step toward explaining how television has been revolutionized.

Notes

Notes to the Introduction

1. Mark Fischetti, "The Future of TV," *Technology Review,* November 2001, 35–40.

2. IBM Business Consulting Services, "The End of Television as We Know It," 27 March 2006, http://www-1.ibm.com/services/us/index.wss/ibvstudy/imc/a1023172?cntxt=a1000062&re=endoftv, accessed 19 April 2006; Adam L. Penenberg, "The Death of Television," *Slate.com,* 17 October 2005, http://www.slate.com/toolbar.aspx?action=print&id=2128201, accessed 20 October 2005; Burt Helm, "Why TV Will Never Be the Same," *BusinessWeek Online,* 23 November 2004, http://www.businessweek.com/technology/content/nov2004/tc20041123_3292_tc184.htm?chan=search, accessed 23 November 2004; Brooks Barnes, "How Old Media Can Survive in a New World," *Wall Street Journal,* 23 May 2005, R1.

3. Josh Borland and Evan Hansen, "The TV Is Dead. Long Live the TV," *Wired,* 6 April 2007, http://www.wired.com/entertainment/hollywood/news/2007/04/tvhistory_0406, accessed 6 April 2007.

4. Michael Curtin, "On Edge: Culture Industries in the Neo-Network Era," in *Making and Selling Culture,* eds. Richard Ohmann, Gage Averill, Michael Curtin, David Shumway, and Elizabeth Traube (Hanover, NH: Wesleyan University Press, 1996), 181–202, 186.

5. Michele Hilmes, "Cable, Satellite and Digital Technologies," in *The New Media Book,* ed. Dan Harries (London: British Film Institute, 2002), 3–16, 3.

6. The distribution of television content on Apple's iTunes in October 2005 marked a significant turning point, and if pushed to identify the beginning of the post-network era, this is the event I would likely propose.

7. The channel allocation freeze encompasses the four years from 1948–1952 in which the FCC granted no new station licenses while it determined a strategy to organize the spectrum. During the same period, CBS and NBC competed to establish the television standard, which included various color and black and white standards that were not always interoperable.

8. The exception being RCA's parentage of NBC; CBS also included the CBS Records division, and ABC had links to theatrical exhibition, but this conglom-

eration is minimal compared with what developed later. See Erik Barnouw, *Tube of Plenty: The Evolution of American Television,* 2nd rev. ed. (New York: Oxford University Press, 1990); Les Brown, *Television: The Business Behind the Box* (New York: Harcourt Brace Jovanovich, 1971); Sally Bedell, *Up the Tube: Prime-Time TV and the Silverman Years* (New York: The Viking Press, 1981); Ken Auletta, *Three Blind Mice: How the TV Networks Lost Their Way* (New York: Random House, 1992).

9. See William Boddy, *Fifties Television: The Industry and Its Critics* (Urbana: University of Illinois Press, 1993); Lynn Spigel, *Make Room for TV: Television and the Family Ideal in Postwar America* (Chicago: University of Chicago Press, 1992); George Lipsitz, "The Meaning of Memory: Family, Class, and Ethnicity in Early Network Television Programs," in *Private Screenings: Television and the Female Consumer,* eds. Lynn Spigel and Denise Mann, 71–110; Mary Beth Haralovich, "Sitcoms and Suburbs: Positioning the 1950s Homemaker," in *Private Screenings: Television and the Female Consumer,* eds. Lynn Spigel and Denise Mann (Minneapolis: University of Minnesota Press, 1992), 111–42.

10. Although, as McCarthy notes, tavern viewing was also common, particularly until penetration levels grew to the point that televisions were common in the home. Anna McCarthy, *Ambient Television: Visual Culture and Public Space* (Durham: Duke University Press, 2001).

Also, Spigel recounts that Sony launched a portable set in 1967. While technologically possible, portability was not a defining attribute of the medium in the way the advent of a technology such as the Walkman fundamentally redefined music use. As Spigel notes, the "portable" sets of the 1960s were often marketed as "personal tv's" to allow individualized viewing. Despite this marketing rhetoric, purchase of such sets was slow, and when purchased, these portable televisions seldom moved. See Lynn Spigel, "Portable TV: Studies in Domestic Space Travel," in *Welcome to the Dreamhouse: Popular Media and Postwar Suburbs* (Durham: Duke University Press, 2001), 60–103, 75. Tracy Stevens, ed., *International Television and Video Almanac,* 44th edition (La Jolla, CA: Quigley Publishing Co., 2001) 4.

11. James G. Webster, "Television Audience Behavior: Patterns of Exposure in the New Media Environment," in *Media Use in the Information Age: Emerging Patterns of Adoption and Consumer Use,* eds. Jerry L. Salvaggio and Jennings Bryant (Hillsdale, NJ: LEA, 1989), 197–216.

12. Paul Klein, "Why You Watch When You Watch" (originally printed in *TV Guide,* July 1971), reprinted in *TV Guide: The First 25 Years,* ed. Jay S. Harris (New York: New American Library, 1978), 186–88.

13. This particular change actually precedes the others, beginning in the early 1970s—although it continues to affect the industry in crucial ways during the period in which the industry negotiates these other changes.

14. John Thornton Caldwell, *Televisuality: Style, Crisis, and Authority in American Television* (New Brunswick: Rutgers University Press, 1995), 11.

15. FOX averaged a share of nine, and UPN and The WB each drew four, leaving ABC, CBS, and NBC with an audience share of only forty-one in 1999–2000. Aggregate cable first draws more prime-time viewers than aggregate broadcast networks in 2003–2004. John Dempsey, "Cable Aud's Now Bigger than B'Cast," *Variety.com,* 20 May 2004, http://www.variety.com/story.asp?l=story&a=VR1117905396&c=14, accessed 20 May 2004. The 1999–2000 figure is from *Broadcasting & Cable*; the 2004–2005 figure is from Monica Steiner, "Primetime Update (Full Season)," *Media Insights,* 27 May 2005, 2.

16. Initiative Media, *Today in National Television,* 9 April 2004.

17. Nielsen Media Research, *TV Audience* (New York: Nielsen Media Research, 2003); Jim Rutenberg, "Much in a Name," *The New York Times,* 15 August 2001, E4.

18. James R. Walker and Robert V. Bellamy, Jr., "The Remote Control Device: An Overlooked Technology," in *The Remote Control in the New Age of Television,* eds. James R. Walker and Robert V. Bellamy, Jr. (Westport, CT: Praeger, 1993), 3–14.

19. Webster, "Television Audience Behavior."

20. Ibid.

21. In his examination of whether new technologies contribute to making "interactive audiences," Henry Jenkins reports Matt Hills' concern about how asynchronous viewing of programming around the globe troubles synchronized fan discussions and interactions with programming online; Henry Jenkins, "Interactive Audiences?" in *The New Media Book,* ed. Dan Harries (London: British Film Institute, 2002), 157–70, 161. Hills contemplates only the beginning of coming issues, as DVRs and VOD technologies as well as the breakdown of network scheduling conventions challenge the likelihood of television viewing cultures experiencing content synchronously even within national or regional contexts. The future model is more likely to be similar to that of film as viewers choose available content on their own schedules, with fans accessing content immediately.

22. In many instances this required co-production with an international market, as in the case of *La Femme Nikita, The 4400,* and *Battlestar Galactica.*

23. Knowledge Networks Statistical Research, "The Home Technology Monitor: Spring 2005 Ownership and Trend Report" (Crawford, NJ: Knowledge Networks SRI, 2005), 40.

24. Dan Harries, "Watching the Internet," in *The New Media Book*, ed. Dan Harries, 171–82, 172.

25. Issues of generation are also noted by Nicholas Negroponte, *Being Digital* (New York: Vintage Books, 1995), and Charlotte Brunsdon, "Lifestyling Britain: The 8–9 Slot on British Television," in *Television After TV: Essays on a*

Medium in Transition, eds. Lynn Spigel and Jan Olsson (Durham: Duke University Press, 2004), 75–92, 85.

26. Neil Howe and William Strauss, *Millennials Rising: The Next Great Generation* (New York: Vintage Books, 2000); Sharon Jayson, "Totally Wireless on Campus," *USA Today,* 2 October 2006, http://www.usatoday.com/tech/news/2006-10-02-gennext-tech_x.htm, accessed 6 October 2006. There are unquestionably factors of class that create substantial differences in the technological access available to the members of this generation.

27. Ann Sweeney, remarks made at The National Show, Atlanta, GA, 10 April 2006.

28. IBM Business Consulting Services, "The End of Television as We Know It."

29. Jason Mittell, "TiVoing Childhood," *Flow,* 3, no. 12 (March 2006) http://jot.communication.utexas.edu/flow/?jot=view&id&1472, accessed 16 March 2006.

30. Bill Carter, "Reality TV Alters the Way TV Does Business," *The New York Times,* 25 January 2003.

31. Examples of early constraining corporate behavior can be seen in early versions of AOL that allowed only paying members to access content and industry efforts to prevent DVR use. Later, AOL shifted to allow anyone access to ad-supported content, and networks made shows available on iTunes for use on personal computers and iPods.

32. Brian Winston, *Media Technology and Society: A History: From the Telegraph to the Internet* (London: Routledge, 1998), 6.

33. A practice with extensive historical precedence; see Winston, *Media Technology.*

34. Todd Gitlin, *Inside Prime Time* (New York: Pantheon Books, 1983).

35. My use of this phrase involves a far more practical dimension than the more theoretical and philosophical meanings found in John Hartley's *Uses of Television* (London: Routledge, 1999).

NOTES TO CHAPTER 1

1. Totals come from hits noted on the site, although these figures are far from definitive.

2. Bill Carter, "Here Comes the Judge," *The New York Times,* 12 March 2006, section 2 page 1; Ciar Byrne, "And the Real Winner Is . . . ," *The Independent,* 16 January 2006, 4; Claire Atkinson, "Marketers Hunger for Idol Reprise," *Advertising Age,* 29 May 2006, 1.

3. To some degree, see John Hartley, *Uses of Television* (London: Routledge, 1999).

4. Lisa Gitelman, *Always Already New: Media, History and the Data of Culture* (Cambridge: MIT Press, 2006), 7.

5. Lynn Spigel and Jan Olsson, eds., *Television After TV: Essays on a Medium in Transition* (Durham: Duke University Press, 2004), 2.

6. Charlotte Brunsdon "What Is the 'Television' of Television Studies?," in *The Television Studies Book,* eds. Christine Geraghty and David Lusted (London: Arnold, 1998), 95–113.

7. Michael Curtin, "Feminine Desire in the Age of Satellite Television," *Journal of Communication* 49, no. 2 (1999): 55–70, 59.

8. This section speaks of dominant norms of this time. Of course exceptions existed as early adopters bought early versions of remote control devices and others utilized portable sets.

9. Nielsen Media Research, *2000 Report on Television: The First 50 Years* (New York: Nielsen Media Research, 2000), 13. See Anna McCarthy, *Ambient Television: Visual Culture and Public Space* (Durham: Duke University Press, 2001), for a critical and theoretical examination of this phenomenon.

10. By using the term "electronic public sphere" I do not intend to invoke Jürgen Habermas. My usage is far more descriptive than analytical and emphasizes the way television made content broadly available; it does not speak to issues surrounding the public sphere that are more theoretically complex.

11. Evident in Horace Newcomb and Paul Hirsch's theorization of television creating a "cultural forum" and John Fiske and John Hartley's explanation of television's "bardic function" in storytelling. Horace Newcomb and Paul Hirsch, "Television as a Cultural Forum," *Television: A Critical View,* 5th ed., ed. Horace Newcomb (New York: Oxford University Press, 2004) 503–15; John Fiske and John Hartley, *Reading Television* (London: Methuen and Co. Ltd., 1978).

12. Todd Gitlin, "Prime Time Ideology: The Hegemonic Process in Television Entertainment," in *Television: A Critical View,* 5th ed., ed. Horace Newcomb, 516–36.

13. This use of the idea of the cultural institution is comparable with Louis Althusser's concept of the ideological state apparatus, and I presume them to function similarly. See Louis Althusser, "Ideology and Ideological State Apparatuses," in *Lenin and Philosophy and Other Essays,* trans. Ben Brewster (London: Monthly Review Books, 1971), 127–88.

14. In fact, a considerable amount of hostility existed between those identifying their work as belonging to the field of cultural studies and those seeing their work as political economy. A 1993 ICA session produced a heated forum for this debate that became legendary; the exchange is captured in a Colloquy section of *Critical Studies in Mass Communication* 12, no. 1 (1995). In that volume, see Lawrence Grossberg, "Cultural Studies vs. Political Economy: Is Anybody Else Bored with this Debate?": 72–81; Nicholas Garnham, "Political Economy and Cultural Studies: Reconciliation or Divorce?" 62–71; James Carey, "Abolishing the Old World Spirit," 82–89. For more on this debate, see also Douglas Kellner, "Overcoming the Divide: Cultural Studies and Political

Economy," in *Cultural Studies in Question*, eds. Marjorie Ferguson and Peter Golding (London: Sage Publications, 1997), 102–20.

15. Paul du Gay, Stuart Hall, Linda Janes, Hugh Mackay, and Keith Negus, *Doing Cultural Studies: The Story of the Sony Walkman* (London: Sage, 1997); David Hesmondhalgh, *The Cultural Industries* (London: Sage, 2002); Andrew Calabrese and Colin Sparks, eds., *Toward a Political Economy of Culture: Capitalism and Communication in the Twenty-First Century* (Lanham, MD: Rowman & Littlefield, 2004); Andreas Wittel, "Culture, Labor, and Subjectivity: For a Political Economy from Below," *Capital & Class* (Winter 1984), no. 84: 11–30.

16. Amanda D. Lotz, "Using 'Network' Theory in the Post-Network Era: Fictional 9/11 U.S. Television Discourse as a 'Cultural Forum,'" *Screen* 45, no. 4 (2004): 423–39.

17. Raymond Williams, *Television: Technology and Cultural Form* (New York: Schocken Books, 1974).

18. Bernard Miege, *The Capitalization of Cultural Production* (New York: International General, 1989), 146–47.

19. Horace Newcomb, "This Is Not Al Dente: *The Sopranos* and the New Meaning of Television," in *Television: The Critical View*, 7th ed., ed. Horace Newcomb (New York: Oxford University Press, 2006), 561–78; Horace Newcomb, "Studying Television: Same Questions, Different Contexts," *Cinema Journal* 45, no. 1 (2005): 107–11.

20. Tom Scocca, "The YouTube Devolution," *New York Observer*, 31 July 2006, 1.

21. Michael Curtin argues this is at least the case of television. Curtin, "Feminine Desire in the Age of Satellite Television."

22. See Anna Gough Yates, *Understanding Women's Magazines: Publishing, Markets and Readerships* (New York: Routledge, 2003); Janice Winship, *Inside Women's Magazines* (London: Pandora Press, 1987); Ros Ballaster, Margaret Beetham, Elizabeth Frazier, and Sandra Hebron, *Women's Worlds: Ideology, Femininity, and Women's Magazines* (London: Macmillan, 1991).

23. Joseph Turow, *Breaking Up America: Advertisers and the New Media World* (Chicago: University of Chicago Press, 1997).

24. A derivation of what Turow describes as "electronic equivalents of gated communities." Ibid., 2.

25. Sub-cultural concerns are also important, but need theory distinct from that which treats television as a cultural institution.

26. Lotz, "Using 'Network' Theory."

27. Fiske and Hartley, *Reading Television*, 66.

28. Austan Goolsbee, "The BOOB Tube Won't Make Your Kid a Boob," *Chicago Sun Times*, 5 March 2006, B3. Although, to be fair to the authors, their method looked at network-era television, which may make their universalizing use of television more defensible.

29. Newcomb and Hirsch, "Television as a Cultural Forum," 503–515; Todd Gitlin, "Prime Time Ideology"; Fiske and Hartley, *Reading Television*.

30. In 1970–71, *Marcus Welby, MD* was the top show with a rating of 29.6; at the time the U.S. television universe was estimated at 60.1 million hence, the show reached 49.2 percent of households. By 1980–81, *Dallas* was the most watched show with a rating of 34.5, but since the television universe had increased to 76.3 million, it reached 45.2 percent of households. Data on top shows drawn from Tim Brooks and Earle Marsh, *The Complete Directory to Prime Time Network and Cable TV Shows, 1946–Present,* 8th rev. ed. (New York: Ballantine Books, 2003). Television universe figures from Nielsen Media Research, *2000 Report on Television: The First 50 Years.*

31. Kathryn C. Montgomery, *Target: Prime Time: Advocacy Groups and the Struggle Over Television Entertainment* (New York: Oxford University Press, 1989).

32. Paul du Gay, et al. *Doing Cultural Studies*; Julie d'Acci, "Cultural Studies, Television Studies, and the Crisis in the Humanities," in *Television After TV: Essays on a Medium in Transition,* eds. Lynn Spigel and Jan Olsson, 418–45.

33. See Patricia Aufderheide, *Communications Policy and the Public Interest* (New York: Guilford Press, 1999), for an account of the regulatory, industrial, and public interest machinations and struggles over the Telecommunication Act of 1996, and Joel Brinkley, *Defining Vision: The Battle for the Future of Television* (San Diego: Harcourt Brace, 1997), on the switch to high-definition television.

NOTES TO CHAPTER 2

1. "Convergence Fulfilled," *The Hollywood Reporter.com,* 13 September 2005, http://www.hollywoodreporter.com, accessed 20 September 2005.

2. Josh Borland and Evan Hansen, "The TV Is Dead. Long Live the TV," *Wired,* 6 April 2007, http://www.wired.com/entertainment/hollywood/news/2007/04/tvhistory_0406, accessed 6 April 2007.

3. In using the frameworks of mobility and theatricality, Spigel does not specify that mobility involves viewing content as it is broadcast—although that was a technological limitation of the period. I emphasize mobility as the function for viewing currently airing content and convenience as the means of mobile viewing of "recorded" content in order to affirm an important distinction in their functionalities.

4. Louise Benjamin, "At the Touch of a Button: A Brief History of Remote Control Devices," in *The Remote Control in the New Age of Television,* eds. James R. Walker and Robert V. Bellamy, Jr., 15–22.

5. Bruce C. Klopfenstein, "From Gadget to Necessity: The Diffusion of Remote Control Technology," in *The Remote Control in the New Age of*

Television, eds. James R. Walker and Robert V. Bellamy Jr. (Westport, CT: Praeger, 1993), 23–39.

6. Jackie Byars and Eileen R. Meehan, "Once in a Lifetime: Constructing the 'Working Woman' through Cable Narrowcasting," *Camera Obscura* [special volume on "Lifetime: A Cable Network for Women," ed. Julie d'Acci] 33–34 (1994): 12–41, 23.

7. William J. Quigley, ed., *International Television and Video Almanac,* 50th ed. (New York, Quigley Publishing, 2005), 15.

8. See Byars and Meehan, "Once in a Lifetime."

9. The launch of some of the most competitive cable networks precedes the mid-1980s, with HBO (1972), CNN (1980), and MTV (1981) seeking audiences years before the industry reaches the 50 percent penetration mark. Major events also follow; DBS systems offer another method of program delivery (although they arguably offer no more additional program providers than those available through cable—especially since the rollout of digital cable systems). Tracy Stevens, ed., *International Television and Video Almanac,* 45th ed. (La Jolla, CA: Quigley Publishing Co., 2000), 9.

10. Meg James, "TV in Your Pocket Is the Next Small Thing," *Los Angeles Times.com,* 1 November 2005, http://www.latimes/news/printedition/front/la-fi-mobile1nov01,1,1902147,print.story?coll=la-headlines-frontpage, accessed 1 November 2005.

11. Knowledge Networks/SRI, *The Home Technology Monitor: Spring 2005 Ownership and Trend Report* (New York: SRI, 2005), 11. Much of this data is drawn from Knowledge Networks' Home Technology Monitor, a report of home technology ownership and trends the company has produced for twenty-five years. The survey relies on calling respondents using a random national sample. A key limit of this data is that it only surveys households with telephones.

12. Ibid., 17
13. Ibid., 27
14. Ibid., 14.
15. Ibid., 17–19.
16. Ibid., 18.
17. Ibid., 19.
18. Ibid., 25.
19. Ibid., 27.
20. Ibid., 30.
21. Ibid., 31.
22. Ibid., 32.
23. 1985: 11 percent; 1990: 18 percent; 1995: 30 percent; 2000: 52 percent; ibid., 39–40.
24. Ibid., 46.

25. Ibid., 57.

26. Ibid., 57.

27. This capability was not introduced in the United States until 2005. Ibid., 59.

28. Although there remained the possibility for expansion in broadband utilization and in the number of phones per household.

29. Mark Dominiak, "Neutralize Clutter to Set Off Message," *Television Week,* 9 May, 2005, 34.

30. MAGNA's estimate was comparable to others; see Brian Wieser, "On-Demand Quarterly," A Publication of MAGNA Global USA, September 2006, 3.

31. Thanks to Jason Mittell for suggesting this phrasing for describing this phenomenon.

32. Steve Sternberg, "Television Insights," A Publication of MAGNA Global USA, 8 November 2005, 1.

33. In 1985, Nielsen reported soap operas constituted seven of the ten most frequently recorded programs. James Traub, "The World According to Nielsen," *Channels* 4, no. 1 (1985): 26–32, 70–71, 70; Josh Bernoff, "The Mind of the DVR User: Acquisition and Features," Forrester Research, 31 August 2004; Steve Hoffenberg, "DVR Love: A Survey of Digital Video Recorder Users," DTV View Lyra Research, May 2004; Brian Hughes, "Nielsen's DVR Impact Assessment Study, Media Insights," A Publication of MAGNA Global USA, September 2005.

34. John M. Higgins, "Empty Screens: If Cable's Video-On-Demand Is So Hot, Where Are All the Good Shows?" *Broadcasting & Cable,* 19 September 2005, 14.

35. By including the Internet, I intend to signal the distribution and viewing of shows over the Internet using peer-to-peer technology (largely illegal at this point), not IPTV (Internet protocol television). As a means of distribution, IPTV receives attention in Chapter 4.

36. Bernard Miege, *The Capitalization of Cultural Production* (New York: Information General, 1989).

37. See Paul du Gay, et al., *Doing Cultural Studies: The Story of the Sony Walkman* (London: Sage, 1997), for an extensive cultural analysis of the Walkman.

38. Diane Werts, "A New Way to Watch TV," *The Columbus Dispatch,* 21 January 2004, F1, 6; John Maynard, "With DVD, TV Viewers Can Channel Their Choices," *The Washington Post,* 30 January 2004, C1.

39. Maynard, "With DVD, TV Viewers Can Channel Their Choices."

40. Werts, "A New Way to Watch TV."

41. Stephanie Rosenbloom, "*Lost Weekend*: A Season in One Sitting," *The New York Times,* 27 October 2005; http://www.nytimes.com/2005/10/27/fashion/thursdaystyles/27dvd.html?ex=1288065600&en=808bc3d02751557&ei=5090, accessed 1 November 2005; Sam Anderson, "The Joys of Rising from

the Cultural Dead," *Slate.com,* 6 April 2006, http://www.slate.com/toolbar. aspx?action=print&id=2139457, accessed 7 April 2006.

42. See Anderson, "The Joys of Rising from the Cultural Dead."

43. Thomas Goetz, "Reinventing Television," *Wired* 13, no. 9 (September 2005), http://wired-vig.wired.com/wired/archive/13.09/stewart.html, accessed 19 September 2005; Business Wire, "Jon Stewart's *Crossfire* Transcript Most Blogged News Item of 2004, Intelliseek Finds," *Business Wire,*15 December 2004.

44. See Anna McCarthy's work on tavern culture in particular. Anna Mc-Carthy, *Ambient Television: Visual Culture and Public Space* (Durham: Duke University Press, 2001).

45. Lynn Spigel, "Portable TV: Studies in Domestic Space Travel," in *Welcome to the Dreamhouse: Popular Media and Postwar Suburbs* (Durham: Duke University Press, 2001), 60–103, 71.

46. Although the primary use of geofiltering involved limiting online downloading to specific national regions to preserve the profitability of international distribution. Amy Schatz and Brooks Barnes, "To Blunt Web's Impact, TV Tries Building Online Fences," *Wall Street Journal,* 16 March 2006, A1.

47. James, "TV in Your Pocket."

48. See Mermigas, [No Title], *HollywoodReporter.com,* 14 September 2005. Accessed through Lexis Nexis 6 October 2005.

49. Daisy Whitney, "Nets Wait by the Phone," *Television Week,* 29 May 2005, 36.

50. Ibid.

51. James, "TV in Your Pocket."

52. Stephanie Whitaker, "True Confessions: 'I Am a Crackberry,'" *The Montreal Gazette,* 28 February 2005, B4; Nick Duerden, "Email of the Species," *The Independent on Sunday,* 17 July 2005, 13–14; Joe Robinson, "Club Med on CrackBerry," *Los Angeles Times,* 4 September 2005, M3. CrackBerry references and discourse about "BlackBerry Thumb" began as early as 2003. Notably, discussions of the devices have been more substantial in Canada and Britain than in the United States as of 2005.

53. Faith Popcorn, *The Popcorn Report: Faith Popcorn on the Future of Your Company, Your World, Your Life* (New York: Doubleday, 1991), 207–33; Faith Popcorn and Lys Marigold, *Clicking: 16 Trends to Future Fit Your Life, Your Work, and Your Business* (New York: HarperCollins, 1996), 51–64. This trend continued through the 1990s, and then the terrorism of September 11th exacerbated it with fears that public venues such as malls, movie theaters, and theme parks might become subsequent targets.

54. Another early adopter use sought a contradictory end. Some used the Slingbox to route content stored on living room DVRs to laptops in other rooms in the house.

55. In fact, Nick Duerden reports a broader popular market for the devices in Britain. Duerden, "Email of the Species," 13–14.

56. McCarthy, *Ambient Television.*

57. Lynn Spigel, "Portable TV."

58. Barbara Klinger, *Beyond the Multiplex: Cinema, New Technologies, and the Home* (Berkeley: University of California Press, 2006), 22–23.

59. Although this discussion of resolution shifts as constantly as the technology, CNet.com has consistently provided the clearest explanations. See David Katzmaier, "HDTV Resolution Explained," *CNet.com,* 12 September 2006, http://www.cnet.com/4520-7874_1-5137915-1.html?tag=tnav, accessed 28 December 2006.

60. For a detailed explanation of the complicated development of HD, see Joel Brinkley, *Defining Vision: The Battle for the Future of Television* (San Diego: Harcourt Brace, 1997).

61. James Hibberd, "Bridging the HD Gap," *TVWeek.com,* 17 August 2006, http://www.tvweek.com/page.cms?pageId=238, accessed 18 August 2006.

62. High definition and digital transmission are difficult to extricate because high-definition functionally requires digital transmission. At an operational level, digital transmission most profoundly changes television distribution capacity, although it provides limited enhancement of the image; by contrast, high definition markedly improves image quality.

63. Some broadcasters decided to use the efficiency of the digital spectrum to "multicast," meaning fit more than one channel in the spectrum. Others "leased" extra spectrum to other service providers. As broadcasters were driven by hopes of maximizing available profit from the spectrum, many of their actions deviated significantly from what regulators hoped the spectrum would provide.

64. Boutique strategies of differentiation are also important in the 1980s, as argued by John Thornton Caldwell in *Televisuality: Style, Crisis, and Authority in American Television* (New Brunswick: Rutgers University Press, 1995).

65. Daniel Dayan and Elihu Katz, *Media Events: The Live Broadcasting of History* (Cambridge: Harvard University Press, 1992), 1.

66. Additionally, in plans publicized for the 2006 and 2008 games, NBC planned to spread content across different applications such as mobile phones. Mermigas, [No Title].

67. This marks an expansion of the trend toward boutique television noted by Caldwell in the early 1990s. Caldwell, *Televisuality,"* 105–33.

68. David Lieberman, "HDTV Sales Strong—Among Wealthier Consumers, Study Says," *USA Today,* 25 October 2006, available from http://www.usatoday.com/printedition/money/20061025/hdtv25.art.htm, accessed 25 October 2006.

69. Also, affluence tends to correlate negatively with television viewing, which makes HD homes more likely to have less frequent television viewers and therefore more difficult for advertisers to reach.

70. See, for example, Phillip Swann's columns and commentaries at http://www.tvpredictions.com.

71. Jodi Kantor, "The Extra-Large, Ultra-Small Medium," *The New York Times,* 30 October 2005, http://www.nytimes.com/2005/10/30/arts/television/30kant.html, accessed 1 November 2005.

72. Claire Atkinson, "TV Ad Effectiveness Drops 7 Percent in Non-DVR Households," *Advertising Age.com,* 16 March 2006, http://www.adage.com/news.cms?newsid=48317, accessed 23 March 2006.

73. Steve Sternberg, "Most Homes Have Only One Set on During Prime-time," Television Insights: A Publication of MAGNA Global, 12 September 2006, 1.

74. In one of my favorite stories, the students recounted three days of National Geographic Channel viewing because they had lost the remote and no one would get up and change the channel. Puzzled students would happen by their room and inquire about why they were watching a documentary about whales and then become engrossed in the show as well.

75. Jostein Gripsrud, "Broadcast Television: The Chances of Its Survival in a Digital Age," in *Television After TV: Essays on a Medium in Transition,* 210-223, eds. Lynn Spigel and Jan Olsson (Durham: Duke University Press, 2004).

76. Nicholas Negroponte, *Being Digital* (New York: Vintage Books, 1996).

NOTES TO CHAPTER 3

1. Quoted in Brian Steinberg, "*Law & Order* Boss Dick Wolf Ponders the Future of TV Ads (Doink, Doink)," *The Wall Street Journal,* 18 October 2006, B1.

2. Although the syndicator or distributor commonly receives 35 percent of gross revenues as a sales commission and an additional 10 to 15 percent to cover costs incurred for marketing, distribution, editing, etc. Howard J. Blumenthal and Oliver R. Goodenough, *This Business of Television,* 2nd ed. (New York: Billboard Books, 1998), 39.

3. By 2003, budgets had increased to $1.6 to $2.3 million, while license fees averaged $1 to $1.6 million. Paige Albiniak, "Deficit Disorder: Why Some Good Pilots Never Get Produced," *Broadcasting & Cable,* 5 May 2003, 1, 27.

4. Bill Carter, *Desperate Networks* (New York: Doubleday, 2006), 130.

5. Paige Albiniak, "License to Thrill," *Broadcasting & Cable,* 8 November 2004, 28; Ray Richmond, "*CSI* 100th: Scene of the Crime," *The Hollywood Reporter.com,* 18 November 2004; Tamsen Tillson and Elizabeth Guider, "CBS

Eyes a CSI Buyout," *Variety.com,* 20 December 2006, available from http://www.variety.com/index.asp?layout=print_story&articleid=VR111795615 8&categoryid=14, accessed 21 December 2006.

6. Maria Elena Fernandez, "CSI: Miami Goes Global," *Los Angeles Times,* 18 September 2006, 12; Daniel Frankel, Ancillary Waters Run Deep," *Variety.com,* 9 July 2006, http://www.variety.com/index.asp?layout=print_story&articleid=VR1117946444&categoryid=2162, accessed 27 September 2006.

7. Steve McClellan, "NBC Still Has *Friends,*" *Broadcasting & Cable,* 30 December 2002, 4.

8. Carter, *Desperate Networks,* 213.

9. Ibid.; Christopher Lisotta, "Sony Sticking to the Flight Plan," *Television Week,* 10 April 2006, 1, 48, 48.

10. Independent stations could also buy programming, but could not afford the same programming as networks.

11. Mark Alvey, "The Independents: Rethinking the Television Studio System," in *Television: The Critical View,* 6th ed., ed. Horace Newcomb (New York: Oxford University Press, 2000), 34–51.

12. Although threats to eliminate the rules began by 1983. See Alvey, "The Independents"; J. Fred MacDonald, *One Nation Under Television: The Rise and Decline of Network TV* (New York: Pantheon Books, 1990); Ken Auletta, *Three Blind Mice: How the TV Networks Lost Their Way* (New York: Vintage Books, 1992), 31; James Walker and Douglas Ferguson, *The Broadcast Television Industry* (Boston: Allyn and Bacon, 1998).

13. John M. Higgins, "It's Not All in the Family," *Broadcasting & Cable,* 23 May 2005, 8.

14. Robert Fidgeon, "FOX on the Run," *Herald Sun,* 26 July 2000, H05.

15. The complexity seen by scholars such as David Hesmondhalgh remains though, as the leading producer in this era is Warner Bros., which funneled only a limited amount of its programming to like-owned weblet The WB. David Hesmondhalgh, *The Cultural Industries* (London: Sage, 2002).

16. Robert W. McChesney, *The Problem of the Media: U.S. Communication Politics in the 21st Century* (New York: Monthly Review Press, 2004); Ben H. Bagdikian, *The New Media Monopoly* (Boston: Beacon Press, 2004).

17. Many proclaimed the shuttering of Carsey-Warner in 2005 as the death of the last independent (Mandabach had left the group a year earlier).

18. In practice, the deficit finance and cost plus models might be viewed on a continuum in which risk and reward relate inversely. Various "in between" arrangements exist whereby production companies receive more substantial initial license fees, but also relinquish a share of ownership to the network. Gillian Doyle, *Understanding Media Economics* (Thousand Oaks, CA: Sage Publications, 2002), 82.

19. Higgins, "It's Not All in the Family."

20. Steve McClellan, "The Graying of the Networks," *Broadcasting & Cable,* 18 Jun. 2001, 32–33.

21. In early 2007, Touchstone, a production studio owned by Disney, changed its name to ABC Television Studio.

22. In early 2005, CBS and Paramount were both part of the large Viacom conglomerate. The conglomerate announced plans that it was considering splitting Viacom into two separate publicly traded entities in March 2005, a decision finalized in June 2005. Both the CBS network and the studio renamed CBS Paramount Television were included in the CBS Corporation part of the split. Josef Adalian, "Eye Mandate Ruffles Rivals," *Variety.com,* 3 February 2005, http://www.variety.com/index.asp?layout=print_story&articleid=VR1117917414&categoryid=-1, accessed 8 February 2005.

23. Joe Flint, "Television Suffers From Loss of Independent Producers," *The Wall Street Journal Online,* 6 July 2005, http://online.wsj.com/article/0,,SB112057535281877372,00.html, accessed 7 July 2005.

24. The panel included Marc Graboff, president, NBC Universal Television, West Coast; Gary Newman, president, 20th Century Fox Television; Mark Pedowitz, president, Touchstone Television, and executive vice president, ABC Entertainment Television Group; and Bruce Rosenblum, president, Warner Bros. Television Group. Las Vegas, 17 January 2007.

25. Many argued that there were no remaining independent producers of scripted series, but definitions of independent varied considerably. Some argued that Warner Bros. was an independent once it no longer had The WB to buy its programming, but it is difficult to categorize a major studio as independent even if it did not have a commonly owned broadcast network.

26. Brandon Tartikoff and Charles Leerhsen, *The Last Great Ride* (New York: Turtle Bay Books, 1992), 14; also recounted in Carl DiOrio, "A Call for More Owners," *The Hollywood Reporter,* 4 October 2006, http://www.hollywoodreporter.com/thr/business/article_display.jsp?vnu_content_id=1003190939, accessed 6 October 2006.

27. DiOrio, "A Call for More Owners."

28. In an unusual move, producers Lawrence Bender and Kevin Brown launched a fully independent company in 2006 after ending an alignment with Warner Bros. The duo explained that the alignment made it difficult to develop series for cable networks and gave this as a key reason for their independent experiment. Josef Adalain, "Bender Moves to Tube Groove," *Variety.com,* 18 January 2006, http://www.variety.com/index.asp?layout=print_story&articleid=VR1117936392&categoryid=1236, accessed 27 January 2006.

29. Paige Albiniak, "Deficit Disorder," 27.

30. Allison Romano, "Crime Pays Again and Again," *Broadcasting & Cable,* 8 August 2005, 18.

31. See Timothy Havens, " 'It's Still a White World Out There': The Interplay of Culture and Economics in International Television Trade," *Critical Studies in Media Communication* 19, no. 4 (2002): 377–97.

32. For more see Amanda D. Lotz, "Textual (Im)Possibilities in the U.S. Post-Network Era: Negotiating Production and Promotion Processes on Lifetime's *Any Day Now*," *Critical Studies in Media Communication* 21, no. 1 (2004): 22–43.

33. See Hesmondhalgh, *The Cultural Industries,* for more on creative labor.

34. Chad Raphael, "The Political Economic Origins of Reali-TV," in *Reality TV: Remaking Television Culture,* eds. Susan Murray and Laurie Ouellette (New York: NYU Press, 2004), 119–36.

35. Film Scape News Center, "1988 Hollywood Writers Strike," 30 April 2001, http://www.filmscape.co.uk/news/fullnews.cgi?newsid988621880,79143, accessed 12 April 2006.

36. Sam Anderson, "The Joys of Rising from the Cultural Dead," *Slate.com,* 6 April 2006, http://www.slate.com/toolbar.aspx?action=print&id=2139457, accessed 7 April 2006.

37. Dave McNary and Ben Fritz, "Guilds Out of the Online Loop," *Variety.com,* 15 August 2006, http://www.variety.com/index.asp?layout=print_story&articleid=VR1117948511&categoryid=18, accessed 18 August 2006.

38. Film shooting in L.A. peaked in 1996 and had fallen 38 percent by 2005. Richard Verrier, "Movies, Schmovies—TV's Taking Over L.A.," *Los Angeles Times,* 19 August 2005, A1.

39. The shifting management of the networks that resulted from the purchase of all three networks also contributed to the demand for cost-savings. Raphael, "The Political Economic Origins of Reali-TV," 122–23.

40. John M. Higgins and Paige Albiniak, "Sunburned: Cable, Broadcast Each Had Summers that Hurt." *Broadcasting & Cable,* 1 September 2003, 1.

41. James G. Webster, Patricia F. Phalen, and Lawrence W. Lichty, *Ratings Analysis: The Theory and Practice of Audience Research,* 2nd ed. (Mahwah, NJ: Lawrence Erlbaum Associates, 2000).

42. The seriality of 24 was so considerable that some audience members waited until the full season of episodes was available on DVD in order to view it at their own pace.

43. David Bauder, "Study: Clutter of Advertising Soaring on Prime-Time Television," *AP News Wire,* 11 April 1999; Susan T. Eastman and Gregory D. Newton, "The Impact of Structural Salience within On-Air Promotion," *Journal of Broadcasting & Electronic Media,* 42 (1998): 50–79.

44. Eastman and Newton, "The Impact of Structural Salience within On-Air Promotion."

45. Jon Fine and Tobi Elkin, "On the House," *Advertising Age,* 18 March 2002, 1.

46. The WB also distributed coffee cup sleeves with an image that changed based on temperature to further promote the supernatural aspect of the show. Chris Blackledge, "They Deserve a Fat Promotion: Nets Angle for Fall Viewers," *NATPE News,* September 2005, http://www.natpe.org/memberresources/natpenews/articles/story.jsp?id_string=200023:X58IMn7ClV8Ry8yPMfzucQ**, accessed 20 September 2005. Meg James, "TV Networks Pursue the 'Super Fan,'" *Los Angeles Times,* 19 September 2005, http://www.latimes.com/business/la-fi-tvbuzz19sep19,1,1350987.story?coll=la-headlines-business&ctrack=1&cset=true, accessed 20 September 2005.

47. Christopher Lisotta, "WB, Yahoo! Offer *Super* Preview," *Television Week,* 5 September 2005, 1.

48. James, "TV Networks Pursue the 'Super Fan.'"

49. John Jurgensen, "Online: Fall TV," *Wall Street Journal,* 12 August 2006, 2.

50. Ben Fritz, "Sci Fi Thinking Inside the 'Box,'" *Variety.com,* 13 August 2006, http://www.variety.com/story.asp?l=story&a=VR1117948373&c=-1, accessed 18 August 2006.

51. Emily Steel, "CBS Touts New Shows in Video Clips," *Wall Street Journal,* 24 August 2006, B2.

52. Wayne Friedman and Christopher Lisotta, "Shows Crave Juice from On-Air Promos," *Television Week,* 21 March 2005, 11.

53. See the five separate stories in the March 10, 2006 issue, including a front-page story about the "real" mafia relative to the HBO series.

54. Ann Oldenberg, "TV Goes to Blogs: Shows Add Extra Information as a Treat for Fans," *USA Today,* 5 April 2006, 1D.

55. Daisy Whitney, "MySpace Video a Boon to *Mother,*" *Television Week,* 4 December 2006, 6, 40.

56. Preliminary findings of research by Vicki Mayer, personal communication, 9 September 2006.

57. Quoted in Sally Bedell, *Up the Tube: Prime-Time TV and the Silverman Years* (New York: Viking Press, 1981), 141.

58. See Susan T. Eastman, "Orientation to Promotion and Research," in *Research in Media Promotion,* ed. Susan T. Eastman (Mahwah, NJ: Lawrence Erlbaum Associates, 2000), 3–18.

59. Jim Bennett, "The Cinematch System: Operation Scale, Coverage, Accuracy, Impact," Presentation made at The Present and Future of Recommender Systems Conference, Bilbao, Spain, 13 September 2006, http://blog.recommenders06.com/wp-content/uploads/2006/09/bennett.pdf, accessed 18 October 2006.

60. This situation is contemplated further in Jason Fry, "O Pioneers!: Watching a Child Who's Grown Up with TiVo Leads to Questions about the Future of TV," *Wall Street Journal Online,* 12 December 2005, http://online.

wsj.com/public/article_print/SB113398924199016540.html, accessed 13 December 2005.

61. Chris Pursell and Michael Freeman, "Studios USA Will Stay the Course," *Electronic Media,* 29 October 2001, 1.

62. In fact, despite his claims of independent status, it is difficult to consider Studios USA in this way. The studio had been part of Universal until 1999, and the relationships it had within that studio and with others remained strong during its two-year "independence."

NOTES TO CHAPTER 4

1. Phil Rosenthal, "On-Demand Deals a New Dawn for TV," *Chicago Tribune,* 9 November 2005, www.chicagotribune.com/business/columnists/chio511090177nov09,1,4745093.column?coll=chi-business-hed, accessed 10 November 2005.

2. The term "original run" (or "first run") is commonly used to refer to programming produced originally for syndication (sale to individual stations rather than networks), but I use it here to include the original run of shows on networks as well.

3. Full service networks typically provided more daily content—for example, while FOX supplied stations with only two hours of nightly prime-time content—NBC supplied three hours of prime time, three hours of the *Today Show, NBC Nightly News,* the *Tonight Show,* and two hours of soap operas. Affiliates of FOX, The WB, and UPN still purchased many hours of programming because the network supplied so little. Jonathan Levy, Marcelino Ford-Livene, and Anne Levine, "Broadcast Television: Survivor in a Sea of Competition," Federal Communications Commission Office of Plans and Policy, September 2002, p. 19, http://hraunfoss.fcc.gov/edocs_public/attachmatch/DOC-226838A22.doc, accessed 9 November 2006.

4. Practices of exclusivity and windowing have been declining in the film industry as well. A 2006 report noted an 11 percent drop in the number of days between the theatrical and DVD release of films. This was the same year some filmmakers experimented with "day and date" release (simultaneous distribution on multiple platforms). Diane Garrett, "Windows Rattled," *Variety.com,* 21 March 2006, http://www.variety.com/index.asp?layout=print_story&articleid=VR1117940116&categoryid=20, accessed 23 March 2006.

5. Markets are generally the zone around major metropolitan areas reached by local stations—so although they tend to overlap with major cities, they exceed city boundaries.

6. A few shows were developed for first-run syndication, but these shows rarely aired during prime time. Mostly first-run syndication includes game (*Jeopardy*) and talk shows (*Oprah*), but also can include scripted series such as *Xena*. These shows operate under a much different financial model and typically

do not rely on deficit financing. The shows are sold to stations in each market, usually for some combination of cash and advertising time.

7. Admittedly, proclaiming a singular first move is difficult. One could also argue that the practice of syndicating series with fewer and fewer episodes marked an earlier procedural shift, but to the degree that this was a slight alteration in an existing norm, this seems less significant than original-run repurposing.

8. Previously a series needed a bank of roughly one hundred episodes before it could be sold in syndication. This meant that it would take four or five years before a series could begin a syndicated run.

9. Notably, this occurs over five years before the NBC/Universal merger that brings Studios USA into the NBC conglomerate. See Joe Schlosser, "Kissinger Tops USA Network TV," *Broadcasting & Cable,* 26 April 1999, 28.

10. See Deborah McAdams and Joe Schlosser, "*Once* Again on Lifetime," *Broadcasting & Cable,* 27 September 1999, 8.

11. John Dempsey, "Shared Runs: Cachet Over Cash," *Variety,* 11–17 June 2001, 11, 54.

12. Traditionally, the license fees broadcasters pay for a series cover only two airings of each episode, a first airing and one rerun. This was part of the networks abdication of Saturday night programming. The costs to program new shows was too high relative to the small audience they would draw, leading NBC, for example, to program repeat episodes from its various *Law & Order* shows on that night. This is different from conventional rerun practices that were typically confined to re-airing programs in the same time period as the network would air new episodes.

13. Steve Sternberg, "Impact on Network Ratings When a Program Is Syndicated," Media Insights: A Publication of MAGNA Global, 17 Jan. 2006, 1–5.

Broadcast networks also received vehement complaints from their affiliate stations which feared the consequence of added competition, especially since this practice diminished the affiliates' status as viewers' only access to the programs. R. Thomas Umstead, "Shows So Nice, They Ought to Play Twice," *Multichannel News,* 28 May 2001, http://www.multichannel.com/article/CA83801.html?q=%22shows+so+nice%2C+they+ought+to+play+twice%22, accessed 30 May 2001. Many of the cable networks that pay high prices for the repurposing licenses were disappointed by the ratings the repurposed series earned for their networks, and most deals prohibited the cable networks from airing these series during prime time (or at least while the original network aired prime-time programming). Many consequently scheduled the series at late hours (11:00 p.m. Eastern), which prevented the cable networks from using these better known series to carry audiences into their original programming. Dempsey, "Shared Runs," 54.

14. Record-setting syndication prices for *CSI* ($2 million per episode) and *The West Wing* ($1.2 million) also illustrate cable networks' eagerness to be associated with top-performing broadcast series. See Susanne Ault, "A

Diminishing Return?" *Broadcasting & Cable,* 30 July 2001, 22. The success of DVD releases of many series may curb repurposing as this second-run market is emerging as a previously untapped revenue stream.

15. Paige Albiniak, "Less Is More," *Broadcasting& Cable,* 10 May 2004, 14.

16. The financial risk of *Significant Others* for NBC was also diminished because it emerged from an experiment with media agency MindShare that was helping get shows in which it was interested on the air by providing financing as early as the script phase. Bill Carter, *Desperate Networks* (New York: Doubleday, 2006), 167–68.

17. ABC held *Sons & Daughters* until midseason; it first aired in March 2006 and failed to find an audience.

18. The *Veronica Mars*/MTV repurposing was in place for the series' first season. In the second season, UPN re-aired the show each week. Since Viacom split its media holdings into two separate companies in 2005 (concurrent with the shift between the first and second season), it was uncertain whether the shift in repurposing was simply the end of the MTV deal or resulted from UPN and MTV becoming parts of different companies after the split.

19. Michael Freeman, "TV in Transition," *Electronic Media,* 28 January 2002, 1.

20. John Lippman, "New Shows Try their Hand at Copying Fox Hit 24," *Wall Street Journal,* 24 March 2006, W7.

21. Lippman, "New Shows"; David Koeppel, "For Those of You Who Wonder How That TV Show Began," *New York Times,* 21 March 2005, C2.

22. Ibid.

23. See Derek Kompare, "Acquisition Repetition: Home Video and the Television Heritage," in *Rerun Nation: How Repeats Invented American Television* (New York: Routledge, 2005), 197–220.

24. Susanne Ault, "Fallen *Wonderfalls* Is a DVD Wonder," *Video Business,* 11 February 2005, http://www.videobusiness.com/article/CA612067. html?text=wonderfalls, accessed 19 September 2005.

25. Anthony Breznican, "*Firefly* Alights on Big Screen as *Serenity,*" *USA Today Online,* 21 September 2005, http://www.usatoday.com/life/movies/ news/2005-09-21-serenity_x.htm, accessed 29 December 2006.

26. The show was also syndicated on cable's Cartoon Network as part of the Adult Swim programming block, where it also performed successfully.

27. Meg James, "Fox Reuniting Itself with *Family Guy,*" *LA Times.com,* 13 April 2005, http://www.latimes.com/business/la-fi-family13Apr13,0,43681. story?coll=la-home-business, accessed 14 April 2005; Jill Vejnoska, "The DVD Effect," *The Atlanta Journal-Constitution,* 3 May 2005, 1E.

28. John M. Higgins, "Fast-Forward; With Scant Notice, TV-DVD Sales Top $1B and Begin to Affect Scheduling, Financing," *Broadcasting & Cable,* 22 December 2003, 1.

29. Ibid.

30. R. Thomas Umstead, "DVDs, Video Games Boost Net Brands," *Multi-channel News,* 19 July 2004, 66.

31. Ibid.

32. The "long tail" derives its name from the chart that tracks number of units sold on its vertical axis and number of titles sold on the horizontal access. It illustrates multi-millions of sales for the mega-hit, then slopes downward and to the right to chart the number of sales of less mainstream hits. The value of this library is not in the number of each book/song sold, but the fact that they are able to sell few copies of so many different items. Chris Anderson, "The Long Tail," *Wired,* 12, no. 10 (October 2004), http://www.wired.com/wired/archive/12.10/tail.html, accessed 2 February 2006; see also Chris Anderson, *The Long Tail: Why the Future of Business Is Selling Less of More* (New York: Hyperion, 2006).

33. Anderson, "The Long Tail."

34. Laurie J. Flynn, "Like This? You'll Hate That. (Not All Web Recommendations Are Welcome)," *New York Times.com,* 23 January 2006, http://www.nytimes.com/2006/01/23/technology/23recommend.html?_r=1& pagewanted=print, accessed 27 January 2006.

35. Data gathered by Forrester Research and presented by Josh Bernoff at the NATPE convention, 26 January 2006, Las Vegas, NV.

36. Daisy Whitney, "VOD Came Alive in 2005," *Television Week,* 2 January 2006, 12.

37. Kris Oser, "Best Online Media Seller: Yahoo," *Advertising Age,* 7 November 2005, M2.

38. Dawn C. Chmielewski, "Studios Not Sure Whether Web Video Innovator Is Friend or Foe," *Los Angeles Times.com,* 10 April 2006, http://www.latimes.com/business/la-fi-youtube10apr10,1,6694137,print.story?coll=la-headlines-business, accessed 12 April 2006.

39. Scott Kirsner, "Low-Budget Viral Videos Attract TV-Sized Audiences," *Boston Globe,* 30 July 2006, E1.

40. Jon Lafayette, "A New Era for TV," *Television Week,* 14 November 1.

41. Jon Lafayette, "Broadband Gold Rush Is On," *Television Week,* 9 January 2006, 1, 27.

42. The pricing standard is relative to timing and commercial-free access. FOX experimented with charging $2.99 in order to download some of its programs before they aired. Others offered programs for less if they included commercials.

43. Kirsner, "Low-Budget Viral Videos," E1.

44. Anne Becker, Ben Grossman, John M. Higgins, and Allison Romano, "How the Google-YouTube Deal Shakes Up TV," *Broadcasting & Cable,* 16 October 2006; available from http://www.broadcastingcable.com/index.asp?layout=articlePrint&articleID=CCA6381202; accessed 18 October 2006.

45. Mike Musgrove, "Video Visionaries Meld Traditional TV and the Web," *Washington Post,* 2 December 2006, D01.

46. Stuart Elliott, "TV Is Getting to Look More Like the Movies," *The New York Times,* 17 May 2006, C3.

47. Gina Keating, "Disney Says ABC Free Web TV a Hit with Consumers," *Yahoo! News,* 19 June 2006, http://entertainment.tv.yahoo.com/entnews/va/20060619/115077305100.html, accessed 23 June 2006.

48. Alison James, "Just Turn Off the TV," *Variety.com,* 4 April 2006, http://www.variety.com/index.asp?layout=print_story&articleid=VR1117940971&categoryid=-1, accessed 7 April 2006.

49. "The Expanding Role of Television Web Sites," *NATPE News,* April 2006, http://www.natpe.org/memberresources/natpenews/articles/story.jsp?id_string=200149:Elo-M6pDKwb9jGTPzHrcuw**, accessed 19 April 2006.

50. Daisy Whitney, "Programs Feeling the iTunes Effect," *Television Week,* 27 March 2006, 40.

51. Steven Zeitchik, "Madness on the March Online," *Variety.com,* 19 March 2006, http://www.variety.com/index.asp?layout=print_story&articleid=VR1117940030&categoryid=14, accessed 23 March 2006.

52. "A Video Discourse from Three Views," *Television Week,* 31 July 2006, 12, 51.

53. One of the areas in which this became most evident was in clearing music rights for back catalog television content. DVD release of many popular shows was significantly delayed by protracted negotiations and expensive fees for music. A number of shows were released without the original soundtrack because pricey music fees would make the DVDs too expensive.

54. Significantly, in the case of CBS's first entry into alternative distribution, only viewers in markets served by a CBS-owned affiliate station could use the new distribution outlet.

55. Statements of Larry Kramer (CBS) and Jeff Gaspin (NBC) at "Digital Strategies: Evolve and Prosper" panel at the NATPE conference, 24 January 2006, Las Vegas, NV.

56. Josef Adalian, "Somebody's *Watching,*" *Variety.com,* 21 June 2006, http://www.variety.com/indcx.asp?layout=print_story&articleid=VR1117945686&categoryid=14, accessed 23 June 2006; Bill Carter, "Sitcom Given Up for Dead Hits the Web. It's Alive," *New York Times,* 3 July 2006, E1.

57. Josef Adalian, "NBC Revives *Watching,*" *Variety.com,* 20 July 2006, http://www.variety.com/index.asp?layout=print_story&articleid=VR1117947160&categoryid=14, accessed 25 July 2006.

58. Half-hour situation comedies typically retained an exclusive first syndication run on broadcast affiliates, while studios normally distributed hour-long dramas first to cable. The number of windows and potential revenue available

to a given program depended significantly on its genre and narrative structure. Episodic dramas such as those in the *Law & Order* and *CSI* franchises earned considerable revenue in cable syndication because of their closed-ended stories that allowed intermittent viewing and for cable operators to play them out of order. As an illustration of this discrepancy, *Law & Order: Criminal Intent* set a new syndication fee record for a drama in 2004 when it was sold for $1.92 million per episode. The heavily serialized shows *Alias* and *24* earned only about $250,000 per episode. See Denise Martin and John Dempsey, "*Sopranos* Reruns Stir Mob Scene," *Variety.com,* 9 January 2005, http://www.variety.com/index.asp?layout=print_story&articleid =VR1117915991&categoryid=14, accessed 9 January 2005. More serialized dramas such as *Alias* and *24* particularly benefited from the DVD sell-through markets, as did "cult" hits such as *Family Guy.* Previously, the international market would have been the only window through which producers of many shows would have earned substantial additional revenue.

59. See Henry Jenkins, "I Want My Geek TV, *Flow* 3, no. 1 (September 2005), http://jot.communication.utexas.edu/flow/?jot=view&id=936, accessed 26 April 2006; Ivan Askwith, "TV You'll Want to Pay For," *Slate.com,* 1 November 2005, http://www.slate.com.toolbar.aspx?action=print&id=2129003, accessed 3 November 2005.

60. There were rumors of an *Arrested Development* movie as I finished the manuscript.

61. Although the article does not note that audience members are not equally valued. David Kiley, Tom Lowry, and Ronald Grover, "The End of TV (as You Know It)," *Business Week Online,* 21 November 2005, http://www.businessweek.com/print/magazine/content/05_47/b3960075.htm?chan=gl, accessed 25 November 2005.

62. Ibid. In industry forums such as presentations at the 2006 International Consumer Electronics Show and National Association of Television Program Executives, many executives would give few specifics because of the nature of the deals they had with Apple.

63. John McMurria, "Long-Format TV: Globalization and Network Branding in a Multi-Channel Era," in *Quality Popular Television,* eds. Mark Jancovich and James Lyons (London: British Film Institute, 2001), 65–87.

64. Daisy Whitney, "Hopped Up on Hope," *Television Week,* 19 June 2006, 1.

65. Rupert Murdoch, "The Dawn of a New Age of Discovery: Media 2006," Speech given for the Annual Livery Lecture at the Worshipful Company of Stationers and Newspaper Makers, 13 March 2006, London England, http://www.newscorp.com/news/news_285.html, accessed 31 March 2006.

66. David S. Cohen, "Wolf Sounds Alarm," *Variety.com,* 20 March 2006, http://www.variety.com/index.asp?layout=print_story&articleid=VR1117940065&categoryid=14, accessed 23 March 2006.

NOTES TO CHAPTER 5

1. Paul Keegan, "The Man Who Can Save Advertising," *Business 2.0*, November 2004, http://www.business2.com/b2/subscribers/articles/print/0,17925,704067,00.html, accessed 11 November 2004.

2. Cited in Scott Donaton, *Madison & Vine: Why the Entertainment and Advertising Industries Must Converge to Survive* (New York: McGraw-Hill, 2004), 60.

3. For more see William Boddy, "Redefining the Home Screen: The Case of the Digital Video Recorder," in *New Media and Popular Imagination: Launching Radio, Television, and Digital Media in the United States* (New York: Oxford University Press, 2004), 100–107.

4. The publication of Malcolm Gladwell's *The Tipping Point: How Little Things Can Make a Big Difference* (Boston: Little, Brown and Company, 2000) has led the television industry and many others to think about the process of change and the existence of a "tipping point" in a very particular way.

5. Claudia Deutsch, "Study Details Decline in Spending on Ads," *The New York Times*, 5 September 2001, C5.

6. Stuart Elliott, "An Agency Giant Is Expected to Warn of Lower Profits, and Analysts Darken Their Outlook," *The New York Times*, 2 October 2001, C2; Stuart Elliott, "Networks Watch Prices for Commercial Time Drop," *The New York Times*, 25 September 2001.

7. For more see Henry Jenkins, *Convergence Culture: Where Old and New Media Collide* (New York: New York University Press, 2006), 61–64.

8. Sponsorship continued into the 1960s, although by that point it was increasingly a residual rather than dominant practice.

9. William Boddy, *Fifties Television: The Industry and Its Critics* (Urbana: University of Illinois Press, 1993), 95–97.

10. Data drawn from Boddy, *Fifties Television*, citing U.S. Federal Communications Commission, Office of Network Study, Second Interim Report: Television Network Procurement, part 2, Docket no, 12782 (Washington, DC: U.S. Government Printing Office, 1965), 736.

11. Boddy, *Fifties Television*, 159.

12. W. L. Bird, "Advertising, Company Voice," in *Encyclopedia of Television*, 2nd ed., ed. Horace Newcomb (New York: Routledge, 2004), 34–37.

13. Christopher Anderson, *Hollywood TV* (Austin: University of Texas Press, 1993).

14. For critical assessments of network and studio behavior in the era see Anderson, *Hollywood TV*.

15. Staff, "Cable's Bucks," *Broadcasting & Cable*, 21 April 2003, 28.

16. Scatter prices can be lower, although broadcasters avoid this in order to prevent angering advertisers that purchase upfront and that the networks will need to sell to again in the next year.

17. Nicole Laporte, "High Prices, Competish Pump a Record Upfront," *Variety.com* 26 May 2003,
http://www.variety.com/index.asp?layout=print_story&articleid=VR111788687
1&categoryid=14, accessed 27 May 2003.

18. Erwin Ephron, "How the TV Nets Got the Upfront," *Advertising Age*, 14 May 2001.

19. Erwin Ephron, "A Short History of the Upfront," *Jack Myers Report*, 2 May 2003, 1–2.

20. On some occasions, however, the networks have guaranteed scatter rates to help increase rates and purchase volume.

21. DVD and syndication sales contributed 20 percent of HBO's operating income by 2004. John M. Higgins and Allison Romano, "The Family Business," *Broadcasting & Cable*, 1 March 2004, 1, 6.

22. R. Craig Endicott and Kenneth Wylie, "*Ad Age* Agency Report," *Advertising Age*, 30 April 2006, http://adage.com/article?article_id=108906, accessed 1 June 2006.

23. Jack Myers, "Communications Planning Will 'Sweep the Industry' in Next 36 Months," *Jack Myers Report*, 25 January 2005.

24. John Consoli, "Shops Form Units for Product Placement," *ADWEEK.com*, 14 February 2005, http://www.adweek.com/aw/national. article_display.jsp?vnu_content_id=1000799577, accessed 20 February 2005.

25. For more on the basic operation of the advertising industry both historically and at this time, see Joe Cappo, *The Future of Advertising: New Media, New Clients, New Consumers in the Post-Television Age* (Chicago: McGraw-Hill, 2003).

26. Jack Myers, "Creativity Moves to Forefront at Media Buying Groups," *Jack Myers Report*, 4 January 2005.

27. Fifteen percent was an old, but eroding industry standard fee. Jack Myers, "Restructuring the Agency/Client Compensation Model," *Jack Myers Report*, 26 January 2005.

28. The introduction of accounting requirements of the Sarbanes/Oxley legislation resulted in micromanagement of budgetary details and contributed to advertisers' demands for definitive information about the return they achieved on their investments in advertising.

29. James Twitchell, *AdCult USA: The Triumph of Advertising in American Culture* (New York: Columbia University Press, 1996).

30. Regulatory prohibitions focused on advertising aimed at children and required disclosure of paid promotion. See Mary-Lou Galician, ed., "Special Issue on Product Placement," *Journal of Promotion Management* 10, no. 1.2 (2004).

31. The norms for cable and broadcast differed until recently. Even as late as 2000, a number of cable channels featured a fair amount of sponsor-produced

programming. See Jim Forkan, "On Some Cable Shows, the Sponsors Take Charge," *Multichannel News,* 4 June 2001, 53.

32. Donaton, *Madison & Vine.*

33. The automaker Ford is a brand while a specific auto is a product. A client may choose to emphasize either depending on the goal of his or her campaign. For example, Johnson and Johnson sponsors annual films on TNT that help reestablish the company's desired brand identification as something safe and reliable for the family. This is different from when it promotes a specific product, such as Acuvue contact lenses. Either a brand or a product might be placed or integrated in television programming.

34. Twitchell, *AdCult USA,* 18.

35. See Donaton for more detailed history and other terms, *Madison & Vine,* 13–16.

36. Significantly, despite the gratuitous placement of the iPod, Apple claims that iPod has never paid for placement because "Apple is cool." The company is well known to have given away millions of dollars of free computers to the Hollywood community that has created substantial goodwill for the company. See Gail Schiller, "Brands Take Buzz to Bank Through Free TV Placement," *Washington Post.com,* 13 April 2006, http://www.washington post.com/wp-dyn/content/article/2006/04/13/AR2006041300272_pf.html, accessed 19 April 2006.

37. Jack Myers, "2004 Gold Award Media Innovators of the Year," *Jack Myers Report,* 18 January 2005.

38. James A. Karrh reviews existing research on the effectiveness and value of placement in "Brand Placement: A Review," *Journal of Current Issues and Research in Advertising* 20, no. 2 (1998): 31–49.

39. Wayne Friedman and Jack Neff, "Eagle-Eye Marketers Find Right Spot, Right Time," *Advertising Age,* 22 January 2001, 2–4.

40. In many cases, products' names must be stripped out of programs syndicated internationally.

41. See Forkan, "On Some Cable Shows," 53, for one of the few examinations of this phenomenon before the resurgence of product placement.

42. Sam Lubell, "Advertising's Twilight Zone: That Signpost Up Ahead May Be a Virtual Product," *New York Times,* 2 January 2006, C1; Jim Edwards, "There's Less than Meets the Eye in TV Placement Economy," *Brandweek* 19 December 2005.

43. Debbie Myers, vice president of media services for Taco Bell reported that producers of *The Apprentice* approached the company with an offer to focus an episode on the company for $5 million (NATPE 2005). Taco Bell declined; trade press reports locate that figure at $1 million for early seasons of *The Apprentice* and $2–3 million by its third edition in 2005. Still, by 2005,

NBC scheduled four, thirteen-episode editions of the series so that integration might offer the network $260 million a season. An industry source reported the primary product association deals in *American Idol* cost as much as $40 million per season. Wayne Friedman, "Placement Bonanza Remains Elusive," *Television Week*, 11 October 2004, 22.

44. "Revlon Pays for Story Line on *All My Children*," *The Associated Press*, 18 March 2002. Industry pundits questioned the success of the *All My Children* deal because of the negative association of Revlon as a competitor to the much-loved villain's corporation.

45. Leslie Ryan, "Passions' Product Pitch," *Television Week*, 28 July 2003, 10.

46. See Virginia Heffernan, "A Gas-Guzzling Revenge Plot Meets Souped-Up Sales Pitch," *The New York Times*, 2 June 2004, E1.

47. Stuart Elliott, "The Diet Coke Empire Strikes Back, Under the Guise of *Friends*," *The New York Times*, 1 January 1996, sec. 1, 51.

48. Gary Levin, "The Newest Characters on TV Shows: Product Plugs," *USA Today*, 20 September 2006, A1.

49. Importantly, within industry discussions, "branded entertainment" is sometimes used as an umbrella term encompassing integration, placement, and the forms I discuss here. Each of these strategies is significantly different and more precision is required for this discussion.

50. The fashion show indicates multiple strategies at work. The year ABC aired the fashion show, it included models in that week's episode of *Spin City*, featured a *Who Wants to Be a Millionaire?* Supermodel edition, and showed the models on *The View*, suggesting a sort of product placement throughout the week.

51. Alice Z. Cuneo and Wayne Friedman, "Spreading Secrets," *Advertising Age*, 22 October 2001, 3. Interview with Ed Razek, Creative Director, Victoria's Secret, in John Watkin and Eamon Harrington, dirs., "A Day in the Life of Television," produced by the Museum of Radio and Television and Planet Grande, aired on CBS 2 September 2006.

52. Cuneo and Friedman, "Spreading Secrets."

53. Zachary Rodgers, "Seinfeld, Man of Steel Reprise Hijinks in New AmEx Spot," *ClickZ News*, 20 May 2004, http://www.clickz.com/news/article.php/3356961, accessed 26 May 2004.

54. Donaton, *Madison & Vine*, 101.

55. Ibid.

56. Ibid.

57. In 2004, Pepsi shifted its *Play for a Billion* promotion to ABC.

58. Andy Meisler, "Not Even Trying to Appeal to the Masses," *The New York Times*, 4 October 1998, 45.

59. "Anheuser-Busch to Launch Bud.tv," *CNN Money.com*, 6 September 2006, available from http://money.cnn.com/2006/09/06/news/funny/bud_tv/index.htm, accessed 25 January 2007.

60. The coming of sponsored outlets and increase of sponsored programming was a refrain repeated by many speaking at the 2007 NATPE conference.

61. Francis Page, personal communication with the author, August 1, 2005, New York, New York.

62. "Loyalty Cards Idea for TV Addicts," *BBC News,* 28 October 2004, http://news.bbc.co.uk/go/pr/fr/-/1/hi/technology/3958855.stm, accessed 30 October 2004.

63. In recent years, ten-second ads have mainly been used in syndicated programming, but concerns about DVRs as well as the federal mandate that all programs feature closed-captioning by 2006 has led other producers to look for the additional revenue a ten-second spot can provide. Producers can offset the closed-captioning cost with a ten second, "closed captioning brought to you by . . ." tag at the end of the program.

64. Wayne Friedman, "Advertisers Seeing :10s as Perfect," *Television Week,* 14 February 2005, 20.

65. Brian Steinberg, "TV Ads Are Challenged By 'Pod' Busters," *Wall Street Journal,* 21 November 2005, B1.

66. Ellen Sheng, "Advertisers Sharpen Their Targeting," *The Wall Street Journal,* 27 October 2004, http://online.wsj.com/article/0,,SB109882501186456295,00.html, accessed 30 October 2004.

67. Louise Story, "A TV Show's Content Calls the Commercial Plays," *New York Times,* 21 December 2006, C6.

68. Cited in David Lieberman, "Cable Firms Make You Easy Target for TV Ads," *USA Today,* 20 February 2005, http://www.usatoday.com/money/media/2005-02-20-digital-ads-usat_x.htm, accessed 7 November 2005.

69. Keegan. "The Man Who Can Save Advertising."

70. Ibid.

71. Ibid.

72. Stefanie Olsen, "Google-Like Technologies Could Revolutionize TV, Other Media," *CNET News.com,* 29 April 2004, http://news.com.com/2009-1025_3-5201803.html?tag+nefd.lede, accessed 29 April 2004.

73. Ibid.

74. Critical approaches to advertising have become multivocal in their outlook on the meaning of consumption. One, arguably more traditional, approach can be found in the work of Sut Jhally and Juliet Schor, who link the rampant consumerism of post-Fordist America with the attendant horrific consequences on the environment and quality of life. Noting that citizens work endless hours and take on credit to purchase unnecessary goods sold to them through lifestyle advertising, they explore the growing economic disparity in the United States as a disproportionately small segment of the population uses incredible amounts of

resources. This critical perspective, which identifies consumption as having an all-encompassing role, focuses on the degree to which people view social power as being accessible primarily through the purchase of goods and services. Hence, this perspective is in accord with social theory that has dichotomized the identities of consumer and citizen and denigrated the activity of the former, arguing that it often comes at the expense of the latter. See Sut Jhally, dir., *Advertising and the End of the World* (Amherst: Media Education Foundation, 1997); Juliet B. Schor, *The Overspent American: Upscaling, Downshifting, and the New Consumer* (New York: Basic Books, 1998).

By contrast, other critical scholars embrace consumption as an expression of agency and theorize participation in commercial culture as an activity with resistant dimensions. In response to a legacy of criticism heavily influenced by Marxist thought that dismissed advertising and consumerism as insignificant or the terrain of cultural dupes, scholars including Meaghan Morris and Hilary Radner, among others, have considered shopping and brand selection as meaningful cultural activities. Their work, which was part of the effort to expand the field of cultural studies to the study of the everyday, treats shopping and consumption as important aspects of life in industrial cultures, as well as noting the gendered dimensions of these activities. See Meaghan Morris, "Things to Do with Shopping Centres," in *The Cultural Studies Reader,* ed. Simon During (London: Routledge, 1993), 295–319; W. S. Kowinski, *The Malling of America: An Inside Look at the Great Consumer Paradise* (New York, Pantheon, 1985); Mica Nava, "Consumerism and Its Contradictions," *Cultural Studies* 1, no. 2 (1987): 204–10; Judith Williamson, *Consuming Passions: The Dynamics of Popular Culture* (London: Marion Boyers, 1986); Hilary Radner, *Shopping Around: Feminine Culture and the Pursuit of Pleasure* (New York: Routledge, 1995).

An alternative critical approach has also developed that intervenes in these two trajectories of scholarship that tend to discount or embrace consumption. This more middle-ground perspective acknowledges consumption as part of citizenship in post-Fordist culture without arguing that it provides such an empowering form of agency. Thus, for example, Thomas Frank uses cultural texts and documents to trace the increasing acceptance of the logic of capital markets during the 1980s and 1990s to the point that the beneficence and propriety of markets becomes part of a dominant American ideology. For his part, Martin Davidson provides more evaluative analysis that acknowledges the complex relationships among consumption and critical theory. See Nestor Garcia Canclini, *Consumers and Citizens: Globalization and Multicultural Conflicts* (Minneapolis: University of Minnesota Press, 2001); Thomas Frank, *One Market Under God: Extreme Capitalism, Market Populism, and the End of Economic Democracy* (New York: Doubleday, 2000); Martin Davidson, *The Consumerist Manifesto: Advertising in Postmodern Times* (London: Routledge, 1992).

Authors such as Frank and Davidson are not diametrically opposed to Jhally and Schor, but their work intervenes in different critical histories. Davidson identifies the cultural significance of branding and the importance of associating a lifestyle with a brand to argue for the study of consumption as a part of life because of its gross absence in much preceding scholarship and a tendency for critical scholarship to take a fairly unsophisticated and naïve view toward advertising and consumption that does not reflect the lived experience of many in late industrial societies (Davidson, 175). Likewise, Frank traces the infiltration and acceptance of the logic of the market fairly dispassionately, while reserving his criticism for a particular version of cultural studies that embraces consumption as an expression of agency. Although written in 1992, Davidson's assessment of the interpenetration of commerce and culture and the attendant impossibility of macro-theoretical explanations of this complexity remain relevant and unimproved nearly fifteen years later.

Here, it is particularly relevant to my discussion to note that Frank spends a chapter exploring and critiquing cultural studies in a manner uncommon for a book targeted to a popular audience. Frank is exceedingly critical of a branch of cultural studies that argues that activities such as fanship and consumerism can provide agency. While aspects of Frank's critique are sound, he allows work that others might define as marginal to cultural studies to define the field in its totality in a manner that makes his point, but in the process misrepresents an intellectual field that is much broader and varied than he allows.

75. Joseph Turow, *Breaking Up America: Advertisers and the New Media World* (Chicago: University of Chicago Press, 1997); Arlene Davila, *Latinos, Inc.: The Marketing and Making of a People* (Berkeley: University of California Press, 2001).

76. Importantly, these studies combine industrial analyses and interviews with industry workers to explain the complex practices involved in this transition, as well as considering the advertising messaging produced as a consequence.

77. Turow, *Breaking Up America*, 2.

78. Davila, *Latinos, Inc*, 2.

79. Canclini, *Consumers and Citizens*.

80. Joseph Turow, "Unconventional Programs on Commercial Television: An Organizational Perspective," in *Mass Communicators in Context*, eds. D. Charles Whitney and James Ettema (Beverly Hills: Sage, 1982), 107–29.

81. Joseph Turow, *Media Systems in Society: Understanding Industries, Strategies and Power* (White Plains, NY: Longman, 1997), 174–235.

82. Anthony Crupi, "FX Pulls in 18–49 Demo with Gritty Fare," *Mediaweek.com*, 16 January 2006, http://mediaweek.com/mw/news/cabletv/article_display.jsp?vnu_content_id=1001844104, accessed 18 January 2006.

83. John M. Higgins, "Edgy Fare Drives FX," *Broadcasting & Cable*, 13 September 2004, 4.

84. Michael Curtin, "Feminine Desire in the Age of Satellite Television," *Journal of Communication* 49, no. 2 (1999): 55–70; Thomas Streeter, "Media: The Problem of Creativity," paper presented at the International Communication Association annual conference, Washington, DC, 26 May 2001; Michael Curtin and Thomas Streeter, "Media," in *Culture Works: The Political Economy of Culture,* ed. Richard Maxwell (Minneapolis: University of Minnesota Press, 2001), 225–50.

85. Production by MindShare also enabled the series to shoot in Canada, which reduced production costs. The issue of runaway production has been contentious for some time, and it is likely that MindShare could shoot in Canada without ramifications from the creative guilds in a way unavailable to ABC or one of the Disney-owned studios. Wayne Friedman, "MindShare, ABC Choose *The Days,*" *Television Week,* 19 April 2004, 3; Cynthia Littleton, "MindShare Investing in ABC TV Series," *Shoot Online,* 12 December 2003.

86. Todd Gitlin provides a network-era comparison in "Another American Dream Gone Astray," in *Inside Prime Time* (New York: Pantheon Books, 1983), 86–114.

87. Admittedly, by the end of the six episodes most of the crises are concluded in the least controversial means possible—neither the mother nor daughter choose to have an abortion and the father goes back to work. Network-era theory offered by Todd Gitlin places considerable emphasis on narrative outcomes. In an environment of such multiplicity of programming and ideas, the negotiation of these outcomes and narrative processing is also of importance in evaluating the ideological perspectives supported by the narrative. The serial construction of *The Days* particularly allocates importance to process.

88. Joe Mandese, "Ad-Supported Media Losing Ground," *Television Week,* 9 August 2004, 17.

89. Ibid.

NOTES TO CHAPTER 6

1. Jon Gertner, "Our Ratings, Ourselves," *The New York Times Magazine,* 10 April 2005.

2. Susan Whiting, personal communication, 16 April 2005.

3. Joseph R. Dominick, Barry L. Sherman, and Fritz Messere, *Broadcasting, Cable, the Internet, and Beyond,* 4th ed. (Boston: McGraw-Hill, 2000), 259; Nielsen Media Research, *2000 Report on Television* (New York: Nielsen Media Research, 2000).

4. Hugh Malcolm Beville, *Audience Ratings: Radio, Television, Cable,* rev. student ed. (Hillsdale, NJ: Lawrence Erlbaum Associates, 1988), 72.

5. Steve Behrens, "People Meters vs. the Gold Standard," *Channels* 7 (September 1987): 72; Steve Behrens, "A Finer Grind from the Ratings Mill," *Channels* 7 (December 1987): 10–16.

6. Peter J. Boyer, "Networks Fight to Delay New Ratings Method," *The New York Times*, 17 April 1986, C29.

7. Brian Dumaine, "Who's Gypping Whom in TV Ads?," *Fortune*, 6 July 1987, 78–79.

8. Joe Mandese, "Prime-Time Rating Points Valued at Nearly $400 Million," *Media Daily News*, 11 October 2006, http://publications.mediapost.com/index.cfm?fuseaction=Articles.san&s=49458&Nid=24151&p=368626, accessed 19 October 2006. A rating point in the 18–49-year-old demographic was estimated at $763.9 million.

9. "NBC Strikes Response Measurement Deal with Toyota," *Ad Business Report* (Email Newsletter), received 24 July 2006.

10. Steve McClellan, "Nielsen: We Just Got Better," *Broadcasting & Cable*, 1 December 2003, 26.

11. Dan Trigoboff, "Nielsen Grows Local People Meter," *Broadcasting & Cable*, 3 March 2003, 14.

12. Nielsen Media Research, "The Facts on Nielsen and Local People Meters;" http://everyonecounts.tv, accessed 14 November 2004.

13. Ibid.

14. Allison Romano, "Measure for Measure," *Broadcasting & Cable*, 11 October 2004, 24; Monica M. Clark, "Nielsen's People Meters Go Top 10," *Wall Street Journal*, 30 June 2006, B2.

15. The Media Rating Council (formerly the Broadcast Rating Council) was established following hearings by the Special Subcommittee on Investigations of the House of Representatives Committee on Interstate and Foreign Commerce in 1963 and 1964. In the hearings, often referred to as the Harris Committee hearings, the committee determined the need for an industry-funded organization to review and accredit audience ratings services. Toni Fitzgerald, "MRC on Its Mission as Media Overseer: Nielsen, Change, and the Media Rating Council," *Media Life*, 26 April 2005, http://www.medialifemagazine.com/News2005/april05/apr25/2_tues/news4tuesday.html, accessed 26 April 2005.

16. Stuart Elliott, "Nielsen Presents a Research Plan to Quell Concerns about Accuracy," *The New York Times*, 22 February 2005. The News Corp.–funded public relations campaign garnered Congressional attention and led Nielsen to create an independent taskforce in July 2004 to help quell the discontent. Congressional hearings that month queried whether Nielsen needed governmental oversight given its monopolistic status, but found the situation warranted no such governmental involvement. Ultimately a combination of more precise counting of cable viewing (which led to losses for broadcasters) enabled by passive rather than active reporting and higher fault rates in minority homes

were likely to blame for the discrepancies between old and new measurement techniques. Nielsen developed a variety of procedures to help address fault rates, many of which related to implementing more culturally sensitive practices in enlisting and maintaining its participants.

17. Joe Mandese, "Navigating Changes in Measurement," *Television Week,* 2 August 2004, 21.

18. Arbitron, Inc., "Regal CineMedia to Participate in Arbitron Trial of Portable People Meter Rating Service in Houston," *PR Newswire,* 28 March 2005.

19. John Consoli, "44 Mil. Watch TV in Unmeasured Places," *Mediaweek.com,* 21 April 2006, http://www.mediaweek.com/mw/news/recent_display.jsp?vnu_content_id=1002383527, accessed 26 April 2006.

20. Arbitron continued development and prepared to launch the device for measurement of radio audiences in the top fifty markets by October 2010.

21. Nielsen Media Research, "Nielsen to Adopt Portfolio Strategy for TV Measurement," 1 March 2006, http://www.nielsenmedia.com/nc/portal/site/Public/menuitem.55dc65b4a7d5adff3f65936147a062ao/?allRmCB=on&newSearch=yes&vgnextrefresh=1&vgnextoid=6658ef8c8c7b9010VgnVCM100000acoa260aRCRD&searchBox=2000, accessed 5 April 2006.

22. John M. Higgins, "Nielsen: Follow the Video," *Broadcasting & Cable,* 19 June 2006, http://www.broadcastingcable.com/index.asp?layout=articlePrint&article ID=CA6344824, accessed 23 June 2006.

23. Joe Mandese, "Hitting the Mother Lode," *Broadcasting & Cable,* 8 November 2004, 24.

24. Steve McClellan, "PPM Could Launch as Planning Tool," *Television Week,* 13 December 2004, 19.

25. "James Bond's BMW and Other Product Placements: New Racier Ways to Advertise," *Knowledge@Wharton* (Marketing Newsletter), http://knowledge.wharton.upenn.edu/index.cfm?fa=viewArticle&id=1093, accessed 15 December 2005.

26. Jack Myers, "Nielsen Losing Value as Custom Insights Gain Status, Says Uva," *Jack Myers Report,* 28 April 2005.

27. Future of TV Seminar, 23 September 2004, Los Angeles, CA.

28. Leo Bogart, "Buying Services and the Media Marketplace," *Journal of Advertising Research,* September–October 2000: 37–41.

29. Members of the MRI panel, for example, would receive a three-hundred-page survey that queried purchase behavior as well as attitudes toward brands and features. This would allow an agency to cross reference different attitude and behavior segments to explore increasingly narrow questions. The data in these surveys tend to be a year old by the time they are published, which limits some of the utility of the surveys.

30. Joe Mandese "Sizing Up Audiences by Body Type," *Television Week,* 8 September 2003, 15; Joe Mandese, "Court TV Makes Case for CPT Viewer," *Television Week,* 5 April 2004, 25; Toni Fitzgerald, "A Truer Measure of Viewer Loyalty: Index Melds Networks' Length and Frequency of Viewing," *Media Life,* 4 April 2004.

31. Steve McClellan, "Nielsen Gives It the New College Try," *Broadcasting & Cable,* 27 January 2003, 8.

32. Michele Greppi, "On-Campus Viewing High in Nielsen Test," *Television Week,* 21 March 2005, 6.

33. Louise Story, "At Last, Television Ratings Go to College," *New York Times,* 29 January 2007, C1.

34. McClellan, "Nielsen Gives It the New College Try."

35. Greppi, "On-Campus Viewing."

36. World Federation of Advertisers and European Association of Communications Agencies, "The WFA/EACA Guide to the Organisation of Television Audience Research," January 2001, http://www.wfanet.org/pdf/WFA_guide OrgofTVaudresearch.pdf, accessed 22 June 2005.

37. Brian Hughes, "Nielsen's DVR Impact Assessment Study," Media Insights: A Publication of MAGNA Global, September 2005. VCRs could be used in this same manner, but Nielsen studies indicated that this was not a regular viewer behavior, except for soap opera taping—which accounted for seven of the top ten most taped shows by the mid-1980s. See James Traub, "The World According to Nielsen," *Channels,* January–February 1985, 26–32, 70–72.

38. Wayne Friedman, "DVR Measurement Hangs in the Balance," *Television Week,* 28 February 2005, 24.

39. Jack Myers, "Upfront Chronicles 2005: Part Two," *Jack Myers Report,* 25 April 2005.

40. Mike Shields, "Researchers: VOD Ads Not Skipped," *Media Week,* 2 May 2005, http://www.mediaweek.com/mw/news/recent_display.jsp?vnu_content_id=1000903610, accessed 3 May 2005.

41. Joe Mandese, "How Much Is Product Placement Worth?," *Broadcasting & Cable,* 13 December 2004, 18; Joe Mandese, "Nielsen Unveils New Service," *Television Week,* 8 December 2003, 17.

42. ErinMedia Corporate Website, http://erinmedia.net/, accessed 5 May 2005.

43. Nielsen Media Research, *2000 Report on Television.*

44. Gloria Goodale, "Before TV Shows Air, They Have to Survive . . . the Lab," *Christian Science Monitor.com,* 4 Aug. 2006, http://www.csmonitor.com/2006/0804/p11s03-altv.htm, accessed 18 Aug. 2006.

45. Joseph Turow, "Audience Construction and Culture Production: Marketing Surveillance in the Digital Age," *American Academy of Political and Social Science* 597 (January 2005): 103-121.

NOTES TO CHAPTER 7

1. A. J. Jacobs, "Let's Talk About Sex," *Entertainment Weekly,* 5 Jun. 1998, 32.

2. For more see Amanda D. Lotz, "If It Is Not TV, What Is It? The Case of U.S. Subscription Television," in *Cable Visions: Television Beyond Broadcasting,* eds. Sarah Banet-Weiser, Cynthia Chris, and Anthony Freitas (New York: New York University Press, 2007).

3. Except in season five, in which the pregnancy of actor Sarah Jessica Parker led to the production of just eight episodes.

4. Kim Potts, "Women Love *Sex*: HBO's Bawdy Comedy Not Just a Pretty Face," *Daily Variety,* 17 September 1999, A1.

5. Toni Fitzgerald, "Where the Real $ Is for Sexy HBO," *Media Life,* 26 February 2004, http://www.medialifemagazine.com/news2004/feb04/feb23/4_thurs/news2thursday.html, accessed 27 February 2004.

6. Previous original HBO series such as *The Larry Sanders Show* and *Dream On* had sold in various other distribution windows, but none earned nearly the revenue of *Sex and the City.*

7. John Dempsey, "HBO Sells *Sex* Reruns to TBS Net," *Daily Variety,* 30 September 2003, 6; John Dempsey and Meredith Amdur, "Tribune Spices up HBO's *Sex,*" *Variety.com,* 10 September 2003, http://www.variety.com/index.asp.?layout=print_story&articleid=VR1117892266&categoryid=10, accessed 11 September 2003; John Dempsey, "*Sex* Sells Its *Sex* to KRON for $10.4 Million," *Daily Variety,* 21 October 2003, 5.

8. Gail Schiller, "It's Not a Plug, It's HBO," *The Hollywood Reporter.com,* 10 December 2004, accessed through Lexis-Nexis Academic, 2 January 2007.

9. Claire Atkinson, "Absolut Nabs Sexy HBO Role," *Advertising Age,* 4 August 2003, 6.

10. Michael McCarthy, "HBO Shows Use Real Brands," *USA Today,* 3 December 2002, 3B.

11. Ibid.

12. Chad Raphael, "The Political Economic Origins of Reali-TV," in *Reality TV: Remaking Television Culture,* eds. Susan Murray and Laurie Ouellette (New York: New York University Press, 2004), 119–36.

13. Bill Carter, *Desperate Networks* (New York: Doubleday, 2006) 67–89.

14. Raphael, "The Political Economic Origins of Reali-TV."

15. Bill Carter, "Survival of the Pushiest," *New York Times Magazine,* 28 January 2001; also see Carter, *Desperate Networks,* 67–89, for a more detailed version of this story.

16. News Corp. traded its control of DirecTV in December 2006 to John Malone's Liberty Media in order to regain Malone's stake of News Corp. shares.

17. Anne Becker and Allison Romano, "Fear Factor Soars on FX," *Broadcasting & Cable,* 13 September 2004, 2.

18. Reported by Bhuvan Lall, managing director, Empire Entertainment Private Limited, at 2004 NAPTE Faculty Seminar, Las Vegas, 17 January 2004.

19. Herbert Schiller, *Communication and Cultural Domination* (White Plains, International Arts and Sciences Press, 1976).

20. See Albert Moran, *Copycat TV: Globalisation, Program Formats and Cultural Identity* (Luton, UK: University of Luton Press, 1998), for a detailed examination of some of the early aspects of format exports.

21. Melissa Grego, "Burnett's New Studio Model," *Television Week,* 15 August 2005, 1.

22. Although this distinction is particular to live-action shows, Comedy Central's *Dr. Katz: Professional Therapist,* various animated Nickelodeon shows and *Mystery Science Theater 3000* had won previously.

23. Interview with Shawn Ryan, http://www.fxnetworks.com/shows/originals/the_shield/interviews/2.htlm, accessed 15 March 2006.

24. Michael Freeman, "An HBO Kind of Respect," *Electronic Media,* 8 July 2002, 22.

25. "TV Out of the Box," Trio Network, 2003.

26. Chiklis was known for a very different police role as the jovial title character of *The Commish.*

27. A. J. Frutkin, "One Tough Show," *Mediaweek,* 16 December 2002; Megan Larson, "Out of the Foxhole," *Mediaweek,* 19 May 2003.

28. Denise Martin, "*Shield* Cops a 7th Season," *Variety.com,* 5 June 2006, http://www.variety.com/index.asp?layout=print_story&articleid=VR1117944652&categoryid=14, accessed 23 June 2006.

29. David Lieberman, "Could Tony on A&E Bring Restrictions to Cable?," *USA Today,* 1 December 2006, available from http://www.usatoday.com/printedition/money/20061201/sleazecov.art.htm, accessed 4 December 2006.

30. Derek Baine, quoted in Larson, "Out of the Foxhole."

31. Larson, "Out of the Foxhole."

32. Freeman, "An HBO Kind of Respect," 22.

33. Personal communication, Shawn Ryan, phone interview, 4 May 2006.

34. Although A&E had purchased *The Sopranos,* illustrating basic cable purchase of a subscription cable series.

35. John Dempsey and Denise Martin, "Spike Wields *Shield* for in Big Deal," *Daily Variety,* 28 July 2005, 5; Christopher Lisotta, "Sony Sticking to the Flight Plan," *Television Week,* 10 April 2006, 1, 48, 48.

36. Lisotta, "Sony Sticking to the Flight Plan," 48.

37. Larson, "Out of the Foxhole."

38. Ari Posner, "Can This Man Save the Sitcom?" *The New York Times,* 1 August 2004, Section 2, p 1.

39. Nellie Andreeva, "Fox Pays Big to Get *Arrested,*" *The Hollywood Reporter,* 26 September 2002.

40. Posner, "Can This Man Save the Sitcom?"

41. Comedy Central had success with *South Park, The Daily Show,* and *The Colbert Report,* but their animation and non-narrative form distinguished these shows from traditional broadcast comedy forms. This is likewise the case for various MTV programs such as *The Tom Green Show* and *Jackass.* A live-action narrative show such as *Arrested Development* would require a substantially higher budget than any of these shows.

42. Michael Schneider, "New Development," *Daily Variety,* 26 September 2002, 5.

43. Josef Adalian, "Hurwitz takes a Hike" *Variety.com,* 27 March 2006, http://www.variety.com/index.asp?layout=print_story&articleid=VR1117940467&categoryid=1417, accessed 30 March 2006.

44. News Corp., "Emmy Award Winning Fox Comedy Arrested Development Finds Post Broadcast Home Online, on Hi-Def TV and on Basic Cable," *Business Wire,* 26 July 2006, http://home.businesswire.com/portal/site/google/index.jsp?ndmViewId=news_view&newsId=20060726005574&newsLand=en, accessed 1 August 2006.

45. Personal communication, Brent Renaud, phone interview, 26 April 2006.

46. Daisy Whitney, "Channel Schedules Limited Series," *Television Week,* 6 June 2005, 22.

47. Ibid.

48. Personal communication, Brent Renaud, phone interview, 26 April 2006.

49. Ibid.

NOTES TO THE CONCLUSION

1. David Carr, "Taken to a New Place, by a TV in the Palm, *New York Times,* 18 December 2005, Sec. 4, 3.

2. For another account of use, see Mitch Oscar, "Does Anybody Really Know How People Watch TV?, *Media Post,* 16 January 2007, available from http://publications.mediapost.com/index/cfm?fuseaction=Articles.show ArticleHomePage&art_aid=53961; accessed 22 January 2007.

3. Diane Mermigas, "Searching for Success in the Interactive Age," *The Hollywood Reporter.com,* 17 January 2006, http://www.insidebranded entertainment.com/bep/article_display.jsp?JSESSIONID=DT%GZpz

ΓGJChBJLTPThiZKvi8I9TsTWdBy42d3vJiiWi4i7T83iiRii!-
13556365448&vnu_content_id=1001844514, accessed 18 January 2006.

4. Jay Sherman, "Digital Age About Community, Says NBCU's Comstock in TVB Keynote Speech," *TV Week.com,* 20 April 2006, http://www.tvweek.com/printwindow.cms?newsid=9808&pageType=news, accessed 26 April 2006.

5. Chris Anderson, "A Problem with the Long Tail." Talk given at iConference, 16 October 2006, Ann Arbor, Michigan.

6. The first use of this comparison that I saw was made by a group of faculty who were tasked to represent the interest of local affiliates in a 2004 IRTS case study competition and offered a well-conceived future path for the affiliates.

7. Joseph Turow, *Breaking Up America: Advertisers and the New Media World* (Chicago: University of Chicago Press, 1997), provides a valuable exception. W. Russell Neuman, *The Future of the Mass Audience* (Cambridge: Cambridge University Press, 1991), also perceives these potential developments before they become clearly manifest.

8. Business Editors, "Examine the Alternative Universe of On-Demand Video," *Business Wire,* 7 September 2006.

9. YouTube figure from Chris Anderson, Keynote Address, NATPE Conference, Las Vegas, 16 January 2007.

10. For example, at the 2007 NATPE Conference, Oxygen president of programming and marketing, Debby Beece, told the audience that Oxygen had found that ratings increased by 10 to 25 percent when they reduced the commercial load—but that the actual increase was dependent on the show.

11. Advertisers supported programs, but consumers have always paid the real price in product costs inflated to finance advertising and marketing budgets.

12. The monthly subscription fee charged by TiVo was about ten dollars, while DVR rental from the cable provider might be a few dollars cheaper.

13. Knowledge Networks/SRI, *The Home Technology Monitor: Spring 2005 Ownership and Trend Report* (New York: SRI, 2005), 23.

14. Damon Darlin, "How to Tame an Inflated Entertainment Budget," *The New York Times.com,* 19 November 2005, http://www.nytimes.com/2005/11/19/business/19money.html?pagewanted=print, accessed 22 November 2005.

15. Bill McConnell, "Never Say Never," *Broadcasting & Cable,* 13 September 2004, 1, 10, 11.

16. Juliet Schor, *The Overspent American: Upscaling, Downshifting, and the New Consumer* (New York: Basic Books, 1998), 15.

17. James Poniewozik, "CRT TV RIP; or, Why You May Soon Be Too Poor for Television," *Time Online,* 8 August 2006, http://time.blogs.com/tuned_in/2006/08/crt_tv_rip_or_w.html, accessed 18 August 2006.

18. Josef Adalain, "Viral Vid Bug Bites Bochco," *Variety.com,* 14 November 2006, available from http://www.variety.com/article/VR1117953949.html?categoryid=14&cs=1, accessed 22 January 2007.

294 | *Notes to the Conclusion*

19. Manuel Castells, *The Rise of the Network Society* (New York: Blackwell, 1996).

20. Work such as that of Nick Browne serves as a notable exception. See Nick Browne, "The Political Economy of the Television (Super) Text," *Quarterly Review of Film Studies* 9, no. 3 (Summer 1984): 174–82.

21. Horace Newcomb, *TV: The Most Popular Art* (Garden City: Anchor Press, 1974).

22. Nicholas Negroponte, *Being Digital* (New York: Vintage Books, 1995), 48.

Selected Bibliography

Althusser, Louis. "Ideology and Ideological State Apparatuses." In *Lenin and Philosophy and Other Essays,* trans. Ben Brewster, 127–88. London: Monthly Review Books, 1971.

Alvey, Mark. "The Independents: Rethinking the Television Studio System." In *Television: The Critical View,* 6th ed., ed. Horace Newcomb, 34–51. New York: Oxford University Press, 2000.

Anderson, Chris. *The Long Tail: Why the Future of Business Is Selling Less of More.* New York: Hyperion, 2006.

Anderson, Christopher. *Hollywood TV.* Austin: University of Texas Press, 1993.

Aufderheide, Patricia. *Communications Policy and the Public Interest.* New York: Guilford Press, 1999.

Auletta, Ken. *Three Blind Mice: How the TV Networks Lost Their Way.* New York: Random House, 1992.

Bagdikian, Ben H. *The New Media Monopoly.* Boston: Beacon Press, 2004.

Ballaster, Ros, Margaret Beetham, Elizabeth Frazier, and Sandra Hebron. *Women's Worlds: Ideology, Femininity, and Women's Magazines.* London: Macmillan, 1991.

Barnouw, Erik. *Tube of Plenty: The Evolution of American Television,* 2nd rev. ed. New York: Oxford University Press, 1990.

Bedell, Sally. *Up the Tube: Prime-Time TV and the Silverman Years.* New York: The Viking Press, 1981.

Benjamin, Louise. "At the Touch of a Button: A Brief History of Remote Control Devices." In *The Remote Control in the New Age of Television,* eds. James R. Walker and Robert V. Bellamy Jr., 15–22. Westport, CT: Praeger, 1993.

Beville, Hugh Malcolm. *Audience Ratings: Radio, Television, Cable,* rev. student ed. Hillsdale, NJ: Lawrence Erlbaum Associates, 1988.

Blumenthal, Howard J., and Oliver R. Goodenough. *This Business of Television,* 2nd ed. New York: Billboard Books, 1998.

Boddy, William. *Fifties Television: The Industry and Its Critics.* Urbana: University of Illinois Press, 1993.

Boddy, William. "Redefining the Home Screen: The Case of the Digital Video Recorder." In *New Media and Popular Imagination: Launching Radio, Television, and Digital Media in the United States,* 100–107. New York: Oxford University Press, 2004.

Brinkley, Joel. *Defining Vision: The Battle for the Future of Television.* San Diego: Harcourt Brace, 1997.

Brown, Les. *Television: The Business Behind the Box.* New York: Harcourt Brace Jovanovich, 1971.

Browne, Nick "The Political Economy of the Television (Super) Text," *Quarterly Review of Film Studies* 9, no. 3 (Summer 1984): 174–82.

Brunsdon, Charlotte. "Lifestyling Britain: The 8–9 Slot on British Television." In *Television After TV: Essays on a Medium in Transition,* eds. Lynn Spigel and Jan Olsson, 75–92. Durham: Duke University Press, 2004.

Brunsdon, Charlotte. "What Is the 'Television' of Television Studies?" In *The Television Studies Book,* eds. Christine Geraghty and David Lusted, 95–113. London: Arnold, 1998.

Byars, Jackie, and Eileen R. Meehan. "Once in a Lifetime: Constructing the 'Working Woman' through Cable Narrowcasting." *Camera Obscura,* special volume on "Lifetime: A Cable Network For Women," ed. Julie d'Acci, 33–34 (1994): 12–41.

Calabrese, Andrew, and Colin Sparks, eds. *Toward a Political Economy of Culture: Capitalism and Communication in the Twenty-First Century.* Lanham, MD: Rowman & Littlefield, 2004.

Caldwell, John Thornton. *Televisuality: Style, Crisis, and Authority in American Television.* New Brunswick: Rutgers University Press, 1995.

Canclini, Nestor Garcia. *Consumers and Citizens: Globalization and Multicultural Conflicts.* Minneapolis: University of Minnesota Press, 2001.

Cappo, Joe. *The Future of Advertising: New Media, New Clients, New Consumers in the Post-Television Age.* Chicago: McGraw-Hill, 2003.

Carey, James. "Abolishing the Old World Spirit." *Critical Studies in Mass Communication* 12, no. 1 (1995): 82–89.

Carter, Bill. *Desperate Networks.* New York: Doubleday, 2006.

Castells, Manuel. *The Rise of the Network Society.* New York: Blackwell, 1996.

Curtin, Michael. "Feminine Desire in the Age of Satellite Television." *Journal of Communication* 49, no. 2 (1999): 55–70.

Curtin, Michael. "On Edge: Culture Industries in the Neo-Network Era." In *Making and Selling Culture,* eds. Richard Ohmann, Gage Averill, Michael Curtin, David Shumway, and Elizabeth Traube, 181–202. Hanover, NH: Wesleyan University Press, 1996.

Curtin, Michael, and Thomas Streeter, "Media." In *Culture Works: The Political Economy of Culture,* ed. Richard Maxwell, 225–50. Minneapolis: University of Minnesota Press, 2001.

D'Acci, Julie. "Cultural Studies, Television Studies, and the Crisis in the Humanities." *Television After TV: Essays on a Medium in Transition,* eds. Lynn Spigel and Jan Olsson, 418–45. Durham: Duke University Press, 2004.

Davidson, Martin. *The Consumerist Manifesto: Advertising in Postmodern Times.* London: Routledge, 1992.

Davila, Arlene. *Latinos, Inc.: The Marketing and Making of a People.* Berkeley: University of California Press, 2001.

Dayan, Daniel, and Elihu Katz. *Media Events: The Live Broadcasting of History.* Cambridge: Harvard University Press, 1992.

Dominick, Joseph R., Barry L. Sherman, and Fritz Messere. *Broadcasting, Cable, the Internet, and Beyond,* 4th ed. Boston: McGraw-Hill, 2000.

Donaton, Scott. *Madison & Vine: Why the Entertainment and Advertising Industries Must Converge to Survive.* New York: McGraw-Hill, 2004.

Doyle, Gillian. *Understanding Media Economics.* Thousand Oaks, CA: Sage Publications, 2002.

Du Gay, Paul, Stuart Hall, Linda Janes, Hugh Mackay, and Keith Negus. *Doing Cultural Studies: The Story of the Sony Walkman.* London: Sage, 1997.

Eastman, Susan T. "Orientation to Promotion and Research." In *Research in Media Promotion,* ed. Susan T. Eastman, 3–18. Mahwah, NJ: Lawrence Erlbaum Associates, 2000.

Eastman, Susan T., and Gregory D. Newton. "The Impact of Structural Salience within On-Air Promotion." *Journal of Broadcasting & Electronic Media* 42 (1998): 50–79.

Fiske, John, and John Hartley, *Reading Television.* London: Methuen and Co., Ltd., 1978.

Frank, Thomas. *One Market Under God: Extreme Capitalism, Market Populism, and the End of Economic Democracy.* New York: Doubleday, 2000.

Galician, Mary-Lou, ed., "Product Placement," special issue of *Journal of Promotion Management* 10, no. 1.2 (2004).

Garnham, Nicholas. "Political Economy and Cultural Studies: Reconciliation or Divorce?" *Critical Studies in Mass Communication* 12, no. 1 (1995): 62–71.

Gitelman, Lisa. *Always Already New: Media, History and the Data of Culture.* Cambridge: MIT Press, 2006.

Gitlin, Todd. *Inside Prime Time.* New York: Pantheon Books, 1983.

Gitlin, Todd. "Prime Time Ideology: The Hegemonic Process in Television Entertainment." *Television: A Critical View,* 5th ed., ed. Horace Newcomb, 516–36. New York: Oxford University Press, 2004.

Gladwell, Malcolm. *The Tipping Point: How Little Things Can Make a Big Difference.* Boston: Little, Brown and Company, 2002.

Gough Yates, Anna. *Understanding Women's Magazines: Publishing, Markets and Readerships.* New York: Routledge, 2003.

Gripsrud, Jostein. "Broadcast Television: The Chances of Its Survival in a Digital Age." In *Television After TV: Essays on a Medium in Transition,* eds. Lynn Spigel and Jan Olsson, 210–24. Durham: Duke University Press, 2004.

Grossberg, Lawrence. "Cultural Studies vs. Political Economy: Is Anybody Else Bored with this Debate?" *Critical Studies in Mass Communication* 12, no. 1 (1995): 72–81.

Haralovich, Mary Beth. "Sitcoms and Suburbs: Positioning the 1950s Homemaker." In *Private Screenings: Television and the Female Consumer,* eds. Lynn Spigel and Denise Mann, 111–42. Minneapolis: University of Minnesota Press, 1992.

Harries, Dan. "Watching the Internet." In *The New Media Book,* ed. Dan Harries, 171–82. London: British Film Institute, 2002.

Hartley, John. *Uses of Television.* London: Routledge, 1999.

Havens, Timothy. " 'It's Still a White World Out There': The Interplay of Culture and Economics in International Television Trade." *Critical Studies in Media Communication* 19, no. 4 (2002): 377–97.

Hesmondhalgh, David. *The Cultural Industries.* London: Sage, 2002.

Hilmes, Michele. "Cable, Satellite and Digital Technologies." In *The New Media Book,* ed. Dan Harries, 3–16. London: British Film Institute, 2002.

Howe, Neil, and William Strauss. *Millennials Rising: The Next Great Generation.* New York: Vintage Books, 2000.

Jenkins, Henry. *Convergence Culture: Where Old and New Media Collide.* New York: New York University Press, 2006.

Jenkins, Henry. "Interactive Audiences?" In *The New Media Book,* ed. Dan Harries, 157–70. London: British Film Institute, 2002.

Karrh, James A. "Brand Placement: A Review." *Journal of Current Issues and Research in Advertising* 20, no. 2 (1998): 31–49.

Kellner, Douglas. "Overcoming the Divide: Cultural Studies and Political Economy." In *Cultural Studies in Question,* eds. Marjorie Ferguson and Peter Golding, 102–20. London: Sage Publications, 1997.

Klinger, Barbara. *Beyond the Multiplex: Cinema, New Technologies, and the Home.* Berkeley: University of California Press, 2006.

Klopfenstein, Bruce C. "From Gadget to Necessity: The Diffusion of Remote Control Technology." In *The Remote Control in the New Age of Television,* eds. James R. Walker and Robert V. Bellamy Jr., 23–39. Westport, CT: Praeger, 1993.

Kompare, Derek. "Acquisition Repetition: Home Video and the Television Heritage." In *Rerun Nation: How Repeats Invented American Television,* 197–220. New York: Routledge, 2005.

Kowinski, W. S. *The Malling of America: An Inside Look at the Great Consumer Paradise.* New York, Pantheon, 1985.

Lipsitz, George. "The Meaning of Memory: Family, Class, and Ethnicity in Early Network Television Programs." In *Private Screenings: Television and the Female Consumer,* eds. Lynn Spigel and Denise Mann, 71–110. Minneapolis: University of Minnesota Press, 1992.

Lotz, Amanda D. "If It Is Not TV, What Is It? The Case of U.S. Subscription Television." In *Cable Visions: Television Beyond Broadcasting,* eds. Sarah Banet-Weiser, Cynthia Chris, and Anthony Freitas. New York: New York University Press, 2007.

Lotz, Amanda D. "Textual (Im)Possibilities in the U.S. Post-Network Era: Negotiating Production and Promotion Processes on Lifetime's *Any Day Now.*" *Critical Studies in Media Communication* 21, no. 1 (2004): 22–43.

Lotz, Amanda D. "Using 'Network' Theory in the Post-Network Era: Fictional 9/11 U.S. Television Discourse as a 'Cultural Forum.'" *Screen* 45, no. 4 (2004): 423–39.

MacDonald, J. Fred. *One Nation Under Television: The Rise and Decline of Network TV.* New York: Pantheon Books, 1990.

McCarthy, Anna. *Ambient Television: Visual Culture and Public Space.* Durham: Duke University Press, 2001.

McChesney, Robert W. *The Problem of the Media: U.S. Communication Politics in the 21st Century.* New York: Monthly Review Press, 2004.

McMurria, John. "Long Format TV: Globalization and Network Branding in a Multi-Channel Era." In *Quality Popular Television,* eds. Mark Jancovich and James Lyons, 65–87. London: British Film Institute, 2001.

Miege, Bernard. *The Capitalization of Cultural Production.* New York: International General, 1989.

Montgomery, Kathryn C. *Target: Prime Time; Advocacy Groups and the Struggle Over Television Entertainment.* New York: Oxford University Press, 1989.

Moran, Albert. *Copycat TV: Globalisation, Program Formats and Cultural Identity.* Luton, UK: University of Luton Press, 1998.

Morris, Meaghan. "Things to Do with Shopping Centres." In *The Cultural Studies Reader,* ed. Simon During, 295–319. London: Routledge, 1993.

Nava, Mica. "Consumerism and Its Contradictions." *Cultural Studies* 1, no. 2 (1987): 204–10.

Negroponte, Nicholas. *Being Digital.* New York: Vintage Books, 1995.

Neuman, W. Russell. *The Future of the Mass Audience.* Cambridge: Cambridge University Press, 1991.

Newcomb, Horace. "This Is Not Al Dente: *The Sopranos* and the New Meaning of Television." In *Television: The Critical View,* 7th ed., ed. Horace Newcomb, 561–78. New York: Oxford University Press, 2007.

Newcomb, Horace. "Studying Television: Same Questions, Different Contexts." *Cinema Journal* 45, no. 1 (2005): 107–11.

Newcomb, Horace. *TV: The Most Popular Art.* Garden City, NJ: Anchor Press, 1974.

Newcomb, Horace, and Paul Hirsch. "Television as a Cultural Forum." In *Television: A Critical View,* 5th ed., ed. Horace Newcomb, 503–15. New York: Oxford University Press, 2004.

Popcorn, Faith. *The Popcorn Report: Faith Popcorn on the Future of Your Company, Your World, Your Life.* New York: Doubleday, 1991.

Popcorn, Faith, and Lys Marigold. *Clicking: 16 Trends to Future Fit Your Life, Your Work, and Your Business.* New York: HarperCollins, 1996.

Radner, Hilary. *Shopping Around: Feminine Culture and the Pursuit of Pleasure.* New York: Routledge, 1995.

Raphael, Chad. "The Political Economic Origins of Reali-TV." In *Reality TV: Remaking Television Culture,* eds. Susan Murray and Laurie Ouellette, 119–36. New York: New York University Press, 2004.

Schiller, Herbert I. *Communication and Cultural Domination.* White Plains, NY: International Arts and Sciences Press, 1976.

Schor, Juliet B. *The Overspent American: Upscaling, Downshifting, and the New Consumer.* New York: Basic Books, 1998.

Spigel, Lynn. *Make Room for TV: Television and the Family Ideal in Postwar America.* Chicago: University of Chicago Press, 1992.

Spigel, Lynn. "Portable TV: Studies in Domestic Space Travel." In *Welcome to the Dreamhouse: Popular Media and Postwar Suburbs,* 60–103. Durham: Duke University Press, 2001.

Spigel, Lynn, and Jan Olsson, eds. *Television After TV: Essays on a Medium in Transition.* Durham: Duke University Press, 2004.

Tartikoff, Brandon, and Charles Leerhsen. *The Last Great Ride.* New York: Turtle Bay Books, 1992.

Turow, Joseph. "Audience Construction and Culture Production: Marketing Surveillance in the Digital Age." *American Academy of Political and Social Science* 597 (January 2005): 103–21.

Turow, Joseph. *Breaking Up America: Advertisers and the New Media World.* Chicago: University of Chicago Press, 1997.

Turow, Joseph. *Media Systems in Society: Understanding Industries, Strategies and Power.* White Plains, NY: Longman, 1997.

Turow, Joseph. "Unconventional Programs on Commercial Television: An Organizational Perspective." In *Mass Communicators in Context,* eds. D. Charles Whitney and James Ettema, 107–29. Beverly Hills: Sage, 1982.

Twitchell, James. *AdCult USA: The Triumph of Advertising in American Culture.* New York: Columbia University Press, 1996.

Walker, James R., and Robert V. Bellamy, Jr. "The Remote Control Device: An Overlooked Technology." In *The Remote Control in the New Age of Television,* eds. James R. Walker and Robert V. Bellamy, Jr., 3–14. Westport, CT: Praeger, 1993.

Walker, James, and Douglas Ferguson. *The Broadcast Television Industry.* Boston: Allyn and Bacon, 1998.

Webster, James G. "Television Audience Behavior: Patterns of Exposure in the New Media Environment." In *Media Use in the Information Age: Emerging Patterns of Adoption and Consumer Use,* eds. Jerry L. Salvaggio and Jennings Bryant, 197–216. Hillsdale, NJ: LEA, 1989.

Webster, James G., Patricia F. Phalen, and Lawrence W. Lichty. *Ratings Analysis: The Theory and Practice of Audience Research,* 2nd ed. Mahwah, NJ: Lawrence Erlbaum Associates, 2000.

Williams, Raymond. *Television: Technology and Cultural Form.* New York: Schocken Books, 1974.

Williamson, Judith. *Consuming Passions: The Dynamics of Popular Culture.* London: Marion Boyers, 1986.

Winship, Janice. *Inside Women's Magazines.* London: Pandora Press, 1987.

Winston, Brian. *Media Technology and Society: A History: From the Telegraph to the Internet.* London: Routledge, 1998.

Wittel, Andreas. "Culture, Labor, and Subjectivity: For a Political Economy from Below." *Capital & Class* no. 84 (Winter 1984): 11–30.

Index

About the Author

Amanda D. Lotz is Assistant Professor of Communication Studies at the University of Michigan. She is the author of *Redesigning Women: Television After the Network Era* (University of Illinois Press, 2006), and many journal articles and book chapters about television.